Issues in English Teaching

**Edited by Jon Davison
and John Moss**

London and New York

2 9 AUG 2012

First published 2000
by Routledge
2 Park Square, Milton Park, Abingdon, Oxon, OX14 4RN

Simultaneously published in the USA and Canada
by Routledge
270 Madison Ave, New York NY 10016

Routledge is an imprint of the Taylor & Francis Group

Transferred to Digital Printing 2007

Typeset in Goudy by Taylor & Francis Books Ltd

British Library Cataloguing in Publication Data
A catalogue record for this book is available from the British Library

Library of Congress Cataloging in Publication Data
Issues in English Teaching / edited by Jon Davison and John Moss.
    (Issues in Subject Teaching)
    Includes bibliographical references and index.
    1. English language – study and teaching – (elementary) – England.
    2. English language – study and teaching – (elementary) – Wales.
    3. English language – study and teaching – (secondary) – England.
    4. English language – study and teaching – (secondary) – Wales.
    I. Davison, Jon. II. Moss, John, 1957– . III. Series.
    LB1576.I89   2000   99-41105
    428'.0071'041–dc21   CIP

ISBN 0-415-20664-2 (hbk)
ISBN 0-415-20665-0 (pbk)

Publisher's Note
The publisher has gone to great lengths to ensure the quality of this
reprint but points out that some imperfections in the original
may be apparent

Issues in English Teaching

Issues in English Teaching invites primary and secondary teachers of English to
engage in debates about key issues in subject teaching.
     The issues discussed include:

- the increasingly centralised control of the curriculum, assessment and
  pedagogy in the teaching of English in schools in England and Wales as a
  result of initiatives such as the National Literacy Strategy;
- new technologies that are transforming pupils' lived experience of literacy,
  or literacies;
- the accelerating globalisation of English and the independence of other
  versions of English from English standard English – a National Curriculum
  with a nationalist perspective on language, literacy and literature cannot
  fully accommodate this wider use of English;
- what has become 'naturalised' and 'normalised' in English teaching, and
  the educational and ideological reasons for this;
- hierarchies that have been created in the curriculum and pedagogy,
  identifying who and what has been given low status, excluded or marginalised in the development of the current model of English.

Issues in English Teaching will stimulate student teachers, NQTs, language
and literacy co-ordinators, classroom English teachers and aspiring or practising
Heads of English to reflect on the identity of the subject, the principles and
policies that have determined practice, and those which should influence future
practice.

Jon Davison is Professor and Head of the School of Education at University
College Northampton. His previous publications include *Learning to Teach
English in the Secondary School* (Routledge 1998). **John Moss** is Head of
Secondary Education at Canterbury Christ Church University College and co-
ordinator of the secondary PGCE English programme. His previous publications
include *Subject Mentoring in the Secondary School* (Routledge 1997).

Issues in Subject Teaching series
Edited by Susan Capel, Jon Davison,
James Arthur and John Moss

Other titles in the series:

Contents

vi *Contents*

Illustrations

Figures

Tables

Contributors

Stephen Bax is senior lecturer in Language Studies at Canterbury Christ Church University College. After some years of teaching English overseas, he took a PGCE in TEFL and English and then returned overseas to teach in countries as diverse as Singapore, Iraq, Sudan and Spain. In 1988 he went to Edinburgh University, where he taught English and studied for his Masters and then MLitt in Applied Linguistics, before moving to Canterbury in 1993. His main areas of professional interest include teacher education for teachers of English as a Foreign Language, sociolinguistics and discourse. His published research includes an investigation into how we can make teacher education more relevant to the contexts in which teachers operate.

Eve Bearne has taught English, drama and language in education in schools and colleges for over thirty years. She was a project officer for the National Writing Project and editor of a number of publications. She is the co-editor of a series of books about children's literature, and has written and edited several books about language and literacy, the most recent of which are *Making Progress in English* (1998) and *Use of Language Across the Secondary Curriculum* (1999). She is Assistant Director in Research at Homerton College, Cambridge.

Hazel Bryan is a senior lecturer in Primary English at Canterbury Christ Church University College, where she lectures on the primary undergraduate and post-graduate courses. She is course director for the Certificate in Higher Education: a programme for Learning Support Assistants. She is currently undertaking research with the UK Reading Association on the Literacy Hour, and is researching issues of teacher professionalism and English.

Gabrielle Cliff Hodges is a principal lecturer and secondary team leader at Homerton College, Cambridge. She jointly co-ordinates the secondary English and Drama PGCE course and lectures in English, language and children's literature on both post-graduate and undergraduate courses. She was formerly Head of English in a Cambridgeshire comprehensive school. She has contributed chapters about teaching speaking and listening and poetry to *Learning to Teach English in the Secondary School* (1997), and has written about the development of reading within the secondary age range in

Voice Off (1996). She was Chair of the National Association for the Teaching of English from 1996 to 1998.

Caroline Daly is involved with several aspects of initial and ongoing teacher education; she currently lectures on the PGCE Secondary English course at London University Institute of Education. She was formerly Head of English in a Bedfordshire comprehensive school, before working on initial teacher education programmes at De Montfort University, Bedford. Her previous publications include articles about literacy, reading and gender, and she contributed to *Learning to Teach English in the Secondary School* (Routledge, 1998). She is currently researching issues connected with boys and English in the secondary phase.

Chris Davies taught English in secondary schools for fourteen years, nine of which were as Head of English at a comprehensive in Oxfordshire. He has worked at the University of Oxford Department of Educational Studies since 1985. In addition to working with PGCE secondary English students, he has been involved in research projects into the teaching and learning of writing across the curriculum at Key Stage 2, and developments in using information technology in education – specifically in the study of Shakespeare texts, and in learning to write in different genres. His publications include textbooks on media education and English and *What Is English Teaching?* for Open University Press.

Jon Davison is Professor and Head of the School of Education at University College, Northampton. After working as a head of English and Media Studies in inner London, he became an advisory teacher at the English and Media Centre, London. He is a member of the NATE publications committee. His recent publications include co-authorship of *Subject Mentoring in the Secondary School* (Routledge, 1997), *History Teachers in the Making* (Open University Press, 1998), *Learning to Teach English in the Secondary School* (Routledge, 1998), and *Social Literacy and the School Curriculum* (Falmer Press, 2000). He is a series editor of the *Issues* series to which this volume belongs.

Viv Ellis is a lecturer in English and Education at the University of Brighton. Previously, he was Co-ordinator of English and Expressive Arts at an 11–18 comprehensive school in the West Midlands. His research interests are in the areas of literacy and technology studies, sexuality and education, and initial teacher education.

Teresa Grainger is a principal lecturer in Education at Canterbury Christ Church University College. Formerly a primary teacher and staff development co-ordinator, she now organises CPD courses in Literacy, works on the PGCE Primary and still manages to teach in classrooms. She is Editor of the UKRA journal: *Reading*, is on the UKRA's publications committee, and is a member of NATE's primary committee. Her publications include chapters and articles about drama, poetry, reading and the language of subversion, as well as a book entitled *Traditional Storytelling in the Primary Classroom* (Scholastic, 1997).

Adrian Holliday is a Reader in Applied Linguistics at Canterbury Christ Church University College, where he co-ordinates research in international language education. He is the author of *Appropriate Methodology and Social Context* (Cambridge University Press, 1994) and is generally interested in the international politics of culture and discourse. He has worked with English teachers and ministries in many locations in the developing world, including ten years in Syria and Egypt as a university curriculum consultant.

Carole King is a senior lecturer in English in the Faculty of Education at the University of Brighton. She has eighteen years' teaching experience in primary and secondary schools. She now teaches on the four year BA in Primary Education with QTS and in Continuing Professional Development. Her previous work includes *Creating Communities of Readers* (1992), a video that pioneered group reading strategies.

Sue Leach taught in a variety of schools within the West Midlands, latterly as Head of Department at a comprehensive school. In 1993 she joined the School of Education at the University of Birmingham, where she lectures in English in Education. Her main responsibility is teaching the PGCE Secondary English course. She has a wide range of research interests, including Literacy and Language, Shakespeare in the classroom, and gender issues in English. She is the author of *Shakespeare in the Classroom*, and the editor of the Oxford University Press *Exploring Shakespeare* series. She chairs Birmingham NATE and is principal examiner for AEB 660 A-Level English.

Janet Maybin is a lecturer in the School of Education at the Open University, Milton Keynes, England. She trained as a social anthropologist, and has edited and contributed to books about socially oriented research into language and literacy. She has also published articles about children's informal language practices. Recent books include *Language and Literacy in Social Practice* (Multilingual Matters, 1994) and, with Neil Mercer, *Using English: From Conversation To Canon* (Routledge, 1996).

John Moss is Head of Secondary Education at Canterbury Christ Church University College, where he teaches undergraduate English and Drama and co-ordinates the secondary PGCE English programme. He is Research Officer for NATE. His recent publications include co-authorship of *Subject Mentoring in the Secondary School* (Routledge, 1997) and three chapters in *Learning to Teach English in the Secondary School* (Routledge, 1998). He is a series editor of the *Issues* series to which this volume belongs, and is currently editing a series of books on citizenship and the school curriculum for the Falmer Press.

Jonothan Neelands is a senior lecturer in Drama Education and Cultural Studies in the Institute of Education, University of Warwick. He is tutor for the PGCE in English and Drama, and programme leader for the MA in drama education and cultural studies. He has been an advisory teacher for English and Drama and an Adviser for Drama. He has published several texts for drama and English teachers, including: *Structuring Drama Work* (Cambridge University Press, 1990) and *Beginning Drama 11–14* (Fulton Press, 1998). Jonothan has also led workshops for teachers throughout the UK, Europe and North America. He is a regular contributor to NATE, and is particularly interested in the links between English and drama in the secondary phase of schooling.

Nick Peim wrote *Critical Theory and the English Teacher* (Routledge, 1993) when he was Head of English in a large comprehensive upper school in Leicestershire. He then worked at De Montfort University, teaching education modules and teaching English and Media Studies in a secondary comprehensive school. Currently, he teaches at the School of Education, Birmingham University. His PhD was on the cultural politics of English teaching. His current research interests include the architecture of state schooling, education and language, literacy and culture. He is currently working on a book on football, culture and identity.

Muriel Robinson is Deputy Head of the School of Education at the University of Brighton. She worked as a primary-school teacher in London for ten years before moving to Brighton as a member of the language and literacy subject team, working first on initial teacher education programmes and then increasingly in CPD. After exploring reading in her MA dissertation, she developed an interest in the relationship between written and televisual narratives, which led to the completion of her PhD in the area, more readily accessible through her book *Children Reading: Print and Television* (Falmer Press, 1997). Since then she has become interested in the linguistic and cultural aspects of house music and in the nature of the writing process as experienced in web-site creation.

Jo Westbrook is a senior lecturer on the Secondary PGCE English programme and the BA (QTS) at Canterbury Christ Church University College. A former Head of English and Media Studies, she taught for nine years in three London comprehensive schools. She then worked overseas as a teacher-trainer with Voluntary Service Overseas in Uganda, where she provided INSET on Gender and Education for other non-governmental organisations. Her research interests are in developing and assessing reading at secondary level, and in home-school literacy links.

Introduction to the series

This book, *Issues in English Teaching*, is one of a series of books entitled *Issues in Subject Teaching*. The series has been designed to engage with a wide range of issues related to subject teaching. The types of issues vary among the subjects, but may include, for example, issues that:

- impact on Initial Teacher Education in the subject;
- are addressed in the classroom through the teaching of the subject;
- are related to the content of the subject and its definition;
- are related to subject pedagogy;
- are connected with the relationship between the subject and broader educational aims and objectives in society, and the philosophy and sociology of education;
- are related to the development of the subject and its future in the twenty-first century.

Each book consequently presents key debates that subject teachers will need to understand, reflect on and engage in as part of their professional development. Chapters have been designed to highlight major questions, and to consider the evidence from research and practice in order to find possible answers. Some subject books or chapters offer at least one solution or a view of the ways forward, whereas others provide alternative views and leave readers to identify their own solution or view of the ways forward. The editors expect readers of the series to want to pursue the issues raised, and so chapters include suggestions for further reading, and questions for further debate. The chapters and questions could be used as stimuli for debate in subject seminars or department meetings, or as topics for assignments or classroom research. The books are targeted at all those with a professional interest in the subject, and, in particular: student teachers learning to teach the subject in the primary or secondary school; newly qualified teachers; teachers with a subject co-ordination or leadership role, and those preparing for such responsibility; as well as mentors, tutors, trainers and advisers of the aforementioned groups.

Each book in the series has a cross-phase dimension. This is because the editors believe that it is important for teachers in the primary and secondary phases to look at subject teaching holistically, particularly in order to provide for continuity and progression, but also to increase their understanding of how children learn. The balance of chapters that have a cross-phase relevance, chapters that focus on issues that are of particular concern to primary teachers, and chapters that focus on issues which secondary teachers are more likely to need to address, varies according to the issues relevant to different subjects. However, no matter where the emphasis is, the authors have drawn out the relevance of their topic to the whole of each book's intended audience.

Because of the range of the series, both in terms of the issues covered and its cross-phase concern, each book is an edited collection. Editors have commissioned new writing from experts on particular issues, who, collectively, will represent many different perspectives on subject teaching. Readers should not expect a book in this series to cover a full range of issues relevant to the subject, or to offer a completely unified view of subject teaching, or that every issue will be dealt with discretely, or that all aspects of an issue will be covered. Part of what each book in this series offers to readers is the opportunity to explore the interrelationships between positions in debates and, indeed, among the debates themselves, by identifying the overlapping concerns and competing arguments that are woven through the text.

The editors are aware that many initiatives in subject teaching currently originate from the centre, and that teachers have decreasing control of subject content, pedagogy and assessment strategies. The editors strongly believe that for teaching to remain properly a vocation and a profession, teachers must be invited to be part of a creative and critical dialogue about subject teaching, and should be encouraged to reflect, criticise, problem-solve and innovate. This series is intended to provide teachers with a stimulus for democratic involvement in the development of subject teaching.

Susan Capel, Jon Davison, James Arthur and John Moss
December 1999

Introduction

Jon Davison and John Moss

Preamble

This book invites primary and secondary teachers of English to engage in debates about key issues in subject teaching. It is intended to stimulate student teachers, NQTs, language and literacy co-ordinators, classroom English teachers and aspiring or practising Heads of English, to reflect on the identity of the subject, the principles and policies, which, in the past, have determined, and now determine practice, and those that should influence future practice. Its editors do not claim coverage of all the issues that could be considered, but they do hope that readers will be encouraged by the book to develop or maintain the habit of mind that asks and attempts to answer important 'why' and 'what if' questions about subject teaching. Each chapter consequently concludes with some questions for discussion and suggestions for further reading.

Since it is anticipated that *Issues in English Teaching* will be used both by readers who will want to identify chapters that explore issues of particular concern to them, and by others who will want to pursue debates and issues through several chapters, this introduction offers both a summary of each chapter and an indication of how individual chapters contribute to the core debates that pervade the book. Readers should note that the book has been written, compiled and edited with a view to making the discussion that takes place in each chapter relevant to the policy and practice of both primary and secondary teachers of English. In some cases, the chapter authors have used examples and illustrations, which they relate explicitly to both primary and secondary practice; in others, the authors invite readers to consider the relevance of discussion to their practice in one or other phase.

Core debates and issues

In this section of the introduction, chapters with a particularly strong emphasis on a core issue under discussion in the book as a whole are identified in brackets.

At a time when control of the curriculum, assessment, and increasingly, through initiatives such as the National Literacy Strategy, pedagogy of school teaching of English in England and Wales, is more centralised than ever before (Bearne and Cliff Hodges; Bryan and Westbrook), the concluding statement of

Adrian Holliday's chapter in this book may seem startling to some readers: 'the direction and ownership of English ... can no longer be taken for granted – by anyone.' However, the past, present and future direction of English is a preoccupation that underlies many of the issues discussed in this book: with the contributors frequently identifying the merits of particular ownership or partial ownership claims, which continue to challenge the dominant view of the subject through a kind of Foucauldian resistance (Moss).

This resistance is partly a matter of putting forward the claims of literary, cultural and sociolinguistic theories for a reconceptualisation of English (Peim; Moss). However, it also reflects awareness of both the rate at which new technologies are transforming pupils' lived experience of literacy, or literacies (Robinson), and the accelerating globalisation of English, or Englishes, as evidenced by the adoption of English as a world lingua franca and the independence of other versions of English from English standard English (Bax; Holliday). In these circumstances, a National Curriculum with a nationalist perspective on language, literacy and literature cannot fully accommodate English. Both global and local perspectives must be allowed to influence what is taught and how (Bax; Bryan and Wetbrook).

It is consequently a characteristic of the book that many chapter contributors are concerned about what has become 'naturalised' and 'normalised' in English teaching, and with identifying the educational and ideological reasons for this. Establishing these reasons frequently involves contributors in presenting some historical analysis, defining the hierarchies that have been created in the curriculum and pedagogy, and identifying who and what has been given low status, excluded or marginalised in the development of the current model of English (Davies; Davison; Maybin; Peim; Robinson). There is some variation in opinion as to whether oppositional or inclusive curricula and pedagogies (Daly; Ellis; Moss; Neelands) offer the most appropriate means of denaturalising (Holliday) 'queering' (Ellis), and exposing the ideological constructedness of this model. However, the 'authoritarian' promotion of the traditional literary canon and standard English in the National Curriculum is subject to much critical scrutiny (Davies; Maybin).

Several contributors locate examples of language in use, including the writing of primary-school children (King), statements by student teachers (Leach), and a variety of 'textual instances' (Holliday), in the discourses in which they appear, and in doing so, identify discourse theory as a powerful concept in any review of the English curriculum (Davison). Contributors insist on the complexity of literacy and learning in English, and the consequent dangers of 'monolithic' tendencies in the curriculum and pedagogy (Bearne and Cliff Hodges; Grainger). Class, race, gender and sexuality are frequently cited as factors that need to be foregrounded in any account of this complexity, and several contributors warn against the simplistic binary oppositions that have often occurred in discussions of these matters and the pedagogy intended to address them, which may reinforce assumptions and prejudices (Daly; Davison; Ellis; Holliday).

Individual chapters

In Chapter 1, Eve Bearne and Gabrielle Cliff Hodges demonstrate that the investigation of the rights and responsibilities of pupils and teachers in relation to the teaching, learning and experience of reading exposes the dangers of attempts to impose a monolithic reading pedagogy. Using examples from primary and secondary schools, they argue that the variety and multiplicity of the experiences that constitute reading, and that are apparent in the diversity of children's methods of learning to read, of the texts they choose to read, and of the ways in which they read them, must be supported by teaching and assessment strategies that stimulate motivation and promote choice. Some of the keys to the development of such strategies include research into pupils' reading experiences and habits, and dialogue with pupils, which can lead to enhanced understanding of the complex individuality of each reader.

Carole King's chapter (Chapter 2) is about the empowerment of writers, and is concerned with promoting a pedagogy through which children can learn 'the power of writing to act in and for their lives.' Referring to Britton's model of writing, King demonstrates that children can learn that writing in the 'poetic mode' has important social and cultural functions, and that writing in the 'spectator role' can help children both to clarify thought and to 'place themselves' in a community of writers. King provides some detailed examples of primary practice that promotes writing 'involving both affective and cognitive processes', and that shows how children become more effective language-users when they understand and are allowed to explore the capacity of writing for meaning making. The practice discussed has applications in secondary schools.

In the following chapter (Chapter 3), Hazel Bryan and Jo Westbrook explore the possibilities for whole-school literacy policies and practice in primary and secondary schools. Setting themselves the task of establishing how teachers can combine the development and retention of their own understanding of good practice with responding to the 'stringency of government requirements', they begin by reviewing the many recent initiatives that have impacted on literacy education. Noting the different emphases of these initiatives and the public recognition that schools need freedom to succeed, they use research evidence of practice in a range of schools to argue for a 'multidimensional view of literacy', which acknowledges that literacy development is 'rooted in social and cultural practices'.

Teresa Grainger (Chapter 4) begins her review of the current status of oracy by acknowledging that its place in the curriculum has been statutorily strengthened, but argues that its value as a 'tool for enquiry, reflection and knowledge construction' has not yet been fully realised. Grainger identifies several factors which militate against oracy's status, including the promotion of *teacher* talk by the National Literacy Strategy, the limited planning and assessment requirements of primary schools, and some ingrained teaching styles and teacher/pupil expectations. The strategies she proposes to further the development of oracy, namely, the improvement of teacher talk, more effective planning for progression, and the development of knowledge about talk, all have applications in both primary and secondary teaching.

Jonothan Neelands (Chapter 5) examines the potential of drama as a liberating force in the curriculum. He begins by identifying the key oppositional positions that have been taken in conflicts over the educational purpose of the subject as: 'drama' versus 'theatre', 'subject' versus 'method', and 'personal and social learning' versus 'cultural induction'. He extracts from a complex recent Ofsted definition of drama, the elements of three common positions that characterise drama respectively as: a method of learning, an arts subject, and part of English. His analysis concludes by identifying an increasing consensus in thinking about the aims of school drama, which he sees reflected in diverse and demanding expectations of the subject and evidence of its increasing status. The models of drama that are considered by Neelands inform practice in primary schools and secondary schools.

Muriel Robinson's chapter (Chapter 6) begins by analysing the history of English, to expose the partially conflicting agendas of 'literacy' and 'literature' lobbies, and by arguing that the dissociation of 'reception' and 'production' in the current process-based curriculum model is damaging to pedagogy in primary and secondary schools. Robinson envisages a redefinition of English, which takes into account the new literacies that are emerging through pupils' increasing exposure to ICT and multimedia texts. She argues that the NLS places a dangerously limiting emphasis on book-based texts, not least because the primacy of written material in children's literacy experiences can no longer be assumed, and concludes by suggesting that, among other cultural experiences, computer gaming and listening to contemporary music develop cognitive abilities that are relevant to literacy and English.

In Chapter 7, Chris Davies explores the polarised positions taken in the debate about whether the objective of language teaching is 'correct' or 'appropriate' English, demonstrating the problems which follow from a rigid advocacy of 'correctness'. Davies argues that any effective pedagogy must take account of the context and purpose of what is being said or written. He discusses the difficulties involved in identifying and teaching 'language rules', drawing attention to the significance of an understanding of language acquisition for practice. He considers some of the factors likely to influence language teaching in the near future, including the ways in which our understanding of literacy and language itself are being changed by developments in ICT. The debate has implications for both primary and secondary pedagogy.

Stephen Bax, in Chapter 8, calls for the development of a new professional dialogue between teachers of TEFL and 'school' English, to promote both a shared understanding of the language issues that confront educationalists in the context of the globalisation of English, and a shared investigative pedagogy. Taking note of what he considers the limited expectations of the 'monolithic' National Curriculum with regard to the understanding of language variation, he challenges school English to treat Estuary English and Singaporean English, for example, alongside standard English, as illustrations of the ways in which language variations bear witness to speakers' and writers' inclusion in and exclusion from groups that may be defined by race, class, gender or age. The practice proposed has applications in both primary and secondary schools.

In Chapter 9, Adrian Holliday argues that because of the increasing use of English as the language of global communication, and because others use English without reference to English users of English, the school English curriculum provides us with an opportunity to 'deconstruct our own ethnocentricity' by exploring the ideological character of discourses that may have been previously considered expressions of the natural. Through the detailed discussion of 'textual instances', Holliday identifies techniques for 'making the familiar strange' by, for example, exposing the 'naturalisation' of discourse, critiquing the authority of genres, and producing meanings that avoid 'otherisation', by distancing reading from stereotyped categorisations. The attitudes to language that Holliday advocates could be adopted by both primary and secondary English teachers.

In Chapter 10, Sue Leach uses research into secondary student teachers' attitudes to English to identify and comment on tensions currently operating in the subject and its teaching. By analysing the responses of a small group of student teachers to three tasks carried out before and during their PGCE year, she establishes that although some student teachers now have considerable knowledge of literary theory, cultural studies and sociolinguistics, their ability to use this knowledge in the classroom is hampered by factors such as the persistence of a pervasive 'classic realist' view of texts and a limiting literature-centred curriculum. Leach argues that while student teachers' pedagogical understanding is often high, English needs to be reconfigured to allow new theories of language, reading and culture to drive practice forward. Primary and secondary English teachers will find it useful to compare their own attitudes to the subject with those of Leach's student teachers.

Nick Peim's chapter (Chapter 11) builds from Leach's observations about the potential of literary theory, cultural studies and sociolinguistics to transform English. Questioning the centrality of literature and the dismissive attitude to popular culture that he finds in the current curriculum, Peim argues that the 'hybridity', flattening of hierarchies and cultural relativism of post-modernism could provide a foundation for the redefinition of English. Having considered the constraints and opportunities suggested by the National Curriculum, the history of English teaching and issues related to the professional identity of English teachers, Peim demonstrates how theory can provide 'technology for thinking' by exploring the potential of post-structuralism, theories of popular culture, and critical language awareness for a projected reworking of the National Curriculum or more radical reforms of English. Peim's illustration of the use of Barthes' narrative codes is suggestive of how a critical technology of thinking can be applied in both primary and secondary phases.

In Chapter 12, Janet Maybin exposes the ideological constructedness of the literary canon by analysing first its history, and then current and future challenges to its definition, status and value. By tracing its relationship with a series of political and cultural initiatives, ranging from the invention of printing to the Leavisite agenda for criticism, Maybin demonstrates the contentiousness of the canon. She explains post-colonial and feminist challenges to it, and accounts for the earlier marginalisation of the voices that they represent. Finally, she considers the probable effects of new cultural studies perspectives, the globalisation of English, ICT and revaluations of cultural identity, on the constitution of the canon. The issues concerning the canon are relevant to a range of curriculum decisions, including text selection, in both primary and secondary schools.

John Moss's chapter (Chapter 13) considers the implications for English teaching of theories that 'locate authority for meaning' respectively in: the reader, contexts, and texts themselves. His discussion of reader-response theory concludes that teachers need to clarify how their practice characterises the text–reader relationship. He then considers the issues involved in promoting reading positions that expose the social, cultural and historical marginalisation of particular groups. Moss accepts the value of a vocabulary that sets out to describe form, but argues that the terminology adopted in teaching need not construct writers merely as controlling manipulators of effects. He concludes that institutionally normalised reading practices can be resisted by teachers who develop pupils' semiotic, generic, cultural and ideological repertoires. The development of these repertoires could influence practice in both primary and secondary phases.

In his discussion of the representation of sexuality in English, Viv Ellis demonstrates, in Chapter 14, the limitations of pedagogical choices and text selections that reinforce a rhetoric in which homosexuality is constructed in binary opposition to heterosexuality, as an 'issue'. He exposes the discourses that normalise this rhetoric, and provides powerful illustrations of the dangers of practice derived from it. Referring to recent developments in critical theory and pedagogy, he then argues that teachers need to adopt strategies for representing sexuality. These should involve unsettling the process of producing meaning, by exploring the identities that are created for, or imposed on, writers and readers as this process takes place, and by asking 'questions about how we read and write sexuality'. Ellis refers to texts targeted at both primary- and secondary-aged children in the course of the chapter.

Caroline Daly's chapter (Chapter 15) is an investigation of the highly politicised debate about gender and achievement in English. Daly challenges the 'capitalist discourse with a male-oriented agenda for education', within which the binary opposition of boys' and girls' attainment in English has been constructed. While noting concerns about matters such as the effect of the 'feminisation' of English and different assessment practices on achievement, she calls for the debate to consider more deeply the ways in which boys' and girls' learning is 'inextricably bound up with their experience of class, race and sexuality'. She finds a way forward in a pedagogy that takes into account the ways in which gender is manifested in the social interactions of speaking and listening, reading and writing. Her detailed proposals in the conclusion should inform both primary and secondary practice.

Finally, Jon Davison's premise, in Chapter 16, is that dominant groups control the curriculum and assessment in ways that protect their own social interests and educational priorities. By documenting how the English curriculum in twentieth-century England has been antipathetic both to the language of the working class and popular culture, he demonstrates how these interests and priorities have become 'naturalised'. Davison then reviews a range of models of English teaching, and argues the case for a democratic and empowering version of English, synthesising ideas from Gee, Searle, Mercer and Lankshear. He makes reference to a detailed reading of Mercer's vision of the construction of the classroom as a 'discourse village', and Lankshear's strategies for the development of powerful literacies. The concepts discussed in this chapter are exerting an influence on cross-phase pedagogy throughout the English-speaking world.

1 Reading rights and responsibilities

Eve Bearne and Gabrielle Cliff Hodges

Controversy about the teaching of reading has a long history, and throughout it there has been the assumption, at least the hope, that a panacea can be found that will make everything right. ... there is no one method, medium, approach, device or philosophy that holds the key to the process of reading. We believe that the knowledge does exist to improve the teaching of reading, but that it does not lie in the triumphant discovery, or re-discovery, of a particular formula ... A glance at the past reveals the truth of this.

(DES, 1975)

What rights and whose responsibilities?

The informed words of the Bullock Report, written a quarter of a century ago, are a reminder that current concerns about reading are part of a long history of debate. What is it about reading that so fires an emotional response in educators and politicians? Just as there is no easy answer to the teaching of reading, there is equally no slick summary of why debates rage so fiercely – in every generation it seems. Part of the answer may lie in the fact that satisfying or satisfactory reading does not just depend on the range of texts available to a particular age group, but on readers, contexts and communities. Since contexts for reading, the experience of readers and the communities they inhabit are not static, it is no wonder that the issues have to be regularly revisited. The fact that every age invents new types of text (see, for example, Alberto Manguel's splendidly wide-ranging *A History of Reading*) is another consideration, and it becomes clear that teaching reading is still a hot issue because the precise nature of reading changes with time (Manguel, 1996).

This chapter explores what reading means for young people and their teachers, in particular their rights and responsibilities. Using examples from students in Key Stages 2 and 3, it asks some key questions such as what do teachers know and what can they find out about readers? How can teachers use what they know to develop fruitful ways of teaching reading?

However, there are some important matters of principle to get into the open before trying to deal with all the complex factors involved in teaching reading. In his wry and incisive book, *Reads Like A Novel*, Daniel Pennac (1994) offers the following as 'rights':

1   The right not to read
2   The right to skip pages
3   The right not to finish a book
4   The right to re-read
5   The right to read anything
6   The right to 'bovarysme' (that is, reading for the instant satisfaction of nothing but our feelings)
7   The right to read anywhere
8   The right to browse
9   The right to read out loud
10 The right to remain silent.

What emerges strongly is the right to be a committed reader, an individual making choices according to inclination as well as need. It would be good if we could make this our target for the nation's children rather than 'reaching Level 4 by the age of 11'! The cool prose of government documents cannot, of course, capture such fervent determination. However, it is not so much the wording of National Literacy Strategy or National Curriculum documents which deserves attention; the new text element that needs scrutiny is the format (with its attendant implications for teaching approaches). For example, the National Literacy Strategy presents a framework for teaching, which, together with its multiplicity of training materials, begins to look very like the kind of 'triumphant discovery' of one particular formula, precisely the approach against which the Bullock Report cautions us. Teachers are having to make space within the framework to meet the needs of individual students' development, interests and preferences. Is space also available for students to exercise their right to choose?

The principle of fostering avid, committed and critical readers can only be realised in practice if students are motivated. If students are not motivated to read, then they will not engage in the breadth and depth of reading necessary for that development to take place. Jerome Bruner's analysis of what he calls 'the will to learn', although written over thirty years ago (Bruner, 1966), provides some valuable pointers to anyone teaching reading. Motivation, says Bruner, is fuelled by the satisfaction of curiosity. Experienced readers learn not just to decode text but also to satisfy curiosity through reading and to sustain their curiosity 'beyond the moment's vividness'. They learn, if given the opportunity, how to channel their curiosity actively to accomplish their own ends, not just passively to meet the demands of others. Bruner goes on to explore another intrinsic element of motivation, namely 'the drive to achieve competence'. Most people know, if given the chance to experience it, the pleasures that can be derived from a sense of achievement. Furthermore, 'we get interested in what we get good at'. However, for pleasure and interest to be sustained we need ultimately to master things for their own sake rather than for extrinsic rewards. A third point about motivation, crucial for teachers of reading, is the power of role models, in reading as in so much else. What Bruner means by 'role model' is 'a day-to-day working model *with whom to interact*' (our italics). Teachers are very well placed to interact with less-experienced readers, not so much because they offer behaviours for students to imitate, but because they are more experienced readers with whom students can engage in dialogues about reading: dialogues which they later learn to internalise.

Bruner's analysis is predominantly sociocultural. It reminds us how important reading is to our concept of what it means to be human. Reading is therefore inevitably political. Being political implies enfranchisement and the right to vote; it also means that the voter carries responsibilities to the community. It follows, then, that if reading is politically situated and a political act, then readers – teachers and students – have both rights and responsibilities. A recent report by an Advisory Group on Citizenship, entitled *Education for Citizenship and the Teaching of Democracy in Schools* (QCA 1998b), reinforces this view, linking the twinned concepts of rights and responsibilities with skills and aptitudes such as the 'ability to use modern media and technology critically to gather information' and the 'ability to recognise forms of manipulation and persuasion'. The more experienced members of a community are those who carry the responsibilities until the younger ones can take full status, so this chapter will give weight to teachers' responsibilities and younger readers' rights, suggesting ways in which these gradually move towards a more equal distribution of each. Since this is a chapter about *teaching* reading, and about what it is to become a reader, it will also be important to look at how success as a reader can be measured. Just what kinds of assessments are most likely to provide useful information for all members of the 'voting' community – for readers, families, educators and employers – about standards of reading?

Reading experience and experiences

One of the most significant shifts in thinking about reading over recent years has been not just the acknowledgement, but the value, given to reading and pre-reading experiences in homes and communities. The greatest emphasis in this area, however, has been given to the early stages of reading. The later years of Key Stage 2 and the early secondary years do not figure as much in discussion of how to teach reading, or in this case of how to build on the experience and experiences of young, already fairly fluent, readers. This lack of attention to older readers reflects a view of reading which measures successful reading according to how well young readers can decode the words on the page and demonstrate this by reading aloud. In its worst manifestation, the idea is that once children can decode and read aloud fluently, then we don't need to teach them any more about reading. Nothing could be further from the truth. Surface-skating the text is potentially more harmful to a young reader than still having problems in articulating complicated text. If you are struggling with a text, you have to be engaged with it in some sense. But if you glide over its surface you never have to get to grips with it at all. Margaret Meek describes her unease about those who 'decontextualise reading in order to describe it':

> The reading experts, for all their understanding about 'the reading process' treat all text as the neutral substance on which the process works as if the reader did the same things with a poem, a timetable, a warning notice.
>
> (Meek, 1988)

A full reading curriculum goes beyond this basic assumption, and considers the range of texts which a reader needs to tackle, alongside the range of reading processes and strategies which might help. It also takes into account the development of reading preferences and reading experience drawn from homes and communities.

There are many assumptions and prejudices about young people's reading at home. Difficulties lie in how reading is being defined – both by students and by those who question them – and in methods of gathering information. For example, pupils are often reluctant to admit to certain types of reading – newspapers, comics, magazines, computer texts, television – because they think that these are not the kinds of things teachers want to hear about and don't count as reading. If reading is much more broadly defined to include everything that students read within and outside the school, then the reality is usually complex and quite a shock.

For example, the responses of one Year 5/6 class in a Cambridge primary school to a questionnaire about home and school reading showed both boys and girls reading twice as much at home as they did in school. Another example involved information gathered from interviews carried out for a small-scale research project with six Year 7 students from a Cambridge secondary school (whose Ofsted report noted that 'pupils do not usually read for pleasure or elect to tackle challenging texts'). The group was mixed ability and included three boys and three girls, for one of whom English was an additional language. For pleasure and interest they read Roald Dahl novels, film and TV tie-ins, e.g. *The X-Files* and *Jurassic Park*, series books such as *Point Horror*, *Famous Five* and *Sweet Valley High*, *Horrible Histories*, humorous poetry, joke books, wildlife books, comics, special interest magazines, local and national newspapers, novels, picture books (with younger siblings), encyclopaedias, books about computer programming, information and letters received from charities and clubs they belong to, CD-ROMs, the Internet, catalogues, and more besides. The EAL student also read letters, forms, and so on, for her mother who knew too little English to be able to do so for herself. Judging by this evidence, if we do not find out about, or pay attention to, the whole picture of young people's reading, then our conclusions about their reading experiences, capabilities and the curriculum we provide for them are going to be simplistic and lacking in precision.

Information from a very large-scale survey directed by Christine Hall and Martin Coles adds to the complexity of the picture. Their *Children's Reading Choices* project sought to replicate Frank Whitehead's earlier study for the Schools Council, *Children's Reading Habits 10–16* (Whitehead et al., 1977). The survey's findings not only support the view that young people, both boys and girls, read a wider variety of texts than we might suppose, but also that within those texts, especially magazines, they encounter an extensive range of genres: fiction, non-fiction and 'faction' (Hall and Coles, 1999).

When students note the television, video and computer reading they do, the range is equally diverse. Teachers, analysing the results of a survey carried out in their Essex secondary school, comment:

> Over and over again pupils made comments like *I watch TV for fiction* and while no-one would want to advocate that this should mean we do not encourage reading of fiction we do need to expand our concept of reading so that we can teach pupils to be critical readers of all sorts of text – fiction, fact and the communications media.
>
> (Spratt and Sturdy, 1998)

Forms of 'cineliteracy' play an increasingly important part in students' reading and have significance not just for the content of the programmes, but particularly for the structures of the verbal and visual texts involved. While soaps depend on dialogue, news coverage combines commentary with analysis. Sitcoms use more visual and verbal humour and are often concise in their plot structures, while film plots cover wide ranges of space and time. The verbal and visual language of advertising and exquisite 30-second narratives offer yet more text experiences, which feed into other kinds of reading. The huge popularity of Baz Luhrmann's film of *Romeo and Juliet* (even taking into account the Leonardo DiCaprio factor), which involves a sophisticated multiplicity of verbal and visual texts, provides evidence of the highly developed cineliteracy of most young people today. Building on the success of the film, as so many did, teachers acknowledged the value of linking the pleasures and interests of voluntary reading with the possibilities of studying Shakespeare's plays in the classroom. Such a wide range of home experience of reading serves as a very strong platform for the reading demands of a varied curriculum.

Several questions for teachers arise from even the limited findings of the small-scale classroom research referred to above. How can teachers find out as precisely as possible what students read beyond the classroom, and how does this relate to their reading at school? How can teachers build on aspects of reading with which students already feel confident, and help them to learn more about the kinds of reading and texts with which they are not already familiar or confident? There are many possible answers to these questions, but one thing is absolutely clear, namely the need to find out about students' home reading in the first place.

Gender and reading

Another issue that is likewise much more complex than some would have us believe, and that needs to be treated as such, is the whole business of boys' and girls' reading. Elaine Millard, in her book *Differently Literate*, points out that: 'it is tempting, when arguing from the kinds of reading undertaken by the majority of pupils, to distribute the subsets of reading genre along gender lines' (Millard, 1997). Elaine Millard researched secondary schools, but gender difference is an aspect of reading practice that can provide cause for concern at a much earlier stage in children's education. Hazel Davies, a primary-school teacher in Essex, wanted to investigate why some of her Year 6 boys had lost interest in reading. After a very carefully observed study, she concluded:

> The reasons are many and complex, but three main issues stand out. Firstly cultural attitudes: *it's not cool to read* and *Dad's only reading is the Evening Gazette, backwards* Oliver told me. Secondly, the reading materials we provide. This has been the main focus of my project, and the very positive response from Chris and Jamie, and all the boys involved in the project, has shown that we *can* provide a range of books that is interesting and stimulating to boys of any age throughout the school. Thirdly, the way in which reading is offered in school. Yes, as teachers, we all appreciate the peace of silent reading, but the part of the reading project which gave the boys the most pleasure was sharing the books: looking at the pictures together, working out the puzzles together and talking together.
>
> (Davies, 1997)

In secondary school, the matter becomes even more complicated. Caroline Daly (1999) observed Year 9 boys using literacy in different subject areas. Their reading behaviours raised for her the question:

> What significance lies in the agreements, acquiescences and resistances that fluctuate in the course of a school day across a range of subjects?
>
> (Daly, 1999)

She concludes that 'boys as well as girls know well how to act like a "reader" '. But there is a problem in using the undifferentiated term 'boys':

> The critical question 'which boys' seems an obvious one. Current initiatives to raise boys' achievement often fail to acknowledge that class and race might have a complicating impact on such an all-embracing objective.
>
> (*ibid.*)

In another recent study, Judith Solsken points out further complexities:

> The learning biographies of the children in this study show that the gender dynamics around literacy in each family involved a highly specific interaction of many factors, including in addition to the mother's predominant role, the participation of fathers in children's literacy activities, the gender and relative age of siblings and their role in each other's literacy, and the treatment by family members of literacy as work or play.
>
> (Solsken, 1993)

A recent Ofsted report on gender and performance also confirms these views, namely that, although there is evidence that boys lag behind girls in literacy performance, 'there are no simple explanations for the gender gap in performance, nor any simple solutions' (Arnot *et al.*, 1998). There *are* solutions nevertheless, drawn together, for example, in publications like the thought-provoking *Boys and Reading* (Barrs and Pidgeon, 1998), the outcome of a working party set up to explore this issue precisely. These include: more focused monitoring of boys' and girls' reading; using different groupings: mixed and single sex; extending the range of texts available; greater involvement of adult role models, especially males, taking account of class and ethnicity; discussions about individual progress with students; planned and thoughtful teacher intervention. As members of that group remind us, however, the solutions are more likely to be plural than singular, given the many-faceted experiences brought by readers – both boys and girls – into classrooms.

Mindful of the relative rights of all students to become satisfied and committed readers, it is important to discover the complexity of what makes a reader like he or she is, not to neglect our responsibility to include a variety of types of text, and to teach as wide a range of approaches to texts as possible. Here, as elsewhere, though, one principle which can guide us in the search for multiple solutions is that of *action research*. This can lead teachers to link their own research findings with planning, teaching and assessment in informed and reflective ways, finely tuned to the nuances of their own classrooms and students. Undertaking such research might be a daunting prospect if it weren't for the knowledge that help is at hand. This help comes not from outside agencies, but from the readers themselves, as they give us access to their responses to reading.

Responsibility and response

Students given the chance to talk or write about their reading in conversations conducted face to face, or through reading journals and reading autobiographies, will often communicate not only huge enthusiasm but also insights of startling perception and clarity. Once again, there is much to learn from these dialogues, not just about what students read or what motivates them to read, but about the very act of reading itself. They provide us with rich material from which to construct different 'frameworks for teaching' rather than leaving us to attempt to fit everything into a single model.

Consider, for example, how the following students' comments provide guidance for their teachers to build on. A Year 5 teacher in an Inner London school established group reading and reading journals as an attempt to raise motivation for reading. Students were asked to give advice to teachers who wanted to help children to improve their reading. Leigh comments:

> One of the best things to make someone a better reader must be confidence
> from whomever they are reading to and self confidence pulls a lot of people

through. Here is a bit of advice for the person who is listening to whom-
ever is reading:

1   Remain calm at all times
2   Try and give the reader help with a word by splitting it up
3   Do not rush the reader on any word
4   Have confidence in the reader at all times.

(Bearne, 1994)

This ten-year-old recognises the affective elements of reading, which do not
appear in the official documentation. Elizabeth sums it up succinctly:

> What I think you need to encourage reading are: a patient teacher, a book
> that suits you and a good imagination.

(*ibid.*)

Spencer gives a complete explanation of the reading curriculum:

> I like to do things like reading books. Every morning my class do reading.
> We fill in a little book called our Reading Record. I have not always liked
> reading. I do not like reading books without pictures, and books that are
> sometimes easy. I like to read books that are challenging. I read a lot of the
> time when I don't even know I'm reading. I like a lot of adventure and
> funny storys. In our class we have group reading. I like this and I like fol-
> lowing storys when other people are reading them. I like all Judy Blume
> storys. My teacher reads us first chapters of books where we write down
> notes and then what we think of the story. In assembly my teacher reads
> books. After she reads them she asks us questions about the story she has
> read to us. I like it when our teacher asks the questions. I like reading
> through my rough drafts of work.

(*ibid.*)

He makes it very clear that he, for one, doesn't see reading pictorial text as
'easy' but that he welcomes the challenges picture books offer. He also
recognises the range of reading experiences on offer in his classroom, including
explicit attention to environmental print, and reading drafts of his own writing.
All of the children in this class, regardless of their fluency in reading, were keen
to talk and write about their reading, knew a range of strategies for getting
meaning out of print and clearly saw themselves as readers who could offer
constructive advice on reading to others.

A primary school in Essex operated a system of reading partners where Year
5 pupils teamed up with Year 3 pupils. The students' comments reveal not
only an awareness of the processes of reading, but a gradual development of a
language through which to talk about reading. The younger children
comment:

I have made a new friend. It helps me and it's fun. I've never had a reading partner before. It's better than reading to the teacher because he's a boy like me. It means we can laugh about it at the end and teachers wouldn't have had time to. As he's older than me he knows more words than me and he can correct me. He sometimes tells me to split words up. Sometimes he tells me to look at the picture.

She is a good reading partner. I knew her before. If I miss out a word by accident she tells me to go back. She says, 'sound words out', or she finds a little word inside a big word. She lives right near to me so it's nice to have her as my partner. With a friend you can look at the pictures afterwards – teachers can't do that because they have other children to listen to. You get more reading time. You can get more clues to what is going to happen in the story, before you read it all at once. With the teacher you only read a bit at a time.

The confident use of meta-language to talk about reading reminds us forcefully of Bruner's argument for interactivity in role-modelling. Furthermore, a look at secondary-school students reflecting on their reading in reading-journals shows that they gradually develop the use of internal and therefore independent dialogue, as we shall see below.

Reading-journals have many benefits, not least that they can provide an opportunity for students and teachers to reflect jointly on the students' reading. Their value lies in students recording in some detail their initial encounters with texts, rather than simply their final ideas and opinions. The accumulated record of reading processes and developments, reflection and response, can form the basis for more carefully shaped course-work at a later stage. What it provides in the meantime, though, is a continuous record of reading, both the texts *and* the processes of reading them. Using journals for responding to whole-class texts as well as independent reading, helps students to learn that similar approaches may be adopted with any text, regardless of who has chosen it or what kind of text it is. By writing about texts studied by the whole class, students learn what kinds of questions or observations it is interesting to ask or record. These can then be applied to their personal reading as well. To list only a few of the important points: students can be encouraged to predict; to reconsider earlier journal entries; to write down questions that they want the text to answer for them at a later stage; and to be explicit about how they are drawing on their own social, cultural or intertextual experiences in order to make sense of what they are reading.

Here a Year 9 reader[1] studying Susan Hinton's *The Outsiders* notes, for example, that reading narrative is not always a straightforward linear process:

I like the way the book goes backwards and forwards so we are always learning more of the gang ... I said earlier that the book keeps going 'backwards and forwards'. This did happen like Johnny saying 'Stay gold'. That didn't make sense when we first heard it but it did at the end.

Another student from the same group demonstrates an understanding of the potential unreliability of a narrator:

> I dislike Ponyboy's part. To me he seems too sure of himself, maybe that's the way they are. He judges other people's character too closely. I quote 'Dally only thinks of himself' but we found out today that it wasn't true.

Not all students like using journals. Why? For some it is because they interfere with the pleasures of reading:

> I don't like journals but they're better than reviews. I'd rather do without journals or reviews and just get on with the book.

Others prefer to talk rather than write:

> I don't like putting books into writing. I just like to say about it instead of writing.

So what would be a better way for teachers to find out about students' reading?

> Ask them!

> Use tapes instead of reading logs because it would be a lot quicker, you'd get more in and save rainforests.

However, others express very different views:

> I like to write a review because when I read a book I like to tell people or write it down so I can read it in the future.

> I find that if I don't tell someone about a book that I'm really enjoying I feel as if I'm going to burst. This is another reason why I like reading journals.

> It helps you to find how your views have changed by looking back on earlier entries and if your predictions were right.

> It gives you more freedom to write your thoughts.

> There are not any set answers in a reading journal.

The kinds of insight that emerge from students' written and spoken dialogue with teachers and each other can be used – by the teacher who is looking out for them – not just to summarise or comment on the stage of reading development that students have already achieved, but more importantly to identify what they might achieve next. Journal dialogues make an ideal site for Vygotsky's 'zone of proximal development', the place where the teacher's instruction is 'that which marches ahead of development and leads it' (Vygotsky, 1986).

While heeding the points made by students who like to talk rather than write about their reading, and ensuring that they have plenty of opportunity to utilise their preferred learning styles, there are equally important arguments for keeping journals, precisely because they *are* written, not spoken. Because there are not any set answers in a reading journal, students can begin to understand that their reading may be as valid as the next person's, without the anxieties that may arise from having to present their suggestions in front of a large group of people. This understanding can increase confidence and develop a more sharply defined awareness of what it means to be a reader. The permanence of the writing enables the subtle and shifting nuances of the reading process to be made visible and can lead students to see more clearly the nature and power of written text.

It must be remembered that the kinds of activities being referred to here will be of only limited use if they are not seen as part of a whole-school approach to reading. This point is made very clearly by Alastair West in 'The production of readers', a summary of research he conducted in the 1980s. Of the three secondary schools included in the study, he writes that all of them:

> placed a high valuation upon reading in their rhetoric, but only one had discovered ways of giving that high valuation any structural form within the working practices and social relations of the institution.
>
> (West, 1986)

For some schools and teachers the National Literacy Strategy offers a structure to help them realise their aims and implement their reading policies. For others, however, it will not be enough. For them the framework is too rigid, the rationale too thin. They are seeking altogether richer and more varied approaches, woven out of a fabric which represents more fully the developing thoughts and feelings of the students that they teach.

Insights, planning and assessment

Comments by students, such as those quoted above, show just how important it is for teachers to have a vocabulary through which to describe what 'getting better at reading' involves in order to model reflective comments for developing readers. Reflecting on reading doesn't just contribute to personal development, but to progress in reading. Most importantly, it contributes to the development of independence and discrimination, making choices about when, what, and how to read. Having an insight into the mind of the reader also allows the teacher to plan for future development. Judging by the teaching objectives (not 'learning' objectives) in the National Literacy framework, criteria for progress would be firmly tied to knowledge about text structures, knowledge about language (at sentence and word level), comprehension and composition. There is nothing wrong with that except for the yawning gap it leaves. What is missing is the essential element of developing preferences and choices, in other words, becoming a reflective, responsive and critical reader.

In an attack on summative forms of testing, based on a wide-ranging study of all the recent research on assessment, Paul Black and Dylan Wiliam argue that standards are only raised by changes that are put into direct effect by teachers and pupils in classrooms:

> There is a body of firm evidence that formative assessment is an essential feature of classroom work and that development of it can raise standards. … Our education system has been subjected to many far-reaching initiatives which, whilst taken in reaction to concerns about existing practices, have been based on little evidence about their potential to meet those concerns.
>
> (Black and Wiliam, 1998)

This raises some questions about SATs and terminal examinations as helpful forms of assessment, especially given the extent to which they are privileged in league tables and media coverage of reading standards. For example, the results for the Key Stage 2 Reading SAT (1998), taken by the Year 5/6 class whose reading habits at home were reported earlier, showed some significant disparities. About a third of the class did not finish the paper, and so about six or seven children were awarded Level 3 when their classroom performance showed that they were much more accomplished readers than this. If the main assessment tools – SATs – are summative, looking largely at the 'comprehension' elements of reading, not at the readers' abilities in making critical choices (in spite of teachers' attention to the structure of texts), then we do not end up with a description of genuine progress, let alone achievement, in reading.

Useful assessment, according to Black and Wiliam, should be related to:

> the quality of teacher–pupil interactions, the stimulus and help for pupils to take active responsibility for their own learning, the particular help needed to move pupils out of the 'low-attainment' trap, and the development thereby of the habits needed by all if they are to become capable of life-long learning. Improvements in formative assessment which are

within reach can contribute substantially to raising standards in all of those aspects.

(*ibid.*)

The writers go on to emphasise that improvements in formative assessment will depend on a properly funded and managed in-service programme, on acceptance of slow development and low-key (at first) dissemination; the removal of teachers' feelings of 'insecurity, guilt, frustration and anger' about assessment; continuing research in 'active development work' about teachers' perceptions and experience, and continuing evaluation of such a programme.

Conclusions

The teachers described in this chapter, and many more whose work is detailed in other texts to which we have referred, are continually discovering for themselves the value and efficacy of reflecting on, discussing and theorising their own classroom approaches to the teaching of reading. They are, to borrow Margaret Meek's words, 'researchers in their own classrooms rather than simply those who carry out instructions' (Meek, 1997). If the teaching of reading is to lead to communities of avid and attentive readers, who read with pleasure and passion, who question and interpret, listen and respond, criticise and initiate discussion, then what is needed is space, time and positive encouragement for teachers to take intellectual as well as practical responsibility for the development of the reading curriculum, and for students to enjoy more of the reading rights to which they are entitled. Reading is a delicate business and requires finely tuned instruments to record and assess progress and development. Pennac concludes *Reads Like A Novel* with a reminder that a sensitive rather than a heavy-handed touch may be the most productive.

> Reading offers [man] no definitive explanation of his fate, but weaves a tight network of correspondences between life and him. These correspondences, tiny and secretive, speak of the paradoxical good fortune of being alive, even while they're illuminating the tragic absurdity of life. The result is that our reasons for reading are quite as strange as are our reasons for living. And no one is charged to have us render an account of that intimate strangeness.
>
> The few adults who have really given me something to read have always effaced themselves before the books, and they've always been careful not to ask me what I had *understood* in these books. To them, of course, I'd talk about what I'd read.
>
> (Pennac, 1994)

What is needed, above all, is that we keep thinking about reading and noting our emerging understanding of the processes and texts that make up reading experience and experiences. For, as Robert Scholes avows:

> Reading is not just a means to other ends. It is one of the great rewards for the use of our capacities, a reason for living, an end in itself.
>
> (Scholes, 1989)

Questions for discussion

1   How can teachers of reading resolve the tension which often arises between the demands of direct teaching and the need to allow time and space for students to develop as discriminating, independent readers?
2   How can teachers' observations and enquiries about developing readers' tastes, preferences and experience be used to encourage more adventurous reading?
3   Formative assessment of reading often relies upon written tasks. What other modes of response (e.g. visual, oral, diagrammatic) can be used to enable teachers to gather reliable evidence of students' understanding and interpretation of the texts they read?

Note

1   The points that follow are taken from a variety of reading journals and taped discussions with secondary-school students over the years. The authors would like to thank all those whose views and comments are represented here.

Further reading

Hall, C. and Coles, M. (1999) *Children's Reading Choices*, London: Routledge.
Hall and Coles' study is based on a detailed survey of what 8000 10–14-year-olds across England choose to read and why. It replicates Frank Whitehead's seminal study carried out in 1977, thus providing important information about children's independent reading over two decades. The evidence from the survey challenges prevailing pessimism about children's reading habits. Hall and Coles' analysis of the texts that children read provides a framework for teachers to judge for themselves the nature and quality of what is read.

Kress, G.and van Leween, T. (1996) *The Grammar of Visual Design*, London: Routledge.
For some of us this is tough reading, but rewarding, as it outlines current theories about the ways in which visual texts are constructed. It is not, however, just another book about media studies, but a thorough and demanding explanation of how social semiotic theory offers a way of talking about visual text design, encompassing oil painting as well as magazine layout, the comic strip as well as the scientific diagram.

Meek, M. (1991) *On Being Literate*, London: Bodley Head.
On Being Literate is a rare kind of book about reading: it shows no signs of age. Written with Margaret Meek Spencer's customary wisdom and enthusiasm, and

covering all aspects of classroom, school and community issues about literacy, it ends with a reminder of just why reading is important. It is that there is no guarantee that literacy will make the world a more benign place, but it helps everyone to consider how it might be different.

Styles, M., Bearne, E. and Watson, V. (1996) *Voices Off*, London: Cassell.
The strength of this collection lies in its diversity. Contributors include authors, picture-book makers, poets, teachers and booksellers, all of whom add their voices to those of the texts they describe and explore. This is a rich representation of what matters about children and their encounters with reading.

2 Can teachers empower pupils as writers?

Carole King

If pupils are to be empowered as writers, then they need to understand the potential of writing: to recognise and appreciate it as an active social process within their own lives. Robinson suggests:

> What is basic to the development of literacy, I would argue, is the same as what is basic to its full exercise: the empowerment of individuals to speak freely in such voices as they have about matters that concern them, matters of importance, so that conversations may be nourished. The most debilitating suggestion in our dominant metaphors for literacy is this one: that a language must be learned, a voice acquired, before conversation can begin.
>
> (Robinson, 1990: 264)

This chapter argues that from pre-school onwards, pupils need to be able to talk about themselves as writers, and value writing as a way of 'constructing' as well as 'conveying meaning' (DES, 1989). It suggests that prescriptive training and teaching curricula will not necessarily enable this to happen unless teachers recognise that progress in writing cannot be measured simply by a growing command of its code and conventions.

The chapter exemplifies approaches to teaching writing which do empower pupils as writers who are able both to explore and share themselves as individuals, through the process of writing within the expressive and poetic modes (Britton *et al.*, 1975). The chapter draws on work within Key Stages 1 and 2 and has implications for secondary English teaching, since the principles which underpin the practices described are valid for all age groups.

Home literacy: why do pupils choose to write?

Five-year-old Hannah, drawing on home-literacy experiences, covers scraps of paper with notes, lists, letters to friends, thoughts and statements about herself, all of which are concerned with sorting out personal relationships and expressing preferences (Figure 2.1). Six-year-old Ann is able to fictionalise herself as the main protagonist in a book full of stories based on family happenings real or imagined (Figure 2.2). Unable to articulate the reason why she writes she says, 'I don't know really what happens. Don't know how the ideas pop in.' But she feels 'good when it's finished. I want to get it done quickly so I can do another one.' Her ten-year-old brother, who initially provided the model for her own independent story-writing, is able to be explicit about his enjoyment, relating it to playing with Lego™ figures, where the toys speak to each other. 'It's like writing a story because you're thinking about what to say, playing it out.' Eleven-year-old Gary, in a class discussion on home writing explains:

> I just write on paper at home. If I've been naughty, about being sorry and it lets me off. I make a paper aeroplane and fly it down with words. Or just because you want to and then read it yourself.

Figure 2.1   Hannah's work

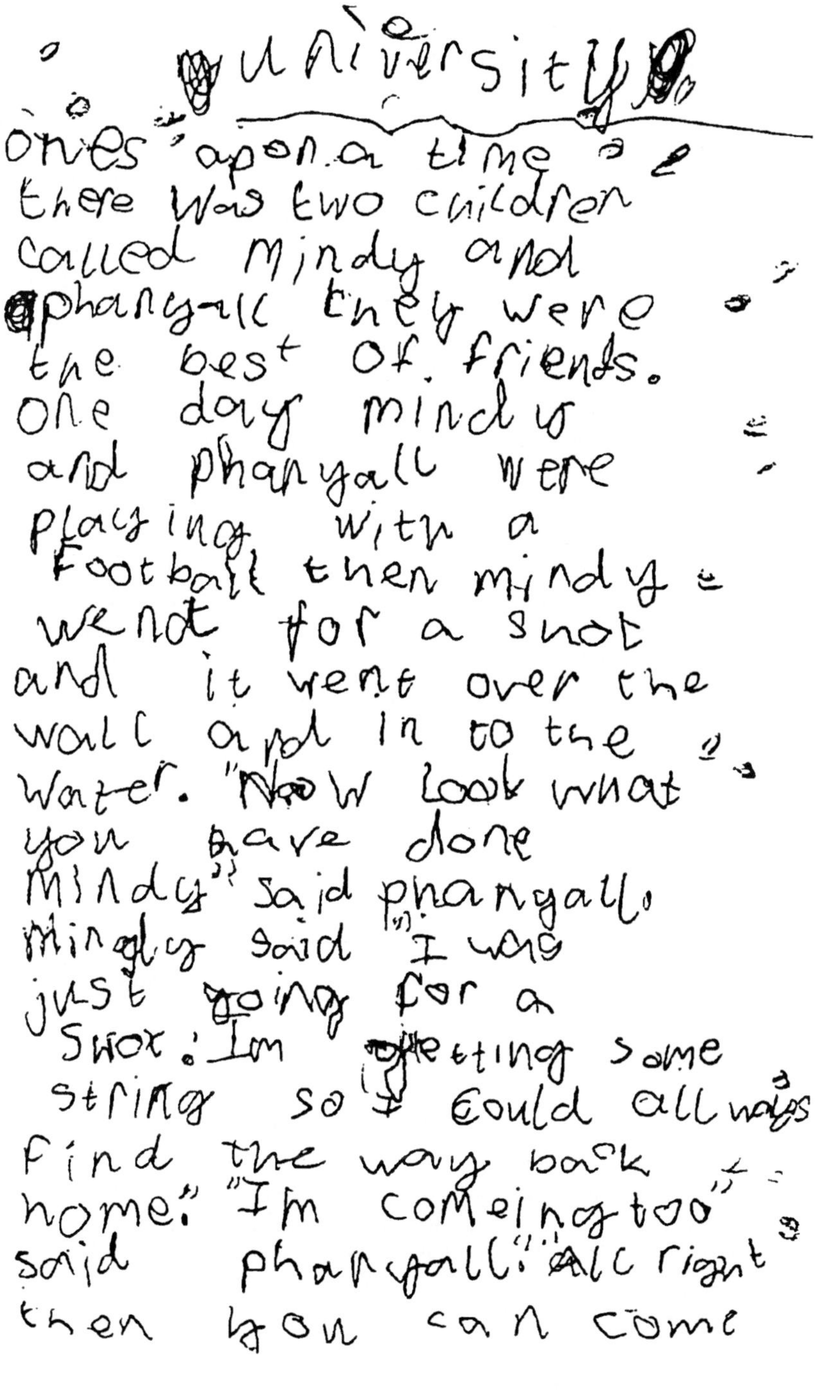

university

ones apon a time
there was two children
called mindy and
phanyall they were
the best of friends.
one day mindy
and phanyall were
playing with a
football then mindy
went for a shot
and it went over the
wall and in to the
water. "Now look what
you have done
mindy" said phanyall.
mindy said "I was
just going for a
shot. Im getting some
string so I could allways
find the way back
home." "Im comeing too"
said phanyall. "All right
then you can come

Figure 2.2   Ann's work

These children have an implicit understanding of the genres they use and have discovered for themselves the power of writing to act in and on their lives. Essentially they write to satisfy personal needs, but their writing has different functions.

Britton's functional writing categories were developed in the 1970s from the work of D. W. Harding (1960), and still provide an illuminating way of looking at what writers are actually doing with their writing and at the roles they take as they write. These are aspects of writing that are easily overlooked in classrooms. Covering the curriculum and achieving good public test results seem often to be the most important reasons for the teaching and learning of writing. Britton summarised his functional categories as follows:

> *language in the role of the participant* designates any use of language to get things done, to pursue the world's affairs, while *language in the spectator role* covers verbal artefacts, the use of language *to make something* rather than *to get something done*.
>
> (Britton, 1993: 28, his emphasis)

The participant/spectator distinction has been a central, though controversial, tenet of Britton's functional linguistic theory, yet Britton always maintained that these should not be seen as mutually exclusive categories. Figure 2.3 shows the relationship between the language functions and the suggested modes of writing. These form a continuum of development, where the 'transactional' and 'poetic' modes typify the participant and spectator roles respectively, and where a third mode, the 'expressive', sits between the two and may well form the basis for more explicit development of either (*ibid.*).

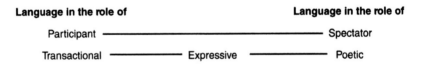

Figure 2.3   Britton's continuum of language development

Writing in the expressive mode shares many similarities with spoken language. It is loosely structured, close to the self, and dependent upon a shared context for interpretation. Its audience is limited to the writer him/herself or one 'assumed to share much of the writer's context' (Britton *et al.*, 1975: 89). Often the reader is the only intended audience; as one Year 6 pupil remarked about her journal writing, 'It's like my face on the page.' Hannah's notes and Gary's aeroplane apologies fall within this expressive mode, and are transactional in purpose.

Ann and Paul, as spectators of real or imagined experiences, craft their ideas into stories. They write in the poetic mode, using:

language as an art medium. A piece of poetic writing is a verbal construct, an object made out of language. The words themselves, and all they refer to, are selected to make an arrangement, a formal pattern.

(*ibid.*: 90)

Applebee (1984) has refined Britton's classification system and argued that the spectator and participant roles are terms that help us to recognise and value the different ways that we represent the world to ourselves through language. They provide vital foci for research (Applebee, 1978). Indeed, Britton's category system has been extensively used for empirical studies of the way that writing for different functions and disciplines may result in different kinds of learning (Durst and Newell, 1989). However, these studies generally focus on the way that transactional writing requires the analysis and synthesis necessary for the reformulation of ideas. They neglect the way that writing in the poetic mode is equally concerned with such cognitive activities.

This chapter recognises the importance of expressive journal writing, but focuses mainly on writing within the poetic mode. Adopting a constructivist view of learning, it advocates that writing poetry and stories need to be recognised and appreciated as learning processes. Writing within the spectator role can enable pupils to review, reflect upon and make sense of conflicting experiences. Existing knowledge can be modified in the light of the new, so that the act of writing becomes another 'way of knowing' (Baker *et al.*, 1996). Genre theory itself highlights the significance of Britton's functional categories as ways of valuing writing. However, its concentration on the transactional forms leads to the neglect of the expressive and poetic as ways of making meanings, which are also dependent on 'a cultural process rather than the solitary invention of the individual' (Willinsky, 1990: 206).

Current models of school literacy: why do pupils write?

Bruner advises that 'the curriculum of a subject should be determined by the most fundamental understanding that can be achieved of the underlying principles that give structure to that subject' (1960: 31). The original National Curriculum (DES, 1989) was generally underpinned by such principles, but this did not necessarily lead to an improvement in the teaching of writing; some teachers misinterpreted the content because they did not understand the principles. It stressed the meaning-making potential of writing and recognised that 'written language serves many purposes both for individuals and for society as a whole, and is not limited to the communication of information' (DES, 1989: 33).

The 1995 revision of the curriculum, while recognising 'the value of writing as a means of remembering, communicating, organising and developing ideas and information, and as a source of enjoyment' (DfE, 1995a: 9) has a greater stress on communicative competence. The 'Initial Teacher Training National Curriculum for English' (DfEE, 1997b), listing the standards to be achieved for qualified teacher status (QTS), has a similar emphasis. The half page given to the teaching of compositional skills makes no mention of children writing for their own purposes, neither is any explicit connection made between writing and learning. The main focus is on teaching technical aspects. This focus is further emphasised by the reports on national curriculum assessments for seven- and eleven-year-olds, where the critical summaries of the strengths and weaknesses of these developing writers foreground technical aspects at the expense of meaning making (Qualifications and Curriculum Authority, 1998d, e).

This concentration on the surface, rather than the deep structures of writing, negates the power of writing, for it implies that the stories and poems that pupils write have no function other than to prove their ability to use structural and stylistic features. Unless teachers themselves understand that writing is about developing meaning, they are likely to view it as a list of skills to be learnt in the practice of a range of 'forms', rather than as a complex social, cultural and historical activity, involving both affective and cognitive processes, some of which are evident in the comments and writing of the pupils quoted within this chapter.

A recent study designed to 'help the Teacher Training Agency and teachers in England to understand more clearly how effective teachers help pupils become literate' found that 'the effective teachers tend to place a high value upon communication and composition in their views about the teaching of reading and writing: that is, they believed that the creation of meaning in literacy was fundamental' (Medwell *et al.*, 1998: 3). This did not mean that technical aspects were neglected, rather that 'they were trying very hard to ensure such skills were developed in pupils with a clear eye to the pupil's awareness of their importance and function' (*ibid.*: 31).

Alhough it was designed to improve literacy teaching, the National Literacy Strategy (Department for Education and Employment, 1998) may well have the reverse effect if teachers fail to understand the need to teach skills in meaningful contexts. Yet this can be difficult for teachers, for though they are all able to write, this does not imply that they understand fully the nature and purpose of written language.

The student teachers who take a writing module as part of their course at the University of Brighton admit that they had not previously given much thought to writing itself. Though well used to writing assignments, most have little recent experience of writing stories or poems and plays. They are expected to be able to help pupils to do so without fully appreciating either the pleasures or problems such writing involves. By participating in writing workshops run on the lines suggested by Elbow (1973), where they are encouraged to respond to each others' writing in structured, supportive but non-threatening ways, all students gain greater understanding of writing and awareness of themselves as writers. In an assignment where she had explored the way that writing itself can develop the relationship between language and thought, one student, Amy, wrote: 'To some extent, the act of writing the assignment made explicit things that I implicitly knew'.

This is a pertinent comment, since it relates to an observation made in the Medwell study: 'although all primary teachers are effective readers and writers ... they have learned these skills without necessarily having become explicitly aware of them' (Medwell *et al.*, 1998). This comment would seem to suggest that such knowledge is likely to produce more effective teachers of writing. Drawing on Britton's work, Amy wrote:

> Having done almost no writing in the poetic mode in the last ten years, I am now aware of the way in which it can convey thought. Expressive writing is the closest mode of writing to speech and most direct link to thought. However, poetic writing can be more powerful because the writer can manipulate the language and writing conventions available to her to enable her thought to become clearer to the reader.

How does explicit knowledge about writing inform practice at Key Stage 1?

First, it enables teachers to help pupils discover what writing is for, as Beryl, a reception teacher and primary-school language co-ordinator, demonstrates. As a keen writer and an avid journal keeper, she is able to draw from her own writing experiences when teaching pupils. She 'tries to provide opportunities for pupils in the nursery to hold on to their experience, to go over it and to evaluate it through writing so that they are encouraged to make sense of the world through writing'. This is evident also in her work with reception pupils. Valuing the role of expressive journal writing as a way of connecting with one's thinking, she introduces her pupils to think books. At the beginning of the autumn term, she models how to use them by writing her own thoughts about a teacher who is ill: 'I am thinking about Miss Bryant who is in hospital.'

The pupils are then given A4 plain paper books, told to write their names on the front, and then write what they are thinking. They all complete the first in their own way, and then, selecting a variety of writing equipment and their own place to write, settle down to transfer thought to paper. Charlie fills the page with linked 'm's (Figure 2.4) and, when asked what she is thinking about, replies: 'I'm thinking about my mummy waiting for me at the school gate.' Throughout the year, these journal entries reveal the pupils' concerns and interests as they record friendships, visits, pets and school events. From the beginning, writing is seen as a powerful way to access thinking, which, as is evidenced later in this chapter, can then be worked on for publication.

Observing Beryl working with a group of Reception pupils at the end of the year, it is clear that they have no hesitation in writing their own thoughts. The pupils have been studying texture and shape as a topic. Having drawn a pineapple, Beryl now wants them to 'respond in words'. Her learning intentions are thus concerned with meaning rather than technical skills. The writing does naturally involve the pupils in using handwriting or keyboard skills, working out

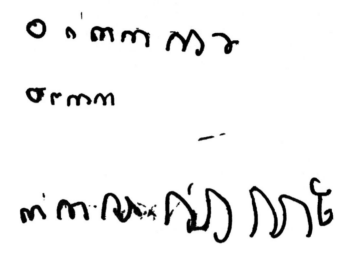

Figure 2.4   Charlie's work

spellings and ordering their ideas, but in pursuit of meaning rather than as a way of ticking off teaching objectives. The session begins with pupils responding critically to each other's pictures before re-examining the pineapple, and suggesting relevant adjectives and phrases which are written, with their help, on a flip chart. These are then removed and the pupils begin to write their poems. There is sustained silent writing for fifteen minutes, the teacher intervening only occasionally to encourage an early finisher to be more reflective or suggest ways of tackling an unknown spelling. At the end of the time the pupils share what they have written and this is scribed on the flip chart for discussion. Amy reads her poem (Figure 2.5):

> It's juicy
> It's spiky
> It's green
> It's nice

Beryl's response, 'There's something about that,' encourages others to begin to be critically appreciative and Fiona suggests, 'It's good words.'

Beryl writes it on the board, correcting spellings and putting in the apostrophe as she does so. She then asks them to read it together and clap the rhythm, praising the writer and saying, 'I like the rhythm.' Later she admits that, 'This is not a teacherly response – a genuine one. This is fun – almost my naive understanding of form.' Thus, in every sharing, the pupils' attention is drawn to the form as well as the words as they bring together their knowledge about, and feelings for, the pineapple. Their language is close to the expressive, but, as they 'shape at the point of utterance' (Britton, 1982: 110), so they show the

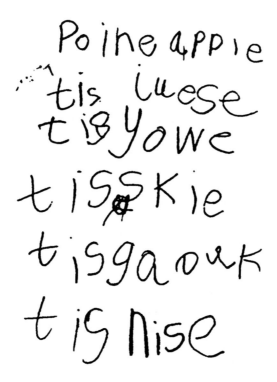

Figure 2.5   Amy's work

beginnings of writing in the poetic mode. In spectator role they write their way between home and school learning, drawing on their past experiences of pineapples and their school discussion and observation.

Although the content is prescribed, in all other ways these pupils have ownership of their work, even to the point of one child refusing to share it until it has been reworked with a friend's help. Beryl accepts this for 'I value the chance when writing to opt out but on the other hand I sometimes need deadlines. It's a question of knowing your pupils.'

This guided writing session exemplifies much that is needed if pupils are to be empowered as writers. As members of this writing workshop they learn about:

- generating and shaping ideas;
- supporting and responding to each other;
- developing critical appreciation;
- writing poetry;
- developing transcription skills as they compose.

The act of literacy here is an empowering one because it enables pupils to use their writing as a way of looking anew at their subject. It also nourishes their self-esteem and respect for each other as writers with something to say.

How does explicit knowledge about writing inform practice at Key Stage 2?

When teachers have little personal understanding of the writing process and of writing as an active meaning-making strategy, then becoming members of a writing workshop is one powerful way of helping them to develop and extend their understanding. Kate, a primary-school teacher, attended a series of writing workshops run over one year in her school as a form of continuing professional development. The teachers were invited to keep journals using the expressive mode to reflect upon both themselves as writers and their practice as teachers of writing. They also experimented with collaborative and individual writing in the poetic mode, learning how to share and respond in the same way as the students at university had done, and as the Reception pupils were learning to do.

From the workshop writing, Kate recognised the value both of explicating her own ideas about writing and of the need to write from real knowledge and experience. She changed her practice. Ceasing to 'pluck a title out of the air', she encouraged her pupils to use topic work as a starting point, maintaining that it was important for them to make connections between school and home knowledge. The value of this approach was demonstrated by the following poem written by Simon, a Year 3 pupil, after completing a unit of work on batteries and magnets (Figure 2.6):

> Temper Temper
> I'm losing my temper
> It's making me mad
> I feel I'm going to do
> Something bad.
>
> Like a magnet my brother is
> Pulling me
> But I repel him easily.

Cognitive and affective processes and formal and informal knowledge come together in the writing of this simple poem, which itself becomes an extended metaphor, symbolising the relationship between himself and his twin brother. As spectator of his own experiences, Simon is able to forge new understanding and see himself anew. This poem enabled Kate to see that 'When we were talking about writing – we write best when we need to say something, some emotion – obviously the same here.' In her next class she wanted her Year 5/6 pupils to feel this need to write, for 'If they haven't felt that, that's what's missing. That's what gives them the power to write what they want and how.' Her pupils had become more fully engaged in their writing, but she was still the instigator, invariably setting both subject and genre.

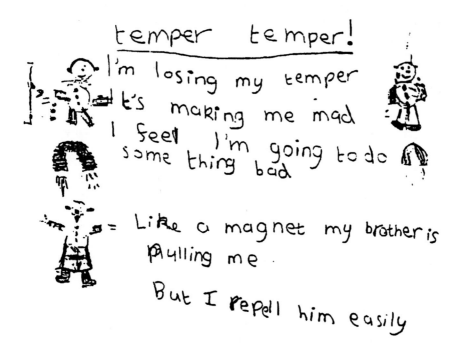

temper temper!

I'm losing my temper

It's making me mad

I feel I'm going to do

some thing bad

Like a magnet my brother is

pulling me.

But I repell him easily

Figure 2.6 Simon's work

Writing in the expressive mode: using think books

As part of the workshops, Kate had benefited from keeping a reflective journal. Like Beryl, Kate therefore introduced think books, where the pupils could write freely, linking home and school concerns, because: 'What's going on in their minds is mostly to do with out of school'.

Through constant discussion, the pupils had become able to articulate their ideas about writing, and could explain how they used their think books for a range of reasons, writing about 'feelings', 'happenings', 'worries' and 'secrets'. While such writing could be 'fun', the comfort of being able to communicate with the page was valued. 'I kind of like, think it talks back ... It makes me happy when I'm lonely, just someone to talk to.' Such replies do reveal how much outside life can interfere with what the pupils should be doing in school, as Kate had recognised. Quarrels with parents and friends, the death of pets, and worries about school work obviously affected the extent to which these pupils were able to give full concentration to the demands of school tasks that must often seem irrelevant to their immediate concerns and needs. The fact that their journals were rarely shared, stressed the personal value of this expressive writing as a way both of coping with present problems and remembering past experiences.

Sally, who struggled both to articulate and transcribe her ideas, not only enjoyed the freedom to write what she liked in her journal, but also the fact that her think book allowed her to write without the need to be correct. She had quarrelled with her cousin and 'can't think straight because I'm thinking about what to say to her next time.' This bears out Kate's comment on pupils' thoughts being mainly concerned with their outside lives. Sally expected that writing about her feelings of anger would help her put them aside and get on with other things, just as writing a poem about her dead budgerigar had helped her to cope with the loss: 'It did make me feel a bit happy but then at lunch time I was sad as I read it.' She also used her journal writing to overcome problems with her mother, for it was 'easier to write to her then talk to her.'

Mark used his journal more cautiously, preferring not to reveal 'his dark feelings like anger and hatred on the page.' As a home storywriter he had discovered that 'I'd express more feeling in a story than I would if I just wrote it down.' Like Sally, he was implicitly aware of the spectator role, but he chose to craft his experiences and feelings into a story or poem. Britton claimed 'that activity in the spectator role represents above all a mode of handling the data of experience' and said:

> If the world we operate in is shaped by the way we represent it to ourselves, then it must follow that the means we employ to maintain the unity, co-herence, and harmony of that representation – its truth to experience as we have felt it – must be of lasting concern to each of us.
>
> (1993: 29)

Writing in the spectator role: sharing stories and poems

Based on her workshop experiences, Kate determined that her pupils should be free to write a story or poem, about anything they wanted, for class publication, using their journals for ideas (an approach to which the National Literacy Strategy gives little importance). She modelled how to do this and:

> Not one of them came to me and said, 'What shall I write about?' When they write because it's personal to them they don't seem to need me so much, apart from editing so they can now sustain different kinds of writing and choose how and what to write with few problems.

Drawing on their autobiographical journal material, some wrote fantasy stories, enjoying inventing and peopling their own worlds, where they were almost always predominant players. Others based their work very much within their own lives. Topsy's confident explanation of her choice epitomises the way in which many of the pupils in this class had by now developed their understanding. She chose to write a poem about her past experiences of being bullied. Writing 'to get it fresh out of my mind,' she explains 'in a story you can fictionalise it or change the time but in a poem you can express more feelings.'

These writers had clearly discovered that when they shaped their raw material into a story or poem, the cognitive processes involved have their own intrinsic value. The writing allows them to review and to make something of their experiences, thus illustrating the power of writing within the spectator role. The chosen genre is a forming influence, for not only does it determine the work's structure, but as the writer struggles to bring his/her material under the direction of that structure and its anticipated demands, then the thinking develops. These writers realised the need to redraft and revise as an inherent part of their writing.

Mark was the most articulate here, being very aware of his own composing processes: 'No. I didn't choose it. It just came'. It is not, however, an easy task, but the enjoyment comes from 'what goes into it. Lots of concentration, very realistic if it's like … horror' and the satisfaction from 'just enjoying myself, using imagination wisely.' Joanne's explanation for revising work echoes many of their concerns:

> Sometimes I judge my work on if it expresses … or if I thought I got what I meant over. Sometimes you write poems and they don't get the point over you wanted. It's the words, they could mean two things at the same time.

Creating a writing community: Emma and Rosie in conversation

Unknown to each other, both writers chose to write about their relationship. Emma chose 'one of the bits with most feeling in' from her journal but, conscious of her audience, changed it 'to make it more like a story.' During the writing, 'all I could think about was her, all the time' and the detailed events of the story illustrate the way that strong feelings raise vivid memories, especially her references to the way Rosie looked at her.

Emma's story is shown below:

> It was just an ordinary day. I pulled up the shutters and the sun shone in my eyes. I crept down stairs to find my mum sitting on the sofa.
> She said, 'Don't forget you're going to Sarah's and the pictures.'
> When I got to school, Sarah was already in class. She is a quiet girl and quite a laugh. She has brown hair, a big smile and a bad temper too! The day passed quite fast. On the way home, I couldn't wait to get to Sarah's house. I got home and changed and was ready to go.
> When I got to Sarah's house she started being fussy. She didn't really like what I was wearing. I could tell she wasn't in a good mood with me. Her mum was a good cook and made a lovely meal. In the car, Sarah and the rest of us were excited. Her mum left us having made sure we were in our seats. She had some shopping to do.
> It didn't feel right or like being Sarah's friend. For once in my life I felt not wanted. I could see the hatred in her eyes. She kept looking at me, giving me evil looks. It was nearly time for the film to start. Sarah looked over every few seconds so I pulled faces back at her and she turned away. I

went to the toilet to get away from her but I could still picture her in my mind. I was going to my seat when I saw Sarah in my seat. I gave her an evil look as she often did to me. She moved, whispering to Claire and I could tell it was about me.

After the film, she continued to be horrible. In the car she was trying to ignore me. That's how it seemed anyway. I was never going to talk to her again. I went home and cried. I thought she was a friend I would never lose.

Writing as spectator of her own experiences encouraged reflective revisiting and evaluation of the events and enabled her to begin to deal with her sadness. Knowing that this work would be publicly shared was also a factor in the writing.

Ironically, Rosie too was concerned with their friendship, but her poems bear little relationship to the events described in her journal (Figure 2.7). She chose to write in a more generalised way, crafting her concerns into a first poem where addressing the audience for help and advice seems to be parallel with Emma's tacit plea for reconciliation. Both girls wrote from very strong feelings. Both were unable to understand their situation. Both expected that writing about it might help. Here is Rosie's first poem:

> Why is she, so horrible to me?
> Why is she so mean?
> I wonder if you know because I honestly don't.
>
> Why do we constantly argue?
> Why do I sometimes feel such hate?
> I wonder if you know because I honestly don't.
>
> Why is there such envy between us?
> Why are we such enemies?
> I wonder if you know because I honestly don't.

Rosie insisted that no spite was intended:

> Me and Emma are always arguing. It wasn't to get back at her. Emma's story isn't all true. I can't remember. She was arguing with me as well and I was getting really angry and we were allowed to fictionalise it. She was nice enough to change my name.

Once the two girls had read each other's work, Rosie wrote a second poem that suggested some reconciliation, and both agreed that sharing their writing had enabled them to 'know how each other feel and stops us arguing. We know both sides.'

> *Arguments with Emma*
>
> Emma always slaps me,
> And I slap her back.

Emma called me stupid,
So I called her fat.

Emma pulled my hair,
And I pulled her's back.

Emma said, 'Sorry',
And I said it back.

These are examples of the writer crafting an artefact in words where the affective is the dynamic force. Emma's narrative account is very simply told but

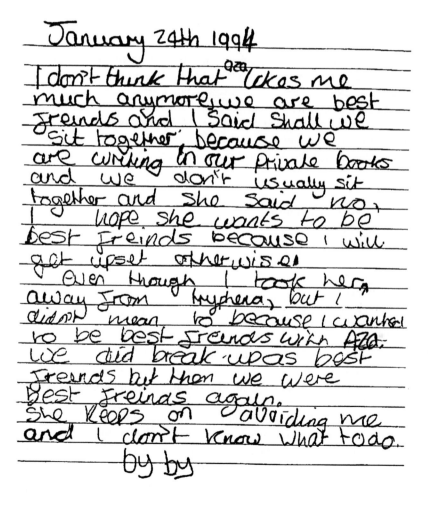

January 24th 1994

I don't think that *aza* likes me much anymore, we are best freinds and I said 'shall we sit together' because we are writing in our private books and we don't usually sit together and she said 'no,' I hope she wants to be best freinds because I will get upset otherwise.
Even though I took her away from mythena, but I didn't mean to because I wanted to be best freinds with Aza. We did break up as best freinds but then we were best freinds again. She keeps on avoiding me and I don't know what to do.
by by

Figure 2.7 Rosie's journal

the feelings are strongly expressed. Rosie's confident and competent handling of two different genres of poetry shows how the form moulds the material, for the first one, with its repetitive refrain, suggests a sense of something to be resolved, which the tight rhyming structure of her second poem clearly defines. The rhyming pattern expresses the balance in this relationship and countermands the power conflict implicit in Emma's story. They are friends again, although Emma is still seen as the protagonist.

Articulating themselves as writers

The pupils selected their own work for a class anthology, while giving reasons for their choices. It was obvious that they valued their work, not just for its technical merits, but because it speaks to them from the page. 'It makes me feel good', and 'This is about my sister leaving home and how I felt when it was happening.' Many comments were related directly to the spectator role in their writing. The observation that 'it made me feel as though I was really there' illustrates the way in which these young writers recognised their power to create and recreate worlds that interest, amuse or concern them.

Eleven-year-old Josh demonstrates this when writing and talking about his poem. Not only was he able to reconcile form and feeling in its creation, but he could also explain how this had been achieved. He also recognised his position in the community of writers within his class; however serious the subject, he knew that his audience would expect some humour.

Leaving

At the end of next month,
I will be leaving,
A new web of school,
I will be weaving.
Six weeks of worrying,
I will be fretting,
And loads more homework,
I will be getting.

Teacher:	Where did the idea come from?
Josh:	I got a brain wave and wrote it in two minutes. I started with 'leaving' and 'weaving' and I thought 'basket', but it wasn't right.
Teacher:	This is where the rhyme sent you … ?
Josh:	To other things. I thought of web and spider. I had a picture of weaving – classes, whole new web as if I've already weaved a web here and know everything about it, so I'd quite like to do a new one.
Teacher:	What kind of things make the web?
Josh:	All my friends, teachers, way round school, dinners. I'll be on the inside spinning towards the outside from year one to the end. And as I weave I'll know it from the inside to the outside.

Teacher: Where did the word 'fretting' come from?
Josh: 'Fretting' – from my mum. She lost her purse and said that she'd been fretting for ages. It was a different word for me; another kind of worry. I was rhyming alternate lines, so 'fretting' and 'getting' came together. The ending is funny because, as I'm serious first, I usually like to have some humour.

In Vygotskian tradition, Josh was perceptive enough to recognise that it is the rhyming pattern that leads him to new ideas (Vygotsky, 1962). He is thus able to create an extended metaphor, which gives him a new perspective on himself. He has shaped his thinking into a genre for publication, and so other pupils are able to share and learn from his insights.

Kate had felt 'that their writing, like their play ought to satisfy both their private and social needs'. Certainly private needs were met, but the pedagogy that had developed in this class had also enabled the pupils to use their writing to meet social needs. Like Anna, the student teacher quoted earlier, they discovered the potential of story and poetry for 'showing the meaning of a person's thought to others'. The forming influence of their chosen genre enabled them to share themselves with their peers by a process of 'metaphorical enactment' (Britton, 1993: 60).

New directions in the teaching of literacy brought about by the introduction of the Literacy Hour and the NLS require that pupils should be much more articulate about the processes of reading and writing. In whole-class and group reading and writing sessions they are actively encouraged to discuss, for example, the way they tackle new words, structure stories and write letters. However, pupils need to appreciate how the discrete elements of writing they daily practise can combine to satisfy 'both personal and social needs'. They must know why they write. This can happen only if teachers themselves realise the nature and function of writing. To achieve this, teachers need to move from tacit to conscious reflexive awareness, so that they, like their pupils, may learn not as objects of a prescribed curriculum, but as subjects of their own.

Conclusions

This chapter began by reaffirming the potential of writing to empower children to find and share their own voices. It advocated a writing pedagogy that would enable children to articulate themselves as writers, so that they could recognise writing as a means of both constructing and conveying meaning in their lives.

Britton's functional linguistic categories were introduced as a way of foregrounding the importance of recognising that writers do adopt different roles when they write. Appreciating the participant/spectator division can enable teachers to realise the learning potential for writing, especially within the expressive and poetic modes. The chapter then considered the way that current curricula for both schools and ITT, together with national testing of writing, are likely to restrict classroom practice, unless teachers become more effective practitioners. To achieve this, they need to develop their own knowledge and understanding about writing.

Using examples of classroom practice at Key Stages 1 and 2, the chapter demonstrated how two teachers were able to draw upon their explicit understanding of writing and the writing process to enable children to:

- use expressive writing in the form of think books;
- adopt the spectator role within the poetic mode to both 'construct and convey' their own voices.

Throughout the chapter, a central theme has been emphasised: namely that children need to be able to become writers who can choose their own subjects and genres, discuss their own composing processes and recognise the learning that can take place through revision and redrafting. In this way, they can be writers whose work does, indeed, empower them to take part in conversations both with themselves and others from the very beginning of their literacy development.

Questions for discussion

1   What provision can be made for teachers to develop their explicit knowledge about writing?
2   What opportunities are there within the normal curriculum for pupils to learn to use writing for their own purposes?

Further reading

Think books/journal writing

D'Arcy, P. (1989) *Making Sense, Shaping Meaning*, Portsmouth, New Hampshire: Boynton and Cook.
Fulwiler, T. (ed.) (1987) *The Journal Book*, Portsmouth, New Hampshire: Boynton and Cook.
For teachers of all age groups who want to explore the possibilities for expressive writing across the curriculum, Fulwiler (1987), which draws on the work of Britton and Elbow (who contributes a chapter), is an interesting source of illustrative material and ideas. D'Arcy (1989) is an engaging exploration of the writing process, and has a useful chapter on think books

Writing workshops

Brooke, R., Mirtz, R. and Evans, R. (1995) *Small Groups in Writing Workshops: Invitations to a Writer's Life*, NCTE: New York.
Elbow, P. and Belanoff, P. (1995) *A Community of Writers: a Workshop Course in Writing*, 2nd edn, New York: McGraw-Hill.
Both of these books are useful for teachers who want to develop the writing workshop approach. The first draws together many of the ideas expressed in Elbow's other works

(see Bibliography) and is an inspiring and practical guide to implementing workshop strategies. The second explores the ideas behind workshop approaches, drawing on student experiences. It has a particularly useful section on ownership. Both books focus on secondary/freshmen work, but the ideas are transferable and would certainly enrich whole-class and group work within the literacy hour for any age.

Genre theory

Cope, B. and Kalantzis, M. (eds) (1993) *The Powers of Literacy: a Genre Approach to Teaching Writing*, London: Falmer Press.

Daiker, D. and Morenberg, M. (1990) *The Writing Teacher as Researcher*, Portsmouth, New York: Boynton and Cook/Heinemann.

This book gives fascinating insights into ways of teaching writing at all levels.

Derewianka, B. (1990) *Exploring How Texts Work*, Melbourne, Australia: PETA.

Freedman, A. and Medway, P. (1994) *Genre and the New Rhetoric*, London: Taylor and Francis.

Rosen, H. (1993) 'How Many Genres in Narrative?' in *Changing English: Domains of Literacy*, vol. 1, no. 1, London: Institute of Education.

Genre theory is essentially concerned with the rhetorical nature of speech and writing: Britton's functional categories are consistent with the concepts of the genre school. They are large categories based on ways of writing and the contentious but crucial participant/spectator roles. The poetic mode must therefore include a number of genres, where both poetry and narrative may be classed, albeit in different ways, as superordinate categories covering many subgenres and registers. Rosen's article explores this aspect.

For the genre theorists, the dominant discourses are those which fall within Britton's transactional categories as being ways of acting in the world. Empowerment comes through mastering these genres. Derewianka's teachers' guide gives explicit and useful guidance for teaching these. She omits poetry, and though she recognises the meaning-making potential of story as 'narrative account with a twist', she emphasises that its public purpose is to entertain (1990: 40). She ignores the way in which literature is a powerful way of sharing new knowledge and understanding integral to social life.

3 (Re)Defining literacy

How can schools define literacy on their own terms, and create a school culture that reflects that definition?

Hazel Bryan and Jo Westbrook

Literacy is a cluster of attitudes, towards oneself, texts and society. Once you see yourself as a literate person – which means other people treat you as literate – then you cannot help learning all the so-called skills of literacy every time you read, or someone helps you to read.

(Smith, 1990)

This chapter is aimed at primary and secondary teachers of English who are interested in a whole-school approach towards improving literacy in pupils. It puts forward the proposition that there is a broad, and changing, concept of literacy in society, with roots in the home and community, which is inconsistent with the increasingly narrow definition of literacy at the core of the centralised curriculum, as measured through its assessment framework. The tensions created by this inconsistency have resulted in a diversity of practice in schools, reflecting their heterogeneous cultures, and differing interpretations of national legislation.

Taking account of this, the chapter argues that schools are increasingly in a position to generate their own definitions of literacy, ones which will engage all staff, pupils and parents, and which are based on 'best practice' as this is derived from legislation, teachers' expertise and the needs of society.

The chapter attempts to answer the following questions:

1   What lies behind recent legislation on literacy, and how should this inform teachers' thinking on literacy?
2   How can schools select ideas from current literacy policy, practice and theory, in order to create their own literacy culture?

Introduction: recent, current and future literacy initiatives

The 1990s' emphasis on literacy across the curriculum revives teachers' sometimes cynical memories of older, broader initiatives such as 'language across the curriculum', which originated in the Bullock Report, *A Language for Life* (DES, 1975). Current policy has adopted the 'language across the curriculum' concept, but linked it to national testing for pupils and targeting for individual schools; schools are now implementing literacy across the curriculum in a more stringent fashion. The question is whether schools can integrate this stringency into what they know to be good practice in terms of how their pupils develop reading and writing, speaking and listening skills. To answer this question, it is necessary first to review recent and current national initiatives.

At the time of writing, it is ten years since the first cohort of five-year-olds enrolled in Key Stage 1 (KS1) of the National Curriculum (NC). Those five-year-olds are now fifteen-year-olds in Year 10. Throughout the decade of their formal schooling, Local Education Authorities (LEAs), schools and classroom teachers have had to respond to many pieces of legislation from the Department for Education and Employment (DfEE) and the Qualifications and Curriculum Authority (QCA), designed to raise standards of literacy. Consequently, many of these pupils have experienced what may appear to be a patchwork of intervention strategies designed to enhance their 'basic literary skills' and help them access the secondary curriculum. These strategies include Reading Recovery, the use of ICT software programmes such as SuccessMaker, Summer Literacy Schools, 'Basic Skills' lessons, withdrawal from the mainstream curriculum, and increased creation of setted classes in both primary and secondary schools. However, some pupils are still part of the 'long tail' who have not responded positively to the strategies designed to help them (Brooks *et al.*, 1996: 10). In addition, these pupils have grown up within the embrace of a popular culture that values new technologies and the visual image more highly than traditional print-based literacy: what schools have offered them has not always seemed relevant.

A key development has been the implementation of the National Literacy Strategy (NLS) in primary schools, which has created significant new opportunities for whole-school discussions of literacy and the development of policy and practice. Other recent initiatives have also contributed to the opening up of a debate about what constitutes 'literacy', and impacted on whole-school approaches.

For example, the implementation of the Code of Practice for the Assessment of Special Educational Needs (DfE, 1994) has seen a 'sharpening of practice' in secondary schools in particular (Westbrook *et al.*, 1998: 31). Identifying and assessing pupils with Special Educational Needs (SEN) is now the statutory responsibility of all teachers, as is the teaching and monitoring of pupils at Level 1 of the Code of Practice.

A focus on the apparent underachievement of boys has also arguably heightened awareness of the need for rethinking of teaching and learning methods. Government concern, triggered by the gender gap in performance at GCSE, has encouraged investigation at national and local level into why boys underachieve (Ofsted, 1993b). One finding is that boys *do read*, but read 'non-National Curriculum' texts: horror stories, science fiction, non-fiction, and computer texts. David Blunkett, Secretary of State for Education, has now requested that such texts are included in the revised NC for English (Cassidy, 1999). The criteria for what constitutes 'works of high quality by contemporary writers' (DfEE, 1995a: 20) would appear to be enlarging in scope.

The number of national initiatives that impact on literacy will continue to increase. Early drafts of the revisions to the NC for the year 2000 show a looser and richer interpretation of English, with a greater emphasis on Speaking and Listening and Drama in KS 1 and 2, and greater acknowledgement of writers from different cultures and traditions in KS 3 and 4. Talking about a text in class as a way of accessing its meaning may thus regain formal recognition after some neglect of oral skills at both primary and secondary level.

The responsibilities that schools have towards their communities have been highlighted from a managerial point of view by Matthew Taylor of the Institute of Public Policy (Taylor, 1999). Taylor writes that schools need 'Freedom to succeed'. He links the need for 'extraordinary management', which he describes as 'the pushing back of boundaries, the generation of enthusiasm and new ideas, team development, issues which go to the core ethos of the organisation', with the new focus on citizenship, which calls for effective partnerships with local communities.

Such innovative practice is already formally endorsed, and funded, by government working in partnerships with local businesses in the 25 Education Action Zones around the country, which allow a relaxation of the NC for schools and experimentation with teaching and learning in the classroom:

> We need to explore local partnerships which build on the roles of schools, local communities and LEAs. They will operate in the context of the national policies to improve levels of achievement in literacy and numeracy.
>
> (DfEE, 1999)

There are, of course, also local pressures on schools' literacy policies from families, ethnic and religious groups, employers, and an increasingly localised politics, some of which may not share the same priorities and emphases as national agencies. Schools have to react to these diverse influences. However, knee-jerk reactions to them may have to give way to measured, reflective ones. Responding actively to the 'best' from both national legislation, and to local community pressures can, when resolutely and creatively done, create a unified and coherent approach to the teaching and learning of literacy. Such a multidimensional approach, underpinned by an agreed pedagogy, can have an impact throughout the school from headteacher to parents, and influence everything from the timetable to display boards. However, despite the larger scope apparently being given to schools with regard to their own practice, they remain locked into an assessment system that narrows the definition of 'literacy' to one of measurable achievement.

Tensions created by narrow definitions of literacy

Literate practices link people, generations and institutions together over time and space. They can create a shared discourse at national, or even global, levels.

Brice Heath (1983) equates the social development of literacy with the need for a 'standard linguistic form', which is often sought because of increasing identification with the state, rather than the ethnic or local community. A common or national curriculum can create cohesion, and theoretically provide equal access and entitlement to full literacy for a whole population. However, for this to be attempted, the concept of literacy is sometimes narrowed down to a purely utilitarian definition, such as: 'The ability to read, write [and speak] in English [and use mathematics] at a level necessary to function and progress at work and in society in general' (Basic Skills Agency, 1999). There is some evidence that Britain has developed a view of literacy linked functionally to the economic well-being of the country: 'Education is the key to creating a society which is dynamic and productive, offering opportunities and fairness for everyone' (DfEE, 1997a).

Defining literacy in terms of a capacity to contribute to the country's economy has been a feature of the 1990s debate over standards in which both the Conservative government and the Labour opposition came to define, and measure, reading standards under the increasingly used umbrella title of 'literacy' (by which they meant basic skills, grammar and spelling). The National Literacy Project was set up by the Conservative government in 1997, in response to concerns that primary schools were not equipping children with the skills to access the secondary curriculum.

The Project, extended nationally as the National Literacy Strategy, was firmly yoked to the 'standards' issue when the newly elected Labour government set a national literacy target in the wake of the 1997 election. The NLS sets out to provide a balanced approach to literacy, including both whole-text work and phonics within its framework. It is explicitly linked to performance as defined by KS2 NC test results, and the magnifying glass of Ofsted is used to monitor the teaching methods and content used to implement it. The drive to deliver pupils with 'basic literacy skills' to secondary schools remains, however, in tension with the richer model of English in the National Curriculum Programmes of Study. The KS2 NC tests, which are used to measure the success of pupils and schools in meeting literacy targets, are based on a narrow interpretation of the National Curriculum Level Descriptions. These are, in turn, based largely on the relatively narrow Key Skills sections of the Programmes of Study (DfE, 1995b). There is, then, the possibility of an imbalance towards a greater focus on phonics and accuracy in the delivery of the NLS, and in an emphasis on key skills and 'teaching-to-the-test' in the delivery of the NC at secondary level, especially KS3.

This tension is exacerbated by the approach of the Code of Practice, which provides a method of labelling and defining pupils similar to that promoted by the KS2 NC tests and the NLS. Pupils with special educational needs (SEN), who are withdrawn from English lessons in secondary schools for help with their basic literacy skills, often regress when returned to mainstream English, where another, more demanding, and wide-ranging set of criteria operate in 'NC English' (Westbrook *et al.*, 1998: 48). Teachers across the curriculum lack knowledge in integrating such pupils' newly acquired basic skills with their subject, and this can lead to regression in attainment.

The emphasis on measurable achievement has created a confusing picture of literacy teaching, a four-tiered system consisting of the NLS in primary schools, 'basic skills', 'Key Skills' and 'NC English', with English teachers also often responsible for literacy across the curriculum in secondary schools. These tensions may be responsible for diverting schools from developing richer, more coherent literacy cultures.

Connecting broad definitions of literacy to national initiatives

> Literacy itself ... has to be redescribed, at least as literacies, to match the new, emergent contexts and kinds of literate behaviours that are prevalent in modern societies.
>
> (Meek, 1991: 230)

The national developments described above and the tensions created by them are leading some schools and teachers to consider how they can offer pupils a richer version of literacy education. A question that secondary schools in particular are beginning to ask themselves is: what kind of literacy education do we want for *pupils*?

Research indicates that five major factors contribute to the development of literacy. These are: first, that literacy is rooted in social practice (Brice Heath, 1983; Meek, 1991); second, that there is a need for a rich visual, linguistic and literary input throughout a pupil's development (Westbrook *et al.*, 1998); third, that opportunities to talk about whole texts significantly add to pupils' understanding (Brice Heath, 1983); fourth, that pupils need help in developing into fluent, autonomous readers-for-meaning (Westbrook *et al.*, 1998); and fifth, that reading and writing are rooted in a social and cultural practice that also embraces 'the semiotic shift' towards the audiovisual 'literacies' of television, film, video and computer-generated images (Kress and Van Leween, 1996: 30).

All these factors are evident in the early stages of literacy development. Children's 'emergent literacy' originates in the recognition of pictures in books, and, increasingly, moving images, 'scaffolded' (Bruner, 1986) usually by a parent or older sibling reading or viewing with them. The development of oral language is intimately linked with literacy development, as parents point out features of pictures and read text aloud, often adding their own comments on a story, and pulling the child into the literate discourse, by referring to the child's knowledge of the world: 'you've got a hat like that, don't you?' Children begin to be able to 'read' the pictures, and ascribe meaning to them, which they will later transfer to the printed text itself. Particular books and cartoons will be favourites because of some linguistic or emotional connection made with them, which gives them particular relevance. These are then read or viewed repeatedly.

The transition from home to schooled literacy need not undermine these processes. Indeed, it is an opportunity to extend the social practice of literacy, by giving children access to: a richer range of texts than those available at home; the stimulation of peers to socialise and collaborate with; and the guidance of professionals who know when and how to intervene in their learning.

Primary teachers scrutinising the NLS for support in sustaining this rich model of literacy education will find support here. For example, the methodologies it draws on include Slavin's *Success for All*, which features 'direct, interactive teaching; systematic phonics in the context of interesting text; a combination of shared and paired reading and writing.' (Slavin, 1996, cited in Beard, 1999: 7) What constitutes 'interesting texts' is worth reflecting on. The NLS specifies an exciting range of books, including non-fiction. It also calls for the use of ICT, comparisons between books and films, and the analysis of pictures, diagrams and charts, all under 'Text level work' (DfEE, 1998). This looks very promising.

Secondary-school teachers might inject a note of caution: they know that while the NC for English for KS3 and 4 appears to encourage wide reading, including non-fiction and media, in practice, it promotes a prescriptive list of texts that mostly reflects a traditional white canon (DfEE, 1995a: 20). However, the NC is – at the time of writing – under review, and is to be aligned with the NLS. There are indications, as already stated, that a wider number of more modern texts, including named writers from different cultures and traditions, will be included. There is, then, increasing potential within the NLS and the NC to include a broad range of texts, which can include those that will interest pupils most:

> If we are building up a popular reading and media culture in which pupils are already immersed, we need to consider how we present choice of texts, range and relevance in ways which encourage variety, breadth and critical reading skills to be developed upon new ground.
>
> (Davison and Dowson, 1998: 102)

Slavin's recommendation of 'shared and paired reading and writing' is also noteworthy. Learning to read and write are sometimes thought of as private activities, requiring a turning inwards which is antithetical to the way that many children experience early literacy development, and to the way that adolescents in particular prefer to spend their time in social groups (Ong, 1982: 74). In the strategies sometimes used to develop the more complex literacy skills, such as essay writing and close reading, secondary-school teachers, in effect, ask pupils to become anti-social in a room holding thirty people. It is hardly surprising that disruption can be the result when these strategies are overused.

On the other hand, if literacy is recognised as being rooted in social and cultural practices, then schools as institutions can utilise this sociability, and unite a class through shared reading, redrafting, collaborative writing, and talking about texts. The evidence is that pupils *like* talking about texts together as a group:

David: Write a letter to the Social Services ... What's the worth in doing that?

Teacher: What would you prefer to do then? Say you break for half the lesson –

Lee: Talk about it, not like writing it down, it's just doing paperwork all the time, we don't never ever talk in here, discuss it, all we do is read and write.

(Westbrook, 1990: 22)

Purposeful, managed talk can enhance pupils' understanding of texts, and provide the social context for writing for a purpose and audience.

The richer model of literacy outlined above is a hardworking one. Its incorporation into a school literacy culture, already defined in part by external pressures and measures, is not an easy option for schools still coming to grips with the basic requirements of new initiatives and the need to improve on whole-school performance. The next two sections of this chapter illustrate the current position.

Selecting what works: the picture in primary schools

Changing fashions in the teaching of reading and writing have resulted in today's teachers having a rich and varied resource pool from which to select appropriate practice for a given child or class at any given time. Personal professional choice, in negotiation and agreement with the English Co-ordinator and whole-school English policy, has been the hallmark of primary practice in recent years. This has been its strength. Some of this knowledge of how children learn has been formalised in the National Literacy Strategy, so that it is possible, for example, to interpret the Literacy Hour as founded on a Vygotskian model of learning (Vygotsky, 1978) and as providing a social constructivist approach to literacy, in which the pupil's learning is scaffolded by the teacher (Bruner, 1986). The argument would be that the Literacy Hour forms a rich and complex cocktail of explicit teaching (15 minutes of whole-class Text level work, 15 minutes of Word and Sentence level work), interaction with other children and texts (whole-class elements, the 20 minutes of discussion during shared and guided reading and collaborative work during independent sessions, the 10 minutes plenary), and opportunities to work independently.

However, while the NLS can be interpreted as embodying good practice at classroom level, there remain concerns regarding teachers' status and 'voice' from a national perspective. The teaching profession has been subjected to training days that have been rigorously designed (the training videos run the message, 'Turn off the tape now'), and a cascade model of instruction has been set up. The messages of good practice that should have been shared have often been lost or simply not heard by teachers who have felt overwhelmed by the new 'rules'. During Staff Development sessions, teachers have started to ask: 'In the Literacy Hour is it OK to ... ?' There has been the feeling that although the NLS has created a new literacy culture, it is one with inflexible rules of practice, and this has created a period of confusion and uncertainty for some teachers. It must be remembered that while the NLS is creating exciting discussion regarding good practice and subject knowledge, not every primary school teacher is an English Co-ordinator or expert, and hence some may feel vulnerable in this newly emerging culture. Wragg and Wragg (1998: 261) note that language co-ordinators in primary schools are seen as the key agents for change, but rarely have any more training than anyone else.

The introduction of new terminology has resulted in many teachers feeling insecure and deskilled, with their professional judgement in the teaching of literacy devalued. The explosion of 'handy tips for your literacy hour'-type books that are flooding the market, glossy, colourful and, apparently, all an overworked teacher ever needed, often provides decontextualised exercises that are not in keeping with the spirit of the National Literacy Strategy. A cursory reading of a poem or story can be followed by one group 'doing' homophones, another apostrophes, and yet another using the dictionary, with no linkages between the tasks. Thus, form can come to signify what being 'literate' is all about, rather than the working out of the meaning of a whole text, and gaining the 'big picture' (Dombey, 1998: 128). Slavin's 'systematic phonics in the context of interesting text' (Slavin, 1996, cited in Beard, 1999: 7) is in danger of becoming a list of parts of speech and terminology tied to a particular year and term, with no relationship to the richness of the 'Text level' section of the NLS.

What has to be remembered is that teachers and their pupils need time to make the given framework 'theirs', and to get the balance right for their pupils. There are indications that schools are beginning to do this, as are the 'messengers': 'The Literacy Advisor tells us we can bring drama and painting into the Literacy Hour – how exciting!' (Headteacher, personal communication, March 1999). This may indicate that the 'rules' of the NLS are being reconceptualised as guidance, and that teachers are seeking out the good practice within them.

As the Literacy Hour framework rolls up through the primary-school years, the implications for all teachers at secondary school are looming large. Increased autonomy, experience of collaborative ways of working, and a greater understanding and application of the forms and functions of literacy could be the hallmark of the Year 7 pupil, assuming that schools take hold of the potential written into the design of the NLS. Secondary schools will need to have some knowledge of this new literacy culture in primary schools in order to provide for continuity and progression of learning. Brief sweeps over KS 2 NC test results, and cursory glances at pupils' Y6 work, will no longer be enough.

Selecting what works: the picture in secondary schools

The nature of the secondary-school curriculum can mean a fragmented, incoherent experience for pupils. As practitioners isolated by curriculum boundaries, it can be hard for teachers to recognise what this fragmentation can feel like. These problems are compounded by the mix of literacy initiatives, pressures to improve examination results, and by subject teachers who are unwilling to teach literacy skills through their subject specialisms.

What follows is a composite picture constructed from interviews with seven Year 10 pupils from seven very different schools in London and the South East (Westbrook *et al.*, 1998). These pupils, four boys and three girls, were interviewed as Year 10 pupils, but talked about their KS3 experience. They were all non-SEN-registered underachievers, gaining mostly Level 4 in the National Curriculum tests in English and other subjects. With the benefit of hindsight, and an extra six months' maturity, they were all able to pinpoint what had failed them in school and at home. In spite of coming from such different schools, there were consistent overlaps in their experience.

A view from below

Paul, a composite pupil, is an articulate white boy in Year 10, who uses a non-standard English dialect, and enjoys football and computer games. He sometimes reads the newspaper to his parents, who think he is doing all right at school because he got a Level 3 in the KS2 English NC tests and appears to be an independent reader. He was placed in a class with others of his reading age (9.7) at secondary school, but was not seen as needing extra support. However, because of his poor performance in English and Science he was put on SuccessMaker in Year 7, and included in a Literacy Project in Year 8. His reading age and confidence shot up, but when placed back in the mainstream, peer pressure to go off task, and his inability to read the Science textbook (written for pupils with a reading age of 11.5) meant that he regressed.

The English and SEN departments are still debating who is responsible for teaching literacy skills. Subject teachers expect English teachers to teach basic literacy skills, and reading-for-meaning. In History, Paul copies chunks of text off the board and reads aloud, embarrassed, for 30 seconds. In RE and Geography he fills in worksheets and cloze passages. He rarely reads for longer than two minutes, or writes more than a paragraph. No teacher has sat down and taught Paul directly where the comma should go, although he does plenty of redrafting for homework. He talks a lot in English lessons, but is actively discouraged from talking in Maths and Geography. He has been sent out of Maths for not having a pencil. His independent reading stopped at secondary school because of the pressures of the curriculum.

He is mostly very bored in school, which can lead to poor, off-task behaviour, interpreted by the teacher as disruption. It was only towards the end of Year 9 that Paul's parents were invited up to school to talk about his disruptive behaviour. Rushing from one lesson to the other, he does not reflect on what he has learnt, or think very much in school. 'You go to the next lesson, trying to figure out what you did in the last lesson and how you can improve it, but with a poor teacher, you get distracted, no time to think' (Westbrook *et al.*, 1998: xvii).

Outside school he is discovering a great interest in the Millennium bug, and reads broadsheet articles and library books on the situation, and has even written a story about the year 2000. However, peer pressure to socialise outside of school is strong, so he often fails to complete homework. 'Football has distracted me from reading – that's what my mum says' (Westbrook *et al.*, 1998: xi). He is one of 63% of pupils who gained a Level 4 in the 1998 NC Tests, but who are not registered as having SEN (Westbrook *et al.*, 1998: 2). He will gain mostly Es, maybe Ds at GCSE.

Missing from this collage is any coherent strategy for the extension of literacy skills across subjects, underpinned by an agreed pedagogical approach. The Literacy Hour has provided a common approach to literacy in primary schools, whatever the subject. In the secondary school, by contrast, other members of staff may not necessarily regard literacy, or 'basic skills' as being their responsibility. However, as the school's SENCO said: 'It is not actually our job to withdraw loads [of pupils], rub the ointment on and send them back cured – which a lot of staff think actually happens. It's a whole school issue' (Westbrook *et al.*, 1998: iii).

Concerns over intervention strategies

Intervention strategies across the curriculum predominate at the present time in an attempt to raise literacy standards. They are characterised by: their intense focus on improving one aspect of literacy, for one particular group of pupils; by testing before and after the implementation of the strategy; by their limited time-scale; and by a lack of integration of pupils' newly acquired skills at the point of re-entry to mainstream classes. The most common intervention strategy is the withdrawal of poor readers, including pupils with SEN, from the literate classroom community in English, to read abridged versions of texts, with decoding skills as the focus.

The Literacy Project of one school in inner-city London targets non-SEN registered underachievers from mainstream classes across all curriculum areas, for one hour every day for a month, to focus on spelling, punctuation, grammar and reading-for-meaning in small groups. The project was designed by a primary teacher specialist, a secondary literacy specialist (now the Head of English) and an SEN teacher. They use and develop materials from feeder primary schools' Literacy Hours for continuity. Another school invested in four Integrated Learning Systems (ILS) three years ago and uses this for pupils with SEN and those who suddenly regress in their reading. The language points from the computer printouts for each child are integrated into lessons. In another school, there have been experiments with Spelling and Handwriting Schemes, Reading Recovery, and a project targeted at disaffected Year 9 boys, but these were only partially successful and became a heavy workload for staff.

What became clear from this research was the patchy, 'sticking plaster' nature of these intervention strategies. They had been put in place by SENCOs wanting to extend their remits to include underachievers, or by enthusiastic Heads of Years concerned about failing boys. The attempts were laudable, but limited in their success by the lack of whole-school involvement. One SENCO stated she had created a 'monster' of disparate literacy strategies that have since collapsed, being too financially costly and too unwieldy for one person to carry.

A multidimensional view of literacy across the curriculum

Below is a second composite picture from the same schools. It pulls together innovative practice already in place, much of it based on the broader understanding of literacy outlined earlier in this chapter. The picture is drawn from interviews with headteachers, English Subject Leaders, and SENCOs, as well from as the more positive points made by the pupils. Only two schools had formed a Literacy Working Party to unite the whole school, although this was a major goal in all seven schools. It was the key, and also the hardest part.

The 'William Shakespeare Comprehensive School' – a case study: NOR 1000, inner-city mixed comprehensive

FROM POLICY TO ...

One starting point was the headteacher's interest in learning about the implications of the NLS in the school's feeder junior schools for the William Shakespeare school. INSET money went towards staff spending a day in a primary school, focusing on reading and writing across the curriculum. The NLS was also a prime focus. Primary–secondary transfer issues were also discussed and fed back into departments.

Back in the William Shakespeare school, a working definition of 'literacy' was used, and revisited throughout the year, until a broad but rich definition was agreed by staff, encompassing functional, school literacy within a wider context of personal growth, family and community involvement. Literacy as a 'cluster of attitudes' was a core theme. Pupils were seen to need a reinforcement of literacy at all levels and from all staff, in order to see themselves as literate citizens in a literate school environment. Wragg and Wragg have noted that, in some schools, 'existing practice was distilled into policy form' when literacy policy was formulated: teachers did not think afresh about what was good practice, and what could be improved (Wragg and Wragg, 1998: 261). At the William Shakespeare school, a Working Party with members from all curricular areas seemed a logical starting point to gather information on existing good practice, and to share practice with advisers and neighbouring schools for greater input.

... TO PRACTICE: A CULTURE OF LITERACY

The headteacher and management team strove to foster a culture of literacy. Literacy became a priority on the School Development Plan, with proper funding allocated to it: funding for SEN was extended to low attainers who are not registered. Extra funding was gathered from RIF (Reading Is Fundamental, part of the National Literacy Trust), and PTA events. The timetable was flexible, with guaranteed time set aside for staff to plan with support teachers. Literacy Support Assistants were assigned to work in one curriculum area for a term. A fifth English lesson was timetabled with a focus on reading-for-meaning.

The Library is the hub of the school and used daily by pupils and teachers, with Book Weeks, Visiting Writers, and Poetry Days woven through the year. Pupils' own books are displayed and published through an in-house publishing company, taking advantage of pupils' knowledge of ICT. The Bookshop is bringing in a profit, with *Goosebumps*, one pound Classics, and subversive, 'attitude changing' poetry books selling best (Lambirth, 1998).

Pupils have a sense of ownership of the curriculum, with high-profile participation in literacy acts: noticeboards, newsletters, reading out work to the class or assembly, and at Open Evenings and Poetry Days. A visible cross-curricular reading culture has been established, and continued: the headteacher carries a novel under her arm; there are reading groups in the staffroom, and amongst pupils; and there are posters displayed with each teacher's favourite book (some read extracts out in assemblies). Funds are used to supply good readers for all tutor groups, who operate DEAR (Drop Everything And Read) every morning for 15 minutes solid. This time is prioritised and no interruptions are tolerated. Each classroom has a library, too, so there are Nature journals, Science Fiction novels, and poems about the Moon in the Science Labs, and biographies of musicians, *Smash Hits*, and a history of the Blues in the Music rooms. Opportunities for pupils to develop a richer literacy, which involves choice and access to texts, as well as a 'schooled' literacy, are thus firmly implanted in the infrastructure of the school.

ALL TEACHERS AS TEACHERS OF LITERACY

There have been INSET days on managing talk, group and pair work and talking-about-texts in the classroom. 'Reading aloud' around the class is rarely used as a means of assessing pupils' reading performance, to pupils' relief, but they are encouraged to do so in small groups for specific purposes. The Performing Arts have a high status within the school for encouraging creative talk and play among pupils.

The core of this multilayered approach is what happens in the classrooms. The Working Party brought together existing best practice, and introduced new literacy strategies through a rolling programme of INSET, set out in a draft Literacy Policy.

There are five basic 'tenets of faith' agreed for all subjects:

1   There is a **rich linguistic input** in lessons translated into meaningful talk-about-texts, backed up by visual displays, and real books as well as work-sheets. This is particularly beneficial for EAL pupils. ICT, especially multimedia texts, is used when appropriate.

2   The **progression from 'basic skills' to reading-for-meaning, to critical literacy** is built into schemes of work and constantly revised. Pupils revisited learned skills, as well as developing new skills.

3   There is a **similarity of approaches to the teaching of reading and writing** across the curriculum. Staff identify text types with pupils and take time for the processing and analysis of texts before expecting any response. DARTS (Directed Activities Related to Texts) are used particularly well in Geography and Science (Gilham, 1986: 164). Particular emphasis is paid to strategies for reading specialist texts, and spelling and comprehension of technical vocabulary. Notions of modelling and scaffolding pupil learning are seen in the use of writing frames (Lewis and Wray, 1995). Staff agree that the aim is to create autonomous learners, with extension tasks for all.

4   There is an **understanding of the gap between reading-for-the-tests, and the wider, richer reading** required for true entrance to the 'literacy club'.

5   There is **consistent monitoring of pupils' independent reading across the curriculum.** Pupils read independently using extensive subject libraries and were set one assessed reading homework a week per subject.

'INTERRUPTION' STRATEGIES

By the end of the first year of literacy policy development, staff were questioning the need for intervention strategies, since all staff were engaged in literacy strategies. Teachers are tired of pupils being 'popped out again for another go'. The issue of entitlement to a curriculum that was seen as generally broad enough for all was one consideration. The SMT decided to phase out most intervention strategies within a year, while providing time-framed support for pupils with SEN. 'Early intervention' is now equated with positive interventions in pupil social groupings, and close parental involvement in both disciplinary matters and the completion of homework.

MONITORING AND ASSESSING THE WHOLE-SCHOOL APPROACH TO LITERACY: A SHARP APPROACH

Previous INSET days on language across the curriculum had resulted in 'Talking Walls' and key words being put up on the board. Now Heads of Department provide an update on literacy strategies for the whole-school Literacy Newsletter every term, and subject teachers observe one another once a term in pairs to discuss management, literacy and individual pupil matters. The SMT, including the headteacher, track a class each term to monitor individual pupils and their work, matching observations with data, and to open up discussions on teaching strategies (Westbrook *et al.*, 1998: xiv).

Pupils are assessed in Year 7, and an analysis of their primary records is carried out. As far as possible, face-to-face meetings are arranged with primary staff about pupils with SEN, to share literacy strategies for continuity and progression. Data received from Year 7 onwards (CATS, London Reading Test, Key Stage 3 tests) are recorded in a database, and discrepancies in scores, together with the evidence of classroom observations, can trigger extra support and monitoring by teachers. Predictions from the data are made for GCSE scores, and communicated in pupil–teacher conferences.

Monitoring of pupils' talk, reading and writing in each subject area, as well as subject knowledge, behaviour, and effort, are used diagnostically, and included in reports to parents. Every term the timetable is suspended and form tutors spend ten minutes with each pupil, discussing targets past and future, short and long term. Each tutor has access to all information on each pupil, and time is allowed to engage with that information.

Teachers routinely write up two or three key assessment criteria for each piece of work on the board, and mark it accordingly. NC test requirements and GCSE syllabuses are simplified and clarified at regular points for pupils and parents, and related overtly to classwork. There is self- and peer-evaluation for each major piece of work. Staff point out irregular points of grammar, spelling and punctuation (GRASP) on each piece of work, and allow time for comments to be read and corrections to be amended within class time. Although they initially found this time-consuming, staff are now seeing the benefits in greater motivation, increased understanding and accuracy.

Pupils are taught time-management skills, note-taking and essay writing in each subject. This work is backed up in PSE, and given more time as exams approach and in KS4. Homework is consistent with classwork and always assessed. Parents are aware of the school's homework policy, and are asked to sign the Home-School Contact book weekly up to Year 11. Parents come into school to help with paired reading with weaker pupils. Form tutors phone home regularly to inform parents about their child's progress, and parents are asked to read with their KS3 children.

Literacy as a 'cluster of attitudes' is thus manifested via a multidimensional approach throughout the school, and supported by the way in which all members of staff incorporate the teaching of literacy skills through their subjects. There is participation in literacy events by all members of the school community, and flexibility in the definition and implementation of literacy. Policy and practice include many recognisable features of existing 'good literacy practice', as well as a sharpening of approach, especially in the assessment and monitoring of pupils, required by national legislation. National requirements are subservient to a richer literacy culture, rather than running the show.

Conclusions

National standards, linked to pupils' ages, within a nationalised curriculum, are here to stay. However, as this chapter shows, literacy encompasses a large canvas, and it may not be possible to narrow it to one definition: 'Literacy, however defined or acquired, or used, or sought, is never static' (Meek, 1991: 238). Schools, at the tail-end of the 1990s, are increasingly aware of this, and the larger scope given by very recent initiatives from Government also seems to offer support for a wider definition. Primary schools need time to work out their priorities in the delivery of the NLS. Secondary schools need to look consciously at what the primary schools are doing, at national legislation, and at the needs of their own communities and to prioritise what best literacy practices they can derive from them. There is the freedom and flexibility to allow them to turn inwards towards their own school cultures, and to iron out discrepancies, despite the external distractions of assessment, benchmarking and target-setting.

Questions for discussion

1   With the NLS working its way up to secondary schools in the form of KS3 'Literacy Hours', are there further more concrete ways in which primary and secondary teachers can share 'best practice', and support pupils who are transferring from one school to another?
2   What is the role of the secondary English Department in a whole-school approach to literacy: advice, consultancy, modelling of good practice, leadership, or as one of a team of departments driving through the approach?
3   The newly revised curriculum for the year 2000 will have a further impact on primary and secondary schools. What will be the influences of the new foci of citizenship and creativity on contracting or opening up debates around literacy?

Further reading

Bearne, E. (ed.) (1998a) *Literacy Across the Primary Curriculum*, London: Routledge.
  Giving a very broad understanding to the notion of language and literacy across the curriculum, this book goes beyond the Literacy Hour to give detailed examples, often drawing on pupils' work, of a whole-language approach in the primary school.

Bearne, E. (ed.) (1998b) *Literacy Across the Secondary Curriculum*, London: Routledge.
  This book gives an in-depth account of one secondary school's implementation of language and literature across the curriculum, including the strategies involved in putting together a Literacy Policy.

Christie, F. and Misson, R. (1998) *Literacy and Schooling*, London: Routledge.
  This is a very thorough introduction to issues in literacy education, and moves through pre-school, to primary and through to secondary school, including good chapters on new technologies.

Raban-Bisby, B. (ed.) (1995) *Developing Language and Literacy in the English National Curriculum*, London: Trentham Books.
  This book gives a good overview of literacy, and draws out useful comparisons with literacy initiatives in Australia. The last section on 'Family Literacy' is very thorough.

4   The current status of oracy

A cause of (dis)satisfaction?

Teresa Grainger

Introduction

In the last century, oracy in schools has grown out of the shadows towards the light. Classrooms in which silent pupils listened to their teacher and only spoke to answer questions and demonstrate their knowledge, have given way to more interactive contexts.

Today, speaking and listening are perceived as vital communication skills and talk is acknowledged as a medium for learning and personal development. Oracy has been officially recognised in the late twentieth century as the first Attainment Target in English in the National Curriculum (DES, 1989; DfE, 1995a), and as an assessed component in GCSE. Indeed, back in 1965, Wilkinson *et al.* argued, 'Oracy is a condition of learning in all subjects, it is not a frill but a state of being in which the whole school must operate'.

While many agreed with him (e.g. Barnes *et al.*, 1969; Barnes, 1976), the development of the oracy movement has been neither rapid nor without problems. *A Language for Life* (the Bullock Report) (DES, 1975) endorsed the use of oral language across the curriculum, but its recommendations were not fully implemented, and nationally, professional attitudes changed rather slowly until the National Oracy Project (1987–1993) fostered development in this area. In-service and innovation, classroom research and curriculum development spread, prompted partly by National Curriculum requirements to plan, monitor and assess pupils' development as speakers and listeners. Arguably, talk has now come to occupy a clear place on the English agenda in primary schools.

However, there is little cause for complacency. Considerable anomalies exist between the rhetoric of the national and school documentation, and the reality and challenges that beset children and their teachers. The most powerful mode of classroom instruction remains teacher-centred, and, with the advent of the National Literacy Strategy (DfEE, 1998), it seems likely that oracy will again be overshadowed by the perceived basics of reading and writing. The high profile currently given to subject knowledge and curriculum coverage mitigates against time for talk, and the dominant mode of classroom organisation is still teacher talk, since deep-rooted Victorian perceptions still persist in much classroom practice.

Strategies to consolidate and enhance oracy are needed because, despite its recent rise in stature, its position remains insecure and it continues to require nurturing. Opportunities for developing oracy abound in all curriculum contexts, but the potential of drama, storytelling, ICT and the Literacy Hour need to be tapped further. Through enhancing pupils' meta-linguistic awareness and teachers' knowledge about progression, as well as through establishing a collaborative climate of enquiry in the classroom, the primary profession can profile and develop speaking and listening, and offer increased access to learning for all pupils. This chapter therefore seeks to discuss the following questions:

1   What status does oracy deserve?
2   What challenges mitigate against a high status for oracy?
3   How can the profile of oracy be enhanced?

What status does oracy deserve?

To establish how oracy has grown and to ascertain what educational status it deserves, research into talk in the early years will be examined, alongside learning theories and the pioneering work of classroom-based researchers.

Learning, talking and thinking at home

Research indicates that young children learn to talk through interaction in purposeful contexts with supportive adults (e.g. Bruner, 1975), mothers establish 'protoconversations' with their babies, accepting their noises, smiles and gestures as intentional and respond accordingly (Trevarthen and Hubley, 1975). The implicitly 'warm, demanding' nature of adult talk and the multitude of informal and incidental learning contexts in the home, highlights the holistic, developmentally appropriate and integrated nature of pre-school talk (Ball, 1994). In sharing life experiences with adults and others, children develop a sense of self and learn how to make meanings in their culture (Halliday, 1978). Indeed, the communicative capacity of five-year-olds is impressive; they are able to use talk for a range of purposes, including reasoned thinking, adopting the speech patterns of their community and furthering their own learning through enquiry and interaction (McTear, 1981). However, research has shown the high level of oral interaction and intellectual effort documented at home is not sustained or developed in school (Tizard and Hughes, 1984; Wells, 1985). In these studies, teacher talk in early schooling was noted as qualitatively different from parents' talk, in so far as it was oriented towards classroom management and focused more upon questioning pupils, who were themselves less involved in decision-making and negotiating than at home. Ethnographic work has highlighted the gap between home and school and showed how schools do not always value children's language (Brice Heath, 1983). While adult/child ratios are significantly higher in schools, and different social and physical features obviously exist, teachers do need to know about the home language practice of their pupils, in order to organise their classrooms appropriately, to build bridges between home and school and to foster talking, thinking and learning that harness pupils' collaborative language experience and cultural practices.

Talking, thinking and learning in school

Collaboration is central at home and also supports learning in school, as audiotaped examples of classroom interaction in secondary schools have shown (Barnes et al., 1969; Barnes, 1976; Barnes and Todd, 1977). Their insightful observations draw attention to talk as a prerequisite for learning, and to the hesitancy and changes of direction which characterise pupils' unformed moves towards making meaning, in speculating, negotiating and hypothesising their way forward. Such exploratory talk is 'one of the means by which the assimilation and accommodation of new knowledge to the old is carried out' (Barnes, 1976). Educational thinking about constructing knowledge is indebted to Vygotsky's work on the interactive nature of language and thought. Following the work of Plowden (1967), the primary tradition of 'child centred' education emphasised children as active, yet solitary learners re-creating knowledge for themselves through action and discovery (Piaget, 1971). Vygotsky argued, however, that talk, as well as physical activity, shapes thought and understanding, and that knowledge construction is not a solitary process but significantly a social and cultural one (Vygotsky, 1978). The implications for the pre-eminence of talk are clear: if learning is social, dialogue will play a critical role as a tool for thinking, so teachers and pupils need to talk together in order to learn together.

> Human learning presupposes a specific social nature and a process by which children grow into the intellectual life of those around them.
>
> (Vygotsky 1978: 89)

Adults 'loan their consciousness' to pupils, and support their conceptual development, enabling them to operate independently (Bruner, 1986), although such a handover is not unproblematic (Edwards and Mercer, 1987; Cazden, 1988). 'Scaffolding' learning in this way involves teachers in finely tuning their talk in order to help pupils articulate their understanding and make sense of their discoveries. Through the internalisation of dialogue, pupils learn to think and to critically examine other people's thinking as well as their own. As one of the primary technologies of thought, talk helps pupils order and re-order their thinking, reason and problem solve, enabling them to take an active and reflective role in their own learning, and in school 'all lessons include, and largely depend upon oral and written communication' (SCAA, 1997a: 6). For these reasons it deserves the highest status, for without it the process of education would simply grind to a halt.

What challenges mitigate against a high status for oracy?

While accepting that oracy has, over the last half-century, been enshrined in government legislation, and received increased status in the eyes of many teachers and pupils, a gap between the rhetoric and the reality of classroom practice remains. Several issues continue to undermine its stature and reduce its pedagogic potential, including: the nature of National Curriculum requirements; the influence of the NLS; assessment; and teachers' ideological positions, teaching styles and expectations. In addition, pupils' views and parental perspectives can inhibit the value of talk in schools. If children are to use spoken language for learning, then each of these challenges to the status of oracy needs to be examined.

National Curriculum limitations

To develop effective speaking and listening, pupils should be taught to:

- use the vocabulary and grammar of standard English;
- formulate, clarify and express their ideas;
- adapt their speech to a widening range of circumstances and demands;
- listen, understand and respond appropriately to others.

(DfE, 1995a: 2)

This statutory summary of National Curriculum requirements across all key stages, and the fine details found in the documents, paint a clear picture: the overall emphasis is on effective speech. However, pupils also need opportunities to use language as a tool for enquiry, reflection and knowledge construction. The vocational stress on developing adequate communication skills in the Programmes of Study, diverts teachers' attention away from these more significant aims, and works towards merely educating children to speak well and to listen carefully. Accuracy, performance and outcomes are profiled at the expense of considering in detail the speculative, and genuinely exploratory talk that characterises much good learning (Doddington, 1998). The ramifications of this stance have led in some classrooms to oral activities that are oriented around performance, and to group discussions that require teacher-set outcomes and a uniform response. It is true, however, that more talk activities, such as 'circle time', have been adopted and timetabled in response to National Curriculum requirements, but, while initially well received, these may fail to thrive in competitive classroom contexts, or where the teacher is perceived as the subject expert and pupils have little sense of themselves as active learners (Housego and Burns, 1994). The National Curriculum also shows little awareness of the cognitive and linguistic benefits of bilingualism, and standard English is asserted as the norm by which other dialects are measured. This adult-needs model of language reflects a functional view of oracy, which reduces its status and undoubtedly widens the gap between the evident value of talk and the reality which pupils encounter.

The influence of the National Literacy Strategy

The National Literacy Strategy (NLS) provides further challenges to the status of oracy, because it focuses upon teaching, not learning, and profiles literacy *instruction*. Despite its protestations that it 'is not a recipe for returning to some crude or simple form of "transmission" teaching' (DfEE, 1998: 8), teacher talk takes centre stage in the hour, and much will depend upon the quality of this talk. The NLS *Framework for Teaching* does acknowledge that teachers should aim for the active engagement of pupils, but the lessons learnt over the last few decades about talk and the influence of the social and cultural context of learning, are not overtly acknowledged in the influential *Framework*. Neither do the teaching objectives focus on the development of speaking and listening. It is likely, therefore, that pressured primary practitioners, anxious to cover the detailed content, may be tempted to inform, instruct, direct and demonstrate, returning to a 'chalk and talk' mentality. Opportunities do exist for teachers to create interactive examinations of texts and to promote investigative approaches to learning, but the quantity of objectives and emphasis on explicit teaching could serve only to reaffirm the dominant pattern of teacher-centred instruction. Separate planning for oracy is not required, so the door remains wide open for busy teachers to let oracy take a back seat as they come to grips with this new national syllabus. The published programmes for the literacy hour have been hard for some schools to resist, yet, almost without exception, independent work activities in these programmes are designed for solitary scribal skills practice. Independent work does not need to equal individual work, but the speed of NLS implementation has rushed many schools in this direction, and more open-ended collaborative work will inevitably have suffered as a consequence.

Therefore, ironically, as literacy targets continue to be profiled for political ends and teachers' energies are focused upon the demands of the non-statutory hour, the statutory requirements for Attainment Target 1 are being sidelined. In terms of planning and assessment, time allocation and attention, talk is not being treated as well as reading and writing. Yet the curriculum depends upon talk, and, if educators neglect it, they not only restrict pupils' access to learning, but also fail to equip them to operate as autonomous adults. The current back-to-basics drive, the new draft National Curriculum and the focus on measurable outcomes, target setting and league tables, pose a real threat to the hard-earned status of oracy.

Assessment

The fact that there is no statutory testing of speaking and listening in primary schools also assuredly undermines their perceived value in this sector. It is true that at Key Stage 1 much learning (in baseline assessment and end of Key Stage tasks and tests) is assessed through talk, but Attainment Target 1 itself lacks official assessment. Many schools, already overburdened, give low priority to teachers' formative assessment of oracy for measuring progress in speaking and listening, and analysing and assessing this transient language form continues to challenge educationalists.

The social, communicative, cultural and cognitive aspects of talk are all influenced by audience, purpose and context, so teachers need to gather evidence of pupils' competence over time and in a wide range of different social and learning contexts. Other factors such as gender, personality and confidence in whatever language is being used will also influence pupils' speech behaviour (Bearne and Elding, 1996). Judging the quality of the talk itself may involve teachers in examining ideational (what is said), interpersonal (how it is said), and textual (the form chosen) aspects, as well as noting the context in which the talk occurs (Wilkinson and Berrill, 1990). Given the pressure of time and numbers, the ephemeral nature of talk, and the influence of context on speech behaviour, it is perhaps not surprising that continuous assessment of pupils' talk and their learning through talk is not a well-recorded, monitored or developed feature of primary schooling. Considerable diversity of practice exists, but without ongoing evidence gathering and self-assessment, teaching opportunities cannot be planned as effectively to develop pupils' use of language, their confidence and competence. Lack of research into progression in oracy has not helped teachers either: although the exemplification of standards materials (SCAA, 1996b) offers some help, there is little evidence that these have been extensively used. Indeed, with the primary school curriculum currently dominated by the Literacy and Numeracy strategies, it is unlikely these (or the Key Stage 2 optional assessment units, QCA, 1997) will influence the reality. The influence of National Curriculum tests on teachers is substantial; since there is no formal oral test, the status of oracy is undoubtedly affected.

Teaching styles

The issue of different teachers' philosophies, and their teaching and pupil-learning styles, lies at the heart of the constraints upon oracy in education. While a rationale for the importance of talk is widely accepted, it is quite another matter to operate in line with this rationale on a daily basis. Examinations of classroom discourse suggest that many teachers implicitly constrain interaction in order to maintain control of both the outcome and the content of the discussion (Barnes, 1976; Edwards and Furlong, 1978; Mercer, 1995). Teachers retain control of the knowledge gained through using a variety of spoken strategies, which, as Edwards and Mercer (1987) argue, include:

- eliciting pupils' contributions;
- marking some contributions as particularly significant, through joint

knowledge markers (e.g. using royal plurals to highlight what has been done and understood);

- cueing elicitations (prompting the required information through heavy clues);
- reconstructing and recapping past activities, (tailoring them to suit the intended reading through 'rewriting history').

While such strategies can succeed in inculcating the children into a shared understanding, they can also deceive and through cued elicitation, for example, create:

> a false impression of the extent to which pupils understand, and are ulti-
> mately responsible for, what they are saying and doing. It can easily mask,
> rather than bridge, the gap between teacher and child that is the basis of
> Vygotsky's developmental process.
>
> (Edwards and Mercer, 1987: 146)

Teacher talk can still be construed as an elaborate guessing game, particularly now that explicit teaching is being highlighted through government documentation, and curriculum coverage dominates. Indeed, the agenda of recent years and the emphasis upon inspection and its attendant administration have directed teachers towards products not processes. During a recent language and literacy course, one teacher noted in her reflective response journal:

> Children working in pairs and talking about their work is a relatively new
> thing for our school. Now we have a busy hum instead of silence. As a staff
> we're beginning to think the children get more done this way; 'two heads
> are better than one'. Up until now, writing was viewed as an individual
> activity here, but when the children co-operate it eases their load and
> enables them to help each other. I don't know why we hadn't realised talk
> was so important before, I guess we've been so busy over the last few years
> with the curriculum tests, with OFSTED and now the Literacy/Numeracy
> hours that we just haven't taken the time to look or listen to their talking
> and learning.
>
> (Sally Langer, 1999)

Her views may not be that extreme or atypical. Indeed, some headteachers, concerned to ensure there is written evidence of learning and to show parents apparently model classrooms of studious silence, also act to reinforce such embedded perceptions. However, many teachers do operate with a more social view of learning and seek to provide opportunities for the dialogic construction of meaning through collaborative talk in a range of contexts (e.g. Eade, 1997; Wilson, 1998). Yet as professionals, all teachers are compromised by the authoritarianism of the school tradition and the requirement to cover the curriculum.

In reality, the majority of primary teachers, while utilising transmission teaching on occasion, also provide some hands-on experiential learning and include discussion as part of their classroom repertoire. So the ideology of cultural reproduction, in which teachers dispense knowledge and maintain the existing social and intellectual order (Apple, 1990), exists uncomfortably alongside a more progressive ideology, in which teachers attempt to facilitate the active construction of such knowledge. This dilemma involves teachers in seeking to ensure that what their pupils learn, through discovery and discussion, conforms to the predetermined knowledge enshrined in the curriculum (Edwards and Mercer, 1987). So, in attempting to turn their understanding about talk into action, teachers are further constrained by their role as curriculum bearers and agents of society.

Teacher and pupil expectations

A number of factors, including teacher expectations, influence whether talk actually serves educational purposes. Such expectations may vary according to the race, gender and class of pupils and teachers and in response to pupils' perceptions of the nature of the task. There is evidence, for example, that white teachers have unconsciously low expectations, perceptions and opinions of black/Asian pupils, which can limit the quality and frequency of their interactions with them and reduce these pupils' access to learning (Levine, 1990; Biggs and Edwards, 1994; Ogilvy et al., 1992). Gender inequalities in classroom talk, which mirror the wider social and political context outside school, have also been documented, endowing males with more power in social interaction than females (French and French, 1984; Coates, 1986). The asymmetrical discourse of the classroom, which provides the teacher with pre-allocated rights, is further skewed by such findings, which show that teachers' questions to boys are often more cognitively demanding, open and challenging than those addressed to the girls (Swann, 1992).

The successful use of oracy also depends upon the status afforded to it by pupils themselves who, within a largely transactional view of learning, may perceive talk as pleasurable but irrelevant (Jones, 1988). Pupils need to recognise that they can learn through talk, for, in coming to value it, they come to value themselves and their peers as meaning makers. Some pupils choose to work alone, and, in their quiet self-containment, disguise their potential, hold themselves back and become invisible learners (Pye, 1988). Talk is ephemeral, and pupils and their parents may feel it has no product, remaining unaware that 'reading and writing float on a sea of talk' (Martin et al., 1976) or that 'conversation is the key in any curriculum' (Cole, 1995). While the value of communication skills in the world of work and relation-ships cannot be underestimated, some parents may have been taught in a more formal didactic manner, and may perceive talk as less relevant in the standards debate than reading or writing. Pupil and parental perceptions do contribute substantially to the profile of oracy in education, but these (like all the other constraining features) can be shaped and developed, widened and enhanced.

How can the profile of oracy be enhanced?

The complex and diverse range of challenges which mitigate against the assured status and development of oracy in schools, should not prevent the profession from acknowledging that real changes have taken place over recent decades. Many schools do inform parents about the role of talk in cognitive develop-ment and help them recognise and value their children's achievement as speakers and listeners. Many offer a wide range of opportunities for talking and learning across the curriculum and others document pupils' oral progression and development. Some schools foster awareness of the importance of spoken language and seek to widen pupils' knowledge about talk, so, through explicit teaching and discussion of meta-linguistic strategies, these schools help pupils learn *through* talk and *about* talk. In such schools a high degree of reflection upon language and learning, by both staff and pupils, is in evidence, pupils' voices are heard and valued, and teachers and pupils work towards a collabora-tive climate of enquiry. To enhance the status of oracy, the profession needs to address these issues, alongside acknowledging the role of unofficial discourses, as well as classroom organisation procedures which foster interaction.

Improving teacher talk

To profile oracy in practice and provide increased access to learning, teachers need to plan carefully, to model and to intervene to extend their pupils' use of language and increase the complexity of their thinking. Teachers can modify their style of talk (Wood and Wood, 1989) and may need to adopt more reflective and speculative stances, demonstrating and modelling increased tentativeness and negotiation, through thinking aloud and using more reciprocal and hypothetical talk (Haworth, 1992). Means by which they signal more overtly the tentative nature of their own knowledge and their interest in alternative views will also need to feature, as will silence, to allow thinking through time.

> Teachers who use dialogue must value the dynamic, ever changing char-acter of meaning-making that results when children are called upon to think for themselves. They must themselves be willing to maintain a healthy uncertainty, to be open to facilitate whatever emerges within the interaction.
>
> (Cole, 1995: 167)

Such teachers will not, however be abandoning the notion of teaching. On the contrary, their understanding of the relationship between language and learning may prompt them to reconceptualise their role as one more focused upon facilitating active knowledge construction, and their classrooms as forums for critical debate and dialogue. Such reformulations in action might begin to reduce the existing gap between theory and practice in this area.

The time devoted to whole-class work could well be harnessed to model genuinely exploratory talk about text, and to encourage pupils to take the initiative, ask questions, hear others' views and articulate their own emerging perspective. The way in which teacher talk influences pupil participation and understanding needs to be investigated further by the profession, and whole staff in-service directed towards questioning, tentativeness and collaboration. Widening the repertoire of teachers' questions – alongside their ability to speculate hesitantly – will not only create more cognitive demands and facilitate pupils' analytical thinking, but should also prompt pupils to take more ownership of their own learning, as they seek to construct meaning in negotiation with others.

Explicit planning for progression

Increased awareness of progression in speaking and listening would aid planning as well as reviewing, recording, evaluation and assessment. Integrating oracy overtly into the hour of literacy, and planning a range of interactive activities at text, sentence and word levels, should not prove difficult for the profession, but such activities must not be randomly selected or eclectically included. In terms of progression, the soundest work to date is that offered in SCAA's own *Framework for Planning and Progression in English at Key Stages 1 and 2* (SCAA, 1997b). This document, written prior to the National Literacy Strategy *Framework*, yet superseded by it, has not been published, but is available on request. It supports the status of oracy by profiling Attainment Target 1 alongside reading and writing, and identifies the following strands of progression that need to be woven across the curriculum (Table 4.1).

Each of the sub-themes is exemplified and developed in termly plans, so, through revisiting the strands of progression over the primary years, teachers can ensure coverage of the range and variety of talk types in different contexts. Detailed planning for progression is an educational prerequisite to ensure pupils' learning through talk, as well as about talk and oracy, is given a genuine status throughout the curriculum.

Drama is the strand of progression which may challenge the profession most, since teachers are not confident about using this largely oral tool for learning (SCAA, 1996a). Perhaps, however, the emphasis on text deconstruction and reconstruction will prompt teachers to use trial drama techniques to explore texts, for example using interior monologues in shared reading in order to examine a character's motives, or using a conscience alley to develop empathy or awareness of narrative options (Neelands, 1992). Such technique manipulation will not develop in-depth 'drama for inner-standing' (Heathcote and Bolton, 1995), but may serve as an introduction to the potential of the medium. It will also offer pupils more collaborative opportunities to enrich

Table 4.1 Progression and development in oracy (KS1/2)

Strands of progression	Sub-themes in each strand
Speaking for different audiences	Reading aloud
	Retelling and telling stories
	Presentation
	Interviews
	Debate
Listening and responding	Talk by adult/expert
	Others in discussion
	Watch (broadcasts, other, plays)
	Persuasive language
	Language variation
Discussion and group interaction	Investigating, selecting, sorting
	Planning, predicting, exploring
	Explaining, reporting, evaluating
Drama activities	Improvisation and role play
	Response to drama
	Writing and performance of drama

Source: SCAA (1997b).

their imaginative capacity and use language for different purposes in fictional contexts. Drama in education can be a process of discovery, an exploration of new ideas and involve the creation of new meanings. It prompts pupils to use a broader linguistic range than is normally accessible, gives them experience of extended utterance, and challenges them to view the world from different standpoints (Grainger, 1998). The current emphasis on citizenship and the exploration of morals and values is well served by drama, but extended time outside a focused literacy hour and further in-service training is needed to ensure that this strand of oral progression is further developed.

Other areas such as storytelling and Information Communications Technology (ICT) provide rich contexts for oral work, and these need to be tapped to extend the range of opportunities provided. Pupils' autobiographical accounts need to be told, to be heard, and to be shared. Traditional tales, myths, legends and fables also proffer rich texts to retell and reshape at the moment of utterance. ICT is an ideal way of promoting negotiation and discussion, for, although computers are designed for individual use, pupils in primary schools often work together at the computer. However, the question of whether such opportunities will prompt collaborative learning is a complex one, which will in part depend upon the pupils' awareness of the intention of the task (Wegerif and Scrimshaw, 1997). It is clear that more conscious awareness of the educational ground rules in small-group contexts can help pupils understand the purpose and nature of their discussion (Edwards and Mercer, 1987; Sheeran and Barnes, 1991).

Profiling reflection: developing knowledge about talk

Effective learners are reflective learners, who not only consider critically what they have learnt, but are also aware of the process of their own learning. To develop the profile of oracy, pupils need to be encouraged to adopt a reflective, analytical stance towards their own language use and that of others. As pupils learn how to work together, they can develop their own strategies to keep themselves on task, share the workload and make negotiated decisions. Pupils can identify guidelines for group work, which serve as principles for effective discussion. Their suggestions might include: don't leave anyone out, share your ideas, listen to others, and so on. Additionally, teachers may offer groups discourse strategies, such as Aim–Review–Question? (ARQ) to help re-establish and shape group discussion when necessary (Hawke, 1991).

John:	What about doing an aim review, because we're all interrupting each other.
Barry:	What's our aim?
John:	What was our question?
Helen:	See what that storm is.
Ben:	Coo look at this!
Barry:	Mm, what's the aim of this? The aim ...
Helen:	The aim is to get to know what thunder storms are, isn't it?
John:	Let's have a review of what we know.
Ben:	Well the thunder is caused by air rising into the cool ...
Barry:	Cooling.
Beth:	Let's all write that down before we set ourselves more questions.

Such strategies can help to guide groups, and work partly by raising awareness of the process of the discourse and partly through establishing group coherence. Once children are aware of the group processes of which they are a part, there is evidence that their collaboration improves (Reid *et al.*, 1989).

Knowledge and reflection are crucial aspects of learning and development, which can contribute substantially to the profile of oracy. Teachers need to identify clear objectives for learning about talk, in order to share their agenda and make implicit knowledge about spoken language explicit, as well as develop their pupils' awareness of the role of talk in learning. Encouraging pupils to talk about talk can involve investigating a range of issues, including those detailed in Table 4.2.

Work focused in these areas could be planned into various curriculum contexts to broaden pupils' knowledge about oracy. During literacy time, examples might include investigating dialects and accents through work on the media, or while reading, e.g. *Johnnie's Blitz* by Bernard Ashley (1995) or Caribbean poetry by John Agard or James Berry. Texts which explore the uncomfortable experience of being extremely shy, such as Berlie Doherty's *The Golden Bird* (1995), or *The Year of the Worm* by Ann Pilling (1984), as well as

Table 4.2 Reflecting upon spoken language

Strands of progression	Sub-themes in each strand
Reflecting upon their own talk	Confidence and competence in a range of contexts
	Choice and appropriateness
	Oral histories
	Using language to learn
	Targets for personal development
Reflecting upon others' language use	How people talk differently in different situations and social groups
	How people use language for different purposes
	How people use language to learn
	Languages, regional and social variations in accent and dialect
	The use of Standard English
Reflecting upon the construction of language	Different kinds of talk
	Differences between spoken and written language
	The history of languages and language development

Source: Adapted from NOP (1991).

texts such as Anne Fine's (1998) *Loudmouth Louis,* which are written from an alternative perspective, can also be useful as issue-raisers.

A wide range of strategies exist to help pupils develop their knowledge about spoken language, (a National Curriculum requirement), but such work is not embedded or well developed in the primary sector. Language investigations into the range of languages used by the pupils, their families and the community can aid their knowledge and respect for language variety. But effective enquiries need not only examine the wide variety of dialects, accents and languages, but also the issues of power and politics which are increasingly evaded in the current climate (Engel and Whitehead, 1996). To widen pupils' knowledge, schools could make better use of NOP (1987–1993) materials, use tape recorders more extensively, and plan language awareness programmes which provoke reflection and consideration of oracy alongside literacy. Such programmes might include some of the following activities, which need to be embedded into the curriculum, and related, where possible, to current work.

Strategies for enabling pupils to reflect upon their own talk are as follows:

- *Questionnaires/Discussions* about talk help learners articulate their perceptions and may reveal limited views which need to be widened: 'If we did all the talking and didn't listen to the teacher telling us things, we wouldn't learn anything';

- *Defining Good Talkers and Listeners* enables pupils to explore features of communication and relationships. They may tend to focus upon surface features (clarity, volume and quantity), but perceptions can be broadened;
- *Learning Logs and Talk Diaries* offer pupils regular chances to make comments about the ways in which they use and introduce self-assessment. 'Kylie and I listened to our story on the tape, we sounded strange. It was a good beginning but we didn't make it sound scary enough, on Friday we're going to add noises and howls and stuff like that.'

Strategies for enabling pupils to reflect upon others' language use are:

- *Drama and Role-play*, which offer opportunities to stand to one side of the action and reflect upon the different language forms, functions and styles used. 'When we swapped roles and I was the policeman, I felt much more in control. I asked lots of questions and expected immediate answers'. Forum theatre is a another useful technique for raising awareness of the influences upon talk and the choices made (Neelands, 1992).
- *Talk Detectives*, which enable individuals to observe a group, make notes, and report back to them what was noticeable about their talk. 'You need to listen to each other more, and let everyone have a say, Sarah was left out you know'.

Strategies for enabling pupils to reflect on the construction of language include:

- *Talking Timelines*, which can document pupils' talk over a short period of time, and can note the kinds of talk used, the purpose and situation;
- *Exploring Speech Verbs*, which can broaden pupils' knowledge of different ways of speaking. Such words can be sorted into categories such as, more frequently used in school/playground/home.

Time to talk about talk is at a premium in a overcrowded curriculum, but in reflecting upon talk and expanding their knowledge about language, pupils come to value talk more and make more conscious and informed choices.

Conclusions

So, should the profession be satisfied with the current status of oracy? Certainly educators have laboured long and hard, investigating and applying theories of learning which stress that, 'most learning in most settings is a communal activity, a sharing of the culture.' (Bruner, 1986: 127)

Dialogue is a central tool in building learning communities, yet for the reasons examined, the press of curriculum coverage, measured scribal outcomes and league tables prevent the full realisation of this goal. Higher priority needs to be given to developing pupils' questioning ability, and space and time must be set aside to embed this reflective and argumentative stance within the curriculum (Phillips, 1992). Professional enquiries need to be fostered so staff can consider together the collaborative construction of knowledge through dialogue, and try out more whole-class and small-group strategies premised upon interaction and engagement. Unless primary schools go back to the basics of consciously teaching thinking, and re-examine the relationship between speaking, listening and learning with their pupils, the principled theoretical arguments will continue to depict a false picture, an educational ideal far from reality. Even today, some children are silenced by some forms of teaching. Their voices deserve to be heard.

If pupils are to learn to think for themselves, teachers must offer them opportunities to share and develop their views, consider and evaluate others' opinions and engage in a collaborative dialogue which seeks to interrogate the content of the curriculum and construct shared understandings in this process. The primary teaching profession should not be satisfied until pupils' voices are more persistently heard to engage in just this critical process.

Questions for discussion

1   In a pluralistic society, there are many minority groups who are disaffected, disadvantaged and seemingly isolated. Is this because they have no voice, are not heard, or are being ignored or rejected?
2   How does the model of communication used in the classroom contribute to citizens' actual experience of democracy?
3   How can teachers come to recognise, develop and utilise the power of informal talk in the classroom, the ongoing conversations, chatter and gossip, jokes and anecdotes?

Further reading

Bearne, E. (ed.) (1998) *Use of Language Across the Primary Curriculum*, London and New York: Routledge.
  This text examines the interdependence of oracy and literacy, and the central role of language in learning. It offers accounts of classroom practice, drawn from across the curriculum and based on an interactive model of language development. The voices of the learners shine through, providing closely observed evidence of pupils using language to learn, learning to use language, and learning about language. The spoken word is integrated within curriculum contexts such as music, maths, art and PE in which all the language modes work together to develop learning. Eve Bearne's model of the English Curriculum highlights the processes of getting information/ideas and the development of discrimination and critical thinking. This is one of the real strengths of the book, as classroom examples show how 'aided by the processes of reflection and evaluation, critical oracy leads to critical literacy' (Bearne 1998: 204). The final chapter offers schools an accessible way forward: a framework for reviewing the use of language in the curriculum and for creating a language and learning policy.

Wells, G. and Chang-Wells, G. N. (1992) *Constructing Knowledge Together: Classrooms as Centers of Inquiry and Literacy*, Portsmouth, New Hampshire: Heinemann.

This book explores socio-cultural theories further, through the use of school case studies. It represents the product of collaborative research with teachers working in inner-city multilingual schools. The nature of knowledge and the communal process of coming to know are examined in considerable detail, and more space is given to evaluating alternative stances. The core of the text (which most appropriately complements this chapter) develops two main arguments: that knowledge can most effectively be constructed in schools which operate as sites for collegial enquiry, and that literate thinking can be attained through collaborative talk. The focus on effective thinking as a prime educational goal is profiled throughout.

5   Drama sets you free – or does it?

Jonothan Neelands

Since the pioneering work of Caldwell Cook, a teacher of English at the turn of the century, there has been a symbiotic relationship between English and drama in secondary schools. Caldwell Cook proposed the then-radical notion that students should perform rather than read the plays of the dramatic canon. Over the next decades, the advances that were made in establishing drama in schools were dependent on both the patronage and the support of policy-makers, managers and theorists in the field of English education. In 1984, Tricia Evans claimed that English teachers taught 75% of drama lessons in the secondary phase (Evans, 1984). While the growth of drama as a separate subject area during the 1980s and 1990s has led to a greater degree of specialism and a growing autonomy from English, drama still depends on its 'mother' subject for protection and as a conduit for influencing future policy. At the time of writing, for instance, drama in secondary schools is once again being seen as a means of meeting priorities in English – in this case the National Literacy Strategy. This is a familiar pattern, in which drama teachers make claims that drama is the most effective means of resolving a wide range of issues and moral panics, which have their genesis in English education – speaking and listening, writing and falling standards in literacy generally. These claims arise out of the understandable insecurities of a minority subject, which is still held in some suspicion in universities, let alone in schools. In trying to free itself from the apron strings of English, drama teachers have sought to carve out their own curriculum territory. However, more often than not, the growth and declines that mark the history of drama in schools have been the consequences of developments and progress in the field of English in schools.

This chapter will examine the current status of drama in schools and identify the key issues and divisions that both stimulate and confound its development as a separate subject. However, the reader will be conscious that the issues and divisions in drama find their mirror image in the field of English in Education. At the heart of this similarity are: the vexed question of literacy; the cultural agendas of class, personal and social identity; and the struggle against authoritarian and bureaucratic control of the curriculum. Drama, like English, is a cultural subject. Through their practices and literary selections, both subjects offer students the opportunities to define themselves and the cultures to which they belong. In addition, culture is of course always an ideological field in which different social groups seek to establish their dominance over others who have competing understandings of what it means to be human and which artistic achievements should be valued over others. The sociologist, Pierre Bourdieu reminds us:

> Schooling serves to reinforce rather than diminish social differences. The culture it transmits is largely that of the dominant classes ... cultural capital thus participates in the process of domination by legitimising certain practices as 'naturally' superior to others and by making these practices seem superior even to those who do not participate, who are thus led through a negative process of inculcation, to see their own practices as inferior and to exclude themselves from legitimate practices.
>
> (Bourdieu, 1993: 23/24)

In terms of the development of drama in schools, Bourdieu's principle has been translated into a set of oppositions that represent the conflict and struggle between those who seek to naturalise and reinforce the cultural practices and objects of the dominant classes and those who seek a more radical and oppositional pedagogy. These oppositions are popularly described as follows.

Drama versus theatre

Drama in schools is often taken to mean the forms of improvisatory and role-taking drama that are characteristic of classroom drama, in which there may be no sense of a 'performance' or 'production' in the orthodox sense. This form of drama is increasingly referred to as 'process drama' and its emphasis is often on the use of drama for personal and social development. Theatre is taken to mean the canon and practices of the bourgeois Western theatre tradition established by Ibsen, Antoine and others in the nineteenth century during the formation of the middle classes. This tradition of theatre is often referred to as the 'Modern Drama' (after Styan, 1981 and others). Historically, this opposition between 'drama' and 'theatre' is centred around the dominance during the 1970s and 1980s of the Drama-in-Education tradition with its emphasis on participatory and content-led forms of classroom drama work at the expense of the formal study of plays, performances and dramatic criticism. The key proponents of this tradition have been Dorothy Heathcote and Gavin Bolton (Bolton, 1992). The most vocal and effective critic of this tradition has been David Hornbrook (Hornbrook, 1989, 1991). The opposition between 'drama' and 'theatre' in drama education parallels the arguments in English between those who have emphasised the use of English for 'personal growth' or 'self-expression', and those who argue for a greater emphasis on the formal teaching of grammar and the literary heritage of the English canon.

Subject versus method

Should drama be used as an efficacious method in other areas of the curriculum – in English and history for instance – or should it be framed as a discrete subject with its own body of knowledge, skills and practices? As drama has become more established in secondary schools – it is the fastest growing subject at GCSE and post-16 – the voice of secondary 'subject' teachers has begun to dominate the field. The Drama-in-Education tradition had flourished when the primary phase model of an integrated curriculum based on topic and theme work dominated the educational agenda. The National Curriculum, with its rigid subject framework, produced a crisis for those who believed in the integrating power of drama, and provided an opportunity for those who wished to put the primacy of the 'subject', or 'body of knowledge' of drama – before the 'subjects', the bodies and minds of the students coming into the drama lesson.

Personal and social learning versus cultural induction

Is the value of drama in school to be placed on its immediate benefits to students in terms of their growth in confidence, understanding and the social skills of communication and interaction? Or, is the purpose of drama to induct young people into the cultural heritage of the Modern Drama?

During the 1980s and early 1990s the divisions caused by the allegiance of individuals and groups to one extreme view or the other produced a deeply fragmented and confusing conception of drama in schools. In the absence of any National Curriculum orders for drama or any consensus amongst the profession, there was, undoubtedly, a sense of professional insecurity amongst teachers and student teachers as to what they should teach in drama and how they should teach it. This fragmented field of drama, in which individuals and groups took positions by denying, even trashing, the positions taken by others and by limiting the potential field of drama to their own narrow, sectarian position is best described by reference to the government's own descriptions of drama in schools.

Drama to order

The most recent and authoritative definition and statement of aims for drama in schools is still to be found in the Ofsted *Handbook for the Inspection of Schools* (Ofsted, 1993a). The manual is a powerful tool for influencing practice in schools because it forms the basis for the inspection of practice. In this sense the document provides a more 'enforceable' interpretation of the National Curriculum than previous orders and non-statutory guidance documents.

The references to drama in the manual provide a view of what inspectors should expect to find in schools and what they might report on. The core reference to drama is contained in one paragraph of the manual.

Drama has a place within English in the National Curriculum. Pupils'
achievements in drama should be judged according to their contribution to
each of the Attainment Targets 1 to 3 for English. In addition, the National Curriculum recognises drama as a subject in its own right, particularly at Key Stage 4 where schools may offer it alongside the other arts. At
all four Key Stages pupils' achievements in drama should be judged within
two main categories: creating and performing drama and appreciating and
appraising it. These categories correspond broadly to the Attainment
Targets in music and will support the evaluation of drama's contribution to
composite courses in the performing arts. Pupils' achievements in drama as
a method of learning in other subjects should also be inspected. Standards
should be judged in the following aspects of pupils' achievements: using
imagination, with belief and feeling; creating drama with conviction and
concentration; responding sensitively to their own work and that of others
in drama; using a range of dramatic skills, techniques, forms and conventions to express ideas and feelings effectively; grasping and using dramatic
concepts appropriately; recalling, recording and evaluating their own work
and that of others.

(Ofsted, 1993a: 27)

There are two other references to drama in the Ofsted manual, which also
encourage a broad influence for drama and emphasise the social and moral
content of drama:

Drama can strengthen and broaden pupils' cultural experience and their
ability to reflect on their own and other societies.

(*ibid.*: 17)

Moral development … in drama pupils may explore complexities in human
relationships: conflict, tension, love, hate.

(*ibid.*: 18)

The apparently unitary construction of the Ofsted definition reveals a
number of different perspectives on the nature of drama in schools and its place
within the curriculum. It is described as being part of English, as an arts subject,
and as a cross-curricular method of learning in other subjects. Each one of these
perspectives places drama in a different relationship to the rest of the school
curriculum; each perspective is accompanied by its own assessment criteria and
standards.

By seeking to include all these perspectives within a single definition of
drama, the paragraph can be seen as being sensitive to, and inclusive of, 'local'
interpretations of drama: conceptions that might vary from one institution to
the next. But it can also be seen as a construction of the space of position-
takings in the field of drama in schools. In other words, the paragraph does not
represent the singular position of drama in the curriculum so much as it

describes the different positions that are taken on what drama is and how it should be placed. There is an analogy here with the Cox version of the English National Curriculum, which also sought to describe and be inclusive of a range of different positions within the field of English teaching (Cox, 1991).

There are, for instance, as we have noted, three quite different sets of criteria for setting standards in drama; each set 'valuing' different emphases within the potential field of drama. It is unlikely that any one school would be operating all three, rather, it would use whichever set belonged to its own distinctive 'position-taking'. The Ofsted definition is, then, a description of the distinctive characteristics of the key positions in the field of drama in schools at the time that it was written. It is an acknowledgement of the range of position-takings that a school's inspector might encounter.

A drama Kama Sutra

There are three positions, which can be identified in the Ofsted account, which will briefly be described here in terms of their distinctive characteristics. They are:

1 Drama as a Method of Learning (referred to as the 'method' position);
2 Drama as an Arts Subject (referred to as the 'subject' position);
3 Drama as part of English (referred to as the 'drama as English' position)

Drama as a method of learning

This position represents the Drama-in-Education tradition by stressing drama's efficacious use as a means of learning in other areas of the curriculum, rather than emphasising the study of the medium itself. The immanent experience of an improvised drama that takes some aspect of another curriculum subject or an issue that is relevant to students' interests, is valued above the study of dramatic traditions and stage craft. There is only an exceptionally weak classification of how it constitutes a distinctive curriculum subject, combined with exceptionally poor recognition of the boundaries between educational knowledge and everyday knowledge. This position claims that the personal and social benefits that students gain from 'doing' drama are too important to be restricted to a single subject identity or to the production and reception of orthodox genres of 'theatre'.

Historically, the Drama-in-Education tradition has insulated itself from the broader fields of drama and theatre, to the extent that it has developed its own discrete history, which is framed as an account of individuals and periods. This history, characteristically, includes Peter Slade's work in the 1950s – the 'Child Drama' period (Slade, 1954); Brian Way in the 1960s – 'Development through Drama' (Way, 1968) and generally concludes with the work of Heathcote and Bolton in the 1970s and 1980s – 'Drama for Understanding'. Dorothy Heathcote is the most influential and internationally renowned teacher associated with the 'method' position. For Heathcote, drama is primarily a means of improving the quality of teaching in schools through its context-centred and interactive methods rather than as an induction into theatre (Johnson and O'Neill, 1984).

> Finally, having spent a long time wondering why I have for years been irritated by the cry of 'let's have more drama in our schools', I now realise why I always wanted to say, don't lobby for dramatics, lobby for better learning!
>
> (Heathcote 1980: 169)

The discourse of the Drama-in-Education tradition seeks to limit the boundaries of the field of drama to its own boundaries – to suggest that Drama-in-Education is the field of drama. This form of position-taking has tended to ignore the reality that teachers of drama have, traditionally, been responsible for teaching a 'set of genres', including the orthodox genres favoured by the 'subject' position, with its emphasis on the study of plays. They have also been responsible for producing school plays and other activities that focus on orthodox theatre concepts and practices.

The emergence of the 'subject' position, which will be described in the next section, with its strategic attacks on the 'method' position, has, however, forced the Drama-in-Education tradition to re-articulate and to regroup, and this has produced a fragmentation of the position into two sub-positions. The 'orthodox' English version of Drama-in-Education has been maintained by the radical left SCYPT (Standing Conference of Young People's Theatre) grouping within the TIE (Theatre in Education) movement, which David Hornbrook has described as:

> An alliance of teachers on the political left, grouped around a concern over issues of class, gender and race, and a commitment to the idea of education as 'empowerment' ... increasingly, during the 1980's, associated with the left radicalism of the T.I.E. movement, this alliance sought to press the dramatic pedagogy of Heathcote and Bolton into the service of revolutionary social change. In short they believed that its revelatory processes enabled young people to see, understand and challenge the 'objective' structures of political challenge.
>
> (Hornbrook 1989: 47)

The second position is occupied by a 'post-Heathcote' grouping, which is disposed to the distinctive student-centred and efficacious characteristics of the 'method' position. However, it does seek to modify the position in order to address both the substantial criticisms that have been made by those who espouse the 'subject' position and the marginalisation of 'child-centred' and liberal pedagogies within the broader field of education.

This second position is concerned with realigning the practices of Drama-in-

Education within both the fields of drama and theatre. It seeks to bring coherence to the complex set of genres and teaching objectives that drama teachers work with, particularly 'performance' and 'theatre', through what has become known as the 'conventions approach' in England and the 'process drama' approach in America and Australia (O'Neill, 1995; O'Toole, 1992; Neelands, 1990). In different ways both these approaches have sought to extend the boundaries of the 'method' position to include some elements of the 'subject' position. The 'conventions approach' goes furthest towards closing the space between Drama-in-Education and other genres of theatre, by abandoning the traditional distinctions and 'differences' between 'drama' and 'theatre', which had characterised the earlier development of the 'method' position. Rather, the approach stresses the 'contexts' and 'developmental stages' in which theatre is used:

> in contexts where theatre is being created by young people and in recognition of the need to define a process in theatre which provides a continuity and development of experience across an age-range that finds its first theatre experiences in play; to a generation which finds its satisfaction in a wide variety of contexts, including seeing and being in plays ...
>
> The conventions and the examples emphasise interactive forms of interchange, even fusion, of the roles of actor and spectator ... The conventions have been chosen to emphasise theatre's traditional role as an educative form of entertainment, which responds to a basic human need to interpret and express the world through symbolic form.
>
> (Neelands, 1990: 5)

Drama as an arts subject

This position represents the 'Theatre Studies' tradition in stressing an educational model of theatre as the performance and appreciation of dramatic literature and an emphasis on the crafts of actor, director and critical reception. This position places an emphasis on the centrality of the playwright and the study of texts, even though it aligns itself with the other arts rather than with English.

There has always been a traditional 'theatre studies' influence, particularly at Key Stage 4 and post-16, and amongst those teachers who favoured the skills and drills of a 'drama school' approach. The theatre studies influence has hardened into an identifiable 'subject' position within the field of drama in schools. Its position-taking has increasingly included assertions of difference of 'aesthetic value' between method and subject, process and product, and, most recently, between 'drama' and 'theatre'. In each case the position-taking has included the assertion that subject is more valuable than method, product more valuable than process, and 'theatre' more valuable than 'drama'. More precisely, it defines itself by foregrounding aspects of 'theatre' that had been marginalised by the 'method' position – plays, directors and orthodox actor–audience relationships.

However, it should be stressed that the orthodox, and Euro-centric, conception of theatre that underpins this position is now highly contested in the academies, and even to those who believe that students have an entitlement to an education in theatre, the descriptions of theatre offered by the subject position must sound somewhat quaint if not downright élitist:

> In the new curriculum, student playwrights, directors and stage managers will tread the boards (*sic*) of the classroom as confidently as their professional counterparts do those of the local theatre; student actors will study their lines, rehearse their parts and perform, knowing that in so doing they join a tradition which stretches from ancient times.
>
> (Hornbrook, 1991: 4)

Both the 'method' and 'subject' position have tended to share the same reductive definition of theatre. Both assume that theatre is no more than the particular tradition that Hornbook characterises above. This would be like suggesting that the socially dominant dialect of 'Standard English' is the only dialect worthy of use and study in schools. This would undervalue the rich plethora of local and cultural variations in language use, just as an insistence on the primacy of 'Standard Theatre' ignores the rich variety of forms and different traditions that are available.

The 'subject' position is itself fragmented into three sub-positions, which all share the basic characteristics of the position, but which seek to extend the position's influence within the field of drama in schools in different ways.

The influential Gulbenkian Foundation Report of 1982, *The Arts in Schools* and the subsequent *Arts in Schools Project* (1990a and b) proposed the 'aesthetic and creative field' as a generic grouping of the arts subjects within the curriculum. Both these projects were addressed to two audiences, teachers and policy-makers, and attempted to schematise the production and reception of the arts into categories and terms that would be accepted by both audiences:

> The second objective was to put the case for the arts as clearly as possible to policy-makers at all levels. Much of the existing literature on arts education had been written for specialists of different sorts: none of it was addressed specifically to the economic and ideological issues raised in the Great Debate.
>
> In the terms of the Great Debate the arts were at risk from two misconceptions. First, to those who argued that the main role of education is to prepare young people for work, arts education evidently seemed unnecessary except for those looking for arts jobs. Second, through the emphasis in some teaching on creativity, self-expression and personal development, the arts had become associated with non-intellectual activities, and therefore seemed to lie outside the priorities of those who argued for a return to traditional academic values.
>
> (Gulbenkian Foundation, 1982: xii)

In seeking to incorporate the field of drama in schools within the field of arts education, the projects also sought to distance themselves from the 'method' position and its nearest ally the 'drama as English' position, which is discussed below: first by distinguishing between the use of dramatic method to focus on content, or meanings, and the study and mastery of form, or 'aesthetic appreciation', and then by creating a hierarchical relationship between the two.

> In describing the roles of the arts in the curriculum, a distinction can be made between learning in and learning through the arts ... In learning through the arts, the prime focus is likely to be on the theme or subject matter, or on personal and social education; in learning in the arts, on the aesthetic and technical qualities of the work.
>
> (Arts in Schools Project Team (1990a) – 84: 37)

> Arts education is concerned with deepening young people's sensitivities to the formal qualities – and therefore to the pleasures and meanings – of the arts and with extending the range of their aesthetic experience and judgement.
>
> (Arts in Schools Project Team (1990b) – 1: 6)

The projects were principally concerned with advocating the arts in a hostile and volatile period of educational reform dominated by the agendas of the radical Right. The schema, discourse and intent of the *Arts in Schools Project* were to build a coherent and consensual theoretical and practical platform for the development of arts education in general. But the projects, and the educational climate that spawned them, also provided a theoretical base for the writings of David Hornbrook, the most recent and confrontational agent within the 'subject' position.

Hornbrook has gone furthest in seeking to create distance between the 'subject' position and the 'method' and 'drama as English' positions (Hornbrook, 1989, 1991). His work is characterised by attempts to replace the essentially liberal progressive, psycho-developmental base of the 'method' position with a conservative 'Marxian' sociology of theatre. (The Marxist antecedents for Hornbrook's work, however, are to be found in the conservative theories of Williams and Lukacs rather than in the radical modernism of Brecht and Benjamin. For a further discussion of the difference between conservative and Marxist aesthetics, see Lunn (1982).)

Hornbrook's project has been concerned with the development of a clearly defined 'subject' position for drama, with strong classification, and therefore distance, between the study of drama and other subjects in the curriculum. He has advocated a 'visible pedagogy' and 'publicly acknowledged' body of knowledge as a way of reducing the weak framing and seemingly idiosyncratic and 'localised' ideological selections of content and form associated with the 'method' position:

> The clear subject identity engendered as a consequence of placing dramatic

art generically within the arts grants educational drama a disciplinary coherence which has been notably lacking in the past ... For most purposes, dramatic art's unequivocal identification with such culturally familiar concepts as plays, theatres and actors, gives it an identity readily acceptable to a wide constituency.

(Hornbrook, 1989: 130)

The emphasis on the 'culturally familiar concepts' of plays, theatres, actors and audiences has produced a 'subject' position within the field of drama in school that reduces the boundaries of the field to these particular concepts. Increasingly, in Hornbrook's own definitions and those that he has influenced – particularly in the authoritative Arts Council document *Drama in Schools* – the boundaries of the field are set at the boundaries of the position.

The Arts Council wishes to add its view of drama as an art form with its own distinct discipline and methodology. While drama is recognised in the national curriculum as an invaluable teaching method, *it is first and foremost an art in its own right.*

(Arts Council, 1992: I; emphasis added)

The third 'voice' within the 'subject' position belongs to Peter Abbs, the poet and lecturer in the aesthetics of English teaching, who has disseminated his own brand of essentially metaphysical and subjectivist aesthetics through the twelve-volume Falmer Press *Library of Aesthetic Education*, published during the 1980s and early 1990s. Drawing on the conservative aesthetic tradition of Peter Fuller and Roger Scruton in particular, Abbs derides the 'method' position for its lack of attention to the European tradition of the arts and proposes an 'apprenticeship' into the arts, based on a study of classical art works. There are close parallels between the stages of Abbs' argument and those of the 'cultural literacy' position of E. D. Hirsch and Allan Bloom. In both cases an argument is made for establishing, and teaching, a stable canon of cultural knowledge – authors, key works and aesthetic movements – based on the tastes and preferences of a governing and dominant elite. For Abbs, the 'method' position, as well as Modernist aesthetics, are literally taken as threats to the future of Western Civilisation 'as-he-knows-it':

educational drama has been culturally provincial, it now needs to widen its range and open itself fully to the whole circle of theatre. It needs to bring a wealth of philosophical conception from the long European tradition to its reformulations, not only the mandatory Brecht and Boal but also Aristotle's Poetics, Nietzsche's *The Birth of Tragedy* and the formulations of, say, Strindberg, Lorca, T. S. Eliot, Arthur Miller, Jonathan Miller and a hundred others. Students of drama at whatever level, need more technical terms, more abstract concepts, more awareness of names, movements, genres.

(Abbs, 1994: 135)

Drama as English

The distinctive characteristic of this position is that drama is an integral part of English rather than a subject in its own right, or a subject within the generic grouping of arts subjects. It is valued for its contribution to the development of language and literacy skills, and for its heritage of dramatic literature. In this position, drama is an essentially verbal and literary art. The position, however, has both conservative and radical 'position-takers' within it. The emphasis on Shakespeare and the literary tradition of English theatre belongs to the former. However, the latter shows more interest in drama's role in helping students to understand the social construction of language and the politics of representation, and, in so doing, to understand more about themselves and their relationships to the worlds in which they live. Gunther Kress and others have described this agenda as a radical form of cultural and ideological enquiry. Kress describes the agenda for English teachers in this way:

> English is the only site in the curriculum which can deal with questions of individuality and responsibility in a moral, ethical, public, social sense … the examination of issues around notions of the individual: of social structures and of destinies; of notions of citizenship; of humans as having social responsibilities and socially produced characteristics as persons …
>
> (Kress, 1995a: 32)

This chapter began with a reference to the work of Caldwell Cook (1917). His *Play Way* was a description of his work on the performance of plays, which were more usually considered as literary objects in the English classroom of the day. This tradition of workshop or school performances of great works of dramatic literature continues and is reflected in the orders for English within the 1995 National Curriculum. Cook established a Modernist and Romanticist foundation for the use of play in education and for this reason he is also identified as a 'founding father' of the Drama-in-Education tradition with its emphasis on drama as an extended form of imaginative play.

> This book sets forth some ideas … on educational method which it is hoped may prove helpful to those teachers who have not shut their minds against proposals for reform.

> The natural means of study in youth is play … A natural education is by practice, by doing things, and not by instruction, the hearing how, as you may see in the flight of a young bird.
>
> (Cook, 1917: xi, 1)

The tensions between 'play' as an educational method and the study and performance of 'plays' has characterised the history of the 'drama as English' position. *A Language for Life*, known as the Bullock Report, described the 'differences' in these terms:

Drama has an obvious and substantial contribution to make to the development of children's language, and its possibilities in this respect have yet to be fully explored ... Essentially drama is a fundamental human activity which may include such elements as play, ritual, simulations and role playing, to give but a few examples. Where the spectators' role becomes dominant in all these activities, they can be said to turn into theatre or conscious art form. Where spectators are absent, or where they become so involved that they cease to be spectators, what results is also a powerful form of drama ... It is inescapably social, for it is about working in a group, often to solve a problem or make a decision.

(DES, 1975, para 10: 31)

While the development of the 'drama as English' position has been influenced by the theoretical and methodological development of the Drama-in-Education tradition with its emphasis on process and improvisation, it has been strengthened by the theoretical contributions of teachers and theorists associated with the post-Dartmouth Conference 'personal growth' position in the field of English – James Britton, James Moffett and Harold Rosen in particular (Dixon, 1975). These theorists, who are associated with the development of a liberal progressive English curriculum, have stressed the pedagogic relationship between language development and drama, and have argued for drama to be given value in the English curriculum as a means of giving students increased confidence and understanding of the social uses of language.

Despite the inclusion of drama within English, the 1989 National Curriculum orders carefully accommodate the 'method' position while leaving space for the 'subject' position. As a method, drama is valued for its 'contribution to children's learning':

the inclusion of drama methods in English should not in any way replace drama as a subject for specialist study.

(DES, 1989, para 8: 3)

Drama is not simply a subject, but also a method; a learning tool. Furthermore, it is one of the key ways in which children gain an understanding of themselves and of others. Planning for drama in the classroom requires a clear understanding of its nature and the contribution it can make to children's learning. Drama is not confined to one strand in the statements of attainment which ceases after level six. It is central in developing all major aspects of English.

(NCC, 1990, D11–13)

A new consensus?

The pace of educational change has been fast and furious since the introduction of the National Curriculum. The Ofsted description of drama was written in

1993, and, in five years, the landscape of drama in schools has already been transformed. Writing in 1997, Mike Fleming suggested that there was now a new 'consensus' in drama in schools, which had replaced the strife and struggle of the position-taking implied in the Ofsted account. Fleming characterises the consensus in these terms:

> The extreme divisions between 'drama' and 'theatre' practice that were characteristic of the seventies and eighties have given way to a more inclusive view of the subject which sees a place for all manifestations of drama in schools ... Publications in drama now largely take it for granted that the dichotomies between 'process' and 'product'; 'theatre' and 'drama'; 'drama for understanding' and 'drama as art'; 'experience' and 'performance' were false polarities.
>
> (Fleming, 1997: 1/2)

In a sense, Fleming has acknowledged a central truth about the teaching of drama in schools, which was often ignored, sometimes wilfully, by the influential proponents of the historical positions within drama. Hornbrook, for instance, bases his entire critique of the Drama-in-Education tradition on his creation of a folk-devil of a drama teacher slavishly following the divine words of Dorothy Heathcote and Gavin Bolton and eschewing all forms of performance, theatre history and stage craft. Of course this teacher did not exist, but Hornbrook's caricature found credence in an age which accepted the routine demonisation of teachers whose agenda was different from, or opposed to, the dominant Thatcherite project of the time. It is more likely that, in practice at least, most drama teachers already worked with an inclusive view of drama. To be a drama teacher in a secondary school necessarily means teaching classroom drama in KS3, often in the genre of 'process' or 'conventions approach' drama. It also means teaching GCSE and A-level theatre studies; putting on school plays; running extra-curricular drama clubs and organising theatre visits. Any teacher who refused, as a matter of principle, to deliver this range would find it impossible to gain employment. It is the range of drama that schools have come to expect.

Some measure of consensus was made inevitable by the pervasive dominance of a subject-based curriculum. In England, at least, the idea of an integrated curriculum based on broad areas of experience, and designed to promote a wide range of intelligences beyond literacy and numeracy, is effectively dead. Those who advocated the 'method' position have been forced to accept and therefore to articulate a subject framework for drama in schools. It is also the case that the growth of drama in secondary schools has at last made possible some debate about progression and continuity across the 11–18-age range (Hornbrook, 1989; Neelands, 1998).

The emergence of a more inclusive conception of drama also mirrored new understandings of drama and theatre in the broader academic field of university theatre departments and academic journals. The rise of post-modern theories of performance and a general awareness of cultural difference raised by post-colonial, feminist and post-structural discourses finally debunked the ethnocentric and class restricted conception of theatre peddled by the 'subject' position in the field of drama in schools.

For the same reason those who took the 'method' position and rejected 'theatre' came to understand that their objection was to the dominance of one genre of theatre and that new alliances could be made with theatre practitioners – like Brecht and Boal – who were also working against the grain of the bourgeois theatre and its fixed conventions of production and reception. As the cultural field of theatre in its broadest sense embraced an increasingly broad range of practices, traditions and cultures it became inevitable that the field of drama in schools would undergo a similar transformation. It is already inconceivable that the 'cultural conservationist' stance taken by Peter Abbs would find any credence now.

In one sense, consensus is to be welcomed. There is no doubt that for a long period the energies available in the field of drama in schools were expended in internal conflicts and struggles and thus diverted from promoting drama within the broader struggles and debates within the fields of education and theatre. But on the other hand, consensus can be a dead hand that stifles necessary struggles within the field. New ideas and directions result from provocations and disputes between the positions. There is no doubt that the iconoclastic sophistry of Hornbrook's provocations in the late 1980s forced the other positions – 'drama as English' and the 'method' position – to reconfigure and re-conceptualise. Hornbrook made it necessary for all involved in the field to re-examine their relationships to both theatre and available curriculum models. In a sense, without struggles of some kind there can be no progress. These struggles are in the end about the legitimate means of cultural representation. As Bourdieu reminds us these conflicts are:

> about the legitimate vision of the world – in the last resort, about what deserves to be represented and the right way to represent it – are political conflicts – for the power to impose the dominant definition of reality, and social reality in particular.
>
> (Bourdieu, 1993: 102–3)

Drama sets you free!

This chapter closes with a view of the most recent survey of drama in secondary schools, published in the autumn of 1998. The Secondary Heads Association (SHA) have produced a report on the status and provision of drama in Secondary schools entitled *Drama Sets You Free!*. This report is remarkable in the sense that SHA is an influential professional association representing the interests of Senior Managers in schools, and tends to be preoccupied with the weighty matters of finance, administration and legislative change. It has never before dedicated a publication to a specific subject in the curriculum.

The report is based on questionnaires returned by 733 of the 5500 secondary schools in England and Wales. Despite the fact that the sample is statistically small and must inevitably reflect the views of those headteachers who are enthusiastic enough about drama to bother to make a return, the sample does represent the largest published review of data about, and attitudes to forms of drama provision.

The report makes interesting reading in the light of the issues that have divided and preoccupied drama in schools. Just as the community of drama teachers, teacher-trainers and others has begun to reconceptualise drama as a subject with discrete aims and objectives, and a framework of progression and assessment, this report seems to suggest that Senior Managers are looking for something different from their drama teachers.

The conclusions of the report are prefaced by four questions, which are raised by the responses to the survey:

• Should it be in the National Curriculum?
• Is too much attention paid to productions to the detriment of educational drama?
• How well used is drama as a vehicle for personal development?
• Are teachers of drama sufficiently well qualified for the task they face?

(SHA, 1998: 29)

Each of these questions reveals new issues and priorities for drama in schools, which readers are invited to consider. A commentary on them is provided here, referring to the SHA report evidence.

Should drama be in the National Curriculum?

Drama has thrived in secondary schools both in spite of not being, and maybe because it is not, a National Curriculum subject. Indeed, many of the SHA respondents see drama as providing a vital alternative to the rigid and technologically based frameworks imposed on other subjects. Whether drama provides a more 'free' and creative space in the curriculum, which has the potential to subvert the narrow agenda of the National Curriculum, or whether it is a 'safety valve', which merely offers the illusion of 'freedom' within a tightly constrained curriculum, is a moot point.

Is too much attention paid to productions, to the detriment of educational drama?

The responses tend to dispel the myth that Senior Managers are more concerned with the obvious public relations benefits offered by school productions than with the quality of the less visible curriculum or classroom drama activity. They give a very strong endorsement of the ethics and principles of the 'method' position, with its emphasis on the efficacious use of drama for a wide range of curriculum and personal and social purposes.

How well used is drama as a vehicle for personal development?

Again for 'vehicle' read 'method'. It is clear from the SHA responses that senior managers do not value drama as a subject with equal status to other National Curriculum subjects. It is primarily valued for the immediate personal and social benefits that students experience from practising drama.

Are teachers of drama sufficiently well qualified for the task they face?

The report makes a strong plea for drama to be delivered by specialist teachers. At the time of writing of the SHA report, the Teacher Training Agency had tried to scrap the seven specialist drama PGCE courses in favour of hybrid English and Drama courses (summer 1998). They backed down in the face of massive opposition from SHA and other significant agencies, and the place of specialist PGCE courses now seems assured. The report is also very critical of the drama being taught by English teachers. The argument is made convincingly that a drama teacher must know how to deliver drama as a subject, and as a method, and must also provide a wide range of extra-curricular activities. The breadth and depth of a drama teacher's role in the school as a learning community requires specialist training in SHA's view.

Conclusions

As the century closes, there are some difficult choices facing drama in schools. In the primary phase of education, drama is in crisis. There are few specialist teachers and the demands of the National Literacy and Numeracy Strategies further depress the priority given to drama for many generalist classroom teachers. In the secondary phase, there is no doubt that drama has done rather well out of not being in the National Curriculum. Would inclusion in the revised National Curriculum of 2001 strengthen drama in primary schools? Would inclusion mean that the last unregulated oasis in the English and Welsh education system – drama at KS3 – would disappear under a welter of specific teaching objectives and an imposition of the dominant culture's view of theatre?

This chapter began with the assertion that English and drama teachers have long been fellow travellers and that drama tends to progress in similar directions to English. Perhaps this is less true today. In reading the SHA report one is forcibly struck by the extent to which the 'grey-suits' of senior management now look to drama to provide many of the qualities of teaching and learning once considered the preserve of English. The report praises drama for its treatment of a wide range of cultural and social issues; its focus on the immediate experience of drama in helping students to come to terms with their emergent personal and social identities and its frequently creative and transformational teaching strategies. The increasingly narrow parameters of the English National Curriculum have meant that consideration of issues of equity, cultural heritage and just attempting to create the time and climate for engaging students in their learning have become marginalised in many English classrooms. Perhaps, it is time for a new alliance between English and drama that is predicated on the desire of English teachers to reclaim ground currently occupied by drama, which could at least be shared.

The final word should go to the 'grey-suits' who conclude their 'summary' with the assertion that:

> A school without drama, is a school without a soul!
>
> (SHA, 1998: 30)

Further reading

These additional titles will give readers further information on the practical dimension of drama teaching:

Banks, R. A. and Marson, P. (1998) *Drama and Theatre Arts*, London: Hodder and Stoughton.
   This is a source book for information about theatre. Each section includes ideas and course-work suggestions for students at GCSE and A level.

Cooper, S. and Mackey, S. (1995) *Theatre Studies: An Approach for Advanced Level*, AEB.
   This is a detailed student text that covers the AEB syllabus requirements. It is also a useful general guide to theatre history studies.

Crinson, J and Leake, L. (ed.) (1993) *Move Back the Desks*, Sheffield: NATE.
   This is an excellent publication, which provides case studies of drama work in English and guidance in managing drama.

Fleming, M. (1997) *The Art of Drama Teaching*, London: Fulton.
   This book explores a variety of theatre conventions, using extracts from dramatic literature and exercises.

Kempe, A. (1997) *The GCSE Drama Coursebook*, Cheltenham: Stanley Thornes.
   This was designed as a student textbook by an author who takes a particular interest in working with scripts. Many of the ideas and extracts are now appropriate to KS3.

Neelands, J. (1992) *Learning through Imagined Experience*, London: Hodder and Stoughton.
   This book describes a range of strategies, which highlight both the value and the possible approaches for introducing learning through drama into the classroom, in the context of English in the National Curriculum.

O'Toole, J. and Haseman, B. (1987) *Dramawise*, London: Heinemann.
   This is one of the first books to look at the teaching of the formal elements of drama within contexts that are relevant and meaningful for students. It is an excellent bridge between 'drama' and 'theatre', which includes projects, lesson plans and exercises for students.

6   What is(n't) this subject called English?

Muriel Robinson

Introduction

This chapter asks the crucial question of what English is, what it does, and what it might offer as one of three particularly privileged (core) subjects in the English National Curriculum. The chapter begins by tracing the development of English as a subject and by showing how recently this subject gained full academic respectability. In doing this, the chapter identifies two pairs of current tensions within the subject, namely between literacy and literature and between reception and production. The chapter then sets this alongside an exploration of what English is in the world outside school, and asks how that relates to what we need to do as teachers of English from Key Stage (KS) 1 to 4. This will allow a consideration of how far this subject called English might need to change to reflect the changing society in which it is now located.

Key questions behind this argument will be:

1   What is – and what isn't – this subject called English, and where did it come from?
2   What is English in everyday life, and how valid are pupils' out-of-school experiences as starting points or points of comparison with the English curriculum?
3   How far does the current curriculum relate to English as used and encountered beyond the classroom, and is this sufficient?

These are all issues that have relevance right across formal schooling (and beyond, since a similar debate could be had about the subject as studied at university level), and so this chapter considers the entire 5–16 age range. However, since one of the points to be made is that the inappropriateness of current policy and understanding is particularly acute in the primary years, there will be a particular focus on KS1 and 2.

Tensions in English: literacy and literature; production and reception

To set the context for this debate about the changing nature of English, it is important to challenge some of the everyday 'givens' which surround it; what

Barthes would call the exnominated concepts of the subject (Barthes, 1973). Barthes' arguments around everyday myths show how we naturalise and de-politicise ('exnominate') fundamental aspects of our lives by taking their underlying concepts for granted rather than by recognising them as socially constructed and so open to challenge and change. We have done exactly this to the subject of English, creating a myth of an uncontested history reaching back through the ages. This myth acts to support certain views of the subject and to resist change by offering a 'common sense', naturalised view of what has always been a highly politically charged site of contested truths.

Central to the myth of English as a school subject is the notion of tradition, and in particular of a long history of an unchanging and unchallenged approach to English in schools and universities. Alongside this goes an everyday view of the content of the subject, which ignores the tensions between literacy and literature and between reception and production. In fact, the subject of English as taught now, and as defined in the National Curriculum, has a complex developmental history from which these tensions have arisen and this history needs to be understood if they are to be considered and resolved.

A brief history of literacy

The subject as taught now actually has two strands of different origin. The first and oldest of these, in terms of the school curriculum, is the part of English that concerns itself with the development of pupils' language skills, and in particular the skills involved in reading and, more controversially at first, writing. There is not space here to explore the whole history of the pedagogy of literacy (but see, for example, Wallbank, 1979, or Gardner, 1984, for fuller accounts of this). However, in brief, the inclusion of literacy training as an aspect of early formal schooling for a relatively wide section of the population can be traced back at least to the dame schools and private schools of the eighteenth century. Although it is commonly assumed that only middle- and upper-class children had access to such schools, in fact, by the nineteenth century, there were also many adventure schools run by and for the working classes (Gardner, 1984). This literacy training was originally for those from more privileged and powerful families, who would then use these skills in later schooling at grammar or public school. Pupils entering these establishments were expected to possess the necessary literacy skills, but the subject of English either as literacy develop-ment or as the study of literature was not a traditional part of the syllabus (Wallbank, 1979).

More controversial was the extension of literacy provision to those who would have no further formal schooling, as can be seen in the debates in the nineteenth century about the wisdom or otherwise of introducing universal state-provided schooling. The potentially empowering effect of literacy was well understood by those who argued against this move, and, in particular, by those who argued against the teaching of production (writing). In other words, it is one thing to have a population who can consume texts, since it is possible at least in theory to attempt to control which texts are available for consumption, but once the means of production is more widely accessible, some sections of the population might use this to produce their own texts, which challenge or question the status quo (Hurt, 1972). This question was not even resolved for all time in the nineteenth century; it is the same issue of empowerment which lies behind the struggles of Freire and other adult-literacy workers in this century (see, for example, Freire and Macedo, 1987), and has even been mooted in Britain as recently as the early 1980s. A secret report emanating from a Department of Education and Science (DES) official reflected on the then-high unemployment levels and implications for schooling:

> We are in a period of considerable social change ... There may be social unrest, but we can cope with the Toxteths ... but if we have a highly educated and idle population we may possibly anticipate more serious conflict. People must be educated once more to know their place.
>
> (Pilger, 1992: 29)

Although there is no direct reference to literacy here, and no evidence that this was ever more than a minority view in the DES, there is a clear recognition here of the relationship between education – of which literacy is such a central element – and power, which is not always made explicit in official documents.

A brief history of literature

Literacy development as an aspect of the study of English, then, is both comparatively recent and still contested. The other strand, that of English as a subject related to the study of literature, is even more recent, only gaining academic respectability this century. Eagleton has shown how the subject finally gained grudging recognition as a discipline worthy of study within the university sector only in the early part of the twentieth century, being seen until then as not sufficiently demanding to take its place alongside the study of the classical languages or sciences (Eagleton, 1983). He shows how the subject came to the universities after it had colonised the Mechanics' Institutes (being seen as an easier way of passing on cultural values and traditions to the emerging educated upper working classes than the classics, since there was then no need to teach Greek or Latin first), and how it was at first seen as very much second class. English was 'a subject fit for women, workers and those wishing to impress the natives', (Eagleton 1983: 29), a view which maybe lingers today in the continued gender imbalance among those on undergraduate English courses. It

> was an upstart, amateurish affair as academic subjects went, hardly able to compete on equal terms with the rigours of Greats or philology; since every English gentleman read his own literature in his spare time anyway, what was the point of submitting it to systematic study?
>
> (Eagleton 1983: 29)

(Again, this attitude can be heard even today as a rejection of the need to include more recent texts or those from different media in the school curriculum.) Only some years after World War I was there a gradual change of attitude to the subject:

> In the early 1920s it was desperately unclear why English was worth study-ing at all; by the early 1930s it had become a question of why it was worth wasting your time on anything else.
>
> (Eagleton, 1983: 31)

Current tensions in English teaching

The subsequent history of English teaching is no more straightforward. Over the years since the Newbolt Report on *The Teaching of English in England* (Board of Education, 1921), as a series of new approaches to the study of literature set up a series of competing views of reading (Eagleton, 1983), succeeding generations of English teachers have contributed to a complex range of approaches to the subject. The most recent parallel to Newbolt, *English for Ages 5 to 16* (DES, 1989), commonly known as the Cox Report, organised this range into five approaches, of which it said: 'We stress that they are not the only possible views, they are not sharply distinguishable and they are certainly not mutually exclusive.' (DES, 1989: para. 2.20). This seems a rather different picture from that painted by Marenbon (1994: 16) of the 'new orthodoxy' which he saw emerging from *A Language for Life* (DES, 1975, the Bullock Report), and would fit more closely with the evidence from a survey of over 110 English teachers, which led the authors to conclude 'There is clearly no consensus here about what is to count as English' (Protherough and Atkinson, 1994: 14).

In post-National Curriculum (NC) schools in England today, tensions and conflicts are still apparent. In primary schools, the division between literacy and literature has been challenged in recent years, but can still be seen. Even today, not all teachers recognise the relationship between story time and the teaching of reading, and particularly in later primary years, story time is too often still an optional extra rather than an integral part of the English curriculum. A university tutor, observing students on teaching practice in the first year of the National Literacy Strategy (NLS), found upon enquiry that at least one teacher in the school was unaware of the text-level work of the NLS, which is designed to develop enjoyment and awareness of narrative structure, and was using a very good children's book merely to teach phonic patterns such as consonant-vowel-consonant (c.v.c.) and word recognition. The reception of stories, either as mediated by the class teacher at story time or in private reading of free-choice literature, has often been segregated from the process of production, both in the gap between encoding the meaning of a story for pleasure and the production of an accurate recoding of an identified text (often from a graded reading scheme), as the child reads to the teacher, and in the gap between stories produced by children and the other stories they encounter. This tension has been identified and alternative approaches offered over the last twenty years or so. The role of the text in teaching reading, and the lessons which stories teach, have also been articulated (see, for example, Meek, 1988, or Mills, 1994), and the relationship between children's progress in writing and their understanding of themselves as authors has been clearly demonstrated by Graves and the writing workshop protagonists (see, for example, Graves, 1982). This chapter will show that not only is there more to be done to promulgate a wider acceptance of these ideas, but that there is a need to develop still further as the nature of English outside school changes.

In secondary schools, the tensions are also apparent in a variety of ways, despite the many instances of good practice. As pupils move through from Year 7 to 13, their own production of original texts becomes increasingly less important and their critical response to the work of others comes to dominate. All of the issues to do with their own literacy and their understanding of language stopped, until comparatively recently, at the end of what is now KS4, where the division between English O-level GCE (which was the demonstration of language competences, as evidenced typically through comprehension, composition and précis) and English Literature, was marked by two separate examining processes. These then mysteriously became inverted over the six-week summer break, so that pupils returning to study A level found that English now meant the study of literature. Even today, although this is changing rapidly, far fewer pupils take the newer A level of English Language rather than study literature, and only a handful of universities offer undergraduate degrees focusing to a significant extent on language rather than literature.

As the subject of English has gradually gained acceptance and become one of the core elements of the curriculum, the debate in educational terms has often focused on the texts used (see Maybin, Chapter 12 of this volume). At primary level this has often been in terms of the need or otherwise to use a reading scheme, but even at KS1 and 2 there have also been concerns about what might constitute appropriate literature (as in the regular concerns about Enid Blyton's work). Although the current National Curriculum is without the suggested reading lists of the Cox Report (DES, 1989), which marked a first attempt to define a canon for KS1 and 2, it still contains some generic requirements. At KS2, for example, the texts used should include 'a range of modern fiction by significant children's authors' and 'some long-established children's fiction' (Department for Education, 1995a: 13), which of course creates an implied canon – who counts as a significant or long-established writer?

At GCSE, texts are defined by examination boards in line with NC requirements where appropriate, and although there is some flexibility here for teachers to select from a range, there are set NC requirements for KS3 and 4:

> An overtly canonical perspective on the value of the classics states that 'Pupils should be introduced to major works of literature from the English literary heritage in previous centuries' (DfE, 1995a: 20) and cites Austen,

George Eliot, the Brontës, Hardy, Swift and Defoe among others as examples of major writers who have written fiction of 'high quality'.

(Baxter, 1998: 23)

The overwhelming emphasis is still on writers from previous generations and is focused on print-based texts (except in the case of non-fiction), a point to be recalled when out-of-school experiences are considered below.

In all this there is a clear division between experiencing texts from a canon (whether explicit or implicit) and the production of written texts by children. As suggested above, this creates a false view of production and reception as separate processes rather than as inextricably connected. Even the act of reading cannot be seen as simply reception, since to read it is necessary to create a viable meaning from the text by re-encoding it into the reader's understanding. When written texts are produced, not only are they destined to be read (even if only by the author), but during the process of production there is a great deal of reading of the unfinished text by the author. This of course is also the case in speech, where the roles of sender and receiver are both active and interdependent (Jakobson, 1960: 350–77). Whether we refer to the development of literacy or the teaching of English, we rely on the learner's growing understanding of this dialectic relationship if the process is to be successful.

These tensions between literacy and literature and between production and reception, or process and product, are to some extent hidden by the current National Curriculum, which divides the subject up into the three Attainment Targets of Speaking and Listening, Reading and Writing (DfE, 1995a). This very process-explicit division, with its emphasis on what pupils can do, not only misrepresents the reading–writing dialectic, but also hides continued tensions and debates about content and the canon, and about what kind of literacy pupils are to develop. These debates can only be understood if we ask what children are learning English for, and what they know about and do with English when they arrive at school, and so the next step in this exploration moves from the classroom to the world outside.

English outside school

Language development: language use

To understand why the definition and containment of English as a subject is so problematic, it is necessary to consider the wider issue of language. English is perhaps the only subject in the curriculum that is so bound up with our everyday living. It has been argued in the past that the subject should be called 'language' rather than English, since essentially it is about our use of what is for many pupils their first language. Also, many of the underlying principles are the same whatever the actual first language being taught. (Of course, there are many issues here to do with the relationship of English as a subject and as a majority language to those pupils and citizens for whom it is not the home language. These issues are beyond the scope of this chapter, but are no less crucial for that.) It can be argued that English is a subject that has to be dynamic and changing because it is essentially about language, which is by nature constantly evolving.

Language is something which has been created by its users, and which would not exist without users, as can be seen in the struggles to keep Cornish alive as the number of its native speakers diminishes, or in the renewal of Welsh, accompanied by a real sense of its worth as a living language, and now used by many people in Wales in preference to English. If language is this dynamic, constantly developing system (as described by de Saussure and succeeding generations of linguists), then the place of the majority language of any country in a national curriculum must of necessity be bound up with the development and use of that language (in the broadest sense, and including the development and use of narrative and poetic forms of the language) in the world outside school.

Not everyone would agree with this view of language. Marenbon, in his critique of the 'new orthodoxy', claims, 'The grammar of English, its range of vocabulary and styles and its literary heritage exist independently of the child who is learning to use them' (Marenbon, 1994: 19). This may superficially appear to be a convincing argument: how can one child have had any major impact on English patterns and structures? Yet, taken to its logical conclusion, this argument separates out language from language users and grants it an independent existence, a view that cannot be sustained, given that language is a symbol system created by its users and has no life unless they continue to use it. As Vygotsky argues, each one of us is in a dialectical relationship with our society and thus has the potential both to change and be changed by it (Vygotsky, 1978). (For a fuller development of this argument and a consideration of the interrelatedness of language, thought and culture, see Robinson, 1997.)

New literacies

In other words, to understand the place of English within our school curriculum it is necessary to consider the world beyond school and the roles which language and texts play in that world. Yet again, this year's lifestyle surveys report that film attendance and Internet use is increasing (Brooks, 1999). More and more homes contain a range of media devices, from televisions and videos through to computers linked to the Internet, to scanners and printers, and to digital video disc players. All of these involve new understandings of reading messages, in that visual images and icons have to be interpreted and understood, but they also require the use of traditional aspects of literacies as we type in our e-mails and web addresses and read on-screen instructions. Even the increasing use of mobile phones requires certain literacy skills, not just to read the manual but also to interpret the stream of on-screen information (including text messaging and e-mail facilities) provided. For an increasing section of the population, electronic organisers such as PalmPilot are replacing more traditional diaries, but they still require literacy skills. All these devices, though, also challenge our traditional views of literacy. Even the QWERTY keyboard raises questions about the traditional alphabetic sequencing of our letters; more fundamentally, the lateral nature of the reading process required by websites and hypertext documents changes what it means to be a reader. Starting at the beginning and following through to the end means something entirely different in a narrative where links can be followed in a variety of sequences, each of which may produce an equally viable and satisfying meaning.

What it means to be literate as an adult in late twentieth-century Britain is thus much harder to define. Where once the tensions in defining literacy revolved around the differences between minimal measures (the ability to sign a name) and what might count as full literacy (see Resnick and Resnick, 1977 for one of the earliest discussions of this, which is still relevant today), now there is a question as to whether literacy can still be seen as a singular concept. There is also the question whether, within the multiple literacies that might replace the notion of an autonomous and culture-free literacy (as challenged by Street, 1984), it is also necessary to extend the term to include the ways in which we read a range of situations and media (Meek, 1991). It is increasingly difficult to separate written and spoken English in many textual contexts. Bookshops and libraries reflect this change, offering not just books but magazines, audiotapes, CD-ROMs, music, and introducing live performances, evening opening and coffee shops.

Before children ever begin school, they have an increasingly diverse set of encounters with the ways in which we use language in the modern world. Almost all will have had access to television, including, but not exclusively, children's programming. One current example serves to illustrate the complex array of interwoven primary and secondary texts to which children have access. *Teletubbies*™ began as a television programme for pre-school children. Every supermarket now has an array of secondary texts related to the series, from sweets and cuddly and squeaky toys, through clothing and videos to spin-off books and comics. All of these texts require an element of meaning-making, from the basic recognition and naming by toddlers (regularly observed pointing and naming: Laa-Laa, Dipsy, Po and Tinky-Winky) to the reading of comics and books.

One such product is a packet of small chocolate bars with a free postcard. The cellophane wrapper, individual bar wrappers, postcard and chocolate all bear the *Teletubbies*™ logo. The cellophane also has a flash detailing the content as '4 milk chocolate bars with Teletubby Post Cards to Collect'. The back has detailed nutritional information in three languages, the confectioner's name and address, and the logo of Ragdoll™, the company which makes *Teletubbies*™. There is also a bar code and expiry date. The individual wrappers repeat the nutritional information, this time just in two languages, and the expiry date. The postcard has a colour illustration, which appears to be a still from the television series, on one side, with the *Teletubbies*™ logo. The other side is laid out as a postcard, with address lines and a space identified for the stamp, as well as another repetition of the logo and the names of the confectioner and production company. Within just this one product, the range of literacy opportunities clearly delineates why it should be seen as a secondary text. There are references to other real world situations through the nutritional and manufacturing information and through the use of the postcard convention. These are coupled with a series of invitations to retell the narrative via such prompts as the logo, the wrapper illustration (of all four *Teletubbies*™) and the still on the postcard, which in this example shows Dipsy and Po. This is not an isolated example; any supermarket has at any time a range of competing characters, often including some from the Disney stable. What is of particular interest is that this is so clearly directed at a pre-school audience and yet still includes so many secondary texts.

When these children do arrive at school, then, many will not only have a knowledge of environmental print and its function, as has been long documented (see for example Goelman *et al.*, 1984), but an awareness of multimedia meaning-making situations and a willingness to experience narrative in ways which transcend media boundaries. This is not to suggest that all children entering school will be totally competent with all the media they have experienced; recent research has suggested that older children may well be less confident and experimental with, for example, home computers than their first responses might suggest (Buckingham, 1999). However, their experience will have been significantly different, in terms of the range of media and narrative sources, than that of their counterparts even a decade ago. The increasing ability of modern society to access texts on demand through video and pay-per-view television has also led not just to a range of texts related to any one narrative (for example, book, video, CD-ROM, PlayStation game), but to an ease of repeated access and control over narrative time previously associated with the written form. This is particularly significant given that a core of familiar, frequently repeated set of texts has been shown to have a role in developing literacy (Bennett, 1991).

Additionally, the primacy of the written text can no longer be assumed, even chronologically; if children see *Babe* before anyone reads them *The Sheep-Pig*, which is the primary text for them? Often there will be a number of competing or contrasting versions of one narrative. A recent study of secondary texts for the film *Men In Black* (itself based on an earlier comic book story) collected around sixty texts in the first three months after the film's release in July 1997, not including any of the Internet sites or television programmes, related to the film, which appeared during the same time. (Mackey, 1999: 48). This study points out both the variety of versions within the retellings and the complex relationship between secondary texts and the original film, reminding us that objects such as screen-savers and posters, which may not immediately seem to have a narrative function, act as memory-joggers for 'instant re-connection' to the original narrative, just as the *Teletubbies*™ chocolate does (Mackey, 1999: 50). This shows how complex an issue literacy has become; which of these texts require reading, and how do we define reading if it includes texts such as screen-savers and chocolate bar labels? It also forces a re-examination of notions of canon, since it undermines, as shown, the primacy of the written text. It is worth considering whether, for example, a study of *The Sheep-Pig* that ignores *Babe*, or of *Romeo and Juliet* that does not relate to the Baz Luhrmann 1996 film version (and the related websites) or even to John Madden's film *Shakespeare in Love* (1998) is any longer a valid way of considering these texts.

Literacy and ICT

An important aspect of pupil (and adult) encounters with computers is the challenge to the traditional linear text created by the linking structures of hypertext. The expression 'surfing the Net', implying as it does a movement across a range of sites, recognises a new development in literacy practice that has parallels in other media. Television viewers channel-surf, people switch rapidly between different sound sources on music systems which have radio, cassette and CD players, newspaper readers skim the pages looking for eye-catching headlines. It has been claimed that such behaviour is symptomatic of a declining attention span and a superficial approach to text, but it can also show an increased ability to process information quickly:

> With a surfeit of stimuli competing for people's attention they are [...] becoming more adept at screening information very quickly, making rapid judgements about whether it is desirable, and 'parallel processing' different materials simultaneously.
>
> (Burbules, 1998: 108)

While this may not be the only strategy we would wish pupils to develop, it could well have advantages as well as limitations; in any case, it is a part of the world they inhabit and as such should be a literacy practice to be taken seriously in school, not least as we learn more about the role of parallel processing in the reading of traditional texts (see, for example, Wray, 1994).

Another aspect of pupils' experience with computers which has a close relationship with the development of the traditional notion of literacy is that of play. For many pupils, computers are synonymous with games. Almost every kind of game can be played on a computer, from traditional card and board games, through chase games, to the fantasy world of MUDs (multi-user dimensions) and MOOs (multi-user dimensions, object-oriented). Meek (1994) has talked of reading as deep play, and suggests that it is when teachers lose sight of this that there are problems:

> We are so keen to make our readers competent, lettered, skilled, that we foreground what is *not* our joy in reading and background the fact that we have been secretly playing games.
>
> (Meek, 1994: 164)

It may be timely for teachers to find ways to make more use of such opportunities for deep play as are offered by MUDs, MOOs and the like within the English curriculum.

Language and music

Another medium which is increasingly significant in young people's lives is music. Popular music has for some years been a fringe element in English curricula, especially in KS3 and 4, but often the main focus has been the song lyrics. It can be argued that the musical form itself can also be seen as another kind of literacy, this time acquired outside school. Modern electronic forms such as house music have structures which can be related to structuralist descriptions of language, with paradigmatic and syntagmatic elements very similar to those involved in language at the level of the sentence. In a sentence, we make a series of syntagmatic decisions, following each word with a syntactically appropriate part of speech. In the sentence 'The cat sat on the mat', we make the choice to follow the article with a noun, because we know that a verb cannot go in this location in English. At the same time, we face a series of paradigmatic choices; we can choose any noun from the bank of nouns we hold in our language repertoire. 'Cat' could just as easily be 'dog', 'child' or 'elephant'; 'mat' could become 'piano', 'carpet' or 'zookeeper'. House music also has musical sequences following the syntactic conventions of the genre. Typically, a bass beat in four–four rhythm is developed by the addition of other sounds, such as a high-hat or the electronic noise known as 'tweaking acid', and so on, each coming in after a sequence of four, eight, or sixteen bars. These musical 'sentences' are linked together through the process of mixing, which creates continuity as different records are joined into each other as seamlessly as the skill of the DJ allows. Again, for each element, there is a range of paradigmatic choices, both as the DJ selects the records to mix and as he/she chooses which drum or tweaking acid pattern to use.

House (in common with related musical genres such as techno and jungle) has a particular relevance in any debate about production and reception, since many young people have the capability not just to listen to such music but to create it. Mixing decks and computer software such as *Cubase* and *ReBirth* are relatively accessible, and music for Sony PlayStations™ is widely available. This experience of the production–reception continuum offers close parallels to more traditional literacies, but tends, at present, to remain outside the English curriculum alongside the more creative experiences of computing described above.

The key issue here is how far pupils' out-of-school experiences should act as starting points or points of comparison with the English curriculum. The account above shows that what people have to do with 'English' in England today before, around, and after formal schooling, relies on an increasing range of competences and a greater flexibility and receptiveness to change than for previous generations. It also shows how the range of texts has developed alongside technological advances. But does this necessarily mean that practices in schools need to change too? To consider the relationship of literacies in and out of school more fully, this chapter now turns to explore current government policy and some of the curriculum development work that moves beyond the somewhat limited requirements of the National Curriculum.

English teaching – policy and practice

Just as literacy has changed, so the territory of English schools changed considerably during the 1990s, as more and more statutory requirements and guidance have been brought into being. These changes, though, bear little resemblance to the developments in literacy charted above. Both the Conservative government, which introduced the National Curriculum, and the Labour government that succeeded it, prioritised literacy; the latter with the introduction of a National Literacy Strategy (NLS) (Department for Education and Employment (DfEE), 1998). This strategy effectively requires all primary teachers to spend an hour a day on literacy teaching, following a closely specified national format (although schools may choose to opt out if they feel secure that they can demonstrate sufficiently high literacy standards on inspection). Whereas the NC subject is called English, the Strategy is about literacy, a significant change of focus paralleled by a shift of emphasis from mathematics to numeracy, and redolent of the original Three Rs of Reading, Writing and Arithmetic. This chapter has already raised the problematic nature of literacy as a singular concept nowadays, but there seems little awareness of this complexity either in government statements about the strategy or within the detail of the National Literacy Strategy itself. It is, of course, impossible to predict for how long this policy will be in place, given the pace of change of the last decade, but certain consistencies can be seen running through the successive versions of the National Curriculum and the Literacy Framework. These can be taken as indicators of longer-term trends, which would appear to conflict both with other aspects of government policy and with research evidence about how children develop as readers.

In terms of government policy, the conflict is apparent when the NLS is set alongside the current major emphasis on information and communications technology (ICT). Both primary and secondary schools are expected to join the National Grid for Learning, with substantial national funding being provided for the necessary on-line connections necessary. Standards for all intending teachers in ICT have been introduced before standards in the third core subject of Science, and so initial teacher education (ITE) students cannot qualify without meeting the standards. A huge professional development operation is being implemented to attempt to update those already in the classroom. All of this would suggest a clear understanding of the need for current and future generations of pupils to be confident and competent in interpreting and creating texts in a range of media (in other words, in reception and production). However, there is little evidence of any relationship between ICT developments and the NLS, or even the National Curriculum for English at KS1 and 2.

Even a cursory reading of the 1998 National Literacy Strategy and the then-current version of the National Curriculum reveals an almost total absence of attention to anything other than book-based texts. Preliminary reports at the time of writing suggest the imminent revisions are unlikely to improve this situation markedly.

This gap between ICT and the NLS is all the more alarming, since much recent research has demonstrated that many of the skills and competences which children develop to interpret texts in one medium have the potential for transferability to other media. In one research project, KS2 children making sense of televisual and written narratives used a similar set of strategies for each, including verbal, visual and auditory information, their experience of other narratives (intertextuality) and their own life experiences. They demonstrated emotional engagement with the characters and speculated on future events. Moreover, when responding to televisual texts, they displayed an ability to draw on several sources of information at once and to follow complex narrative structures, skills not required in many narratives written for children (Robinson, 1997). Recent work on a number of research projects by the Centre for Research on Literacy and the Media, a joint initiative from the British Film Institute and King's College London School of Education, suggests that 'there may be an even stronger link between moving image media and print literacy than that implied by Robinson' (Parker, 1999: 34). An Australian study of children in Years 3, 5 and 7 (crossing the English Key Stages 1 and 2) found that the children were learning about codes and conventions from their experience of computer gaming; here again there is potential for development into other forms of literacy (Smith and Curtin, 1998: 219). Although, as media use and the available technologies change, there will be a continued need for more research, it is already clear that what children learn about literacy outside the classroom has significance both for their development of literacy in school and for their future lives.

Many teachers are already developing their teaching of English to draw on a much wider range of texts and literacy practices, and to help pupils develop their existing competences and take on new ones (see for example the revised curriculum suggested by Campbell (1999) for KS4, or the work by Goodwyn in bringing print and visual texts together (Goodwyn, 1998a)). However, unless such initiatives are allowed to influence national policy and lead to explicit suggestions for such practice within such documents as the NLS, the practice of this significant minority is unlikely to become mainstream. What is needed is a change in focus and approach, which draws on the ideas behind these alternatives but which also allows the subject of English to refocus on what it could and should include if it is to prepare pupils for their future beyond school.

Conclusions

This chapter has argued that English, both as a language out of school and as a school subject, is and always has been dynamic and changing. This means that the range of texts produced and the ways in which they are interpreted will also continue to develop, and so the subject must be one that remains open to change. By showing both how this has been the case in the past, as English became a part of the curriculum, and how the uses and practices of everyday life are developing new ways of reading and creating texts, this chapter has sought to argue that whatever the subject is called, it has to be continually redefined. However, it also suggests that one of the ways in which it needs to be redefined is in terms of a clearer view of the dialectic relationships inherent in the production–reception, reader–text relationships. It is in the creative interplay between reader and reading that the text is created, and, as texts are read (received), the reader creates a new encoding (production). The sender and receiver roles in the communication of a message are not mutually exclusive. Some of the situations in which this relationship is most transparent involve non-traditional texts such as hypertext narratives, yet these do not yet feature in government guidance on the teaching of literacy, particularly at KS 1 and 2. Neither, however, are they explicitly forbidden, and imaginative teachers will continue to bring such resources to their pupils. This is simply not sufficient; it is time that the subject of English as defined by National Curriculum documentation was revised to include the full range of language situations and literacies necessary for a full and creative adult life in modern Britain.

Questions for discussion

1   Given that the National Curriculum documents do not specifically exclude work that develops pupils' understandings of other literacies, how far is it possible to create opportunities for pupils to explore a wider range of texts and still meet the requirements of the National Curriculum, even at KS1?
2   How can teachers accommodate the increasing range of pre-school experiences of literacy which pupils will bring as new technologies continue to infiltrate some but by no means all homes?
3   If the subject of English is continually changing, can official policy ever keep pace with the change? If not, how do we balance the legal requirement to define a Programme of Study with the impossibility of this reflecting English as it is outside school?

Further reading

Brindley, S. (ed.) (1994) *Teaching English*, London: Routledge/Open University.
   This brings together some very useful articles, some originally published elsewhere, which reflect on the nature of English teaching. It includes several chapters exploring media literacy and cultural studies, all of which extend the debate in this chapter and offer new perspectives.

Reid, M. (ed.) (1999) *English in Education*, **33**(1).
   This themed edition of *English in Education* explores many relevant issues and offers clear and helpful examples of classroom practice that has worked within English to

extend the range of texts and experiences offered to pupils. (Many other issues would also be useful, as would many of the articles in *The English and Media Magazine*.)

Snyder, I. (ed.) (1998) *From Page to Screen: Taking Literacy into the Electronic Era*, London: Routledge.
The articles in this collection all come from what was to have been a special issue of *The Australian Journal of Language and Literacy*, but which grew into a book instead. This gives some idea of the quantity of relevant material offered; the quality is equally impressive. The chapters include a great deal of information about the actualities of electronic literacy in general, as well as much direct reference to educational implications.

Wray, D. and Medwell, J. (eds) (1994) *Teaching Primary English: The State of the Art*, London: Routledge.
As with the Brindley book, this brings together some of the most significant writers of the moment in a collection of articles about primary English. Although it contains less specific references to newer literacies, it offers a good broad base from which to reflect on the nature of English today.

The following websites are well worth checking out:

http://www.hollywood.com/videoguide/movies/ and
http://www.etonline.com/html/Movies/, to see some different ways of reading these texts.

7 'Correct' or 'appropriate'?

Is it possible to resolve the debate about which should be promoted in the classroom?

Chris Davies

When children leave English schools today, few are able to speak and write English correctly; even fewer have a familiarity with the literary heritage of the language. It is not hard to see why. Among those who theorize about English teaching there has developed a new orthodoxy, which regards it as a conceptual error to speak of 'correct' English ...

(Marenbon, 1987: 5)

One of the disadvantages of the prescriptive approach to language teaching is its negative aspect. ... This kind of teaching has often inhibited a child's utterance without strengthening the fabric of his language.

(DES, 1975: 170)

Introduction

This chapter will attempt both to outline the main positions in what has, for many years, constituted an area of some disagreement between educationists and the wider public, and to discuss ways in which current developments in the world of education and communications might eventually render such a debate obsolete. The first section will characterise the polarities of this debate, while the second section will explore these issues in a less oppositional way. The third section will consider the question of whether rules of correctness do actually provide an effective means of helping young learners in the process of acquiring native language skills. The final section looks at current developments – especially those arising from government initiatives – and speculates on future developments that might change the way we think about the whole question of teaching young people how to write correctly.

The character of the debate

What is the debate about 'correct' and 'appropriate' English, and how has it developed?

Debates of this kind occur at the meeting point between educational professionals and society at large: a place where different priorities, and different ways of talking about those priorities, tend to collide in overheated and frustrating ways. In any field where the outside world takes an interest in what the professionals are up to (not normally the case in relation to the production of, say, petrol pumps or paper clips), the representatives of the outside world often find it hard to understand why the professionals must make everything so complicated. Why can't they just get on with it? The professionals themselves, however, do actually seem to cherish the complexity of what they do.

The long-running debate about English teaching has always been a rich source of moral panic and indignation, in which English teachers themselves have been presented as either villains or fools for deliberately steering clear of telling children how to use their own language correctly. The *Mail on Sunday*, for instance, claimed on one occasion to have come across a secret dossier from the National Association for the Teaching of English, which revealed how left-wing professors and teachers were 'violently opposed to the formal teaching of English grammar' (31 January 1993). The most familiar line of attack has focused on the emphasis by English teachers on *creativity* during the 1960s, during which the notion of 'personal growth' through English was seen as central to the subject. It is certainly the case that, during this period and for some time afterwards, an over-insistence on accuracy was at times spoken of as being positively harmful:

> To deride or insult a child's work is to do his spirit, his being, an injury ... To avoid such evils, we must, above all, recognise what the child's work means to him.
>
> (Holbrook, 1961: 136)

In the mid-1970s, the Bullock Report – *A Language for Life* – looked at the same question in a more linguistically focused way, and very carefully attempted to argue a case against an over-reliance on prescriptive language teaching by emphasising issues of *how* children learn to use language accurately and effectively. At the same time, it took up the idea of teaching children to think above all about what kinds of language are appropriate in specific contexts. Eventually, this line of argument, too, was used to represent the wilful refusal of English teachers to simply get on with the job of teaching children right from wrong. This is illustrated by the following extracts from pamphlets that were written from outside the teaching profession in order to influence the agenda of the newly proposed National Curriculum:

> competence in language is not seen as very much to do with an ability to write correct Standard English. Bullock does not accept the concept of correctness in English, but prefers to talk of 'appropriateness'. Prescriptive approaches to grammar, spelling and punctuation are dismissed by the report, not so much with contempt as with amusement.
>
> (Marenbon, 1987: 8)

Noting the close links between the acquisition of language and any sort of learning, the report rejects any notion of English as a distinctive subject, with a body of knowledge and a set of techniques that its teachers should transmit. The teacher's function is, rather, to help children in their 'process of discovery'. The report rejects 'correctness' as a concept to be used in judging speech, preferring 'appropriateness' as the criterion.

(Lawlor, 1988: 12)

This notion of *appropriateness* can be traced back to the *Language in Use* project, based on the work of M. A. K. Halliday (Doughty *et al.*, 1971). This introduced a sociolinguistic perspective to secondary-school English teaching, especially for those children who made up the bulk of the comprehensive school population. The chief emphasis in this, and other work developed for use in schools around the same time, entailed 'rejecting the notion of correctness' and replacing it 'by the concept of appropriateness' (see Mathieson, 1975: 147–8, for a more detailed account). This concept of appropriateness involved, above all, the argument that language use is inevitably influenced by the *context* in which it is being used. On this basis, all choices about aspects of language use, such as vocabulary and syntax, do not in reality involve reference to the exact requirements of a fixed and unvarying 'standard English', so much as locate what is being written or said in terms of the varying degrees of formality that the English language so uniquely allows, and within the richly varied registers and dialects of the language.

In fact, John Marenbon, the author of one of the pamphlets attacking the current orthodoxies of the English teaching profession, presents quite a convincing case *for* the notion of appropriateness, in trying to characterise what was wrong with it:

Different circumstances call for different types of language. The grammar and vocabulary used in casual conversation will be different from that required for an interview or public speech; biographical reminiscence or a short story will be written in a different manner from a piece of technical description, a business letter or an advertisement. The English teacher should help children to use the type of language appropriate to each of the various common situations of life; and he should judge each use of language 'in its own context of use, and not by the standards of other uses which it was not intended to satisfy'.

(Marenbon, 1987: 11)

His own argument against this viewpoint seems far less compelling. The best he can manage is that an emphasis on appropriateness would somehow leave the way clear for 'reformers who wish to change social patterns of language-use in order to remove the pre-eminence of standard English'. Although it is true that the sociolinguists referred to – figures such as David Crystal in *Child Language, Learning and Linguistics*, 1976, Donald Trudgill in *Accent, Dialect and the School*,

1975, and Michael Stubbs in *Language, Schools and Classrooms*, 1976 – did indeed see dangers in an unbending emphasis within formal education on the prescriptive teaching of standard English, there is no evidence that they were interested in abandoning it as a language form. Rather, their concerns were with the long-term harmful effects on working-class pupils that might arise from the negative attitudes to their non-standard uses of language that they might encounter in school, and more widely in society. They argue against the validity of such negative attitudes by trying to point out that all varieties of English – i.e. standard and non-standard – can be viewed as equally elaborate, rule-governed, and flexible. In other words, non-standard forms are not linguistically inferior: they are merely accorded inferior prestige. Such a viewpoint is powerfully characterised by another sociolinguist, Dwight Bolinger, when he talks of the unquestioned need for a standardised form of the language:

> The desired uniformity could be achieved by adopting the forms used by the underprivileged, but it never is – they are the ones who must demote their own language and learn a new one, replacing the threads that join their minds and feelings to reality – like the operation of reconnecting the flesh and nerves of a severed limb.
>
> (Bolinger, 1980: 52)

The line argued against this by figures such as Marenbon and Lawlor is that standard English is simply the most effective form of the language, which must be insisted on:

> A better approach to English teaching in schools would recognize English as a subject – no more and no less: the subject in which pupils learn to write standard English correctly and thereby speak it well ... The teacher would not hesitate to prescribe to the children on matters of grammatical correctness.
>
> (Marenbon, 1987: 33)

In the end, this turns out to be little more than a rhetorical stance, which was not based on any detailed analysis of actual practice. There is very little evidence to suggest that there has ever been a time when practising English teachers have not insisted on accuracy and correctness in their pupils' writing. However, English teachers have never felt comfortable about directly addressing the ways in which their pupils speak, preferring at most to set up opportunities for exploring a variety of spoken registers through activities such as role-play, in the firm belief that criticism of someone's normal way of speaking entails criticism of that person's family and social background. English teaching has, over the last twenty years at least, preferred to help children use their natural resources of speaking in order to express and develop their own ideas in the classroom, rather than to take on a new identity through adopting prestige forms of speech. In this aspect of language use especially, the emphasis on the notion of appropriate language use has proved particularly crucial.

Balancing correctness and appropriateness

Can a balance between correctness and appropriateness be
sustained in policy and practice?

The following statement from a comprehensive school English department's policy document written nearly twenty years ago is a fairly typical instance of how practitioners tried to sustain a balance between an emphasis on correct and appropriate language use:

> We should aim to correct what is wrong because it is ugly, unclear or not conforming to accepted standards. The terminology of grammar should be subservient to our need to help pupils with their expression, and not an end in itself. Be flexible on common usage, warning pupils of the possible consequences of errors like 'it's me', while accepting that it is a commonly spoken form.
>
> (unpublished secondary-school English department policy document, 1980)

Beneath the expression of traditional linguistic values, it is possible to discern a degree of commitment to flexibility and sensitivity to pupils' own language usage. The reference to 'errors like "it's me" ' demonstrates how very difficult it is in reality to make definitive statements about what is and is not correct. In the end, the only helpful answer to that problem would be to consult not Fowler's *Dictionary of Modern English Usage*, but one's real-world knowledge about context and degrees of formality. It would be possible to think of occasions when it would be more effective to write, or even speak, the words 'it is I', but most young language users would intuitively know that, in most situations, 'it's me' is considerably more appropriate. To teach young learners otherwise would not only be linguistically inaccurate: it would entail disregarding their own real-world linguistic knowledge and experience.

Even if teachers now would mostly be uncomfortable with the first sentence of the above extract (to be fair, quite possibly written in order to placate the outside world of parents, governors and inspectors), one can certainly expect to find teachers today grappling with the same basic dilemma. As English teachers they are, in one respect, charged by the society which employs them to maintain the language in good order, and to produce new generations of language users who won't destroy this particular national heritage – a point that Michael Stubbs recognises when he says that standard English 'has a central place in the educational system, and is in fact partly defined by the place it occupies there. In practice, every time a teacher corrects pupils' spelling or a grammatical form, some process of standardization is taking place' (Stubbs, 1986: 84). On the other hand, they see their job as primarily being about *developing* the language capacities of their students. This, in effect, involves helping young people to extend and strengthen the already considerable (whatever their social prestige) language resources they bring with them.

At most levels within the profession, it is likely that there is general agreement about the need for English teachers to treat the fragile confidence of learners with considerable care, as they become conscious that their own forms of language do not match – in ways that they are not yet able to define or deal with – the language registers of formal education. At a basic level, this requires that teachers show sufficient patience and restraint to balance the identification of errors, whether in writing or speech, with the identification of the linguistic achievement. Sometimes that merely means simply not marking every error in red pen, or interrupting a speaker in mid-flow, but in more positive terms it entails the conscious effort by teachers to recognise and acknowledge what has actually been achieved in novice attempts at literacy.

Sensitivity to the anxieties of learners is not the whole story, of course. We also owe them a firm conceptual framework upon which to develop their own capacities with language. English teachers would, for the most part, view the notion of appropriateness as providing this, in a far more powerful way than the rather more simplistic notion of correctness. This, it must be understood, constitutes no more than a starting point for helping children to develop the literacy and oracy skills and understandings that will carry them through their education and out into the adult world, but it is one that possesses sufficient conceptual coherence to provide a useful foundation for thinking about language use.

The notion of appropriateness recognises the simple linguistic truth that there is always, *always*, more than one way of saying anything – and that it is the job of any mature language user to choose what will work best for their particular purpose. This is the case whether writing an academic essay, or a love letter, or an analysis of investment possibilities, or a note on the fridge door for your mum. Decisions about tone of voice, level of formality, tentativeness vs. assurance, humour vs. solemnity, etc., all come down to decisions about what kinds of vocabulary and syntax – what register – will be most appropriate in order to communicate whatever it is you must communicate to the listener or to the reader.

The crucial point here is that, underlying all such decisions, the notion of correctness is never abandoned – indeed, it is always central. But the question is less likely to be 'is this correct or not?', as if there was only one permitted way of saying or writing anything, but 'what would be correct in the case of this particular register?'. In effect, the central question to be asked in relation to any task involving speaking or writing is: *what language will work best in order to achieve this particular goal?* Conceptualising speaking or writing tasks in terms of appropriateness does not mean indifference to whether the job has been done correctly – rather, it means thinking about what constitutes *correct* in any particular context. Thus, when we concern ourselves with the question of what is appropriate in language, we are also implicitly concerned with questions of correctness.

Accommodating language acquisition and language rules

How should what we know about language acquisition and the
complexity of the rules of language influence the debate?

None of this means that English teachers do not actually also correct pupils'
work, or try to teach them right from wrong in the ways they should write and
speak. There are times, indeed, when the notion of appropriateness is not
particularly relevant. There are certain rules of written English which apply to
any job of writing, even if on occasions they might then be deliberately broken
for effect: writing must be legible; syntax must follow the logic of the English
language, and punctuation needs to reinforce that logic; spelling should be
correct. Even where progress has been made in encouraging teachers across the
curriculum to engage actively with language in their teaching, English teachers
still have a unique responsibility to teach pupils what is right and wrong in
these respects, steadily and incrementally and helpfully, drawing on all the
resources of support and guidance available to them. The learning of such skills
is inherent in learning to do any writing task in an appropriate way, and it
would be difficult to find any English teacher who didn't see that as a priority in
their teaching.

But while there is little empirical evidence to suggest that English teachers
are not concerned with accuracy, the fact still remains that many interested
parties from outside the profession often express anxiety about the standards of
accuracy in the English of young people in school, and after they have left
school. Employers and those in higher education often claim, in particular, that
children are given insufficient instruction in how to write correctly when they
are at school, and parents have a right to worry about such things. Are there
any grounds, in reality, for questioning whether an emphasis on appropriate
rather than unvaryingly correct language use might be so ingrained in English
teachers' thinking that they refuse to contemplate teaching a basic curriculum
of clear rules about how to speak and write? Might it be the case, despite all
that has been argued above, that the emphasis on appropriate language has,
despite all best intentions, resulted in bad, 'soggy' teaching – teaching that
evades the particularly difficult problem of teaching people how to use their
own language accurately?

Research into language learning does suggest that it is, in fact, very difficult
to teach effective rules about how to use one's own language correctly.
According to one expert in second language learning, reference to rules about
language use does not really play a significant role in mother tongue learning:

> Language acquisition is a subconscious process; language acquirers are not
> usually aware of the fact that they are acquiring language, but are only
> aware of the fact that they are using the language for communication. The
> result of language acquisition, acquired competence, is also subconscious.
> We are generally not consciously aware of the rules of the languages
> we have acquired. Instead, we have a 'feel' for correctness. Grammatical

sentences 'sound' right, or 'feel' right, and errors feel wrong, even if we do not consciously know what rule was violated.

(Krashen, 1982: 10)

What is more, Krashen goes on to claim that 'evidence from child language acquisition confirms that error correction does not influence acquisition to any great extent' (*ibid*.: p. 11). It could, in effect, turn out therefore that English teachers' efforts both to teach correct usage prescriptively and, in response to children's written products, to correct their errors are largely wasted. This is, of course, particularly likely to be the case with speaking, whereas writing can perhaps more reasonably be viewed as a distinctive code in which the learning of explicit rules may be more feasible. But even there, the negative outcomes that teachers experience when correcting the same mistakes time after time in exercise books, and on the blackboard, do suggest that a largely prescriptive and error-hunting approach to language use is not in itself particularly fruitful.

Even if the teaching and learning of a set of rules about using one's own language could be shown to have a direct impact on the accuracy of mother-tongue language use in principle, there is also a very great problem in establishing a sufficiently concise and digestible set of rules about English usage. Sheila Lawlor's attempt to define a simple English curriculum, whose 'requirements should be minimum', unfortunately ended up as a mixture of idiosyncrasy (for instance, in the following definition: 'Syntax which is neither simple nor complex is "ordinary" syntax') and entirely familiar (to English teachers, at least) generalities:

> write legibly, in print and cursive script; use the full range of simple vo-cabulary and a variety of current vocabulary in their writing; construct sentences in simple syntax with a fair degree of accuracy; use capital letters, full stops, commas, question marks and apostrophes correctly; organise writing into paragraphs; spell correctly most words belonging to a simple vocabulary and many words belonging to current vocabulary.
>
> (Lawlor, 1988: 26)

Disregarding the thoughtful and helpful chapter on 'Teaching Standard English' that was produced by the first working party on the National Curriculum for English (DES, 1989: ch. 4), the attempts by the writers of various National Curriculum documents to specify the teaching of standard English struggled in fairly similar terms with the same problem:

> Standard English is characterised by the correct use of vocabulary and grammar. Pupils need to be able to speak and to write in standard English in order to enhance the communication skills necessary for social and professional development.
>
> (DFE, 1993: 9)

Use of language

Pupils should be given opportunities to develop their understanding and use of standard English and to recognise that:

- standard English is distinguished from other forms of English by its vocabulary, and by rules and conventions of grammar, spelling and punctuation;
- the grammatical features that distinguish standard English include how pronouns, adverbs and adjectives should be used and how negatives, questions and verb tenses should be formed; such features are present in both the spoken and written forms, except where non-standard forms are used for effect or for technical reasons.

(from the *General Requirements for English in the National Curriculum*, DfE, 1995a)

The English language is, in effect, less susceptible to reduction into simple rules than people generally tend to recognise. The main issues that concern critics outside the profession involve a few simple issues, such as spelling, common errors (e.g. the differences between *their, there* and *they're*), punctuation, and handwriting. Beyond those general pre-occupations, people tend to express idiosyncratic and inconsistent concerns about things like split infinitives, prepositions at the end of sentences, and specific things that they themselves recollect being taught at school (i.e. the need to avoid the word 'get' – the use of which was viewed in textbooks of the 1950s as a lazy substitute for more precise verbs, usage such as 'different *from*' in favour of 'different *to*', and the dangers of double negatives, etc.). Taken individually, as they invariably are, these instances seldom seem to add up to much and therefore appear to represent a relatively compact and manageable curriculum. It is only when, as a professional, one faces up to the full range of what potentially must be learnt in order to be sure of avoiding language errors, that the immensity of the task becomes apparent – as does the unfeasibility of teaching such rules either on a prescriptive basis, in advance of need, or through the relentless correction of multiple errors in written work. As the detail of the new National Literacy Strategy demonstrates, a comprehensive list of all possible appropriate learning is quite an awesome and daunting prospect.

Developments in the debate

What developments are taking place in the debate?

The current government is enacting a strong commitment to the improvement of children's language use, in the form of its National Literacy Strategy. The emphasis in this goes far beyond the enforcement of correctness. It is interesting, indeed, that – despite the immense amount of detailed grammatical work contained in the learning proposed for the daily Literacy Hour – the prescriptive teaching of correct English is not explicitly emphasised:

> Through Key Stage 2, there is a progressive emphasis on the skills of planning, drafting, revising, proof-reading and presentation of writing. The range of reading and writing increases and, with it, the need for pupils to understand a wider variety of texts, their organisation and purposes. Of course, pupils also need to continue to work on autonomous strategies for spelling and correcting their own mistakes.
>
> (DfEE, 1998: 5)

The Strategy does, though, require the teaching of a vast amount of knowledge about language which will, it is hoped, provide a firm foundation upon which children can learn to develop their own language resources. The spirit of this guidance attempts to be non-prescriptive, with its emphasis on helping children to develop autonomous literacy strategies, and to correct their own writing. There is also a firm commitment to the idea of appropriate language use: the very last instruction – out of several hundred directions provided to cover the full spread of education – is that pupils should be taught 'to select the appropriate style and form to suit a specific purpose and audience, drawing on knowledge of different non-fiction text types' (*ibid.*: 55). It is too early to say whether this really represents a satisfactory balance between prescriptivism and the provision of support for the learner – the initial impression is that the authors of this particular document have not entirely overcome the problems of bulk inherent in specifying a comprehensive language learning curriculum. (Reports of its implementation do suggest that the Literacy Hour itself has introduced a marked degree of relentless seriousness into the early literacy experiences of young primary-school children.) It does, though, constitute a radically new approach to the whole issue, and may possibly develop into something very important when the practical efforts of working primary-school teachers have perhaps succeeded in eliminating some of its excesses.

A number of efforts are also coming currently from QCA (the Qualifications and Curriculum Authority, responsible for determining the content of the National Curriculum) to establish a meaningful kind of grammar teaching at the secondary level. It does not appear to be the intention here, either, to prescribe correct language behaviour so much as to introduce the technical understandings about sentence construction, and the composition of whole texts, that are potentially as much implied by the word 'grammar' as the more rigid notions of correctness that the word traditionally represents to the outside world. In effect, in the same spirit of the National Literacy Strategy, the hope is that a more intensive effort to provide children with a varied technical language about the workings of language will result – among other things – in a population of more accurate, flexible and autonomous language users. Whether or not this will prove to the case only time will tell, but the spirit of these attempts is considerably more ambitious and far-reaching than anything advocated by the traditionalists from outside the profession.

At the same time, educational policy-makers seem now to be trying hard to address the issue of Information and Communications Technology, which has, until now, had relatively minor impact upon formal education (in comparison, at least, with the impact first on commerce, and then on home use). The guidance coming from the Teacher Training Agency in this respect provides a principled foundation for developing English and literacy-related work in the classroom, but the inadequacies of both the hardware and software currently available in most schools make such guidance seem somewhat optimistic in the short-term. Nonetheless, the full impact of that technology will eventually make itself felt in school-based education, and when it does it is conceivable that our whole relation to the written word – including that of young learners – will be transformed for ever after. Sooner or later, this technology will take upon itself most of the difficulties and decisions that writers currently face in writing accurate, standard English. Even now, word-processors offer guidance on spelling and grammar, which, with every upgrade, becomes both more competent and more intrusive. It is not at all fantastic to envisage a time when word-processing packages will be programmed with sufficient syntactical, lexical and semantic knowledge to provide highly accurate and dependable guidance on spelling, sentence formation and punctuation. Sooner or later, a line will be crossed in which we no longer see such decisions as our responsibility, any more than we see decisions about how our bank account receives, counts and distributes our money to be our job.

There is also a real problem of homogenisation implied in progress of this kind. It could be that stylistic variation will be sacrificed, or regularised, in the interests of painless text production, which will potentially have a reductive effect on the range of choices available both when writing *or* speaking (because, as Kress points out, the way we do one is influenced by the way we do the other: 'The syntax of the spoken language is constantly being invaded by forms from the syntax of writing. This is particularly so for those speakers who wish to gain social, economic and political power' (Kress, 1994: 10). Equivalent reductions in the variability of speech are already under way as a result of the explosion in mass communication, over satellite and cable TV, the Internet, and as a result of the role of English as an overwhelmingly dominant world language. We are therefore already possibly witnessing the beginnings of a rapid disappearance of non-standard written language, along with the birth of a hybrid spoken non-standard.

Although schools will experience these changes only gradually – mainly because the cost of the technology has long meant that schools are the last places to benefit from such progress – the identification of this trend is important for the way that it focuses our attention on the longer-term question of what should be the central priorities of literacy teaching in the future. English teaching has, in fact, moved a very long way from the passionate but inward-looking concerns of creative/expressive writing in the 1960s: nowadays

– as initiatives such as the National Literacy Strategy inescapably demonstrate – we have learnt to view literacy as a basic right of all young people, and something that is considerably more sophisticated than the notion of unvarying correctness could ever permit us to contemplate:

> The great divide in literacy is not between those who can read and write and those who have not learned how to. It is between those who have discovered what kinds of literacy society values and how to demonstrate their competencies in ways that earn recognition.
>
> (Meek, 1991: 9)

Literacy is about far more than accuracy, and concerns more than just the written word:

> Literacy unites the important skills of reading and writing. It also involves speaking and listening ... Good oral work enhances pupils' understanding of language in both oral and written forms and of the way language can be used to communicate.
>
> (DfEE, 1998: 3)

As the National Literacy Strategy also emphasises, literacy is above all about the autonomous capacity to manage complex language resources in one's own interests. Literacy learning is in great part, therefore, a conceptual activity: it requires an understanding of the purposes that language can serve, and its use can only be developed effectively when learners recognise and desire the benefits and rewards of literacy for themselves. As the Strategy demonstrates in awesome detail, it does not *only* involve conceptual understanding, but the value of that detail depends on the extent to which learners are helped to think about the purposes of their uses of language, and about the most effective ways available to them of achieving those purposes. Within such a conception of language use, a primary emphasis on the notion of correctness must surely seem rather limp and inadequate.

Conclusions

The debate described in this chapter has too often been acrimonious and counter-productive. English teachers have in recent years learnt to distrust their own expertise in dealing with the complex problems of helping young people develop effective and accurate literacy skills, and the general public has too often been encouraged to doubt that expertise by the press, and by the actions and words of central government. I believe that it would be ludicrous to suggest that English teachers have worked out all there is to know about how to help children use their own language effectively. However, the inventiveness and flexibility that has long been a hallmark of English teaching in this country does provide, I would argue, the best possible basis upon which to continue to build good practice. Ultimately, we should continue to focus our energies on teaching children to use language accurately and appropriately, in ways that are responsive both to – rather than prescriptive about – the realities of how language is used, and how young people learn to use it.

Nevertheless, the fact is that those realities are changing fast, and in ways that are both exciting and bewildering. To be literate in the twenty-first century will involve interacting with Information and Communications Technology in ways that we are only now beginning to think about. Above all, however, these will require that we learn how to be served by technology that can do on our behalf what previously we had to do for ourselves. To a certain extent, that technology will relieve us of many of our worries about correctness, and will also increasingly offer us predetermined forms of appropriateness. Our freedom as communicators in general, and as writers in particular, will be both more extensive and less autonomous. We need to start thinking about how we want to use these possibilities, and about how we want to teach young people to use them, right now.

Questions for discussion

1 To what extent do English teachers actually teach spoken standard English, either at primary or secondary level? In what ways do they correct their pupils' speech, if at all? Are there times when this would be a helpful thing to do?
2 What aspects of traditional grammar teaching might directly enable the production of appropriately written, or spoken, English?
3 What are the implications of the programme of learning detailed within the National Literacy Strategy at primary level for teachers of secondary pupils? Will that entail a radical redesign of the secondary English curriculum?
4 Would any of the arguments in this chapter actually provide reassurance to parents concerned with the fact that their child's writing is full of errors?

Further reading

Bereiter, C. and Scardamalia, M. (1987) *The Psychology of Written Composition*, New Jersey: Lawrence Erlbaum Associates.
  The text needs to be read selectively, but contains a well-researched exploration of the problems children face in learning to write, and especially the ways in which technical aspects of writing tend to overwhelm other crucial aspects of thinking about writing composition.

Brice Heath, S. (1983) *Ways with Words: Language, Life and Work in Communities and Classrooms*, Cambridge: Cambridge University Press.
  Here Shirley Brice Heath provides a powerful study of how the learning of language skills is intimately rooted in the community within which children grow up.

Czerniewska, P. (1992) *Learning about Writing*, Oxford: Basil Blackwell.
This book is a helpful overview from the Director of the National Writing Project during the 1980s.

Leech, G. and Svartvik, J. (1994) *A Communicative Grammar of English*, 2nd edn, London: Longman.
The notion of the varying degrees of formality that the English language allows is very effectively illustrated in this useful textbook (see p. 29f).

Norman, K. (ed.) (1992) *Thinking Voices*, London: Hodder and Stoughton.
This is a wide-ranging collection of articles arising out of the work of the National Oracy Project.

Russell, S. (1997) *Grammar, Structure and Style*, Oxford: Oxford University Press.
Although this text is written for A-level English Language students, it provides an excellent introduction for beginning teachers on ways in which grammatical knowledge can help with the production of both writing and speaking.

8 Variation in English

Looking at the language from the outside

Stephen Bax

This chapter looks at the ways in which speakers of English vary their language in particular ways and for particular purposes. It then examines:

- the reasons why we need to take account of this variation in our teaching of English;
- ways in which we can do this in practice;
- resources which can assist in this endeavour.

Introduction

English is growing in influence around the world, and looks set to continue to do so in the foreseeable future (Graddol, 1997). Likewise, the Teaching of English as a foreign language (TEFL) is now a huge world-wide industry, employing many people and bringing large revenues to English-speaking countries. Britain, through agencies such as the British Council, has been actively involved in the promotion of this area of the language.

Since they involve the same language, there could in theory be a close link between TEFL and English teaching in British schools, but in practice there exists a strange gulf between the two. It is clear to those who, like myself, are trained or qualified in both the teaching of English in the British state system and also in TEFL, that the two are different worlds – TEFL has established its own methodology, its own jargon, its own qualifications and its own 'culture', and is striving for a more professional status quite separate from that of state teachers of English.

This division is understandable to the extent that the two educational areas have different contexts, features and aims – for one, TEFL by definition treats English as a 'foreign' language and not as student's first language, and therefore needs to use a different methodology. Even so, it is remarkable and regrettable that there is so little dialogue between the two fields. There are certainly signs of more communication – TEFL teachers are realising that they can learn from good practice in British state schools, for example in the teaching of drama, the use of drama in teaching language, in the teaching of literature, the use of literature to help teach language, and so on – but nonetheless the exchange could, I feel, be more systematic and more deliberate than it is at present, to the benefit of both groups.

One area where TEFL could perhaps contribute is in its more global view of the nature of English itself. English is evolving rapidly around the world, both in its system (vocabulary, grammar and pronunciation) and in its use. The precise nature of these changes and their eventual effects on Britain and British speakers is not clear at this stage, but mere mention of them surely serves as a warning that what we teach in British schools and how we teach it require constant and careful attention. The alternative – a complacent sense that we are fine as we are, 'English, our English' – will see the world move on without us.

Complacency about the nature and role of English cannot be beneficial, either at a national or an individual level. The examples that Holliday offers (Chapter 9 of this volume) show pointedly how such complacency can make Anglo-centric British speakers and writers seem too arrogant and limited to the outside world. Holliday argues for a greater awareness of ideology in language; someone who wants to develop this kind of awareness must necessarily, it seems to me, acquire a perception of the English language as something dynamic and rapidly changing, with diverse varieties and manifestations at different places and different times, rather than something unchanging and static.

In other words, we need to ensure that our concept of English and our attitudes towards it suit the changing world scene. We also need to ensure that in the sphere of education our pupils leave school with an appropriate perception of the language, one that will help them cope in changing social and work environments. We need to ensure that they have the full range of linguistic skills to enable them to function at the highest levels of effectiveness in changing global conditions.

This is particularly true in view of the fact that many British schools have pupils for whom English is indeed their second or third tongue. For their sakes, and the sakes of their peers and communities, the view of English that we adopt in the classroom cannot afford to be a parochial one.

In practice, though, there is little evidence that our schools and teachers are moving in this direction, or are equipped to do so. This may not be their fault – considering that linguists are hardly able to keep up with developments, it is hardly surprising that teachers too might struggle to cope. Nonetheless, most of us would agree with Cheshire and Edwards (1993), that many teachers and pupils would benefit from an enhanced awareness of the sociolinguistic dimension of English, including the ways in which it varies within a speech community, the ways in which it varies beyond their town and county boundaries, and the ways in which it is used beyond Britain, to include its global dimension.

To take one example, namely the attitudes of teachers and pupils towards different varieties of English, Edwards shows in his comprehensive review of attitudes towards English in society and education that views are often stereotyped and limited; for example, 'teachers – like other members of the population – do maintain stereotyped and often negative views of certain language varieties and their speakers' (Edwards, 1982: 30). The fact that teachers hold these views is important – since they are 'in a position directly to hinder a child's early success if they hold and act upon overly generalized views [of language]' (*ibid.*: 30), but are equally able to have positive influences: 'teachers are [also] well placed to help children overcome the negative evaluations made of them and others and, in some cases, by themselves' (*ibid.*: 30).

Variation

To put it succinctly, this chapter deals with what I will call '*variation*' in English and how English teachers can deal with it. 'Variation' is intended in a wide sense, to include, for example, the ways in which my accent and dialect 'vary' from yours, the ways in which language 'varies' across time and place, the ways in which language differs between old and young, male and female, between one racial group and another, even between one person and a neighbour. This variation is extensive and pervasive – its role is greater than was once thought and far more extensive and influential than is realised by non-linguists (*ibid.*).

The challenge for English teachers, then is to take this awareness of linguistic variation, its extent and its importance in social interaction, locally and globally, and to equip their pupils with the awareness and skills to deal with it to their advantage. Given that English teachers may feel ill-equipped to do this, this chapter attempts to map out the areas that could be covered and ways in which it could be done, as well as resources which teachers could draw on in this area of their work.

English as a monolith: the National Curriculum

What impression do pupils have of English at the moment? It could be that they see English as the 'best' language, the only one worth knowing. It is probable that they also see it as a relatively stable, fixed and unchanging thing – particularly if their exposure to it has been limited to their own geographical region and the mass media. Those who are exposed to other languages at home or in their immediate environment may not have quite so limited a view, but, generally speaking, research suggests that people have fixed and rather unsubtle ideas about their own language – meaning that monoglot English speakers will probably see English in a relatively limited way. Cheshire and Edwards (1993) report a number of studies which suggest this, including the fact that 'experiments have repeatedly shown that speakers with Received Pronunciation … are considered to be more intelligent and more competent than speakers who have a regional accent' (*ibid.*, p. 42).

This limited view of language, and in particular the attitude that variation is relatively unimportant, tends to be reinforced by areas of the National Curriculum for English. Take the attainment targets for speaking and listening in English for Key Stages 1–3, for example. 'Exceptional speakers', the highest band in the level descriptions, are characterised as follows:

Exceptional performance

Pupils select and use structures, styles and registers appropriately in a *range of contexts*, *varying* their vocabulary and expression confidently for a *range of purposes*. They initiate and sustain discussion through the sensitive use of a *variety of contributions*. They take a leading role in discussion and listen with concentration and understanding to *varied* and complex speech. They show assured and fluent use of standard English in a *range of situations* and for a *variety of purposes*.

(DfE, 1995b, my emphasis)

The ability to cope well with variation in language is prominent here: I have emphasised no fewer than nine references to it. This is surely appropriate, since we would expect an exceptional speaker to be able to deal with linguistic variation in many areas of life, across time, place and situation. But is it right to see this as 'exceptional'?

If we look at Level 5 attainment – the middle band of what is expected of the majority of pupils by the end of Key Stage 3 (what we might expect of an average pupil at this stage of schooling) – far less is expected:

Level 5

Pupils can talk and listen confidently in a *wide range of contexts*, including some that are of a formal nature. Their talk engages the interest of the listener as they *begin to vary* their expression and vocabulary. In discussion, they pay close attention to what others say, ask questions to develop ideas and make contributions that take account of others' views. They begin to use standard English in formal situations.

(DfE, 1995b, my emphasis)

What is interesting here is not so much what is included as what is omitted. While there is reference to dealing with linguistic variation, there is no mention of dealing with different accents, dialects, non-standard forms of language, differences relating to age, gender, race and so on. In other words, we can picture a pupil at this level as being relatively unaware of how language differs across time and place, and relatively unable to cope with such differences as they arise – and this is meant to be the norm.

This is not to say that we should expect pupils at this stage to be fully efficient speakers in all areas of life – they will continue to develop and learn as they get more experience of different linguistic domains. But the fact remains that if we set ourselves low targets in dealing with language, we give pupils (and teachers) the message that English is a kind of monolith with little variation, and that we, as speakers of English, therefore don't need to try very hard to deal with that variation – which would be a false impression. We need to ensure that pupils have an enhanced awareness of how language varies and how they can respond to it.

What should we teach? How should we teach it?

If we adopt the position, then, that it is important to give pupils an enhanced sense of how and why English varies, and the effects this has on communication, the next step is to discover what we should teach and how we should teach it.

As noted above, the National Curriculum does recognise the existence of linguistic variation, but English teachers are offered relatively little guidance as to how this can usefully be studied, what learning outcomes they might aim at, how such study of variation might progress through the different year groups, and so on. In addition – given the fact that research into language variation is moving quite swiftly, and now has a considerable body of literature behind it – it is unlikely that most English teachers will feel confident in teaching all of those aspects of linguistic variation that are important to pupils.

These areas will therefore be the focus of the remainder of this chapter. I shall try to address in turn the key aspects of variation in English, aiming to outline their importance and the ways in which they are currently viewed in the relevant literature. I shall also in each case attempt to give brief consideration to how the teacher might in practice address these issues in class, and the kind of resources that might prove valuable.

The fact and extent of variation in English

Few speakers of a language are consciously aware that their own language contains as much variation as it does – they are too busy using it as a tool for other purposes. But the first step towards accepting variation and being able to respond effectively to it in everyday life is to be aware of how much and in what ways it occurs. In particular, it means that we need to challenge the idea that language offers a small and fixed set of choices.

In practice this means that pupils at school need to be exposed to a wide variety of types of English, oral and written, from different periods and places, in a more explicit and deliberate way than happens at present in many classes. This should include spoken and written texts, modern and old, British and non-British, from a range of voices and writers. This is best done in a systematic way, which means in effect that the English teacher needs to keep track of the kinds of language to which pupils have been exposed in the classroom, and to ensure that the range is a broad one.

This may already happen in many classes – but on its own it is not enough. Teachers need, as the next step, to devise strategies that raise awareness of variation in pupils' minds whenever possible, and to cover the full range of variation – in pronunciation, in grammar, and in vocabulary. This needs to be done explicitly – in my experience merely exposing pupils to linguistic variation is not enough. Since pupils usually aim to extract the message, the medium (the language itself) often goes unnoticed. For this reason, the teacher needs to make the point explicitly that language varies widely in phonology, vocabulary and grammar, and then to take every opportunity in subsequent work to point out illustrative examples.

At what stage can this be done? Day (1982) shows that children at the age of three already have a clear sense of language variation and what it means in society – he further shows that their attitudes 'tend to reflect stereotypes of the majority culture' (*ibid*.: 131). This means that the issue of language variation needs to be addressed as early as possible, and that doing so may have a useful effect in countering prejudice.

In practice, of course, young children can grasp the concept of language variation quite readily, if only because they will have encountered and noticed variation in their own peer group, on television and elsewhere. The teacher can use these real cases (for example of different use of words, of accent and of vocabulary) to make the point that different people use language in different ways, and then to get across the idea that young people's language differs from older people's, women's differs from men's, old books have different language from newer books, and so on. Such explicit emphasis on variation can then be followed up by small projects investigating words that are 'old-fashioned' and words that are new, for example, or other areas that pupils notice.

If children start to gain such an awareness early and consistently, this can provide a good base upon which the teacher can build whenever additional examples of variation arise. If this is applied consistently throughout the child's schooling, she or he can gradually develop a sense that language varies in many ways, that this variation is widespread, and that it is important.

The functions of variation

The next issue which needs to be addressed is why this variation exists. Change and variation in language are often viewed negatively, as some sort of disease or laziness (Aitchison, 1997). Writers whom Milroy and Milroy call 'language guardians' tend to promote this view in letters to the newspapers and elsewhere as part of what has become known as a long-standing 'complaint tradition' (Milroy and Milroy, 1985), and the implication of their arguments is that variation is somehow negative and to be avoided.

Besides the fact that variation is not, of course, avoidable for the most part, and that most attempts to prevent language variation have proved spectacularly unsuccessful, it is undoubtedly more fruitful to see variation in language as achieving certain purposes, and as fulfilling a function which can be positive. Pupils should be made aware, for example, that language often acts to create or deny *solidarity* (social closeness) between speakers (see Holmes, 1992) and that we often subconsciously or consciously adopt forms of pronunciation, vocabulary and grammar in order to fit into a particular group in the short or long term, or to deny others entry into a group or a piece of discourse. (An example of the latter is jargon, such as legal courtroom language or medical language.) Therefore pupils can usefully be made aware that variation of this kind is not only widespread but that it can have important effects in various areas of life, and that if it is mastered it can be useful.

Another factor behind variation in social settings is the *formality* of the setting and the relative *status* of the speaker and listener. We all adjust our language according to our perception of the formality of the setting and the status of the listener relative to ourselves, but this kind of variation is often unconscious and can usefully be highlighted in the classroom.

It is important that pupils are aware of these points in order that they can eventually turn this theoretical understanding into the practical skill of adjusting their language to suit their purpose. This awareness can best by achieved, in my experience, through case studies (such as those in Holmes, 1992), which are essentially short examples that pupils can read and comment on, designed to illustrate ways in which variation can achieve various functions. These can easily be devised and can generate interesting discussion of how the language we choose reflects our closeness to the listener, or our social status relative to the listener, or the formality of the context.

Gender, age, class and race

I have so far identified three main factors behind language choice that we can usefully teach in school – solidarity, formality and status. But there are many other reasons why we may choose one word, phrase, structure or pronunciation over another. In general, we modify what we say according to our view of ourselves, our view of our listeners and our view of our surroundings, and four of the most important determinants are the *gender, age, social class and race* of both speaker and listener. These affect language choice in ways which are not yet fully defined, as they are remarkably complex and interact with many other variables, but it is nonetheless important for pupils to be aware to some extent of their influence, as it will doubtless affect their lives.

As mentioned above, short case studies or scenarios are a useful introduction to these areas, and these can lead to role-plays and short dramas, even with younger children. Source material that is useful in this regard may include cartoons and comics, and works such as Tannen (1994) and Coates (1993) on gender differences, and Holmes (1992) on other areas, provide an excellent discussion, which can be adapted for older children.

Historical variation

Variation of language through time is particularly stimulating – children are exposed to a lot of language which is old-fashioned or outdated, and this unconscious resource can be made more explicit in order to raise awareness of the processes and effects of language change. Old films, old news clips and literature of various kinds – including older children's literature – can be used to point out ways in which vocabulary and even aspects of grammar change through time. Older pupils can also be shown old texts in English – Freeborn (1992) is an excellent resource here, as he offers authentic texts in their original form, carefully chosen and explained – and they can be asked to pick out features such as pronouns, different verb forms and so on, whose changes can then be charted.

Dialect, accent and standard English

Research indicates that the British have quite clear views on the relative value of different British accents and dialects. But equally it appears that they are relatively unaware of the nature and extent of these accents. Resource books such as those by Hughes and Trudgill (1979; 1996), with recordings of different accents and dialects of Britain, offer the teacher much useful and stimulating material to generate informed discussion about dialect and accent differences.

The precise role and status of standard English, although mentioned in a number of places in the National Curriculum and in the media, are relatively poorly understood. It is crucial that students should be equipped to deal with standard English, but also that they have a good understanding of, and appreciation of, regional variations, but it must be said that a lot of the literature in this area is not particularly helpful for teachers. Cheshire and Edwards go even further, reporting that 'for the most part, teachers have had to try to establish the differences between standard and non-standard dialects of English without the help of linguists' (1993: 35). Fortunately, however, this is not so true as it once was – teachers could now look to Perera (1994) or Wilkinson (1995) for succinct discussion and advice on how to deal with the issue in the classroom, and both would generally agree with the Cox Report:

> All children should be supported in valuing their own dialects ... but they should also be able to use Standard English when it is necessary and helpful to do so in speaking as well as in writing.
>
> (Cox, 1991: 128)

Making language work for you

So far, I have presented language variation as *reflecting* the way our social world is organised – as if its speakers merely change their language in *post hoc* response to events and circumstances. But pupils also need to see that our choice of language can *change* social facts – they need a sense that language, as Bolinger (1980) claimed it in the title of his book, is a 'loaded weapon', a tool with power. If we want, for example, to change our social distance relative to someone else, we can adjust our language accordingly, altering the intonation, choice of address term, or something else.

These points are best taught through examples – hence my reference to case studies. The teacher could borrow these from Holmes or elsewhere, or construct new ones, but the best ones perhaps come from pupils themselves – so that project work investigating how we vary our language in order to reflect facts and to achieve certain ends could be most productive. Cheshire and Edwards (1993) offer a good deal of guidance on how this sort of project work could operate, and how to involve children as participants and as 'experts' in a highly motivating way to collect language data and examine it.

A world perspective

So far I have concentrated on English spoken in Britain. But in line with my comments at the start of this chapter regarding English as a world language, and Britain as a multicultural society, it is equally important to draw examples and scenarios from further afield. Pupils can be exposed to a range of non-standard dialects within Britain, as we have noted, but it is also important that they hear and begin to respond appropriately to other varieties of English. These include, of course, Australasian and American forms with which they will usually be familiar from the media, but increasingly they will need to handle other 'Englishes' (as they are called; see Kachru, 1992). Indian English, Singaporean English and others are strong regional standards in their own right, and, in future, our pupils will increasingly be faced with such varieties. I am not of course advocating that in an already crowded curriculum they be 'taught' these varieties, merely that from time to time they be exposed to varieties of English that come from outside Britain, in order that they are aware of their existence and are to some extent able to respond to them appropriately.

I have implied above that in teaching pupils about variation we can take our examples and case studies from English. But, in many cases, the examples could well come from other languages too. This would raise awareness about how other languages work, but also of how English works by comparison. When teaching about formality, to take one example, the teacher could show how English expresses formality, and then give examples from Japanese and Thai of how the whole pronoun system is affected by attention to social status and formality – the speaker must abase himself/herself before a superior and choose a particular lowly form of pronoun. Examples from other languages are in fact readily available – in this respect the *Culture Shock* series of books (e.g. on Thailand, Cooper and Cooper, 1991) represent excellent source material, as does Crystal's *Encyclopaedia of Language* (Crystal, 1994).

Language change today

Variation need not be presented as something far away. Pupils need to be aware that language varies and changes all around us. Besides projects on how different speakers use language and how language has changed historically, projects on current and recent change often offer a motivating way of raising awareness of variation. These could look, for example at slang, jargon (e.g.

computer jargon), at the phenomenon known as Estuary English (using accessible accounts such as Coggle, 1993), at the way sounds change, and so on.

A simple example could be one aspect of pronunciation, such as what is technically called 'yod insertion' or 'yod deletion' (Bauer, 1994). Some speakers – my own parents are examples of this – would pronounce 'issue' as 'is-y-oo', whereas I and my brothers and sisters all pronounce the same word as 'i-shoo'. It would seem, then, that the 'y' sound (technically the /j/ or yod) is present in this word in the older generation of my family but absent in the younger generation, and this appears to be a phenomenon observable in other speakers too. Other words where this yod deletion is observed are 'suit', 'suitable', 'new' and so on. There is some evidence (Bauer, 1994) that this is a change occurring throughout the language – with younger speakers 'deleting the yod' in many of these words, but it is not clear whether it is an import (e.g. from the USA) or a British dialect feature which is spreading, or something else. Once pupils have been introduced to an example like this, and given some background information and guidance, it is straightforward and motivating to set up a mini-research project to try to find out what kind of speakers say 'sootable' and which say 's – yoo – table' and in which contexts.

Many other examples could be offered. Slang words could be discussed and then pupils could do a school survey to see which words are used in which age-groups, which by boys and which by girls, and so on. Others could look at television and newspaper language.

And finally ...

In this chapter I have argued that pupils need to be equipped with a view of English not as a monolith but as a dynamic, changing entity. It was suggested that the National Curriculum, while recognising language variation as important, does not give enough guidance as to how this variation can enter the English classroom in practice. For this reason, some of the key areas of variation in English were examined, with suggestions as to how they might be approached in class.

It is not assumed, however, that this will be a short and easy task. Children quickly develop attitudes to language that resemble those of their parents and of the community at large, and very often these attitudes are relatively entrenched and difficult to alter. As Edwards puts it: 'social judgements are not only endemic and powerful, they are also by their nature singularly resistant to change' (Edwards, 1982: 30). One reason for this is the 'yawning gap' between public perceptions of language on the one hand and linguists' views on the other (Milroy and Milroy, 1991) – a gap which can be reduced only by education in various forms.

In this light, the problem is seen to be a large one, involving societal change as much as local educational change. The English teacher has to see the process of change as long term, and in the absence of specific guidance in the National Curriculum as to how to structure and organise that process, the teacher needs to create this vision in relative isolation. In a sense, there needs to be an additional, unwritten curriculum for dealing with language variation during the years that the pupil is at school, during which time the issue of variation can usefully be viewed as a key part of the English curriculum as a whole. At times, it will be considered explicitly, but often it will remain in the background, to be mentioned when the opportunity arises.

The ultimate aim, of course, will be to enhance pupils' understanding of the nature of language itself, and to enhance their ability to use it effectively in the widest possible range of domains – it is an empowering aim. This might, in addition, help us to learn modern languages, improve our understanding of other cultural groups in society, give a clearer perception of the role of English in Britain and around the world, and so on. It will enlarge our perspective of language itself, and of its links with culture.

The role of English is changing; the nature of English is changing. This will undoubtedly affect the ways in which we in Britain communicate, and the way we perceive our language. If we are to adopt a broad view of education and our role in it, and to equip pupils to manage in these new domains in which they will surely find themselves, then awareness of language variation – its nature, extent and types – must form a central part of the English curriculum and of classroom practice.

Questions for discussion

1   To what extent do English teachers currently address issues of language variation in their work? What methods do they use?
2   This chapter has suggested that pupils – and the public at large – are largely unaware of the ways in which language varies. To what extent does this claim correspond to, or differ from, prevalent attitudes towards English in and out of school?
3   This chapter has suggested various practical ways of addressing issues of language variation in class. In what other practical ways can pupils be made more aware of these issues in the English classroom?

Further reading

Bauer, L. (1994) *Watching English Change*, Harlow, Essex: Longman.
   This book offers a wealth of discussion related to how English has changed in the recent past and is changing now, in the areas of vocabulary, grammar, pronunciation and elsewhere. It is essentially a source of information, some of it quite technical, rather than a class resource book, but it can be used to give teachers valuable background information and ideas of areas for project work.

Freeborn, D. (1992) *From Old English to Standard English*, Basingstoke: Macmillan.
   This is designed as a resource book for educational use. It offers many original texts from all periods of the development of English, together with excellent background notes, good commentaries and attractive charts and summaries. Teachers will find it

an invaluable resource for teaching the ways in which English has changed, though they will need to be selective and adaptive in using it with younger classes.

Holmes, J. (1992) *An Introduction to Sociolinguistics*, London: Longman.
   An excellent and readable introduction to the area, with accessible case studies and examples, and a wide coverage of all the areas discussed in this chapter. This will be an ideal companion to the English teacher wishing to touch on sociolinguistics areas in class.

9 Exploring other worlds
Escaping linguistic parochialism

Adrian Holliday

This chapter argues the importance of developing a more worldly view of English in secondary education. It is motivated by three factors in a changing world:

1   With an increasingly global role, English is used more as an international language than as a language of any particular 'English-speaking' nation. Indeed, English is probably used more by second-language speakers communicating with each other across the world in different ways in a wide range of media, institutional, professional and technical discourses which transcend national boundaries, than by first-language speakers within Britain, North America or Australasia.[1]
2   Ideology and prejudice is deeply embedded in the everyday use of language, supported and legitimised by group, institutional and professional discourses which form the fibre of society.
3   The forces in (2), operate naturally within a parochial, Anglo-centric English to reduce and degrade the 'foreign' other both abroad, and at home, within an increasingly multicultural Britain.

Growing up in such a world, it would seem that young people in Britain need an awareness, if not a use, of English that goes beyond the parochial Anglo-centric. I shall begin with a brief exploration of the importance of a more worldly, non-parochial vision of English. Then I shall demonstrate how this vision might be facilitated through a process of making the familiar strange, by looking at a series of instances in which the 'expected' construction on 'us' and 'them' in English texts is changed and thus promotes a critical, non-parochial view.

The need for non-Anglo-centric vision

I use 'parochial' to refer to a state of mind in which a particular language is thought of as characterising and belonging to a particular people or nation. In some cases, this may seem a straightforward relationship, where all and only the people of one nation are the speakers of a particular language. This is arguably the case with, for example, the Japanese. Even if Japanese is heard in Bradford, it is most likely that it is spoken by a Japanese person, and the Japanese speaker of Japanese is easily assumed the norm. Arabic can also be considered parochial, but less so than Japanese. In one sense, all the first-language speakers of Arabic are Arabs. Indeed, one definition of 'Arab', is 'someone who speaks Arabic'. However, the span of Arabic is geographically far greater than Japanese, across many countries. Furthermore, not all first-language Arabic speakers would be equally comfortable with the label 'Arab'. For many Egyptians 'Arab' refers to people living in the Gulf, unless they are invoking 'Arab nationalism' as a concept to unite 'Arab World' countries against the rest of the world. There is no consensus about which is the 'best' or 'standard' spoken Arabic; and there is a strong feeling that 'everyday' Arabic is far removed from the 'pure' Arabic of the Koran.

One would think that English is rather like Arabic in this sense. Both languages have been carried by colonisation to different parts of the world, where they have taken root and acquired very different regional standards (see Bax: Chapter 8 of this volume). English can, however, be seen to have a far less parochial character. There is no word like 'Arab' to tie all English speakers together. There is no concept of international 'English nationalism'. Moreover, English is not always used as a national language. It is spoken as competently, though very differently, in many places where it is not officially a first national language. For example, it is still the most frequent language for Internet users all over the world; it is the language of Microsoft, and thus dominates world computer software; it is used as a lingua franca between businesspeople all over the world (Graddol, 1997: 13). From my own experience, whereas British teachers of French would normally speak English outside the classroom, English teachers in many parts of the world would always use English in front of their students both in and out of the classroom, and often when talking to each other. I once came upon two Egyptian colleagues speaking English to each other. When I asked them why they were not speaking in Arabic, they retorted 'Why shouldn't we use English? Why should you British feel you have a monopoly on the language?' In such contexts, English is considered an important socio-economic resource. In Singapore, although there has been popular concern that English is eroding 'Singaporean culture', many parents do not want to risk their children missing the advantage of English-medium education (O'Brien, 1999).

It can therefore no longer be simply thought that English belongs, as the first language, to Britain, North America and Australasia, or that it is this same, 'native' English which is taught as a second language to the rest of the world. This long received, Anglo-centric notion of English has given us the straight forward idea that (from an Anglo-centric viewpoint) 'we' educate 'our' young people in the complexities of 'our' English, and that 'we' teach a simplified version of this same English to 'foreigners' so that 'they' can talk to 'us'.[2] This is no longer the case. Other people are using English as their own; and very often they do not need 'our' English. Increasingly, English is a world language which 'we' use in a particular way as one community among many, each of whom use English in other particular ways, making 'us' just one partisan, albeit influential, political player in this community of English users.

I am not pursuing this argument simply to put 'our' English in its place, or to suggest that 'we' should stop teaching 'our' English at secondary level. I wish instead to propose a new dimension through which we can enrich the way in which we see 'our' English. Seeing 'our' English as an interactant in a much larger scheme of things can provide a window on to worlds not previously encountered. In educational terms, 'we' are wasting a valuable resource in understanding ourselves and others, by only being concerned with our own parochial use of English. We need to see and appreciate how our English is perceived in other worlds, and that there are *other* people using *their own* English about us. This will help us to deconstruct our own ethnocentricity and to become more worldly in the way we live with others in an increasingly multicultural society. We must all come to terms with how English is also 'foreign', how we can also be 'foreign' English users to others, and how the 'foreign' is also 'normal', within our own society as well as within the world. We need to acquire a worldly, non-Anglo-centric vision – really to see things from the 'other' side – the 'foreign' as normal, ourselves as foreign, and taken-for-granted discourses as ideological. This will help us counter racism and to see how the ethnocentricity of our own position can lie in our own language. The three characteristics of a changing world defined at the beginning of this chapter require a completely different way of thinking about 'us' and the 'foreign'. Kress expresses this sentiment as follows:

> I happen to think we are in a period of truly epochal change; and in that it may be that existing ways of thinking will no longer serve in all respects, and that new ways of thinking may be called for in some crucial areas.
>
> (1988: 6)

To be citizens of this changing world and align ourselves with international, multicultural society, we must work first on ourselves – seeing how 'we' are strangers to others, and how others can use our English in different ways.

Kress goes on to assert:

> The cultural diversity of societies – pluri-, multi-, or polyculturalism – will not be reversed ... A newer understanding of equity will be based on the realisation that all groups in society have goods, cultural goods, to which all others will need to have access as an absolute prerequisite for producing a culture of innovation. Equity will need to be seen as a matter of reciprocity.
>
> (Kress, 1995b: 8)

I would like to consider English as one of these 'cultural goods'; and if it is accessible to others, 'we' can learn from how they use it, and expand ourselves accordingly.

The impact of escaping the parochial and seeing 'our' English from other directions can be seen in what Kress has to say about suddenly living in another, strange world of a foreign country where everything was different and even the simplest things could not be taken for granted:

> In the First World I had never paid any attention to the physical mechanisms which held my life together. It never occurred to me to figure out how the flush of a toilet worked, which secret route a gas pipe actually took, what a spark plug's purpose was. Their intrinsic nature had never concerned me ... To me the inner life of mechanical objects was as abstract as a cubist painting.
>
> (Marciano, 1998: 76)

Similarly, we need to become aware of the inner life of 'our' language – to see ourselves as strange – to make us understand better the normality of others and their worlds.

Making the familiar strange

In the major part of this chapter I am going to present a series of what might loosely be called textual instances, each of which force an alternative perception that facilitates a liberation from linguistic parochialism. Each instance involves a fragment of English that is either interpreted by, has impact upon, or contains elements of, other worlds than those normally associated with 'our' English. Some of the instances will present the text itself for analysis; other instances present how the text was interpreted by others. As the discussion proceeds, I will refer to three disciplines through which to approach these texts and interpretations, and to work this liberation from linguistic parochialism:

Making the familiar strange – a central discipline in interpretative ethnography – enables the observer to distance her or himself from the easy, prescribed agendas most likely to dominate perception.

Critical discourse analysis – based on the work of Fairclough (e.g. 1995) – confronts implicitly the ideological nature of texts by connecting language forms with the social forces which surround them.

Consciousness of the ways in which 'our' language otherises 'them' – or reduces the 'foreign' other to something simple and inferior – provides an ongoing monitor.

Each of these disciplines will be elaborated as the textual instances are investigated. I see making the familiar strange as overarching with respect to the other two, as it is often only by seeing things strangely that ideology and otherisation can be detected. Although each discipline derives from complex interpretative and critical traditions in social science, I hope to demonstrate how they may be accessible to the secondary English curriculum.

'Their' view of 'our' English

The first textual instance involves a user of English as a second language interpreting a text from the British press: I recently showed a copy of *The Guardian* to Sara, 19, who lives in a 'developing' country. She has never travelled abroad or seen a British newspaper before. Although this is illegal, she has seen CNN and BBC World television in friends' homes, and listens regularly to the BBC World Service on the radio. She has learnt English at school and is an enthusiastic member of an 'English group' – friends who meet regularly to practice their English. Her parents speak English, as do many of their educated compatriots.

She read the newspaper eagerly from beginning to end, moving quickly over the extracts of the newly published tapes in which Clinton talked about his relationship with Monica Lewinsky. What she commented on in particular was a full-page article about famine relief in an African country. She wanted to know why the newspaper had chosen to publish this article at this time, when famine was ongoing, and why the journalist's name was highlighted at the beginning. She asked if the real purpose was to project the image of a 'caring' media who employed 'caring' journalists, while at the same time reducing the people in the African country to a starving 'foreign' other?

My own interpretation of her reaction – for there could be many – is that here is a member of a society acutely aware of the way in which the media – what people are told, can or cannot say – is an instrument of political power. She is thus automatically critical. This compulsion by people from politically oppressed societies to 'read' more 'between the lines' is suggested by Wallace, who cites the banned Czech writer Sdener Urbanak's statement that:

> You in the West have a problem. You are unsure of when you are being lied to, when you are being tricked. We do not suffer from this: and unlike you, we have acquired the skill of reading between the lines.
>
> (quoted in Wallace, 1992: 59, citing Pilger)

I am not sure that, as Urbanak continues to say, 'in Britain today we need to develop this skill urgently' because 'as freedom is being gained in the East, it is being lost here' (*ibid.*). Sara comes from a farther 'Eastern' place, the name of which I do not disclose in order to protect her, where 'freedom' in whatever form still cannot be compared to that which we enjoy in Britain. Nevertheless, I am arguing in this chapter that we *do* need to acquire a greater skill in reading between the lines, not only in the press, but also in our own language, so that we may practise our freedom more fairly.

More to the point, though, is Sara's attitude to English. She comes from a background where there is considerable ambivalence with regard to English, which she associates with the West, which on the one hand represents international commercial, educational and cultural opportunity, and on the other, dubious cultural and political power. At the same time as finding a potentially corrupt President is 'nothing surprising', she challenges the more 'innocent' famine article. She problematises the style and choice of content in the newspaper as an artefact of the way in which British society sees itself. Thus Sara, without instigation, asks some of the basic questions that are recommended in critical discourse analysis 'to help raise awareness of the ideology of texts' – about *why* the topic is being written about in the first place, *how* it is being written about, what other *ways* there are of writing about it, and why in *this* case it is being written about in *this* way (Wallace, 1992: 71, citing Kress).

There is nothing really new in the substance of her critical discourse analysis. One might say that Sara is overdoing her critique. However, it does not actually matter whether she is right or not. It is the nature of the questioning that is important. Sara's critique is an important example of how seeing the (to us) familiar as strange makes one think twice about what 'we' are doing with our own English. In Fairclough's terms, to 'us' the way the journalist is presented in the article on famine has become 'naturalised'. It has become '*natural* and legitimate because it is simply *the* way of conducting' things (1995: 91, his emphasis). Sara is an outsider, so she sees the article as 'strange', and sees through this naturalisation.

Innocent ideology

It is important to pause a moment to consider the nature of naturalisation. I have found it useful to divide the concept into three, as depicted in Table 9.1 (see p. 137). These levels are entirely my own, which I am imposing on Fairclough's work for the sake of this argument. In terms of public awareness, *Level 1* is relatively unproblematic. Much of the British public in the 1990s, with the talk of spin doctors in politics, and after the revelation, which came with the 'mad cow' crisis, that even science can be ruled by rhetoric, are aware of the way in which language is manipulated in the press, image in advertising, and statistics in what 'research has shown'. Although we may be taken in daily, we generally know that we are, and are in a position to pay back, by choosing to 'buy' or not.

Level 2 is more problematic. Here Fairclough is concerned at how our society undergoes a more subtle change, in which, for example, education and the health services become the new 'commodities' (Fairclough, 1995: 35). His work contains examples of how university prospectuses and government pamphlets have been 'invaded' by the discourses of consumerism and 'the customer'. Although the instigation of much of this change may have been through government policy in Level 1, in Level 2, as naturalisation advances, we become less aware of how citizens', patients' and students' charters are only 'apparent' in their democracy. It is very easy for us to forget as we all begin to take part in the 'synthetic personalisation' evident in much media, work-place and professional interaction (1995: 89). 'The simulation of private, face-to-face, person-to-person discourse in public mass-audience discourse – print, radio, television' leading to 'the breaking down of divisions between public and private, political society and civil society' can easily be

Table 9.1 Levels of naturalisation

	Source	Ideology	Mode	Awareness
Level 1	Government, media, science	Thatcherism, New Labour, short-termism	Language manipulation, image, spin doctors, advertising, statistics	Very aware, resistant, knowingly taken in
Level 2	Institutional, professional	Commodification of education, health, charity, the military, quality assurance	Semi-naturalisation of technical discourse in documents, reporting, charters, professional talk	Semi-aware, initial resistance, gradually taken in
Level 3	Everyday language	Sexism, racism, bullying	Naturalised words, phrases, emphasis, chauvinist discourse	Often unaware

interpreted as a rational means whereby, for example, doctors are more effective if they talk to patients in a friendly manner. However, it also results in a ' "political functionalisation of speech" ' (*ibid.*: 80, citing Thompson). Fairclough considers how the 'counselling ... now used in preference to practices of an overtly disciplinary nature in various institutions' – as in staff appraisal – is in effect a 'hegemonic technique for subtly drawing aspects of people's private lives into the domain of power' (*ibid.*: 81).

At this Level 2 we may thus be initially aware, but are gradually taken in. I remember myself and colleagues being acutely resistant to the discourse on quality assurance when it first arrived more than five years ago; but with the need to use and be involved with its technology, although resistant to a degree, we now conform to it as we daily speak its language.

The most problematic of all is *Level 3*, at which it is easy for us to be 'standardly unaware' of how ideology has become naturalised in our own everyday language (Fairclough, 1995: 36). This is where we are racist or sexist without knowing, at the frontier of political correctness. This is where we so easily fall in with, and are seduced by the discourse of our peers, to label and taunt the 'other' in our midst. 'Ideology' here is not necessarily in the sense of political movements such as Marxism or fascism. It can be any 'systematic body of ideas organised from a particular point of view' (Clark, 1992: 121n, citing Kress and Hodge). Ideology can thus be present in everyday 'common sense' assumptions' that certain states of affairs or being, often represented by 'relations of power', are 'natural' (Fairclough, 1995: 2).

Everyday talk

Two examples come to mind here. The first is again from my own experience. I was washing the dishes when Rachel, an eighteen-year-old friend of my daughter's, came into the kitchen and said, '*You're* well trained'. Here, Rachel utters what at the time seemed to me a sexist, and therefore ideological, comment. I felt she was expressing surprise that I, a male, should be doing a task 'normally', in her terms, reserved for females. However, it is very difficult here to see whether she was knowingly being sexist. Indeed, it was not clear that she was even aware that her comment carried any ideology at all. On the one hand, 'you're well trained' could have been phatic, in that it is a very common phrase that is commonly said to men in circumstances like this, as a piece of mild banter – a comment that Rachel might have heard used many times without attaching any particular significance to it. On the other hand, she might well have been making a bald on-record statement, analysing me washing up in the kitchen, without realising that it was sexist. Whichever way, the sexism is deeply naturalised in common, everyday language, and difficult to see.

Another example of apparently innocent phatic talk is described by Lansley (1994: 52–3) within a teachers' room setting. Teachers talking about their students are heard to say: 'He's really thick. He's not worth bothering about', or 'Arab students always have terrible spelling problems, don't they?' Other teachers collude silently. Even if they disagree, they do not wish to confront the speaker over such a small issue and 'reflect' or 'mirror' her or his statement to show solidarity. Although the second statement approaches racism, it might seem admissible while 'only' talking about students. It is 'only' staffroom talk. However, it gets more serious when colleagues are allowed to say: 'Women are terrible drivers, aren't they?', then 'Pakistanis are taking over the area, aren't they?' Nevertheless, collusion is still easier than disagreeing. The use of the question tag helps make it sound as though the obvious is being stated and that disagreement is all the more inappropriate. Lansley labels this type of talk as 'moral illiteracy', and sees it as one of the building blocks to prejudice (*ibid.*).

It is at this *Level 3*, that foreign, outsider Sara sees things going on in the newspaper article that we might not. She can see the ideology in what to us seems neutral because she is able to see our familiar as strange. It is this Level 3 on which secondary-school English could easily focus through analysis of text and school talk.

'Our' English in 'their' world

My second textual instance involves a text written by 'us' that has an impact on 'their' society, and how it might be perceived by second-language English users in that society. It demonstrates the direct impact of English on another world where English has an authentic value. It is taken from a popular tourist guide, *Morocco: The Rough Guide* (Ellingham *et al.*, 1998: 260):

Temara Zoo (open 9.30am–dusk) is an unexpected delight. Most 'zoos' in Morocco are scrubby little enclosures with a few sad-looking Barbary apes ... Amid the imaginatively laid-out grounds there are lions, elephants, gazelles, jackals, desert foxes, giraffes and monkeys; there is a lake too, with pelicans and wading birds.

This piece is written for a British audience of tourists in Morocco, for whom it is supposedly a harmless description. However, when seen from the Moroccan viewpoint it is a text from the West about how tourism, which plays a major role in their own economy and is relevant to the lives of many people in their country, is constructed by outsiders.

I recently showed this text to a group of Moroccan secondary school teachers, who noticed the implicit (Level 3) ideology that implies something substandard to the British expectation (see Holliday, 1998). There is the obvious derogatory description, 'scrubby little enclosures'; but more significant is the veiled expectation in the understatement of 'unexpected delight' and the use of inverted commas in 'zoos', which imply a British civilisation pronouncing, between the lines, about the rest of the world. After this, 'imaginatively', in the third line, emerges as almost patronising, as the 'foreigners', who know so little about 'real' zoos, try their best. Nevertheless, as Level 3 ideology, as with Rachel's comment about being 'well trained', one cannot even say that the writers *intend* anything derogatory. Like us all, they are caught up in the texts of our society.

My analysis is of course highly interpretative; others may see the text quite differently. It would however be difficult for a text describing the society of others, especially as 'foreign' as sub-Mediterranean Morocco, to be ideologically neutral. For the Moroccan secondary-school student, this text reveals not only a British, Western attitude to their own society, but also the way in which the potential tourist psyche is played to and constructed by the writers and publishers of tourist guides.

Genre and society

This brings me to another important point. The Temara Zoo text represents the disciplined genre of tourist guides, and, despite its brevity, is rich in the features of this genre – bold head-word, with bracketed information to quickly denote place and opening times, followed by concentrated information, aided by lists, which appears neutral but is in fact loaded with opinion. Fairclough defines this genre as the 'socially ratified way of using language in connection with a particular type of social activity' (1995: 14). Put another way, the text is:

Embedded in larger shared public practices ... Language *is* social practice in which meanings are made, fixed, and shared publicly. Language *is* the practice of linking signs, rules and patterns in agreed ways within larger shared and purposeful material practices.

(Lankshear *et al.*, 1997: 23)

The Temara Zoo text thus represents real social practice, not only in British, but also Moroccan society, where tourism takes place. Moreover, as a representative of an established genre, validated by publishers and the tourism discourse community, it represents the authority of society.

If presented in an educational setting, whether in Morocco or Britain, the language in the Temara Zoo text needs therefore to be treated as part of the disciplined genre of tourist-guide writing, thus making it clear that it has an institutionalised professional base, and that it is not simply a body of description and opinion about Morocco. When this is established, the students will find the encounter with the ideology of the Temara Zoo text even more poignant. 'Most "zoos" in Morocco are scrubby little enclosures' is not simply an opinion about Morocco. Socially located within the discourse of tourism, it represents a concerted ideological power that the student must confront. Just like subject boundaries in other fields of education, genre boundaries in language education present a firm foundation of authority against which students can measure their own thoughts, thus contributing to the learning tension (Bernstein, 1971a). Moreover, because the genre has authority, and the student has to conform to it in order to participate in it, a very critical learning tension is set up. It is by having to negotiate a position with regard to the more negative ideological elements of the text, presented as authority, that the student will become autonomous in the struggle and learn to 'write into the discourse'. Classroom activity thus becomes authentic in that, as in the rest of social life, individual language-users are caught in a social matrix of genres within which they need to struggle to maintain their own text. 'Texts become an arena for struggle', in which a 'struggle over meaning takes place' (Clark and Ivanic, 1997: 173–4, citing Volosinov).

Reducing the 'foreign' other

The overall impact of the Temara Zoo extract can be seen as the otherisation of aspects of Moroccan society. Otherisation can be defined as the process whereby the 'foreign' is reduced to a simplistic, easily digestible, exotic or degrading stereotype. The 'foreign' thus becomes a degraded or exotic 'them', or safely categorised 'other' (Holliday, 1998). This phenomenon has perhaps been given most popular attention as underlying 'Orientalism', as defined by Said (1978), where 'our' conceptualisations of, in particular, the Middle East, are constructed by our own agendas:

> suggesting not only a whole culture but a specific mind-set. It is very much the case today that in dealing with the Islamic world – all one billion people in it … – American or British academic intellectuals speak reductively and, in my view, irresponsibly of something called 'Islam'.
>
> (Said, 1978)

Said (1978: xi) argues that the process of otherisation is easily extended to what the 'modern metropolitan West' considers 'its overseas territories'. It is presented everywhere in our society, in literature, painting, the media and advertising (e.g. Kabbani, 1988, Holliday, 1996, Moeran, 1996). An example of this preference for stereotypes over a more complex reality is exemplified in a television programme on Bosnia (Vulliaumy, 1993), when it suggests that whereas the British public, often encouraged by the media, prefers the image of the fundamentalist Muslim, many Muslim Bosnians eat pork, drink beer, dress in Western clothes, and enjoy music just as Western Europeans do. A woman reports how journalists showed disappointment when she put on make-up and fashionable clothes for an interview, because this was not the headscarved, puritanical image that their readers expected (Holliday, 1996: 127).

Otherisation is not however restricted to 'our' view of 'overseas territories'. It is deeply intertwined with racism, sexism and other '-isms' everywhere. I would maintain that otherisation is also at the root of bullying – where the 'different' schoolchild or employee is placed as the 'other' by the dominant 'in' group – someone perhaps not prepared to collude with the group's dominant discourse – not prepared to agree with the staffroom statement that 'Pakistanis are taking over the area, aren't they?' (cf. Lansley's discussion above). The 'other' is thus no longer in distant lands. With the increasing movement of different types of people and their multicultural embedding in each other's societies 'Orientalism is dated' and 'has itself become a cliché' (Ahmad and Donnan, 1994: 5). Jordan and Weedon argued that in ' "postmodern" societies: the celebration of difference and the commodification of Otherness' is everywhere (1995: 149). They state strongly that:

> Blackness, for example, is often *celebrated* in the dominant – that is to say, racist – culture, especially by those in the dominant group who regard themselves as liberal, avant-garde and/or cosmopolitan ... The celebration of racial and cultural difference is a marked feature of the radical twentieth-century avant-garde (both modernist and postmodernist) in the West.
>
> (*ibid.*: 150, their emphasis)

This point of view may seem extreme, but to question is important:

> Our questions simply are these – Isn't the Cosmopolitan often inadvertently a Racist? – How innocent is shopping for difference? ... Doesn't this particular recreation often reproduce again, inadvertently – racist imagery and fantasy?
>
> (*ibid.*)

Such questions are not far removed from Sara's questioning about the famine article (above).

In multicultural Britain, otherisation feeds 'the ideology underlying the construction of minority group cultures based on the principle of differences'

(Sarangi, 1995: 11). Baumann, in the introduction to his ethnography of the uses of the concept of 'culture' in Southall, observes that:

> In Britain this Ethnic reductionism seemed to reign supreme, and the greater number even of academic community studies I read seemed to echo it. Whatever any 'Asian' informant was reported to have said or done was interpreted with stunning regularity as a consequence of their 'Asianness', their 'ethnic identity', or the 'culture' of their 'community'.
>
> (Baumann, 1996: 1)

Sensitivity to the 'negative stereotyping' implicit in otherisation is currently present in Britain in many circles. This is seen in the *Right to Reply* programme on television, where complaints about the way in which various vulnerable sectors of the population, such as ethnic minorities and the disabled, are aired and the authors of various media are required to answer. There is thus concern and discussion about how, for example, the new Asian character on *Coronation Street* is depicted. My concern in this chapter is how this sensitivity can be methodically integrated into the secondary-school English curriculum. This concern belongs in the English curriculum because it has to operate deep in the everyday language which we all use (Level 3 in Table 9.1).

Baumann suggests a methodology, implicit in ethnography, connected with the principle of making the familiar strange, in an attempt always to look at things differently to what one would automatically. He tells us that while working as an anthropologist in South Africa, ' "an African miner is a miner" was a neat phrase that ... served as a slogan against reducing people's culture to their tribal or ethnic identity' (Baumann, 1996: 1, citing Gluckman). Similarly, within a British context, he suggests that it is more objective to think that: 'a Southallian Sikh is a Southallian', and whether or not I have to refer to their 'Sikhness' or their caste to understand what they did would be a matter of finding out, rather than knowing in advance (*ibid.*: 2).

This is in effect distancing oneself from the 'easiest' label. It is part of the basic ethnographic discipline of distancing oneself from the most obvious agenda and opening to less obvious channels. In this way, the observer allows perceptions to emerge from the evidence displayed, rather than working from preconceived stereotypes.

Making the 'foreign' one of 'us'

I shall take as an example of how this may be done with my third textual instance, this time an extract from Hanif Kureishi's story, 'My Son the Fanatic'. This is a difficult text to describe in terms of 'us' and 'them', because ostensibly the writer and all the characters are British. The story is nevertheless about 'Asians' in 'our' society. In the story, Parvez, a taxi-driver, is a father who is disturbed by his son, Ali, becoming a religious 'fanatic'. I am going to suggest two readings of these extracts:

A   in which Parvez is interpreted as a member of the 'Asian culture', which many British people would regard as 'them'. Using Baumann's familiar–strange methodology (above), this Asian taxi-driver becomes primarily Asian.

B   in which Parvez is simply one of 'us', thus countering the dominant discourse of ethnicity and cultural difference in Britain. Using Baumann's methodology, this Asian taxi-driver becomes primarily a taxi-driver.

I would like to suggest that the two readings are each dependent on which parts of the extracts the reader focuses on most in forming a picture of Parvez. In the following extracts I have italicised those parts which would support reading A. The non-italicised parts would, I think, support reading B.

Parvez had grown up in Lahore where all the boys had been taught the Koran. To stop him falling asleep when he studied, the Moulvi[3] had attached a piece of string to the ceiling and tied it to Parvez's hair, so that if his head fell forward, he would instantly awake. After this indignity Parvez had avoided all religions. Not that the other taxi drivers had more respect. In fact they all made jokes about the local mullahs[3] walking around with their caps and beards, thinking they could tell people how to live.

(Kureishi, 1997: 123)

Parvez couldn't deny that he loved crispy bacon smothered with mushrooms and mustard and sandwiched between slices of fried bread. In fact he ate this for his breakfast every morning.

(*ibid.*: 125)

On one occasion Ali accused Parvez of 'grovelling' to the whites; in contrast, he explained, he was not 'inferior'; there was more to the world than the West; though the West always thought it was the best. 'How is it you know that?' Parvez said, 'seeing as you've never left England'.

(*ibid.*: 129)

I am aware that I am leading the reader here, which is unavoidable within the constraints of this chapter. English teachers might like to turn this example into an activity, in which students are invited to find focuses that support each of the two readings for themselves – and, indeed, to evaluate the whole supposition I am making. My argument is that Parvez does undoubtedly have a Pakistani upbringing that *is* very different from, and culturally 'foreign' to that of the majority of British people, and that does influence his view of the world and of himself. This is represented by the italicised parts. This does not mean to say, however, that he cannot be *like* the majority of British people in other ways, and at the same time. His love for crispy bacon might be something he has developed in Britain, because it *is* British food, of a sort unlikely to be found easily in Muslim Pakistan. Nevertheless, he has the normal human capacity to eat crispy bacon if he wishes, when it is available. In this way, his likes, dislikes and capacity for a variety of behaviour are as complex as anyone else's. Reading A would see this differently – that he is essentially narrowed in his behaviour by a reductive, otherising notion of Asianness, and that eating crispy bacon is somehow a *loss* of 'culture' brought about by him becoming 'Westernised' – no longer a 'real' Asian. This is how his son sees him, accusing him of 'grovelling' to the West. Reading B would of course see his son's behaviour as characteristic of any revolution of youth, which sees loss of integrity of identity in the old.

Put in other terms, Reading A represents a narrow view of 'culture', in which difference excludes and limits. Reading B represents a more creative view of 'culture', which allows diversity and complexity, allows ordinary people to be 'us' as well as 'them', and does not see the embracing and absorbing of 'other' behaviour as a loss. Reading B makes Parvez travelled, worldly, and cosmopolitan – more so perhaps than those who might be seduced by Reading A. The film of the story (Prasad, 1998), unfortunately 18-certificated and not accessible to secondary English students, makes much of Parvez going down to his cellar to find his own private space, where he can drink whisky and listen to Frank Sinatra and jazz. This is not, however, the act of a man 'grovelling' to the West and losing his Asianness, but of someone being his fullest self.

Perceptions of 'us' in 'their' English

My last textual instance is an extract from an Egyptian novel, *In the Eye of the Sun*, by Ahdaf Soueif, about an Egyptian research student, Asya, who goes to England to study. Significantly, the novel is written in English, not translated from Arabic – in itself evidence of an English that has travelled, but also a rare example for us to see, in an English of which 'they' have taken ownership, how 'they' think about 'us'. This extract describes the study of Asya's British university tutor – an aspect of 'our' education system in 'their' English:

> A room with modern furniture. Teak effect. But then, she was silly to expect anything else here. To expect deep leather armchairs, an enormous nineteenth-century desk, books piled up on the floor, a silver tray with drinks and biscuits, a window-seat looking out over the white sunny quad – with cloisters.
>
> (Soueif, 1992: 329)

Hence, 'silly to expect anything else here', refers to 'our' system as strange, while her reference to 'their' system remains positive and richly resourced. In another extract, we see 'their' inability to accept what 'we' might consider normal. When Asya arrives in her hall of residence room:

> On the floor there is a brown rug of the same texture as the bedspread, only thicker ... She looks at the room again, then she takes two paces and bends down. Using the tips of her fingers she folds up the rug and pushes it under

the bed. She lifts the bedspread a tiny bit and peeps: white cotton sheets and a beige blanket. She peels back the bedspread, folds it up and pushes it under the bed next to the rug.

(*ibid.*: 324–5)

By 'richly resourced', I mean that 'their' society is far from the reduced, simple and therefore otherising stereotype we might have of it. Finding 'leather armchairs', 'quads' and 'cloisters', which 'we' might normally associate only with 'our' society, within this otherness makes it many-faceted and complex.[4] Without this varied richness, Asya's difficulty with fluffy British rugs and blankets, which may seem to her less clean than the plain white sheet and smooth floor, might seem simply a 'cultural difference'. With this varied richness, such a simple view is problematised. As with the images of Parvez above ('their'), images of Egyptian life on an evening with Asya's family in 1979, with Rod Stewart and brandy seen as normal parts of life, play with our preconceptions of the foreign 'other':

They sit on the balcony looking silently at the sky. A warm, moonlit, July night. Rod Stewart is on the record-player and a supper of cheeses, cold roast beef, salads and yoghurt … Mint tea is brewing in the teapot and three small glasses stand ready for it … Hamid Mursi, wrapped in his woollen cloak with his beige shooting cap still on his head, sits in a woven armchair and longs for a brandy.

(*ibid.*: 9)

An account by a foreigner which makes 'our' normality strange may seem a simple reversion with which to end my textual instances; but perhaps the whole issue *is* simple. The response to Sara's basic questions (above) might be simply a matter of from whose point of view one is looking. Almost any text could be rewardingly rewritten from 'their' rather than 'our' point of view – a feasible exercise for any secondary-school English class.

Conclusions

I shall now try to retrace the basic arguments in this chapter. Each of the four textual instances were selected to demonstrate how 'we' must think carefully and be critical of what 'we' are doing with 'our' Anglo-centric English as one partisan player in a wider world of international English. Sara (first instance), a non-Anglo-centric English user, perceives 'our' English as an ethnocentric artefact. The second instance, of tourist writing about Morocco, shows the impact of 'our' English as an ideological force in 'their' society. These realisations lead to an analysis of how ideology is embedded in 'innocent', everyday language, and can reductively misrepresent the 'foreign' other both abroad and at home, and form the building blocks of social '-isms', from race to common bullying. Moreover, the struggle to reveal and address this ideology is part and parcel with the struggle of individuals to write themselves into the maze of genres that underlie the authority of society. The third instance demonstrates how the ethnographic discipline of making the familiar strange can induce a different reading of text and avoid the reduction of ordinary people, like taxi-driver Parvez, to a 'foreign' or 'ethnic' other. The fifth instance, of a description of 'us' by a non-Anglo-centric writer, shows how simply perceptions can be changed completely, depending on who is the writer.

The overall message I have tried to purvey is that English is often far from what it may seem; and that different viewpoints must be brought to the most 'innocent' of English texts – that their Anglo-centricity must be revealed and addressed if we are to be appropriate players in an increasingly pluricultural world of English. Moreover, this sensitivity must be begun at school, and it requires disciplined, critical investigation.

Despite the simplicity of the final textual instance, this critical approach may seem over-complex for the secondary English curriculum. In my defence, Kress makes the following point. Although he is talking specifically about orthography, the principle can be transferred across all aspects of language. 'Complexity is not a matter for anxiety ... but it is *directly* a question of the challenge posed by the structure of the world for the child' (1988: 13, his emphasis). Furthermore:

> English has always been an enormously complex subject – the subject that has provided a curriculum of the resources of communication; a curriculum of cultural values; a curriculum of aesthetic considerations; a social curriculum of questions focused on how we can and should live together; and a national curriculum addressing the issue of what it is to be English.
>
> (*ibid.*: 9)

I am basically arguing in this chapter that the direction and ownership of English – 'what it is to be English' – can no longer be taken for granted – by anyone.

Question for discussion

How far is it possible for teachers of English to agree with the final assertion in this chapter?

Notes

1 In an increasingly plurilingual world, all terms like 'mother tongue', 'native speaker', 'first', 'second' and 'foreign' language become problematic. Throughout this chapter I shall use 'first' and 'second' language to refer roughly to a language spoken from birth, as distinguished from one learnt later in life. I shall not attempt to distinguish 'second' (normally associated with another language with an established role within a particular country) and 'foreign' (normally another language belonging to another country).

2 Throughout I shall assume an Anglo-centric viewpoint in the use of 'we' and 'us'.

3   Moulvis and mullahs are people with specifically religious, priest-like roles.
4   It could be argued that these are essentially British residues embedded artificially in a 'pure' Egyptian culture through colonialism or Western-oriented globalisation (e.g. Pennycook, 1994). I would instead maintain that such influences are a normal part of the complexity of any society. This is not so much a cultural hybridity as normal social complexity (Holliday, 1994a).

Further reading

Jordan, G. and Weedon, C. (1995) *Cultural Politics: Class, Gender, Race and the Postmodern World*, Oxford: Basil Blackwell.
This is a comprehensive introduction to contemporary cultural politics and would prove a useful starting point for anyone wishing to pursue the ideas developed in this chapter.

10 Student teachers and the experience of English

How do secondary student teachers view English and its possibilities?

Sue Leach

Introduction

In this chapter I want to discuss some aspects of PGCE English students' attitudes to English as a subject, and to themselves as teachers of English.[1] I shall be using three main sources of evidence, all provided by the students: lesson plans that my applicants are routinely required to produce as part of the interview and selection process; students' self-audits produced during the first two weeks of the course; and students' responses to a short questionnaire completed during the first half of their second teaching practice placement. In the course of this discussion, I shall be demonstrating something of the current position of English, the challenge inherent in attempting to shift entrenched and 'naturalised' approaches and expectations, and the possibilities for future change. My analysis of this material is to some extent informed by adherence to the alternative practices posited in Chapter 11. In many instances, the implications and positions are very much drawn out of the material itself: the students themselves may not have been explicitly aware of what their words denoted within the kind of context I am exploring here.

I am conscious that the material is open to interpretation from a range of perspectives (gender, age, educational background, and so on) and that each of these may indeed have helped shape the students' responses. However, as I shall be focusing exclusively on the students' expressed attitudes to English, I shall not be subjecting their words to scrutiny from these other viewpoints. In order to keep this discussion manageable, I shall be using evidence from five students only.

Pre-course lesson planning at interview

Students at interview are asked to produce a lesson plan for a single lesson, in which they are to decide how to use a very short poetry anthology, while working with a class in Years 7 to 11 (any one of these age groups), and for which they are required to suggest not only their methodology but the learning outcomes that they are aiming at. The anthology offers them the choice of 17 poems about the weather and seasons by nineteenth- and twentieth-century poets. They are not given a time limit, and produce the plan on their own in a quiet environment. Applicants do not know in advance that they will be asked to produce this plan, so what they produce is possibly more nearly indicative of what they 'really' think at this stage, than if they had prepared in advance. Possible, and indeed likely, features that they may quite consciously react to are the canonically loaded nature of the anthology and the tenor and direction of the questions they have just been answering during the formal interview.

Three lesson plans from these five students are available, which I shall discuss in terms of what they reveal about students at this stage from a range of perspectives, as indicated by the subheadings.

Students' approach to the teaching of poetry

At this stage of the students' lives, I am assuming that most of what they say about teaching and English is likely to be based on their own experiences as pupils in school. For some of them, degree work will have added other understandings, but the strong influence of GCSE and A-level teaching can be clearly discerned in all their writing. One student talks of wanting to help pupils understand 'the effect metaphor and simile can have upon a poem'. Another student focuses attention on themes, another key element of the 'traditional' approach, even though she embeds this discussion within a methodologically and pedagogically 'progressive' framework. This student is concerned that she teaches the pupils 'the correct terms used for discussing poetry', but she also wants them to enjoy the lesson, and to empower them 'to make decisions about what appeals to them'. The third student has different views, and aims to help students see 'how a poet "taps in" on our senses, especially vision, in order to convey a message or evoke a response.' This student also sees the possibilities of alternative interpretations, and wants to help pupils 'consider different interpretations of the imagery of a poem, or different responses to it.' However, she too wants to consider poetic devices such as metaphor, allegory and simile. The two latter students demonstrate a lively understanding of the importance of reading poetry out loud.

The approaches demonstrated here can be summed up as follows: *the effect metaphor and simile have on a poem, themes, correct terms for teaching poetry, helping pupils decide what appeals, tapping in to senses (especially vision), alternative interpretations, reading aloud.* The expressed intentions generally reflect what is commonly seen going on in English classrooms, embracing as they do a mixture of text-centred and pupil-centred approaches. Within this implied methodology there seems to be little understanding of the text as an artefact, or of the different reading practices that can be applied to texts. Rather, texts are understood and interpreted according to what one might call a 'traditional' approach, which owes its practice to an unmediated classic realist view of literature, in which the author has a particular status (high), and the text somehow exists beyond and behind the language through which it is expressed.[2] Pupils are sometimes placed at the centre of these approaches, and their emotional response encouraged, while the *reading aloud* of the poems suggests some grasp of the importance of shared experience. The attention to *poetic devices* (a dominant feature in all candidates' lesson plans, not just the five selected here) also reflects students' past experience of being 'taught' poetry, and may well say a great deal more about current common approaches to poetry in the classroom than I have space to investigate here. The emphasis on *the effect metaphor and simile have on a poem* seems to be based on the notion that there is a poem already in existence to which the poet adds these poetic devices. The *reading aloud of poetry*, which might be considered to be a *sine qua non* in view of the ways in which poetry foregrounds the sound of words, is a curiously ignored practice in too many classrooms. The focus on *themes* is a characteristic part of much English literature teaching, particularly at examination level, which, at its worst, limits reader interaction with the text, and at its best does little to promote the kind of alternative reading practices advocated elsewhere. The pupil-centred nature of some students' ideas is discussed later.

Students' views of themselves as teachers

The teacher stance implied by these lesson plans is also of interest, demonstrating as it does in all instances an internalised set of English classroom practices, many of which appear to have little to do with intentional and explicit teaching. One student talks of 'encouraging' the pupils, giving them 'the ability to recognise and appreciate poetic devices', 'offering advice and help where needed' (while pupils write a description of the classroom using metaphor), 'entering into a discussion with the pupils', and 'hoping' that pupils would be able to 'feel like they had achieved something as a class, as well as as individuals'. Mixed in with some quite explicit teaching intentions is some curiously tentative language, which is echoed by another student. She states clearly some actual teaching aims, but she also sees the teacher as responsible for 'enabling', 'encouraging', 'developing pupils' confidence', 'developing pupils' personal response' and being 'hopeful' that pupils will do certain things. The third student sees herself as 'helping pupils see', hoping that 'pupils will get involved and be active' and encouraging pupils 'to read aloud if they feel confident'. All three students at this stage see themselves as what I might call 'progressive' English teachers in the Dixon/Britton/Holbrook[3] mode; they see themselves primarily as enablers, and the pupils primarily as young people who may or may not be enabled, but it's all a bit in the lap of the gods. 'Hopefully' it will happen, but it may not. This implies that what is being enabled, within this discourse, is just 'there' somehow, obvious, clear and uncontested, and the growth and nurturing metaphors emphasise the students' untheorised notions of pupils as large seeds, awaiting the application of a gentle rain from heaven. This attitude may also signal the common position of students at this stage *vis-à-vis* pupils; they want to be 'on their side' and 'friends', a stance found quite frequently in younger post-graduates, who have not long left their own schooldays behind them.

Students' views of classroom management and English pedagogy

In addition to the approaches outlined above, the students did show awareness of a range of techniques for bringing about the desired response in their pupils. Two of the students showed some sophistication in their suggested classroom and lesson management, which indicated an understanding of pupils and learning. One student, who talks of 'applying' his lesson to Year 10 pupils, implies quite a formal stance in his plan, even though his underlying impetus is towards encouragement. He would be anchored at the front of the class, using the blackboard to collect ideas, and then go round the room to oversee individual work. The classroom layout is not described; one might infer that the pupils are facing the front, in rows. He talks of 'discussion' without showing any awareness of how it might be organised. This student is in effect reproducing a model of English teaching, the pedagogical basis of which was evidently never made explicit to him as a pupil, and which follows the pattern of: introductory 'discussion'; exemplar work; second brief discussion; application of what has been 'learned' to a new situation; sharing of what has been written by pupils; second discussion; with the pupils finally creating their own writing. The student sees him or herself very much as the centre of attention here, even though his/her desires for the pupils appear to be genuinely supportive.

Another student talks of using a range of methods to engage pupils' attention, such as playing a tape recording of one of the poems, reading another poem herself, using group discussion, or getting pupils as a class to read aloud. However, she too talks of giving them a written task that she will supervise with 'one-to-one' interchanges as she moves round the room. This student was quite clear about having a horseshoe arrangement of desks, with the teacher's desk as the focal point; a not untypical arrangement, which again focuses attention on the teacher, but does allow some unforced interaction between the pupils.

The third student also employs reading aloud as a technique, but expects pupils to be able to answer questions on a poem after only one reading aloud. However, she does understand something of the need for time limits and short-term aims, shows a clear grasp of ways of using group discussion and interaction, and sees the importance of summing-up the lesson. This student actually writes down the words she would say at the end of the lesson, and is clear about its structured nature.

These three rather different approaches all exist within English teaching generally; the first one is relatively mechanical, and the student shows little or no awareness of the pedagogical implications of his/her chosen method. The two others implicitly show their understanding of the need to set up lessons to achieve engagement, through types of activity, opportunities for structured interaction and discussion, and the quality of teacher response and reinforcement. Their pedagogical understanding is already at quite a high level, and their lesson plans show their real desire to bring about learning. However, as suggested earlier, these classroom methods are often put to the service of teaching a model of English that remains under-theorised and undeveloped, but in which may be discerned elements of Cox's five National Curriculum[4] models, on to which have been superimposed some methods of covering the grammar teaching requirement of the current National Curriculum[5].

Students' audits

Students were asked a range of questions in these audits. For the purposes of this discussion, I am going to focus on how the five students defined English as a subject, including their view of the place of literature and language within English; themselves as readers and writers; and their understanding of literary and cultural theory.

Students' definitions of English

All five students show that they see English as predominantly to do with the teaching and reading of literature. Their own love of English (nearly always given as the main rationale for wanting to teach English) has often been based on a love of reading, and the moments of illumination, which pushed them in the direction of English studies and English teaching, are often rooted in the reading of one particular text. One student refers in this way to her reading of *Frankenstein* for example, and describes her orientation towards English as one based on books and literature: 'I have always felt that I had a love of books. As I have got older, I feel that this has developed into an appreciation of literature'. Another student is concerned that the National Curriculum will make it difficult to 'ensure that children develop a love of reading, an enthusiasm for language and literature'; in other words, she is worried that pupils will not be able to make the same connections with English that she herself has made. In this regard, it is appropriate to mention that this literature is almost exclusively *English* literature, and that few students have any experience of literature from other cultures, other than Black American women's writing. One student, however, does show a strong commitment to other literatures, and expresses concern that the National Curriculum appears to exclude 'literature of other cultures than white English', and is alert to the tension that this causes for her, recognising as she does that 'every child has the right to access the high quality, English literature that "we've" decided reflects our culture and represents our heritage, whatever that child's social or economic background.' Her implicit grasp of the cultural and ideological choices that have helped frame the National Curriculum is reflected in some of what this same student says later about literary theory. Another student voices a similar concern, feeling that 'in its reinforcement of the canon, the National Curriculum is ignoring the multicultural make-up of the classroom and wider society.' This student can also see how the importance of women writers is not recognised 'even though their role is being increasingly acknowledged within the academic world'.

However, there are clear indications that, in addition, some students do also see language as constituting the matter of English, although by no means all of them believe this. (One interesting feature of interviews, for example, is the clear surprise shown by some candidates when asked about the place of language within English, implying a view of English exclusively focused on the reading and appraisal of literary texts.)

One of the students, coming from a degree background that included sociolinguistics, regards 'language as fundamental to all learning', and, with some insight, sees problems in reconciling pupils' home languages with the National Curriculum standard English requirement and entitlement. Another student focuses on meaning as central to English; he is interested in 'accessing meaning by detour and search for new untrodden and perhaps more user-friendly entrances'. A third student is strongly committed to the idea of English as communication, and sees this as an integral part of language teaching: 'Once a person has confidence in self-expression, I believe that they open themselves up to much wider life experiences. Thus one cannot underestimate the importance of language teaching.'

The view of English as a service subject is strongly held by most of these students; one believes that English 'is crucial' to children in that it is 'the means by which they access other curriculum areas. I believe that it allows the development of complex ideas when children have a thorough grasp of language, and that it allows expression of emotions and ideas in sophisticated and effective ways.' Another, coming from a strong drama background, echoes this ('I feel that English informs all other subjects.') before taking off on the wings of hyperbole: 'I think it is fair to suggest that its subscribers and contributors are the mass of tributaries that create the fast-flowing, ever-changing river that is human experience and knowledge.' A third student, writing from a slightly different and down-to-earth viewpoint, thinks that 'English is the most important subject taught in schools.'

The general view of English demonstrated here is that it is about the teaching and learning of literature, with some attention to language, that it equips pupils for life and success, and that the National Curriculum worryingly narrows the range of literature that pupils might experience. None of this comes as any surprise, and is in many ways well in line with the notions of English implied in these students' lesson plans. However, the implicit tensions between these three dominant views of English, as a service subject, a preparation for a successful 'life' in material terms, and as giving access to experience through literature, are not usually recognised by students.

Students' views of themselves as readers and writers

Students' responses to this part of the audit are in many ways the most interesting and revealing of all, particularly if these views are taken to be indicative of what students felt (at this stage) about reading and writing within English. Students' key remarks, with regard to themselves as readers, include the following:

I am a 'good' reader – fairly fast, focused and committed. I read at every available opportunity and am always interested in new and/or different areas of writing.

Reading is a very personal part of me, an activity I prefer to pursue in isolation. I tend to be a quick reader.

I regard myself as a technically slow reader, with very thorough comprehension of the text. I'm a 'social' reader, rather than 'academic'; it is very much a recreational activity to me

I can read quickly, I enjoy it, and understand the vast majority of what I read. I am comfortable reading aloud.

I am a skilled reader.

These statements are interesting for several reasons. They convey an understanding of being a reader that is very narrow, concerned almost entirely with reading as a private individual activity, in which students feel they have more or less facility, and which is focused, by implication, on the reading of prose writing. Although there are one or two indications that being a reader implies having a range of skills, in the main the students appear to see reading as a personal, private experience. One can only speculate about the reasons for this kind of response: is this the only notion of reading that comes to mind because of the context of the question? Is this really the only way in which students perceive themselves as readers? Does this indicate that they have no other ideas about reading? Does this indicate that they have few, if any, ideas about reading practices and strategies? Have they ever been asked to consider reading and their own reading practices outside the framework constructed at A level and degree level?

I have no answers to these questions at this stage, as this audit was not followed up with the students, but I do want to draw attention to these responses, as I feel that they indicate, yet again, the relative narrowness of experience and understanding that students are bringing to their PGCE year.

Some key statements made by students about writing include:

I have always achieved good marks for essays, but find writing less pleasurable than reading; I'm a fairly private person in some ways, so I find writing tasks more difficult.

I feel that it is necessary to distinguish between factual writing (essays, letters etc) and creative writing. My more formal writing is clear and very structured. I go through phases with my creative writing. I write some poetry but I usually write short stories.

As a writer I'm more colloquial than academic in style. I think my style of writing emanates from my Theatre and entertainment background.

I think my strength in writing is to be able to structure my writing, but my weakness is sometimes clumsy expression.

I have tried to adopt a more informal written tone, to replace the rather stilted style I adopted in university based essays.

As degree essays and university studies were still recent events in these students' lives, it is not surprising that they mention essay writing in their responses here. However, a similar worrying narrowness dominates their ideas about themselves as writers, and, apart from the student who does creative writing, they all seem to see writing as a formal activity, operating more in the public than the private domain, and concerned with the finished product rather than the process. As with the reading section of the audit, it may be that students responded in this way because of the context within which the question was asked. Otherwise, as potential teachers, they appear not to feel that it matters whether they are confident writers or not. This raises the key question of how they think they will draw on their own experience and expertise when they are called on to develop pupils as writers, and what they think 'teaching writing' involves.

Students' understanding of literary and cultural theory

It is evident, both from the students' responses in these audits, and from interview replies, that most post-graduates with English as a substantial part of their degree have some acquaintance with literary theory. However, modules devoted to literary theory often seem to occur towards the start of a degree course, when their radically different approach to text is often in direct opposition to everything that students have experienced heretofore. This opposition becomes more and more evident as students and their practice in schools are examined. The dominance of the prevailing modes makes it difficult for students, as learner teachers, to resist them. My reflections follow at the end of this chapter, on how the dominance of certain modes of working with texts might be explained and challenged. The students' comments on their experience of literary theory are given below:

I have encountered Eagleton, Said, Fanon and Achebe, Cixous, Gilbert and Gubar, de Beauvoir and Adorno, amongst others, but have little familiarity with cultural studies.

This was rather a difficult area for me as I tended to view it as an attempt to turn literature and its study into a science. I felt it denied the reader a passion for the work. However, later I began to understand the relevance of this form of study. I have a working knowledge of structuralism with some knowledge of Saussure, and have familiarity with terms such as *langue*, *parole*, *signified* and *signifier*. Also the Marxist literary school, Bakhtin, Lukacs, Macherey and associated terminology. Limited knowledge of feminist literary theory confined to Julia Kristeva.

I have a wide knowledge of literary theory from historical theories to feminist theory to postmodern literary theory. Literary theory is an area of strength as I enjoy researching it and developing arguments I've read about. A moment of illumination was discovering literary theory and being enthused by the freedoms of interpretation it made possible.

I am aware of the many objections that have been made to the application of some of these rather ethereal ideas to something as concrete as the teaching of English literature and language in a modern school. I am aware that I only know some theory, and that post-colonial and Marxist theory remain obscured to me.

These comments demonstrate a number of key aspects of the relationship between literary theory and school-based English teaching. Students cannot see any way in which to make a link, or to reformulate and adapt what they know for application with pupils in classrooms. The teaching they have had, and the reading they have done, apart from being difficult for many of them, has not been geared to application at a non-academic level. Students clearly see their experiences in this field as existing in another sphere: one of them quite aptly calling theory 'ethereal ideas', and only one of them writes with any conviction about her grasp of the possible links between teaching English and her revelatory experience about 'discovering literary theory'. In the lesson plan exercise discussed earlier, it was clear that literary theory played no part at all in students' thinking about English teaching, and until their attention was drawn to it in this audit, it is clear that it never would have. However, a general feeling does emerge from these responses, i.e. that students would like to pursue literary theory, and learn more about it. They also would like to know how it might be applied in the classroom, but their later experience during the PGCE year suggests that teaching-practice placements are not necessarily the best time for this learning. The question remains to be asked: when is a good time to learn?

So far, I have described and commented on the views of a small sample of students, without wider reference to the overarching questions that I am posing, which are: Do I feel that students have had any opportunities to arrive at their 'own' view of English and English teaching? Have students shown any inclination to formulate possible alternative views? To what extent is the prevailing mode a result of current English imperatives, and to what extent might it exist anyway, whether or not English teachers had found themselves corralled into a government-constructed enclosure?

In considering the last set of responses from these students, I aim to attempt some answers to these questions.

Short questionnaire

The questionnaire was designed to get students to think about their own development as teachers, to think about the kinds of English they had seen in the classroom, to offer some brief examples of lessons seen and taught, and to consider whether their school-based experiences had in any way changed their views of English. Three of the students responded.

In an effort to define the English teaching they had seen, they commented as follows:

Student A

> I have seen approaches which focus predominantly on developing pupils' imagination and creativity; others which seem to concentrate primarily on oral and dramatic elements of the subject, and still others which seem to have pupils writing for much of the time.

Student B

These comments are worthy of inclusion in full, summing up as they do much of current practice:

> Both English departments pursue the teaching of English with great enthusiasm and passion. Has been taught with dedication, and systematically. Very planned and structured. However, I have detected a degree of despair and exhaustion at the constant changes that have occurred in education generally. Also resentment towards the 'apparent' structures of the National Curriculum and 'apparent' resulting erosion that this had had on English teachers' individual teaching style. I say 'apparent' because I don't hold with the attitude that the curriculum is restrictive and prescriptive. In both schools there is a division of attitude between those who see English as now being dull, overstructured and geared only to producing a result that satisfies the curriculum criteria (sterile hoop-jumping!).

> the view I subscribe to which is that the curriculum is a national education train which I (pupils and teachers) are riding on. The train is moving in an agreed direction passing attainment stations with a specific destination ahead. I ... in conjunction with the cooperation and input of the pupils, parents and community ... fashion and design the vehicle in which I travel. Its colour, style and enjoyment are in my hands and I have the freedom to make the journey as good or bad as I choose.

> Some teachers are presenting dull prescriptive didactic lessons, designed to follow the curriculum. I call it 'teaching by numbers'.

Some are following the curriculum to the letter, but doing so innovatively, entertainingly, collaboratively and imaginatively.

There is a camp of bored professionals who hark back to a golden era and a camp of enthusiastic 'curriculum pioneers'.

There are those who believe Shakespeare must be read line by line right the way through, and those who recognise its three-dimensional existence, that it was written to be performed and seen.

My big interest is in the teaching of grammar and metalanguage in innovative ways. Also in new and exciting ways of teaching poetry.

There is on the whole a mini-revolution at work and a battle royal going on. It's all very exciting!

Student C

At my first placement school, English is presented to the students as a challenge to be enjoyed for its own sake, rather than as a means to exam success. English is taught to mixed ability groups and is seen as a means to successful communication as much as being about literature. The school has a progressive attitude to English, yet some tendencies towards 'authorial intention' and 'historical facts' render some aspects of English teaching there quite traditional. At my second placement school, English is split about 50/50 between progressive 'textual analysis' methods and traditional 'author based' methods. English is taught to setted groups.

What is worth commenting on here is not so much the picture of English teaching and English practice painted by these observations, interesting though they are, but the implicit attitudes of the students, two of which come across as highly engaged, thoughtful and critical in a positive way. I sense much intelligent observation and thinking going on, and a more than hinted suggestion that both these two students are thinking out their own view of the subject.

The question on lessons seen and taught revealed a very wide range of teacher approaches, including some drama, role-play, collaborative sharing of reading, group work with a clear purpose and method, Shakespeare study for Key Stage 3 SATs, a wide range of writing activities, and much speaking and listening embedded in many lessons, even if it was simply 'class discussion'. By and large, the most interesting and innovative lessons were those taught by the students themselves. The most dispiriting lesson, which outraged the student who observed it, was on *Great Expectations* with a Year 9 class, who were required to read the novel silently for 50 minutes while the teacher marked books, had a cup of tea, and discussed private matters with another member of staff.

These lesson reports go some way to explaining the students' initial views of what English is, as revealed by their interview lesson plans, and their audit responses; that is, they substantiate the notion that English is about literature. Of the 30 lessons reported by the three students:

- fifteen were solely concerned with reading, discussing or working on a literary text;
- seven were literature-bound, but included some aspects of language (not necessarily made very explicit to the pupils) – that is, pupils used their reading experience of a text to spark off some written or visual work;
- one was literature-bound, using drama as a means of exploring the text (taught by a student);
- one was literature-bound, with a focus on speaking and listening, in which the pupils' rehearsed performance of part of the text was tape-recorded (taught by a student);
- six were solely focused on language – sometimes overtly – as in working on compound adjectives, but sometimes less so – as in preparing and holding a debate.

These were lessons chosen from many by the students for inclusion in the questionnaire; they appear to have decided to offer a range that illustrates some of the practices at their schools. With regard to their own practice, these lessons serve to confirm that it is usually the students who are attempting alternative ways of engaging pupils in lessons, but their teaching is still dominated by literature. It is possible to see the requirements of the schools closing in on the students, with choices of reading material determined by availability and curriculum needs, and the demands of examinations apparently closing down the options for wide-ranging textual practices.

The last question, which asked students to consider whether their school placements had changed their view of English and English teaching, produced the following responses:

Student A

> I need time to sit down and reflect. My impression is that hidden underneath all of these experiences that I am trying to assimilate is the same view of English that I had at the beginning – that it should change and develop from a focus on language in the early stages, and then to an appreciation of literature, as competency in using and understanding language develops. But all comments on what English is, including my own, seem always so vague and woolly.

Student B

> My view has not changed. It is pretty much as I expected.

Student C

> I now see English as an interactive subject best enjoyed and learnt by students when they actively participate in lessons. English teaching and classroom management are inextricably linked, so therefore it is particularly useful to incorporate drama exercises and speaking and listening exercises in lessons where there are more 'challenging' students. I can now see the value of English as a means to successful communication, as well as a way of analysing literature and so-called 'high culture'. I used to have a very restricted view of grammar and defined it in terms of word classes. I can now see how sociolinguistics and other language analysis is incorporated into grammar. I have become even more confused about whether I should have Standard English, and whether it is justifiable to advocate one kind of English over another. I now view literary terms such as imagery, structure, plot, as a meta-language with which I can analyse text more comprehensibly.

These three last responses neatly sum up some common positions for students at this stage, varying from the need for more time, to an unchanged perception, to a realisation that understanding has been developed although some areas still remain problematical. It would be rare indeed, in my experience, to find students able to articulate a fully rounded view of English and English teaching by the middle of the PGCE year.

Conclusions

In so far as literary theory and cultural studies can offer significant opportunities to rethink English teaching, and indeed have already played some part in redirecting some of the focus of work with printed and media texts within English, it is worth considering how consciously available these approaches are to students once they start teaching practice in partner schools. General experience of school English departments, and of classroom approaches to English teaching, does suggest the existence of some key factors that militate against the application of literary theory, and make it extremely unlikely that established classroom teachers will ever feel the need to make it part of their practice. Among these is the strong adherence to the 'traditional' approach to the teaching of texts at Year 10 level and beyond. This very often results in an emphasis on 'meaning' usually linked to some exploration (futile) of what the 'author intended'. This approach is also concerned to lay bare the means whereby the author 'produces her/his effect' on the reader. Rarely are pupils asked to consider texts from the kinds of perspective suggested by Peim (Chapter 11, this volume) and few teachers appear to have any understanding of them. This means that student teachers are very unlikely to come across any hint of literary theory, in any of the schemes of work, lesson methodology, department resources and departmental targets they come across during their teaching practice time. It also means that they are constrained into set methods of teaching, and predetermined content, where they are even less likely to be able to experiment and explore this area. The extent to which it is possible to generalise about the practices of the teaching of English demonstrate the powerfully consensual nature of teachers' sense of what English is. The same kinds of expectations, attitudes and methods can be seen across all the schools connected with this course, applied with varying degrees of enthusiasm, commitment and expertise, and resulting in differing levels of attainment. None of these practices links overtly with any explicit application of literary theory, even though some of the thinking made possible by literary theory has clearly become embedded in an unexamined and unattributed way in a range of English teaching materials and approaches.[6]

The key factors referred to above include not only the direct daily work of the department, but the requirements of the National Curriculum, Key Stage 3 SATs, GCSE and A-level examinations. Because the experience of English teachers over the last 10 years or so has been of almost unremitting pressure, nearly always in the direction of a narrowing of scope and disincentive to creative autonomy, the current classroom picture is inevitably very similar across schools. There is simply no incentive or time to be experimental, to consider alternative ways of thinking about the subject, or to look at ways of opening up pupils' experience of English by applying literary theory to work on texts of all kinds. (Student B above makes some interesting comments on this in his response to the questionnaire.) The teachers' general response to the increased testing load is to devise ways to teach to the tests. They would rather do this than to take the wider view that pupils empowered by a wide range of textual experience (based on an understanding of reading practices and strategies and bolstered up with some explicit 'teaching for the examination') are more likely to attain at higher levels. However, there are some interesting features associated with 'teaching to the tests': a recent example is of a teacher feeling that she must compel the student to read through the whole of *Romeo and Juliet* with the Year 9 pupils before embarking on any detailed exploration, rather than using alternative ways of making the pupils familiar with the 'story and characters', thus leaving them free to focus on the set scenes for the SAT tests. The attitude to the texts that are set for testing or examination is currently unproblematised and untheorised in much of the teaching that I see, and is in itself a rich area for discussion.

There also appears to be a tendency for teachers systematically to underestimate what pupils can do, and to favour a linear approach to English teaching. This type of approach allocates the teaching of particular 'skills' and certain texts to particular year groups, and which in no small part contributes to the alienation of some pupils, who are simply not sufficiently challenged. When students do attempt to offer pupils work of a more challenging nature, which requires pupils to think creatively, to read text with 'difficult' vocabulary, and to interact in planned ways during the lesson, students are often discouraged by teachers, who are convinced that the pupils 'won't be able to do it'. In all the cases that I have come across where students went ahead anyway, the pupils not only 'did it', but performed in ways which really surprised the teacher, while deriving great satisfaction from their experience. I would not argue that this shows how students are influenced by literary theory, but simply that it is difficult to envisage change occurring within the current school context.

In university-taught PGCE English sessions, it becomes evident that few, if any, students are able to apply any kind of alternative reading strategy to any kind of literary text, other than the one that I characterise as the dominant liberal/traditional mode, in which the pinning down of character, theme, plot, authorial intention, meaning and some aspects of writers' use of language, such as imagery and other 'poetic devices', is the desired objective. The role of theories about language in underpinning much literary theory could offer students and teachers ways in to more useable classroom applications.[7]

Obviously the role of mentors is of key importance in the development of student teachers' subject knowledge and subject application, as well as of their classroom management skills. Of crucial importance is the ability of mentors to move students on from basic classroom management issues to more fundamental engagement with the subject within the context of some understanding of current theories of learning and of critical theory. Mentors who encourage experimentation; who can resist the impulse to dictate approaches and lesson content; who can offer students suggestions for wider reading within the subject; and who themselves recognise the need for constant development of their own ideas about the subject, are those most likely to allow students the space within which to continue their explorations of the nature of English. This may or may not be an English rooted in literary and critical theory, and cultural studies, but it is unlikely to be an English that simply rehearses all the accustomed practices over and over again.

The findings from this material would therefore seem to suggest that the ability to reach a personal, thought-through, view of English varies from student to student. Individual starting-points will inevitably affect the outcome, as will mind-sets and attitudes. Of key importance also are the schools, and the mentors that students work with. The most perceptive student above, Student C, was placed with a particularly committed, supportive and visionary mentor, but it was clearly her own disposition, in conjunction with her experiences at the school, which allowed her to develop her views. Alternative approaches to the teaching of texts, for example, seem to be neither encouraged nor envisaged in many English departments. Even within the very good department mentioned above, the student found that there are still what she called 'tendencies' towards considering authorial intention and historical facts. Although I would suggest that these students have clearly maintained a strongly personal view, I have not yet seen any convincing evidence that they have had any realistic opportunities – while in placement schools – to develop alternative, theorised, individual views about English. Discussion and exploration of alternatives are apparently the province and the inclination of only a few English departments. Therefore, as students have only the most subordinate status within schools, they are rarely in a position to begin challenging institutional inertia.

Questions for discussion

1   What kind of teaching programme might be constructed for student teachers on teaching practice that would support them in developing their ideas about English?

2   What kind of programme of mentoring might allow mentors to engage creatively with students in this enterprise?

3   How might English departments be empowered to set up ongoing explorations and investigations within the subject?

4   To what extent do the National Curriculum for English, examination and SAT syllabuses dictate particular kinds of classroom teaching of English?

5   How might classroom teachers, as well as student teachers, be given opportunities to take on approaches to English based on literary and critical theory?

Notes

1   It might be useful to consider this chapter alongside Andrew Goodwyn (1997) *Developing English Teachers* and Chris Davies (1996) *What is English Teaching?*.

2   See Catherine Belsey (1980) *Critical Practice* for a useful exposition of classic realism, and discussion of the work and theories of Jacques Derrida (1967a, b), Michel Foucault (1975) and Wolfgang Iser (1978).

3   See David Holbrook (1961) *English for Maturity*, John Dixon (1967) *Growth Through English* and James Britton (1970) *Language and Learning*.

4   See DES (1989) *English in the National Curriculum, The Cox Report*.

5   See DfE (1995a) *English in the National Curriculum*, Key Stages 3 and 4, *Standard English and Language Study* in each of the sections *Speaking and Listening, Reading* and *Writing*.

6   Much material published by the English and Media Centre, and latterly by NATE, clearly owes its approaches to text to some of the deconstruction theories of Jacques Derrida (1967a, b), discourse theories developed by Michel Foucault (1977), and the reader-response theories of Wolfgang Iser (1978).

7   The work of Jacques Lacan (1992) and Ferdinand de Saussure (1974) in opening up theories of signs and semiotics is of relevance here.

Further reading

Goodwyn, A. (ed.) (1998b) *Literary and Media Texts in Secondary English: New Approaches*, London: Cassell.

Morgan, C. and Morris, G. (1999) *Good Teaching and Learning: Pupils and Teachers Speak*, Buckingham: Open University Press.

Poulson, L. (1998) *The English Curriculum in Schools*, London: Cassell.

11 The cultural politics of English teaching

What possibilities exist for English teachers to construct other approaches?

Nick Peim

What kind of subject is English?

Why read *The Tempest*? For its undying human truth? For its narrative structure? For the insight it gives us into Shakespeare's mind? Or maybe to deconstruct its colonial, patriarchal and ultimately sexist ideology? These questions, raised by Hawkes (1992), Holderness (1985) and Dollimore and Sinfield (1988), lead to others.

Is *The Tempest* intrinsically worthy of study? Is it just as ideologically loaded and questionable as *Coronation Street* or *Who Wants to be a Millionaire*? Does Shakespeare automatically claim a place at the centre of the English curriculum by natural authority? If not, what's it doing there at all? In other words, why does English in the National Curriculum remain so much dominated by literature, by Shakespeare, and why, by the same token, does it neglect to deal with so much textual material beyond the limits of literature?

This series of questions raises the fundamental issue of the purpose and range of English in education. Is the centrality of literature in English acceptable, given contemporary cultural conditions? Are the reading practices of English in accord with contemporary thinking on meaning? Are the ideas that inform language work in English teaching, especially language assessment, compatible with current knowledge about language and how it works in education? Is English teaching intent on teaching specific texts, rather than intent on teaching certain kinds of critical reading practices? How are such reading practices formulated? What reading techniques do they deploy? What theoretical frameworks support them?

What happens if we start to read Shakespeare critically, as surely we must, if, like the girl in a Year 10 class I recently witnessed, we find the ending of *Much Ado about Nothing* 'cheesy' and 'dodgy' in terms of its gender politics? What happens if we reread *Much Ado* in terms of gender politics, alongside *Home and Away* or *East Enders*? Or, by the same token, what happens if we set up a comparison between *Othello* and *The Cosby Show* or, perhaps more problematically, Othello and O. J. Simpson? The cultural authority of Shakespeare as a naturally superior form of fiction is difficult to sustain if we reread it through the categories of gender and race. The same is true of literature in general. If so, what are the implications for the identity of English – in so far as English remains organised around the special textual category of literature? Unless we are simply prepared to accede to the claims of tradition and to accept the given form of the National Curriculum in English, these questions are worthy of exploration.

This chapter attempts to address questions about the *cultural politics* of English teaching in terms of:

- critical theory and issues related to meaning;
- ideas about texts and textuality drawn from Media Studies and Cultural Studies;
- current knowledge about language, including critical language awareness and sociolinguistics.

'The Time is Out of Joint': English teaching and contemporary culture

A fairly common resolution to the problem of textual authority in English teaching is to make a qualitative distinction between 'the popular' and 'literature', and to simply dismiss the realms of popular culture ('I'd rather eat worms', as one English mentor put it recently in a discussion about watching soaps). An alternative is to accept, grudgingly, the brute reality of soaps, while lamenting their inferior quality. This is what one recent writer in the *Secondary English Magazine* would have us do: 'Soaps are transitory, they deal with stock situations and melodramatic incident, and they can encourage a kind of vicarious involvement among their followers which is passive and unthinking. But they're there.' (Francis, 1999). Not only does this position deny the validity of all the recent work done in audience studies, it also implies that other kinds of texts are more worthy and more challenging. It also has the rather unfortunate consequence of downgrading a significant element of a majority of people's cultural experiences.

One way of addressing contemporary cultural conditions is through the idea of the post-modern (Lyotard, 1986; Harvey, 1991). This way of looking at things is not guaranteed to resolve all the complex issues of language and culture facing English, but it does provide one means for thinking through cultural political questions.

English in its current dominant form has been unconcerned with important developments in cultural theory. According to theorists of the post-modern, contemporary culture is characterised by *hybridity*. In this new world order of mingling experiences and identity, our cultural bearings are likely to be many and varied. Post-modernism might be described as a flattening of hierarchies and undermining of canonical foundations. Cultural objects, processes and experiences are seen as mingling and merging and losing the distinct differences that might have given them a singular identity in a world gone by. We now seem to inhabit a multicultural supermarket where we might eat Vietnamese food, listen to Jamaican music while wearing American clothes, and so on.

Moreover, we are all positioned differently in relation to these things: positioned by age, gender, class, cultural inheritance, local cultural practices. The world of stable meanings and fixed cultural bearings – if it ever really existed – seems to have vanished in a welter of intermingling forms.

The traces of the colonial period are evident in every aspect of culture, and have generated a rapid increase in rates of cultural interpenetration and mixing. Then there's the complex phenomenon of globalisation, where local cultural practices react with – and against, in some cases – general global cultural trends, where communications systems and forms have changed significantly. We're told also of the collapse of the great meta-narratives of religion, the crisis of progress, the resurgence of new nationalisms and the new emphasis on measured performance, corporate and state efficiency and competitiveness. What's more, recent times have seen a vast intensification and multiplication of media representations and their considerable impact on communities. In our media-saturated world, some have claimed that representation has become the means through which we largely experience the world – whether through news media constantly conveying a sense of the world at large and our place in it, or media fictions with their representations of gender, identity, the family and social life. The proliferation of representation argues for a rethinking of the business of literacy – and by the same token makes the textual concerns of English, as well as its language practices, look rather limited and anachronistic.

Post-modernism is a theory of cultural relativity. It speaks of the cultural diversity of the world and keeps a wary eye on the imperialist tendencies of Western cultural forms and products. Some may celebrate this relativity and some may lament the loss of traditional values that at least seemed to give our thinking about cultural matters some sense of direction. The category of literature, though, surely poses problems, both in terms of contemporary cultural conditions – and in terms of who is already well placed to access and respond appropriately to it. Literature – whether strictly defined as canonical literature or liberally defined as stories, drama and poems – remains theoretically questionable in terms of definition and limits. Nobody knows where it begins and ends. We know what's likely to be included, like Shakespeare, and what's likely to be excluded – like *Eric Cantona: My Story* and *Diana: Her True Story*. However, can we say for sure that either one of these popular texts is less worthy of attention, less susceptible to critical reading or less culturally significant than *The Tempest*?

In the early days of English teaching, when the subject was being advocated as the central element in state education, there was no ambiguity about the centrality of canonical literature. The Newbolt Report of 1921 was clear that literature must be at the centre of English for social and cultural reasons – to bind the people together in the face of potential political unrest and to cement national identity. The Newbolt Report's concern for standard English was a concern for the linguistic hygiene of the nation – set against what were held to be impoverished or inferior forms of the language. When George Sampson wrote *English for the English* in the early 1920s, it was with a clear sense of the missionary work needed among the culturally and linguistically heathen elements in the national population. In contemporary terms, that idea of a cultural missionary position is surely as improper as the book's monocultural title.

The important issue of the cultural exclusivity of literature can be approached by rethinking what it is that we're doing when we read texts with pupils in English classrooms. It may be more positive, and less culturally exclusive, to consider English teaching as an educational practice that is centrally concerned with reading practices, and that is interested in different texts and how they may be read and interpreted. This approach opens the textual field limitlessly and resolves the problematic issue of canonicity. It implies a significant extension to the reading practices of English teaching. Character study, themes and plot may be acceptable when working on *Hamlet* or *Terminator 2*, but won't yield much of interest when examining almost any other kind of text – from TV news items to magazine adverts or memorial inscriptions. There is a wealth of material on reading practices, including narratology, semiotics, deconstruction and other communications theories that can radically extend the world of reading for English teaching. The question of language in English teaching can be equally simply rethought. Current acceptance of standard English as the necessary norm against which other language forms are positioned and negatively misjudged, is clearly a problem, especially for the liberal tendencies of a subject that promotes a rhetoric of inclusivity. The subject faces important questions about where it stands on language issues. Sociolinguistic, critical linguistic, and discourse-oriented models of language can make the language practices of English much less monolithic and more exploratory, and open to a full range of pupils with their very varied language orientations.

The concept of the post-modern is certainly not uncontroversial. Even if we reject the post-modern description of contemporary culture and society, it nonetheless remains important to keep some debate stirring on the question of the cultural conditions of our work as English teachers. We certainly need to theorise the relations between the cultural practices we promote through teaching, and the cultural practices of the populations we teach. Applied to English – along with some modern theory about texts, language and culture – a post-modern perspective might be radically critical of its central concerns, habits and practices. It might at the same time liberate the subject from some of the anachronistic preoccupations that bind it. Cultural and linguistic theory will tend to demand a radical rethinking of the foundations and constitution of the subject. In the meantime, such theory might even suggest ways of making the National Curriculum, despite its limiting traditionalist bias, interestingly and adventurously interrogative, enabling the exploration of texts like *Hamlet* and *Terminator 2*, *Romeo and Juliet* and *Home and Away*, and a host of other written texts, media texts, 'spoken texts' – language and textuality in general – to become the focus of the subject's concerns.

Before suggesting some of these lines of development, it might be useful to rehearse what makes English what it is.

The structure of the subject

The National Curriculum

The National Curriculum in English has significantly closed down the traditional openness of the subject celebrated in the Bullock Report (DES, 1975) or the Cox Report (DES, 1989). The model of English teaching that the National Curriculum expresses is a contradictory amalgam of instrumental, traditional, liberal and personalist creative models. The ideas that dominate, however, are literature and standard English. The 'constitution' of the subject before the National Curriculum was already based on these two dominant principles. The unwritten constitution of the subject – that defines how English teachers see their role, how examination assessment is conducted, and how language issues are dealt with – remains similarly attached to literature, and to an acceptance of standard English as a desired or at least necessary norm for language competence.

In spite of developments in sociolinguistics and in cultural theory that have offered alternative models of engaging with the field of language and textuality that English addresses, teaching and assessment in English has remained hinged around a limited range of responses – often characterised under the general heading of 'personal response' or 'comment and appreciation' – and closely tied to evaluations of linguistic performances against a normative endorsement of standard English. The National Curriculum in English endorses and confirms this view with its compulsory Shakespeare, pre-twentieth-century literature and anachronistic conception of reading practices. In terms of the latter, the National Curriculum remains problematically fixated with standard English as *the* model.

The culture and history of English teaching

Although the National Curriculum is a fixed structure, there are strands in the history of English teaching that suggest different possibilities for the subject. Early documents on English teaching, like the Newbolt Report (Board of Education, 1921) and George Sampson's *English for the English* (1921), emphasise the social cultural mission of English teaching in terms of a desire to sustain the national culture, and a desire to sustain the national language – both of which were felt to be under threat from dangerous political and cultural developments. F. R. Leavis was influential in giving English teaching a powerful sense of the moral value of literature, setting literature against the malign influence of popular culture.

Other movements shifted the thinking and the practices of English teachers in different directions. English teaching was influenced at various stages by progressive teaching methods. Teaching styles, derived from active learning through drama, migrated into English. During the 1960s and 1970s, language and equality became a significant issue in English teaching for a brief period, raising questions about the dominance of standard English. Educational psychology influenced thinking about language and learning in the 1960s and 1970s. This combination began to give rise to more consciously inclusive and exploratory language practices in English teaching. During this period the trans-Atlantic Dartmouth seminar (1967) took place (written up in John Dixon's *Growth through English* (1967)), and advocated creative writing and the use of literature for self-exploration and for exploring the world. Later, especially in the late 1970s and the 1980s, multicultural literature became a significant concern of English teaching. With the emergence of Media Studies in the 1980s, increasing interest in teaching the media in English became evident. At the same time, there was a consciousness developing of 'other' literatures, as multicultural literature became a significant practice in liberal English teaching.

The practices represented by these strands of development can be identified as existing almost independently of official syllabus content, and are not necessarily tied to any particular subject model. The recent research that I have conducted indicates that the following are established practices of English teachers:

- close, exploratory and critical textual reading;
- textual interpretation through gender;
- some inclusive and non-corrective language practices, especially in oracy;
- genre-based work on reading and on producing writing;
- drama-based work on reading positions and perspectives;
- directed group talk and presentations;
- work on language variety;
- work on film and other media forms.

These practices bear the traces of the subject's recent history. They are not necessarily central to the subject's constitution. While their presence in English teaching is uneven and varied, they nevertheless indicate the potential of the subject for realignment. For example, while much of the language work that English teachers do with classes and pupils is productive, positive, and fosters development – it is little informed by knowledge of sociolinguistics. Media work in English, while well intentioned, is often limited to critical readings of specific media products – often uninformed by Media Studies knowledge and theory. Interesting, critical, analytical work on a variety of texts goes side by side with the persistence of literature.

The relatively open culture of English teaching, and some of its more recent historical trends, offer some opportunities and grounds for its practitioners to rethink the terrain of the subject and to renegotiate the closed curriculum in English. The cultural and linguistic theory that is advocated here provides a sharp focus for the modification of the professional identity of English teachers.

The professional identity of English teachers

For secondary English teachers, questions of subject models and practical questions of curriculum delivery come together. Theory about textual matters, language, and the role of English in education can come into collision with, or be overridden by, specific departmental practices in schools. Pressures for teachers to adopt existing working models may suppress any desire to negotiate the historical and constitutional complexities of the subject. Under current conditions, significant tensions in English teaching are often deflected by demands for classroom competence and for curriculum conformity. Surely, though, it is important for teachers to keep in focus the cultural and social implications of English teaching? Subject models are highly significant in negotiating the cultural and social orientation of the subject practitioner. Dealing with language and textuality gives English considerable importance in terms of the cultural politics of education. After all, language and literacy are key elements that define how we see ourselves, and are significant aspects of social identity. English teachers are not automatically equipped to confront complex issues around language. Their awareness of subject identity is likely to be coloured by their degree of experience of literature-based English courses and the embedded textual practices used to engage with this literature – often tempered with an honest but vague sense of promoting instrumental language competence and rich language experience. Where English teachers may have some awareness of different models and approaches to English, the various pressures of professional life are unlikely to provide much opportunity for developing alternative practices.

Theory – as a kind of technology for thinking – is vitally important in motivating significant transformations of the subject for student teachers and for qualified teachers. The term 'theory' signifies ideas that address the fundamental business of the subject – language, textuality and identity – and enable us to explore more explicitly the relations between these things and the social dimension of education. Current discourses of school improvement, professional proficiency and competence fail to address questions in this area of the cultural politics of English teaching. It is important for English teachers to be involved in a revival of professional debate about subject identity and the governance of English. This involves rethinking the governmental view of the role of English teachers, especially in relation to fundamental matters of literacy and language. We devalue the professional status of the English teacher if we neglect these questions in favour of a pragmatic accommodation to the given order of things. The process of rethinking the subject has to be negotiated and contested with student teachers, and has to be related to their experiences in English departments in schools.

Plenty of evidence exists to suggest that PGCE student teachers and NQTs are involved more or less consciously in developing theories of teaching and subject knowledge. (e.g. Hatton, 1988) For English teachers entering the profession, I'm proposing three significant sources of theory for the realignment of professional identity and practice:

- post-structuralist theories of language, meaning and subjectivity;

- media studies and cultural studies;
- sociolinguistics.

Failure to theorise at fundamental levels of subject identity means the inevitable domination of the subject by what is deeply conventional, ritualised and – as I have argued – deeply questionable.

Theory: tools for rethinking English teaching

Post-structuralist theory: rethinking language and textuality

Post-structuralist theory provides some of the materials for a rethinking of discourses, textuality, language and subjectivity – or personal identity – all of which are key elements of English teaching (see Peim, 1993 for a more extended account). Post-structuralism questions the very idea of intrinsic textual identity, a fundamental tenet of traditional and liberal models of English. According to the logic of post-structuralism, texts are not discrete and clearly bounded units. They operate with language, codes and conventions that constantly refer to things outside of the immediate text. Post-structuralism also questions the very conceptions of meaning that English has operated with. Meanings are not simply contained in stories, for example, to be later released by reading. Neither can meanings be the free productions of 'personal response'. The business of meaning is far from personal. The impersonal forces at work in producing contexts of meaning, ways of thinking, speaking and writing are foregrounded in key aspects of post-structuralist theory. In the work of Michel Foucault there appears an explicit critical inversion of some of the key oppositions at work in English. Foucault's theory of discourses emphasises the historical relativity of some of our favourite concepts: literature, the author, creativity, the idea of the personal, and so on. All of these, it appears, are much more recent and much less secure than we had imagined (Foucault, 1981; 1988; 1977); see also Weedon (1987), Harland (1987) and Seldon and Widdowson (1993) for accounts of related ideas by Jacques Derrida (1967a, b) and Jacques Lacan (1992).

Within the post-structuralist view of the universe, meanings are not fixed (not by themselves, anyhow), institutions and institutionalised practices like English teaching determine the meanings that we live by. The very (liberal) idea of the creative individual mastering language and their environment is also brought into question by post-structuralist theory. Language uses us more than we use language. Language represents a ready-made symbolic ordering of the world, constraining, as much as enabling, our perception of and dealings with the world. At the same time, by problematising the stability of identities, post-structuralist theories of language, text and meaning enable the institutional forces at work in the realm of signification to become more visible, and open the possibility of a textual politics. This serves to save reading from the ghostly domain of pure interpretation. It also enables us to see how institutionalised meanings and values might be challenged, re-read and rewritten.

Post-structuralist theory offers the possibility of rethinking key areas of English teaching – textuality and language, meaning and discourses. In deconstructing our familiar habits of thought, post-structuralism reveals more clearly the operations of institutionalised power in the curriculum, in the classroom, and in the ideas and practices of English teaching and teachers. The social dimension of education cannot be kept separate from our dealings with individuals. English cannot be thought of as the free space of open creativity that we may have wanted it to be. Whenever we make judgements about pupils' abilities, about their linguistic capacities, or about their examination potential, or whenever we mark or adjudicate pupils' work, we are entering into processes of distinction and discrimination that can have social implications. There are important issues about cultural difference, linguistic normativity and legitimate authority in what we had for so long considered to be purely innocent, purely educational activities like reading, speaking and writing in the classroom.

If a main effect of this theory is to challenge and deflate our most cherished assumptions, it also offers the positive prospect of new possibilities. Post-structuralist theory opens new vistas, giving a new handle on the subject's relations with the realm of the social. If the textual field becomes dynamic and unbounded – and if literature must be seen as only a small portion of that field – textually focused work in English may range into entirely new territories. These areas may include a significant emphasis on the everyday world of textual encounters: media texts, popular fictions and non-fiction texts of all varieties, from TV news items to *Dawson's Creek* and radio phone-ins, as well as all the more formal kinds of texts that we may encounter in education and in general social life. In the long run, we may be required to shift our conceptions of those pupils who may not have been very strongly or very positively engaged by canonical literature. If language is fundamentally social, and meanings are not individual but socially constructed, then our view of pupils whose language performances don't match the absolute requirement for standard written English – which gets wrongly interpreted as good writing – will also have to change. This will mean that practices in the teaching of writing can be organised in much more inclusive ways – while explicitly emphasising questions about the form, style and social dimension of writing. It implies much less emphasis on normative assessment of language in English, and much more emphasis on a genre-related teaching of writing.

The relationship of English to contemporary cultural life might also have to shift, in order to reread the world of text and language in which we operate. This reorientation implies immediate changes at the 'mundane' level of everyday classroom practice. A set of new and different questions will come into operation, to engage with almost any kind of text and almost any manifestation of language that we care to mention. The key questions – What do you feel about this text? or What does it mean? – might be displaced by a number of other questions: Where does this text come from? How does it work? What kind of signs does it deploy? How are they organised? Who might read it? In what different ways might it be read? How does it connect with other texts we know? What social practices are associated with this text? Post-structuralist theory has implied these changes, while newly emerging subject areas – Media Studies and Cultural Studies – have developed new practices in the realms of communications and culture to follow such changes through.

Cultural Studies and Media Studies – theories of the popular

English teaching has tended to neglect the fact that Media Studies has a significant and demanding theoretical content – and is about much more than teaching pupils to be sceptical about adverts, stereotypes and media manipulation. Theories of popular culture and audience-oriented work in Media Studies, for example, propose alternative models of communications theory, and challenge the centrality of literature in educational practices (see Fiske, 1987; Easthope, 1991; Storey, 1993). From a Media Studies perspective, not only is canonical literature oddly exclusive, limited and indeterminate (nobody knows how to draw its boundaries), but its cultural politics are deeply questionable. From a Media Studies perspective, the general category of literature is extremely restricted. The apparently free category of personal response is, in fact, much more constrained than has been represented. In English teaching, the dominant model of media analysis remains one of inoculation – enshrined in the National Curriculum's dismissive and anachronistic statements on the topic. The relations between English teaching and Media Studies have been characterised by the divide between media theory and English practices. English has incorporated Media Studies into itself entirely on its own terms, without revising its cherished beliefs and practices about text and language according to the alternative perspective that Media Studies powerfully offers.

Media Studies actually has important ideas to offer English teaching, in a number of ways. A dynamic sense of meaning is central to the sense of textual encounters in Media Studies, deriving from linguistics and communications theory. Media Studies has reworked the idea of textual relations through the idea of the *audience*, reviewing the significance of varying interpretations and valuations of texts – once more making the business of meaning and interpretation more mobile, dynamic, and at the same time more socially rooted. Media Studies is alert to the social forces that actually determine meanings, and that set the limits on the meanings in the public sphere. In relation to obvious social issues like gender, or race, for example, it is easy to see how ideas and practices might be of great significance in teaching about the generation and reception of meanings in the social sphere, and how these might be questioned, modified or resisted. A range of reading techniques – derived from semiotics and narratology, for example – are intrinsic to Media Studies approaches, and might usefully migrate into English to extend its range of textual encounters, in order to make them more rational, visible and coherent. If English teaching is to take its textual dealings systematically beyond the limits of personal response, character and themes, and to extend its textual aspirations beyond the limits of literature, Media Studies has a great deal to offer – usefully and positively challenging the premises of the subject's textual orientation. Once again, it promises a wide range of texts and of reading techniques and procedures, beyond the current remit of English.

Sociolinguistics and critical language awareness

If post-structuralist theory enables a rethinking of textuality and textual relations in English teaching, and of fundamental aspects of language, meaning and institutions, then sociolinguistics demands a more steady focus on the specific realities of language practices in education and their effects. Some of the effects of sociolinguistics had entered into the consciousness of English teaching in the 1960s and 1970s, but only partially, and without shifting perceptions at the constitutional level. In mainstream models of English teaching, classroom talk has been of increasing importance in English. 'Oracy' became a central element in active learning through speech. A new (post-1970) emphasis on language and learning was conceived of as essentially democratic, and aimed to embrace warmly all the varieties of language found among the pupil population (Britton, 1970). Temporary controversy was aroused in the early 1970s by Basil Bernstein's researches into working-class underachievement in schools – related directly to language (Bernstein, 1971b). Meanwhile, in the USA, William Labov's crucial linguistic work on education has been critical of the systematic devaluation of non-standard forms of English in schools (Labov, 1973).

In Australia, M. A. K. Halliday's sociolinguistics has provided approaches to education and to English teaching, significantly displacing literary studies in the school curriculum, addressing a more inclusive textual field and deploying a range of reading practices emphasising the social dimension of language (Halliday, 1979). Systemic functional linguistics has been applied, in the form of genre theory, to the arena of secondary schooling, and has offered techniques for reading as well as promoting persuasive policies on language practices for schools and education authorities. Systemic functional linguistics has a great deal that is challenging to put before English teachers, in terms of rethinking the teaching of grammar. The challenge of sociolinguistic perspectives to mainstream English is vital at the most mundane level of practice, in terms of how pupils' linguistic competencies are understood, how their work gets marked, and how their progress as users of language is judged – all things that are quite fundamental to English teaching. The related field of critical linguistic studies offers a varied set of processes, concepts and techniques for the analysis of the social construction of texts. Norman Fairclough's writings in the field of critical discourse analysis offer clear and accessible examples of working with the relations between language and power, in specific ways that have a great deal to offer textually focused teaching (Fairclough, 1989).

Gaps and possibilities: reworking the National Curriculum

The current National Curriculum takes a relatively narrow view of the textual field, of reading practices and of language and language competence. Linking reading to the category of literature, it limits the range of the subject. Ideologically it is contradictory, although it does pay uncritical homage to the notion of literature and to the idea of a textual hierarchy in which popular forms are of less significance and value, as well as validating the idea of standard English as common currency, thus representing language development itself as the competent performance of standard language forms. To this extent, the National Curriculum has generally been recognised as signifying a restriction imposed on English teaching that at least keeps out alternatives. Nonetheless, it does seem plausible that approaches to the National Curriculum could enable a teaching of English that extended beyond its ostensible limits; that could provide a more relevant and inclusive set of ideas and practices; and that could, at the same time, offer pupils more than adequate opportunities for success within the National Curriculum. While this is a partial and constrained ambition, it is one that, within present conditions, may free English teachers from reading practices mainly concerned with extracting meaning, which focus on character, plot and theme. Here it is only possible to sketch an approach that might exemplify the kind of alternative practices proposed.

Some implications for practice: exploring textuality

Terminating Hamlet

Subjecting some of the fixed categories of English to 'play' might demonstrate the implications of some of these issues for practice. By playing around with fixed textual identities, exploring the construction and the potential meanings of texts, we can release the constraints that delimit approaches to texts, and that determine a limited textual field. The category of literature might provisionally be seen as providing occasions for exploring textual issues that go beyond the limits of the single text, i.e. issues that explore textuality and the signifying practices. Reading a poem – any poem – might then be seen not so much as getting in touch with a special literary experience as providing the occasion for some reflections on language, for some 'semiotic' work on networks of meaning and symbolic references. Reading any narrative text can lead into a consideration of narrative as a category, and might encourage some taxonomical accounts of the many and varied narratives that we live among.

A useful teaching technique for opening up questions of textual structure and identity is to place two apparently contrasting texts against one another. The characteristic features of both may be revealed, and questions about meaning and textual status can be explored. An approach might begin by focusing on texts from the point of view of how they work as texts, examining generic features and semiotic effects, and how they may link with similar texts and contrast with different texts. Roland Barthes' (1970) narrative codes provide a handy way of beginning to examine perspectives on narrative content and structure. They are as follows:

- **the proairetic** – actions, sequence, development;
- **the semic** – components, constituent elements;
- **the symbolic** – theme, symbol, contrasts, echoes;
- **the cultural** – knowledge, references, implied information;
- **the hermeneutic** – questions, enigmas, answers, gaps.

It is easy enough to translate these codes with their unfamiliar names into exercises pupils can readily work with. The proairetic code can be activated simply by asking: 'How can we divide this text into sections? How does one section relate to another?' This kind of exercise gives rise to a consideration of narrative sequencing, and may be considered in relation to questions about texts and time and textual editing – the gaps that are left, where they occur, their effects and how we, as readers or spectators, fill in or interpret those gaps. The proairetic code can provide some consideration of the idea of action and agency in texts and how it is distributed. In *Terminator 2*, interesting questions about the logical sequencing of action arise from the deployment of the time-loop paradox. Parallels can be drawn with the figure of the ghost in *Hamlet* and the relations between past actions, present knowledge and future orientation towards action. The proairetic code can operate at a very simple level, as a teaching technique for indicating fundamental narrative sequencing – from disruption, through action towards resolution – or can be used to ask funda-mental questions about how texts work, about editing, reading and the activation of codes and conventions.

The semic code might ask pupils to identify the key places, objects, identities and events in a text. This approach tends to deal with the elements of meaning in narrative texts and offers a simple and direct way of examining the relations between meanings that circulate in relation to identities, and how these get caught up in textual threads. Ophelia, for example, can be understood only if we already have some field of knowledge about feminine identity, and exactly the same is true of John Connor's mother in *Terminator 2*. Where these figures stand in relation to that field is of course different, and indicates something about each text and its relations with ideas about the feminine. It might be interesting, from a quite different perspective, to identify the different kinds of weapons in each text and their different symbolic resonances, as well as their common meanings. Another approach might concentrate on different places in these texts and how they constitute elements of a symbolic landscape – identifying the symbolic meanings of place in each text, from the apocalyptic desert in *Terminator 2* to the other-worldly battlements of Elsinore.

The hermeneutic code could be easily explored in relation to these two texts by asking questions like: 'What questions does the text ask? What questions are answered and what unanswered? What information are we given? What information does the text not provide?' This might give rise to interesting speculative reading practices. In *Hamlet* there are unanswered questions about Hamlet and his father, about his parents' marriage, about the precise nature of Hamlet's relationship with Ophelia. In *Terminator 2*, a similar cluster of questions can be imagined around various logical and technological issues – indicating perhaps significant differences between the texts. *Terminator 2* raises questions about the relations between the past, the present and the future, and about technology and its relations with human values, for instance.

The cultural and symbolic codes similarly provide techniques for analytic work on texts. The cultural code provides useful material for identifying frames of references and context. Pupils could consider specific pieces of vocabulary that might refer to a cultural context, such as the word 'husbandry' or 'arras' in *Hamlet* or the use of robotic and apocalyptic images in *Terminator 2*. This practice can also serve to identify how texts of different types deploy different languages, and can also be a useful way of indicating how textual meanings constantly refer outside of themselves to meanings that are current (or not, as the case may be) in general cultural practices and discourse. The symbolic code also addresses the relations between texts and the systems of ideas they refer to and operate within. Contrasts at work in *Hamlet* and in *Terminator 2* – between action and inaction, between the human and the technological, for example – connect with some of the powerful binary oppositions that shape our thinking in general and that form part of the world of meaning that we inhabit. These phenomena can be usefully explored in relation to these two texts, through the application of the codes I've referred to here. These practices can be keyed into other theoretically informed modes of textual engagement: semiotic analysis, for example; examining the relations between texts and contemporary discourses; linguistic analyses of various kinds and so on.

It is important that these codes can be deployed in relation to *Terminator 2*, just as much as they can to *Hamlet*, but also to any other narrative that you care to mention: a news item, a joke, a TV soap opera or a historical account. They invite an analytical attention to textual material, and highlight generic and intertextual features, making work on texts less focused on the unique properties of the texts themselves than on a transferable sense of how texts work. There's no special reason to begin this type of exploration with *Terminator 2*. But then again, there is no reason to begin with *Hamlet*, either. Putting them together, however, provides opportunities for rethinking the textual field in English and for exploring the very idea of textual fields.

New bearings in subject identity

Rethinking the process of constructing the professional identity of English teachers must involve knowledge that reaches beyond the idea of competencies and classroom efficacy. PGCE training for English teachers needs to provide space and means for the consideration of models of subject identity – and for the alternative practices that they may engender. In contemporary cultural conditions – call them post-modern or otherwise – it seems essential to encourage English teachers to reconceptualise literacy, perhaps using their own real and varied experiences of reading (*all* kinds of reading), but also exploring the reading of their pupils in a more open spirit. A sense of how both individuals and groups become *differently* literate might furnish a starting point for the construction of an inclusive notion of literacy – an idea that doesn't privilege one special category of fictions, for example, above all others. Similarly, knowledge about language would seem to be highly significant to teachers of English, although many will have no degree knowledge in this area, just as many English teachers may have little knowledge of significant perspectives on education and literacy.

Models and materials exist for moving the habitual study of textual material in English classrooms away from the literary. Media Studies, critical linguistics and Cultural Studies all offer techniques and materials in abundance. Within English teaching there has developed a tradition of working with women's writing and women's issues in literature, for example, that, implicitly at least, acknowledges that reading habits and practices are determined significantly by social identities. Work on gender might be productively developed using a number of methods – including ways to positively break down the textual hierarchies and begin to develop understandings of the phenomenology of reading practices. Gender is potentially a key category for creating a more explicit consciousness of issues in the area of reading, literacy and society within the arena of English teaching. Recent panics about boys' performance in English have already given rise to some serious attempts to rethink the relevance of a literary-based English curriculum.

In relation to language in English teaching, work with genres, forms and frameworks already provides prototype models for subject development. The range of types of writing in English classrooms is now likely to include significantly more non-fiction, and more explicitly generic writing, than was previously the case. Techniques for – and examples of – the framing of writing: explicitly referring to registers, discourses and generic features, also exist to some extent in practice. At the same time, a sociolinguistic awareness of language issues in education seems urgently vital for contemporary English teachers, especially in a context where traditionalist aspects of language teaching may be imposed externally in answer to perceived public pressures for standards. Approaches to marking, and rigorous policies for non-corrective forms of response to pupil writings in English teaching, appear to be vital. Just as vital is the cultivation of techniques for the teaching of writing, including the explicit teaching of the form and content of the valued models for all pupils, as well as training English teachers to recognise the power of expression in their pupils' non-standard writings. Why not draw from the rich resource promised by *non-prescriptive* grammars, developing writing through explicit teaching in the varied fields of syntax, semantics and semiotics of language? Semiotics takes us into the idea of the extended field of writing: including discourses and language games, crossing boundaries between different textual types and forms, and enabling pupils to gain access to ideas about signs, meaning and the social sphere. Semiotics can also provide a vocabulary and technique to define procedures for 'reading' specific texts and for constructing intertextual readings. Using this 'semiotic' model, reading is perceived as the deployment of specific techniques – techniques that can be *taught* and *learned* – rather than as the expression and reflection of personal qualities or social habits.

The tradition of pedagogy in English teaching is well suited to make the kinds of transitions of material that have been proposed here. The characteristic flexibility of the English teacher signifies a range of productive teaching techniques that can be deployed for a host of purposes. The English teacher's familiar pedagogical repertoire includes integrating and moving among: explicit class-based teaching, workshop models, group work, practical work growing out of theory, devising and monitoring individual programmes of reading and writing, encouraging autonomy, and encouraging critical thinking. All of these established practices are congenial to a more inclusive approach to textuality and language. While the changes proposed here might mean that English teachers have to ditch their time-honoured professional attachments to literature, to literary models of reading, and to standard English, the effect of this renunciation may be positive. It may open up new vistas and fresh possibilities across a vastly extended range of textual encounters. Similarly, it may allow the language to be worked with, by using more inclusive and productive perspectives.

This chapter begins with some questions about *The Tempest* and English teaching. At the end of *The Tempest*, Prospero promises to throw down his staff and drown his book. This might be read as a metaphor for the necessary shedding of patriarchal and colonial authority that he has exerted on his remote and isolated island. This is, of course, only one way of reading the end of *The Tempest*, but it seems to be one that reverberates with significance for the future of English teaching in its contemporary context.

Questions for discussion

1 What might be the key questions to ask about texts, and are they applicable across the complete range of genres?
2 Would a post-modernist approach to the subject divorce the English curriculum from values?
3 What possibilities for comparative work in English are suggested to you by this chapter's discussion of narrative codes?

Further reading

For introductions to post-modernism: see Lyotard (1986) and Harvey (1991). For introductions to post-structuralism: see Foucault (1975); Weedon (1987); Harland (1987); and Seldon and Widdowson (1993). For the fundamental theory of Media Studies and Cultural Studies: see Easthope (1991) and Storey (1993).

12 The canon

Historical construction and contemporary challenges[1]

Janet Maybin

Introduction

The 1995 revised National Curriculum for English presents a familiar roll-call of great authors. Shakespeare comes first, and is followed by lists of pre-1900 stipulated and post-1900 suggested writers. These range from Chaucer through Spenser and Milton to Romantic poets like Wordsworth and Shelley, nineteenth-century novelists like Charles Dickens and Charlotte Brontë, and twentieth-century modernists like T. S. Eliot and James Joyce. This is the canon of English literature, the backbone of university courses, the focus of literary criticism, and the staple of the publishing industry. It looks very similar to my own school English literature curriculum in the 1960s: an authoritative cultural tradition that we were taught to appreciate through 'analysing and discussing' themes, meanings and techniques of plot and characterisation. However, although the same literary heritage appears, apparently unchanged and unproblematical in the 1995 orders, this canon has been substantially challenged and debated over the last twenty years.

For some critics and educationalists, the English literature canon represents the highest form of literary art, 'the powerful and splendid history of the best that has been thought and said in our language' (DES, 1988). It provides universal models of beauty and excellence in the use of English, and an important humanising influence on students' minds. For others, however, the canon is élitist, tied up with narrow notions of 'Englishness' and a particular approach to literary criticism. From this second point of view, the canon is by definition exclusive; it is defined as much by the genres, the uses of language and the cultural experience it omits as by those which are authorised. Terry Eagleton puts forward a strong version of this argument:

> the so-called 'literary canon', the unquestioned 'great tradition' of the 'national literature', has to be recognised as a *construct*, fashioned by particular people for particular reasons at a certain time. There is no such thing as a literary work or tradition which is valuable *in itself*, regardless of what anyone might have said or come to say about it.
>
> (Eagleton, 1983: 11)

What is clear is that questions about the canon are not only questions about English literature. They also raise social and political issues about language and art, and about cultural and national identity. For instance, how do individual works achieve greatness, and who decides which literature is worth preserving? Who and what get left out of the limited field we criticise and theorise about? Will the English literary heritage as we think of it now still be a relevant standard of excellence in the increasingly globalised, multimodal community of the twenty-first century? In this chapter, I shall argue that the history of the English literature canon is closely intertwined with the history of standard English, and with the development of English cultural and national identity in ways that are becoming particularly controversial at the turn of the century. I shall look at how the traditional English literature canon has been challenged by writers from former British colonial countries, feminists, and new theories about communication and reading, and finally suggest some important questions for the future.

The history of the English literature canon

First, where does the idea of a 'canon' come from? In ancient Greece the word 'Kanon' meant literally 'any straight rod or bar', with the associated notion of a standard of measurement. As early as 454 BC, Polycletus' 'Kanon' set out a series of standards for the representation of the human body in art, which were used by sculptors as an authoritative guide for several hundred years. The idea of a canon of divinely inspired texts was established in early Christianity (after considerable argument and controversy), and this canon also included rules for religious observances, and linked the Christian community together through shared beliefs and practices (Gorak, 1991). There is evidence that literary texts were connected from the earliest times with cultural identity and the spirit of nationalism. Virgil's *Aeneid*, for example, was part of a larger literary development that was a deliberate attempt to create a Roman national literature to rival the classical Greek tradition (Zetzel, 1983). So how do all these meanings and associations of the canon – the notion of a standard, a set of inspired authorities, associated practices and teaching, and the defining of a community with a common cultural identity and shared past, apply to the development of the English literature canon?

Although the English literary heritage is presented as if it has always been there, the idea of literature in the twentieth-century sense (poems, plays and novels), only emerged in the nineteenth century. Before then, the term 'literature', adapted from the French in the fourteenth century, meant polite learning, and included a wide range of learned texts from across the arts and sciences. Indeed, late nineteenth-century lists of 'Great works of English literature' still contained the Bible and names such as Francis Bacon, Isaac Newton, Adam Smith, Edmund Burke and Thomas Macaulay. The term 'canon' is still sometimes used today to refer to this kind of wider collection of learned texts, and often includes works from the classical literature of Greece and Rome.

Our contemporary notion of a literature canon of imaginative writing is a subset of this older notion of a broader literary heritage. Over the first half of the twentieth century, English as a subject moved to a central position within the humanities. I shall explain in more detail below how the canon used in English literature teaching today was largely constructed in the 1930s, together with an approach to literary criticism, which still dominates the curriculum.

While the English literature canon is in this sense not very old, neither is it exclusively English. From the earliest times, authors of English literature have drawn on ideas for the content and style of their work from sources outside Britain. In the late fourteenth century, Chaucer, often seen as the father of English literature, used material from French and Italian sources, and, in the fifteenth and sixteenth centuries, authors in England, as in other parts of Europe, looked back for inspiration to the classical scholars of Greece and Rome. More recently, in the early twentieth century, modernist writers like T. S. Eliot (an American), James Joyce (an Irishman), and Joseph Conrad (a Polish emigré) were strongly influenced by French poets and novelists. Yet their work has been appropriated into a canon that is still seen as essentially 'English'.

As well as representing a wide range of cultural influences, the canon also includes works with diverse literary styles. Many texts now seen as canonical were rebellious and iconoclastic in their own day. For example, in 1798, Wordsworth's celebration of the rustic life of ordinary people in his *Lyrical Ballads*, and his idea that 'a poet must express himself as other men express themselves' were seen as highly unconventional in relation to 'polite learning'. John Clare, also writing in the first half of the nineteenth century, was asked by his publisher to change the local dialect he used in his poetry to a more correct form of the then-emerging standard English. He retorted 'grammar in learning is like tyranny in government – confound the bitch I'll never be her slave'. And at the beginning of the twentieth century, the modernist writers' experimental uses of imagery, symbolism and narrative style were part of a broader European reaction against the realism and naturalism that had dominated literary style in the nineteenth century.

English undefiled

Having established that the canon is neither purely English, nor uncontentious, how then did it achieve its present status? One of the earliest records of a writer's work being promoted as a standard of excellence is in the fifteenth century, when Caxton selected the first books to print and pronounced Chaucer's writing from the previous century to be 'ornate and fair'. Caxton was not, however, referring to the literary qualities of Chaucer's work in the modern sense, but to his use of the English language. With the invention of printing, 'literature' in its 'polite learning' sense, quickly became closely associated with the printed word, and printed works of literature could be used to provide models of the best English. Thus began the long association between English literature and the emergence and codification of standard English.

During the sixteenth and seventeenth centuries, England, like other states in Europe, was in the process of developing its own language and cultural identity. The crucial issue for English writers and scholars was to establish the authority and pedigree of the language in a country which for three hundred years after 1066 had been ruled by French-speaking monarchs, and which took its learned literature from Greece and Rome. Greek and Latin were still seen as the highest ideal, but between 1500 and 1700, English authors added over 30,000 new words to the language, often from Latin sources, to make it more 'eloquent'. The mid-sixteenth to mid-seventeenth century saw a flowering of English writing in the work of many subsequently canonical authors, including Edmund Spenser, Sir Philip Sidney, Francis Bacon, Christopher Marlowe, William Shakespeare, John Donne, Ben Jonson, Robert Herrick, John Milton, Samuel Butler and Andrew Marvell. The publishing of The King James Version of the English Bible in 1611 and Shakespeare's plays in 1623 were high points for both the English language and English literature, and knitted language, literature, Christianity and national identity more closely together. Even at this time, there was a sense of looking back for 'purer' uses of English, along with some reaction against the new Latinate vocabulary. Spenser, a poet, referred to Chaucer as 'the well of English undefiled'; and the translators of the 1611 Bible chose to use a style of English from a few hundred years previously, with fewer French and Latin terms. Difficult Latinate words were referred to in a derogatory way as 'inkhorne terms', and a manual for poets by Puttenham in 1599 advised against their usage.

While the eloquence of English had now been proved, there was still a need to 'fix' the language and to protect it, like the nation, against barbarism and degeneration. In compiling the first comprehensive English dictionary (published 1755), Samuel Johnson famously pronounced: 'tongues, like governments, have a natural tendency to degenerate: we have long preserved our constitution, let us make some struggles for our language'. For standards of good English usage, he turned to English literature, looking backwards as others had done before: 'I have studiously endeavoured to collect examples and authorities from the writers before the restoration, whose works I regard as "the wells of English undefiled", as the pure forces of genuine diction ... From the authors which rose in the time of Elizabeth, a speech might be formed adequate to all the purposes of use and elegance. If the language of theology were extracted from Hooker and the translation of the Bible; the terms of natural knowledge from Bacon; the phrases of policy, war and navigation from Raleigh; the dialect of poetry and fiction from Spenser and Sidney; and the diction of common life from Shakespeare, few ideas would be lost to mankind, for want of English words, in which they might be expressed' (quoted in Leith and Graddol, 1996: 159). Johnson did not go any further back than Sidney to look for his 'wells of English undefiled', as older varieties would have been too different from the contemporary usage.

Romanticism and reform

Up until the eighteenth century, then, literary works in English were praised and promoted not so much for their creative qualities as for what was seen as an eloquent and correct use of the national language. By the late eighteenth century, however, the influence of European Romanticism was beginning to shift the meaning of literature towards the more specialised modern concept of imaginative and creative writing with an emphasis on 'sincerity', 'intensity' and 'organic unity'. At this time, the idea of a more imaginative national literature became increasingly important to the unity and cultural identity of individual European states. In England, the nineteenth century was a period of researching and publishing texts from the literary past, alongside a growing national consciousness and profound social change. As the British Empire expanded and Britain became the most powerful nation in Europe, industrialisation brought the emergence of new middle classes, and developing scientific knowledge undermined the religious institutions that had bolstered up the old social order. Between 1750 and 1850 the British population grew from six and a half million to 18 million, and the Reform Bill in 1867 nearly doubled the electorate, giving the vote to working men in towns. The 1870 Education Act for the first time introduced compulsory elementary education in Britain, and by the end of the nineteenth century, with mass secondary education and the provision of academic places for women, a different base for the curriculum was needed to replace the traditional élitist foundation of Greek and Roman classics.

The promotion of English literature, as a basis for education that would provide the spiritual guidance formerly associated with religion and draw the nation together, is closely associated with the ideas of Matthew Arnold, the Victorian poet, critic and school inspector. For Arnold, literature (which he saw mainly as poetry), offered 'the best knowledge and thought of the time, and a true source, therefore, of sweetness and light' (quoted in Trilling, 1982: 271). Arnold identified key writers in English and the classics, whom he believed set the standards for all other writing, and he identified 'touchstone' passages in the poetry of Homer, Dante, Shakespeare and Milton to exemplify the highest forms of literary and moral expression. This weaving together of Romanticism, religion and national unity shaped the beginnings of literature study in British schools, and, together with older ideas about polite learning and eloquent uses of English, laid the foundations for the development of the English literature canon in the twentieth century.

For centuries the classics had been seen as central to training the intelligence and sensibility of the English upper classes, and arguments to establish English as a respectable school subject during the early years of the twentieth century were couched very much in terms of proclaiming its equal value with Greek and Latin, and its greater suitability for a general, national education. The work of the English Association, formed in 1907, culminated in the Newbolt Report (Board of Education, 1921). This set English teaching at the heart of a national educational strategy for cultural renewal after World War II, presented an argument for its serious study at university level, and set out recommendations for the training of English teachers. The Newbolt Report, like Matthew Arnold, saw literature as 'an embodiment of the best thoughts of the best minds', 'a great source of pride', and 'a bond of national unity', invoking a golden Elizabethan age. It developed further the notion of a specifically English literature, which ranked 'among the two or three greatest in the world'. Although classical and European influences were acknowledged, these had been absorbed into 'a stream native to our own soil'. Elementary pupils should learn to appreciate the grandeur of the national language and literature (thus acquiring standard English), while, in secondary education, English literature should be used to fire the imagination and inculcate superior moral values.

The Leavisites

During the 1920s and 1930s, the position of English at university level was strengthened, producing the first graduate English teachers, and the subject was finally consolidated and codified (and, some would argue, masculinised), through the work of a group of Cambridge critics in the 1930s, which included F. R. Leavis, T. S. Eliot and I. A. Richards. The Leavisites came from strongly middle-class backgrounds, and it has been suggested that their canon and practical criticism established not only an essential and continuous Englishness in literature, from Anglo-Saxon poetry to modern novel, but also a charter and sense of function for middle-class professionals at school and university (Doyle, 1989).

The Leavisites, like Arnold, saw literature as a way of saving England from the pernicious influences of industrialisation and secularisation. They took up the idea of great literature as timeless, humanising and morally uplifting, and looked back to a golden age of English pastoralism and linguistic purity. Their most significant contributions to the development of the subject were their establishment of a canon that has influenced syllabuses ever since, and a form of literary criticism that has become the chief method for studying literature in school and university. Leavis argued that only a small cultural minority was capable of making literary judgements, and that they had the responsibility for ensuring the survival of the finest human experience of the past, and for maintaining the purity of the language. The greatest literature displayed a combination of moral, aesthetic and 'English' qualities that recalled the lost golden age of an organic, rural Utopia. Truly 'English' English was classically demonstrated in Shakespeare's work, in writers like Donne, who embodied its 'sinew and living nerve', and in Wordsworth, whose poetry demonstrated an eighteenth-century English rural 'social–moral centrality'. Milton, on the other hand, was seen as too Latinate, and Shelley as not concrete enough. In *The Great Tradition* (1948), Leavis produced a canon and a critical discourse for the novel, a genre that until then had held a rather tenuous place in the literary heritage, in comparison with poetry and drama. *The Great Tradition* opens: 'The great English novelists are Jane Austen, George Eliot, Henry James and Joseph Conrad – to stop for a moment at that comparatively safe point in history'.

Eagleton describes the Leavisite construction of an English literature canon through their journal *Scrutiny*:

> With breathtaking boldness, *Scrutiny* redrew the map of English literature in ways from which criticism has never quite recovered. The main thoroughfares on this map ran through Chaucer, Shakespeare, Jonson, the Jacobeans and Metaphysicals, Bunyan, Pope, Samuel Johnson, Blake, Wordsworth, Keats, Austen, George Eliot, Hopkins, Henry James, Joseph Conrad, T. S. Eliot and D. H. Lawrence. This *was* English literature; Spenser, Dryden, Restoration drama, Defoe, Fielding, Richardson, Sterne, Shelley, Byron, Tennyson, Browning, most of the Victorian novelists, Joyce, Woolf and most writers after D. H. Lawrence constituted a network of 'B' roads interspersed with a good few cul-de-sacs. Dickens was first 'out' and then 'in': 'English' included two and a half women, counting Emily Brontë as a marginal case; almost all of its authors were conservatives.
>
> (Eagleton 1983: 32–3)

Leavisite 'close reading' and 'practical criticism' treats literary texts as independent, self-contained objects, with a fixed meaning and literary essence waiting to be discovered by the skilful reader. The Leavisite critics' approach to analysing language and style, in order to extract explicit and implied meanings, and their expectation that readers should engage with themes and ideas to develop an informed response and extend their moral and emotional understanding, have become consolidated in the examination system for schools and universities, and are repeated in the 1995 National Curriculum for English. In many ways studying English at secondary school and university since Leavis has meant learning to be a critic, and learning how to produce criticisms, along Leavisite lines. His decontextualised approach to 'great works' is echoed in the alphabetically arranged lists of names in the 1995 National Curriculum, which give no indication of a historical, or any other relationship, between the various authors' work. It has been argued that this individualistic approach to authors leads to the promotion of those who conform to a particular ideal of the writer, and can most easily be studied in a decontextualised way. For instance, Wordsworth the genteel Romantic recluse now occupies a much more prominent place in the canon than does his contemporary Southey, with his common provincial background and international orientation. Southey was more highly respected when they were both alive, but his work and influence are more difficult to appreciate today without a knowledge of his links with other early nineteenth-century writers in Britain and Europe (Butler, 1987).

Challenges

Leavisite élitism ruled out of discussion whole areas of popular culture and radical art. It has been criticised for elevating writing produced by and about a particular Anglo-Saxon class and gender, so that the 'universal meanings' it embodies are only universal for those who define the world from that perspective. Other people are not only under-represented as authors in the canon, but have to read about themselves and their experience as constructed by authoritative others. Raymond Williams (1973) pointed out the narrow exclusiveness of Leavis's definition of 'culture', and argued that a truly popular culture representing the voices and interests of the working class should be supported and valued. Critics have complained that people from cultures outside Britain are presented in the Leavisite canonical texts (if at all) as alien and inferior, women are represented as the objects of male desire and defined in their relation to men, and the working classes are depicted as pitiful or quaint. The existence of this canon as a whole may be experienced as a form of oppression, and a denial of everyday personal experience.

Colonialism and the canon

Some writers from former British colonial countries, particularly the first generation of those writing in English, have found the canon alien in terms of its subject matter, the history it invokes, and the forms and styles of language used in high literature. Brathwaite (1981), the Caribbean poet and critic, pointed out that the English literature of Shakespeare, Austen and Eliot taught in Caribbean schools had very little to do with the pupils' life, or with Caribbean culture and history. The South African critic, Nkosi, argued that T. S. Eliot's cold, abstract pessimism seemed very foreign to the optimistic humanism of African experience: 'We live on a substitute culture borrowed from other lands' (Nkosi, 1965: 120). He objected to 'white academicians dealing with African art and literature who find it convenient to judge African works of art entirely by European canons of description' (Nkosi, 1965: 49). Some writers have suggested reshaping the use of English to reflect their own traditions more accurately. For the Nigerian novelist, Achebe, the English of African writers could be 'a new voice coming out of Africa, speaking of African experience in a world-wide language' (Achebe, 1965: 29). Wole Soyinka, the Nigerian playwright, describes how he draws on African forms:

> African drama is sophisticated in idiom. Our forms of theatre are quite different from literary drama. We use spontaneous dialogue, folk music, simple stories and relevant dances to express what we mean. Our theatre uses stylised forms as its basic accepted disciplines. I am trying to integrate these forms into the drama of the English language.
>
> (Soyinka, quoted in Nkosi, 1965: 108)

Others have suggested changing the form of English itself: for Brathwaite, Caribbean experience and its brutal, disrupted history could be better expressed through a variety of English or 'nation language' that drew on African syntax; replaced the rhythm of the pentameter with the dactyls of the calypso; and was performed in what Brathwaite calls a 'total expression' in which the oral music of words and audience involvement are an intrinsic part of the poetry. There remained for him the problem of the oblique relationship between the Caribbean poets' true feelings and their use of English, however much they creolised it, and this ambivalence towards the English language is echoed by Rao, an Indian novelist:

> The telling has not been easy. One has to convey in a language that is not one's own the spirit that is one's own. One has to convey the various shades and omissions of a certain thought movement that looks maltreated in an alien language. I use the word 'alien' yet English is not really an alien language to us. It is the language of our intellectual make-up – like Sanskrit or Persian was before – but not of our emotional make-up.
>
> (Rao, 1938: vii)

For some writers, English is hopelessly contaminated as the language of imperialism, racism and Western associations of cultural superiority. In 1981, the Kenyan author, Ngugi wa Thiong'o (1981) explained that for these reasons he was going to stop writing in English, and would from that point on use either Gikuyu, his first language, or Kiswahili, the Kenyan national language.

If English has been seen as an instrument of colonial oppression, so too has the canon. Viswanathan (1990), a literary historian, explains that when the 1935 English Education Act prescribed English literature teaching in India, it was feared that exposure to the wrong kind of Western literature might encourage thoughts of freedom and independence. The colonial administration selected a canon of particular texts for the English literature curriculum, to implicitly convey the Christian values of the Missionary Societies and produce docile and obedient subjects, thus safeguarding British commercial interests. Shakespeare was argued to contain 'sound Protestant Bible principles', Addison's *Spectator* papers included the 'strain of serious piety', Bacon and Locke displayed a 'scriptural morality' and Adam Smith's work taught 'noble Christian sentiments'. As in Victorian England – where Arnold hoped literature would take religion's place and calm the rebellious spirit of the working classes – English literature in India was seen as standing in for Christianity to produce compliant colonial subjects.

Since the Heinemann African Writers series in the early 1960s first made the writing of Chinua Achebe, Peter Abrahams and James Ngugi wa Thiong'o generally available in England, authors, poets and dramatists from Africa, India, the Caribbean and other English-speaking parts of the world have become widely read. Today, writers like Achebe, Abrahams, Ngugi, Narayan, Naipaul, Walcott, Nichols and Soyinka are accepted as great writers across the English-speaking world, and carry off prestigious literary awards. A second generation of writers has also emerged, for example Salman Rushdie, Ben Okri and Toni Morrison, and many would argue that the most important literature in English at the end of the twentieth century is being produced by writers at the margins, or outside, the traditional English cultural centre. Different histories in India,

Africa and the Caribbean have produced different readings of the English literature canon, and new kinds of writing. The experience and work of these writers challenge the way that the canon has been constructed and used, the privileging of the printed word and a particular set of genres and the cultural hegemony of the stories the canon contains. The existence of these different voices and perspectives is briefly acknowledged in the 1995 National Curriculum, not in the canonical lists, but in a broad requirement to read 'texts from other cultures' under the more general preceding comments. Thus these texts and authors are separated off from what is presented as the heart of English literature, and their problematic relationship with the canon is not addressed.

Feminist challenges

The canon has also been challenged by feminists for its privileging of a particular kind of gendered writing and experience. The lists of authors in the 1995 National Curriculum contain fifty-two men and nine women, seven of whom are primarily novelists. Are women under-represented because they write less well than men, or do they have less opportunity to get their work published? Is there something about the process of canonisation that excludes women's writing? Historical reasons to some extent account for the lack of canonical texts by women in the areas of poetry and drama. Poetry, with its particularly privileged and prestigious position within the canon, was traditionally closely connected to the Greek and Roman classics taught to boys at public school and university, where girls were not admitted until the end of the nineteenth century. Major women poets are difficult to find, and are often associated with a male poet, for example Elizabeth Barrett Browning with Robert Browning and Sylvia Plath with Ted Hughes. In the area of drama, women writers are even rarer. As part of the public commercial world, theatres in past centuries were not considered appropriate places for respectable women to work, either as actresses or dramatists. The dramatist Aphra Behn (1640–89) achieved notoriety rather than respect during her lifetime, and is only now being taken seriously as an important writer. Two out of three of the main canonical literary genres, then, have until recently remained virtually inaccessible to women. Novel writing, which did not depend on a classical education or access to public institutions, was the one area where women did begin to make their voices heard; but even here they often used male pseudonyms in order to get published. For example, Charlotte Brontë wrote as Currer Bell and Mary Evans as George Eliot. The less prestigious private genres of diary and letter writing, which are more commonly used by women, do not usually fall within the boundaries of imaginative writing, and, with a few exceptions (for example Samuel Pepys and Anne Frank) have not become part of public literature.

In the past then, women have had restricted access to education and to the public world with its theatres and publishers, and male publishers and critics have been unwilling to take their writing seriously. Women's writing still counts for less than 9% of the contents of contemporary British and US literature and poetry anthologies, which are almost all edited by men, and reviews of books by women, or reviews by women critics, seldom make the front pages of literary magazines (Morris, 1993). Feminists claim that women still find it hard to break into the literary world because those in positions of power are largely men, and male perspectives and values dominate the way in which books, plays and poems are read and evaluated. Particularly masculine-centred readings have been dubbed 'phallic criticism' by feminist critics like Elaine Showalter, who provides the following example from the critic Irving Howe, on the opening scene of Thomas Hardy's *The Mayor of Casterbridge*, when the hero sells his wife and daughter at a country fair. Showalter argues that Howe not only ignores the response of women readers, but also distorts Hardy's text:

> To shake loose from one's wife; to discard that drooping rag of a woman, with her mute complaints and maddening passivity; to escape not by a slinking abandonment but through the public sale of her body to a stranger, as horses are sold at a fair; and thus to wrest, through sheer amoral wilfulness, a second chance out of life – it is with this stroke, so insidiously attractive to male fantasy, that *The Mayor of Casterbridge* begins.
>
> (quoted in Showalter, 1986: 129)

Male dominance of the canon has been challenged by feminists through re-readings of texts, criticism and history, and by the increasing circulation and promotion of women's writing through publishing initiatives and university courses. But women's work has not yet achieved a central, established position within the institutional network of publishing, reviewing, marketing, advertising and teaching, which has been developed around the canon.

Shifting models of communication

Feminist and post-colonial readings and writings have called into question the Leavisite canon's assumptions of cultural and moral excellence, its view of literature and its promotion of particular ways of reading. Their arguments about the importance of readings 'against the text', reflect a more general shift in ideas about communication, which has been occurring over the last thirty years, alongside widespread questioning of established notions of culture, value and tradition. In broad terms, there has been a general move away from the transmission model of communication, which is based on the idea that an individual's thoughts are transmitted, via the conduit of language, to an audience. In this model, texts are coherent and complete, containing a specific meaning and a special literary essence that can be discovered and appreciated by the reader through authorised critical methods. This transmission model has been called into question by post-structuralist theories about communication and reading, which suggest that meaning is more open and provisional, because there can always be new interpretations. Possible meanings of texts are related to wider discourses connected with institutionalised practices (for example, schooling, literary criticism, film tradition), and to the reader or viewer's own changing life experience. In this sense, a text is shaped by the writer's dialogues with other writers and texts, and by factors in the historical and cultural context in which it is written. Furthermore, its meaning and significance is constructed not so much by the author, as through its readings.

The location of meaning in readings rather than texts problematised the notion of a text as an independent entity and, therefore, the idea of a canon as a collection of great works. In addition, the proliferation of different media within American and British popular culture in the 1960s and 1970s suggested different ways of reading that could not be encompassed within traditional conceptions of print literacy or literary criticism. Critics argued that the increasing importance of the spoken word in radio, television, film and popular music for all social classes in contemporary cultural life was undermining the authority of printed texts and 'unmaking notions of canonicity on a daily basis' (MacCabe, 1987: 6). The focus of English studies should therefore no longer be a set of canonical texts tied to the printed word, élitist critical practices and a 'mystic national identity', but should instead be reconstituted as 'Cultural Studies', focused more broadly on the questions and problems posed by contemporary culture and supported by a variety of contemporary media resources as well as by relevant classic texts. As time changed, so would the questions, and fresh questions would generate new reading lists. This shifting of the focus away from canonical printed texts and on to contemporary issues was echoed in a number of educational initiatives in the United States in the 1980s. In 1988, Stanford University replaced its undergraduate programme in 'Western Culture' with a new course called 'Cultures, ideas and values'. It was felt that thus would more accurately reflect the range of cultural identities within the United States, and the histories of its successive waves of immigrants from Europe, Africa, Asia and Latin America. Rather than setting up an alternative canon, it was seen as more important to find ways of looking at a common set of problems. Changes like the Stanford University curriculum were interpreted by conservative educationalists in the United States as a move to dismantle the authority of the traditional canon, and replace it with cultural pluralism and 'political correctness'. A backlash has reasserted the importance of European and Anglo-American 'cultural literacy' (Hirsch Jr, 1987) and advocated a return to the 'great books' (Bloom, 1995).

What of the future?

Behind the list of texts in the 1995 National Curriculum for English lies a complex history about the cultural functions of canons, and the particular factors that have affected the development of literature in English. The history of the English literature canon has been closely related to the history of the standardisation of English, and to the emergence and consolidation of English national and cultural identity. I have shown how this canon has been challenged by writers whose perspectives and experience are devalued or excluded, and who suggest alternative kinds of language art, and ways of reading and writing. The privileging of the printed word and the existence of a canon at all have been called into question by new theories about language, the development of different media, and changing ideas about cultural identity. What, then, is the future of the English literature canon in the twenty-first century?

There are a number of reasons why the close intertwining of language, literature and nation in the canon becomes problematical at the turn of the century. The first concerns the relationship between the canon and standard English. During the sixteenth and seventeenth centuries, English developed as the language of an autonomous state, and during the eighteenth century, its standardisation was closely associated with the literature believed to exemplify eloquent and correct use. The close relationship between standard English and 'great texts' is constantly reiterated, from Johnson's turning to literature in order to compile his dictionary, to Newbolt's belief that standard English should be inculcated in children through their study of English literature. The importance of English today, however, is increasingly that of a world language, spoken by people who have a wide range of different histories and cultural allegiances. Many of these will have first encountered English as a world language not through its literary heritage, but through the global dissemination of American popular culture. There are currently estimated to be 370 million speakers of English as a first language, 375 million speakers of English as a second language, and 750 million speakers of English as a foreign language (Graddol, 1997). Trends in language shift suggest that the largest group of English speakers in the next century will be those using it as an additional language. There are already a number of different standard Englishes in various parts of the world, as well as many local varieties, and the global future of the language will be shaped by its increasing use as a second language for international communication in new genres on the Internet and elsewhere. English will continue to change and develop as a language, but the most significant changes will probably happen in areas of language use for which the national literature may no longer be a relevant standard.

The second issue concerns the relationship between the canon and technology. The invention of printing was crucial for the codification and standardisation of the language and for the related development of English literature. Print literacy became the linchpin of educational practice. How far will new developments in computer-mediated communication undermine the prestige and authority of canonical printed texts? Teaching the literary heritage today involves considerably more use of audiovisual media than thirty years ago, when most teachers and pupils relied exclusively on print. Print is still a central reference point in literature teaching, but in other areas its role as the primary source of authoritative knowledge is being challenged, for example through the more extensive use of images in information texts. Tools to create visual texts and disseminate them globally are increasingly available, and words, typology and pictures are now woven together to form multimodal texts (Goodman and

Graddol, 1996). The canon has already been criticised for being too wedded to the printed word and to particular conceptions of critical reading, both by critics coming from cultures with a strong oral tradition, and from the point of view of cultural studies. New technologies have created an additional and perhaps more fundamental challenge, and it remains to be seen how canonical processes will translate into the new media genres and literacies of the twenty-first century.

The third problematic relationship is between the English canon and cultural identity. In its Elizabethan heyday, England was an emerging nation with a blossoming literature in the developing national tongue. In the nineteenth century, when Britain stood at the head of a vast colonial empire and led Europe's technological development, a literary heritage was constructed to celebrate the language and cultural identity of a mighty nation. Since World War II, however, Britain has declined as a world power, and the spread of English has had more to do with the influence of the United States, which has taken over Britain's former political and economic leadership. During this period, there has been an outpouring of literature from countries that were formerly part of the British Empire, and much of the most highly respected literary writing in English at the end of the twentieth century has come from outside the United Kingdom. This writing, however, has a problematic relationship with the cultural values and perspectives that are encoded in the traditional English literature canon, and with its orientation towards an idealised national past closely tied up with an inward looking English cultural identity. The cultural allegiances and identities expressed through new literature in English are redefining its points of reference. It is not clear how relevant the English literature canon, as represented in the National Curriculum, will be to English speakers inside or outside Britain in the shifting cultural landscape of the early twenty-first century.

There is an inherent tension in the canon between the notion of inspired works and operation of the institutions like education, publishing and literary criticism that are built up around the canon and that tend to reinforce centralised authority and regulate how texts are read and used. In the past, the canon has been used to proclaim cultural and national unity, but it has operated through principles of exclusion, which confirm the very divisions that it claims to heal. In this sense, canons may always contain the seeds of their own destruction. It has been suggested that in the struggle between cultural transmission and cultural change, each new generation kicks against some aspect of the canon, particularly at times of social turbulence when dominant ideologies and assumptions are being more generally questioned. In the struggle between different political, economic and political forces at the turn of the century, when rapidly developing technologies are opening up possibilities for new kinds of texts and identities, questions about the future of the English literature canon are part of wider debates about language, literature and culture and technology. These will become increasingly important for students of English in the twenty-first century.

Questions for discussion

1   What works should be included in an English literature canon for students in the early twenty-first century? How would the selection of texts be justified?
2   How far should the English literary heritage represented in the National Curriculum be treated as independent from its history?
3   Is the argument that the canon is exclusive and oppressive a convincing one? Are there ways in which it could be made more open?
4   Does the idea of a literature canon have to be tied to print literacy?

Note

1   Parts of this chapter draw on J. Maybin (1996) 'An English canon?', in J. Maybin and N. Mercer (eds) *Using English: from Conversation to Canon*, London: Routledge.

Further reading

Cox, B. (1995) *The Battle for the English Curriculum*, London: Hodder and Stoughton.
This is a very readable commentary on the controversies surrounding changes in the National Curriculum for English, between the publication of the Cox Report in 1989 and the Revised Orders in 1995. Cox explains the context in which the 1995 lists of authors are provided, makes a number of points about the use of the canon, and criticises its 'Little England' mentality.

Fiedler, L. A. and Baker, J. R. (eds) (1981) *English Literature: Opening Up the Canon*, Baltimore, Maryland and London: Johns Hopkins University Press.
This book was an important landmark in debates about the canon during the 1980s. Its contributors attacked what they saw as the conservatism, sexism and racism of the contemporary English literary establishment, arguing that it should be transformed in the light of the increasing importance of English as a world language, and in the cause of social justice.

Gorak, J. (1991) *The Making of the Modern Canon: Genesis and Crisis of a Literary Idea*, London: Athlone Press.
This is a scholarly and erudite account of the histories of canons in literature and in cultural life more generally. Gorak reviews the major critical work, which has produced and attacked literature canons, taking the position that they will continue to be an important way of organising art and history in the future.

Graddol, D., Leith, D. and Swann, J. (eds) (1996) *English: History, Diversity and Change*, London: Routledge.
This book traces the spread of English throughout the British Isles and into different parts of the world, and provides the main source for my discussion of the early history of English literature. Many of the issues that it raises about English as a language are also relevant to the development of literature, and the canon.

Knight, R. (1996) *Valuing English: Reflections on the National Curriculum*, London: David Fulton.

Knight reviews the recent history of National Curriculum English at secondary level, from the point of view of a belief in the centrality of literature to all aspects of English teaching. He argues strongly for the imaginative and moral importance of literature, and attacks the 'barbarism' of social theorists like Eagleton.

13 How should critical theory inform English teaching?

John Moss

Introduction

For the purposes of this chapter, critical theory will be described as a set of perspectives on, or configurations of, relationships among writer(s), text(s) and reader(s), which may or may not take account of: aspects of the context(s) of those relationships; the significance of other texts to them; and the systems within which readings are produced (see Figure 13.1).

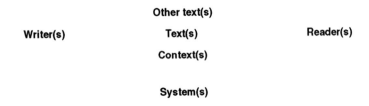

Figure 13.1   Elements contributing to the meaning(s) of reading(s)

Individual theories, or perspectives on this set of relationships, may pay most attention to one or more of the following areas:

1   choices of text, and how one text relates to another;
2   writers: who they are and what they do;
3   texts, and how they work;
4   readers: who they are and what they do;
5   the social, historical and cultural contexts in which texts are produced and received;
6   the systems in the operation of which the location of the authority for meaning is determined.

The emphasis that a theory places on one or more of these areas tends to be related to the author's view of the location of an authority for meaning, and whether that lies primarily in:

- tradition and culture;
- the writer's intention or psychology;
- the meaning inherent in the text or that can be derived from its procedures;
- the process of reading as it represents the text or the reader's identity; or
- the influence of social and historical factors on the areas that writing and reading practices include or omit.

This chapter needs a means of grouping theories for the purpose of discussing how different types of theory should inform the English curriculum. In Figure 13.2, the place where a theory primarily locates its authority for meaning has been used as the criterion to construct a rough taxonomy of theory types.

Such a taxonomy needs to be treated with caution for several reasons. No individual theory locates the authority for meaning wholly within one particular area of attention dealt with by critical theory. Individual theorists often make use of the resources of several theoretical positions, and range across the areas of attention. In addition, some critical theories make use of strategies taken or adapted from the work of others. Moreover, there is not the scope in this chapter to offer even simplified definitions of the theoretical positions listed here, let alone to justify the allocation of theories to the areas of attention that are proposed. However, the terms included in Figure 13.2 can all be investigated easily, using as recommended starting points either Culler (1997) or Baldick (1990), which are respectively, a short introduction to literary theory, and a dictionary of literary terms.

Other texts
Canonicity ...
... Intertexuality

Writer(s)
Authorial Intention
Psychoanalysis

Text(s)
Formalism
New Criticism
Structuralism/Semiotics
Linguistics/Stylistics
Narratology
Poetics

Reader(s)
Phenomenology
Reader–Response
Psychoanalysis
Hermeneutics

Context(s)
New Historicism
Marxism/Cultural Materialism
Post-Colonialism
Feminism
Queer Theory
Minority Discourse

Systems
Deconstruction
Post-structuralism/Post-modernism

Figure 13.2   Taxonomy of types of critical theory (according to the primary location of the authority for meaning)

Nevertheless, the contest over the location of an authority for meaning in critical theory is real. It is, moreover, echoed in the long-standing contest over rationales for the English curriculum and the teaching of English. These competing rationales have been defined and discussed in many places, including by Moss (1998). Broadly speaking, the proponents of a 'cultural heritage' view of English locate primary authority for meaning in tradition and/or the individual writer, whereas adherents of English as 'personal growth' stress the significance of the reader, while those who engage in 'cultural analysis' emphasise the significance of social and historical contexts. A text will be analysed in different ways, using a particular set of critical tools, by the theorists in each of these three traditions.

It is noticeable that the taxonomy proposed suggests that little current theory privileges the author or tradition as the location of meaning. The proponents of 'cultural analysis' have routed the theoretical positions that were used to promote the 'cultural heritage' view of English. The notion that English should transmit a canon of texts has been undermined by questions about the cultural determination of canonicity, and also by the recognition that, for real readers, a multiplicity of intertextual references, uncensored by canonical exclusiveness, is triggered in the act of reading. Similarly, the notion of the single authoritative writer, the producer of a single text, has been challenged by numerous critical approaches, which deny the simplicity or single-mindedness of either writer or text. These include New Historicist approaches, which focus on disjunctions in the culture in which a text was produced, and textual investigations of drafting, which point at shifting authorial meanings. Consequently, although *English in the National Curriculum* (1995), SATs, GCSE requirements and the A-Level English Literature Core have left the idea that at least one primary location of an authority for meaning is the traditional canon, which remains embedded in the curriculum, it is clear that critical theory has provided the tools both to interrogate canons and to demonstrate how intertextuality applies in reading processes.

This chapter is concerned with investigating the contest over the location of an authority for meaning that takes place among those theories that give primacy to the reader (and often with a 'personal growth' pedagogy), and those which give it to the social, cultural and historical contexts of reading and writing (and often with a 'cultural analysis' pedagogy). It will make reference to theories that give primacy to the text, and the contest for control of the text between theories that give primacy respectively to the reader and to the context.

Its questions are: what are the implications for English teaching of theories that locate authority for meaning in:

- the reader;
- the social, historical and cultural contexts in which texts are produced and received;
- the text itself?

Theories locating authority for meaning in the reader

Reader-response theory

> We have to decide how to balance the power of the writer with the power of the reader as part of teaching literacy in school.
>
> (Meek, 1991: 65)

The focus of reader-response theory on readers and the act of reading makes its significance for pedagogy particularly apparent. Numerous writers in recent years (for example: Benton *et al.* (1988), Dias and Hayhoe (1988), Hayhoe and Parker (1990), Martin and Leather (1994) and Protherough (1983)), have proposed models and strategies for teaching texts in either the primary school, the secondary school, or both, which are based on the insights of reader-response theorists such as Fish, Iser, and, most frequently, Rosenblatt.

While reader-response theories share a common emphasis on the reader as the primary location of meaning in the writer–text–reader relationship, individual theorists continue to offer accounts of this relationship that 'balance the power of the writer with the power of the reader' in different ways, as historical accounts show (Tompkins, 1980). The response of educators to this problem is sometimes to suggest that one theorist offers the best formulation of the text–reader relationship. For example, Benton *et al.* (1988: 13) recommends Rosenblatt's 'transactional theory' (Rosenblatt, 1978: 151) and her concept of 'recreative reading', as offering a 'sense of how best to define and develop response to literature in such a way that neither text nor reader is "over-privileged" '.

However, a key statement by Rosenblatt, which Benton *et al.* (1988: 15) regards as 'her clearest formulation about recreative reading', contains evidence of the problems inherent in her 'balanced' position: 'the process of understanding a work implies a re-creation of it, an attempt to grasp completely the structured sensations and concepts through which the author seeks to convey the quality of his sense of life. Each must make a new synthesis of these elements with his own nature, but it is essential that he evoke those components of experience to which the text actually refers' (1970: 113).

The tentative self-expression of an author who '*seeks* to convey' something, and the struggle of a reader making 'an *attempt* to grasp' meaning 'completely', are curious contrasts with the apparently unproblematic question of identifying that 'to which the text *actually refers*', something which it is the teacher's task to determine when, for example, making an assessment of a response. The relationships here are very slippery, which is one reason why so many versions of reader-response theory exist.

However, even if its account of the text–reader relationship could be considered secure, Rosenblatt's statement both mystifies learning processes and attaches value to particular aspects of response in a way that raises difficult questions for both pedagogy and assessment. In relation to learning, the word 'implies' in the observation that 'understanding a work *implies* a re-creation of it', masks a problematic issue about how (subjective?) re-creation can be transformed into the (objective?) understanding, which appears to remain Rosenblatt's ultimate goal. This problem is highlighted by an observation from Margaret Drabble about a favourite poem: 'I don't really know what it means, but I respond to it very strongly' (Martin and Leather, 1994: 15). In relation to assessment, despite Rosenblatt's insistence about what the reader *'must'* do, she does not explain either why this one type of reading is required, and with what authority, or what kind of response to a text – whether this is one that is spoken, written, or a dramatic or multimedia presentation – can demonstrate both the ability to 'grasp completely' what is 'structured' in it *and* 'a new synthesis of these elements with [the reader's] own nature.'

Furthermore, the statement makes no kind of foregrounded reference to the economic, social, cultural and historical contexts of the production and reception of texts. This kind of omission is characteristic of some versions of reader-response theory and can create blind spots for educators in both research and pedagogy. For example, Martin and Leather, whose book uses a metaphor from drug culture to describe the escapism and involvement that they rightly see as essential to reading development ('Before long you are hooked and cannot do without a regular fix' (Martin and Leather, 1994: 7).), prioritise engagement to the exclusion of all other considerations: discussing their decision to use an extract from Blyton in research with pupils, they patronis- ingly dismiss 'adverse criticism about the sexism, classism and every other kind of -ism' in her work as irrelevant because of her power to absorb young readers (*ibid*.: 53). They see *'Extratextuality'* merely as 'the extraneous cultural knowledge assumed by the text' (*ibid*.: 42), which can be packaged and supplied as contextual information for readers. Similarly, Benton's *'flexible methodology'* for poetry teaching pays no further regard to context, other than the provision of 'preliminary information about particular poem(s)/poet(s)' (Benton *et al*., 1988: 205).

The next part of this discussion pursues the contention that while reader- response theories validate a wide range of pedagogical activities, it is important for teachers and, in some circumstances, pupils, not to use and experience these activities as though they are a homogeneous collection representing a single view of the reader–text relationship. Teachers must understand how the strategies that they use characterise that relationship, and why it is appropriate to characterise it in one way at a particular point in the educational experience of their pupils.

Tompkins' (1980) excellent account of the history of reader-response criticism demonstrates its heterogeneity: an examination of some of the tenden- cies that she identifies can be linked to observations concerning both the messages about the text–reader relationship that may be conveyed by particular kinds of pedagogy, and the implications for pupil assessment of each perspective.

Some theorists focus attention on the ways in which texts construct readers. Gibson (1950) for example, 'reveals the strategies the author uses to position his readers with respect to a whole range of values and assumptions he wishes them to accept or reject' (Tompkins, 1980: xi). In a similar way, Prince (1973) makes a telling distinction between the 'narratee', the fictional character to whom a text is explicitly or implicitly addressed, and the 'virtual reader', whom the writer imagines reading the text (Tompkins, 1980: xii). An example of this distinction might be between the absorbed and naïve reader of Ruth Brown's *A Dark, Dark Tale* (1983), who is enticed by its language into increasing fear as the story progresses, and the more sophisticated reader who is, at least on a second reading, alert to its method. A teacher wanting to use this insight could invite pupils to present the different responses of these two constructed readers, one of whom they might identify with more than the other. The method would provide a way of distinguishing between 're-enactment' and 'understanding', which could allow teachers to explore, with a class, the functions of both in reading. However, it would also suggest that power is primarily located in the writer's ability to construct readers, just as the teacher using it would retain considerable power over the form and content of the different kinds of pupil response that would be generated.

In the theories of both Poulet (1972) and Holland (1975), intersubjective communication between writer and reader is a major constituent of the reading process (Tompkins, 1980: xiv, xx). However, whereas for the phenomenologist Poulet, the reader's self has to be annihilated to allow communication with the writer to take place, Holland's psychoanalytic methodology sees interpretation as a function of the identity of the reader. Classroom activities derived from these positions would include the promotion of sustained, 'absorbed' reading and empathetic role-play or writing on the one hand, and tasks that encourage the reader to use the text as a stimulus for self-exploration on the other. The connection between the first group of activities and formal, analytical writing might be difficult to achieve, and the last sounds like the kind of 'invitation to fantasise', for which Benton believes that the 'text acts as a regulator' to prevent in worthwhile reading practice (Benton *et al.*, 1988: 15). However, these problems only emerge if the requirement for formal writing is seen as essential to the educational endeavour. Poulet and Holland's ideas suggest that equally valid 'readings', which are no less sophisticated than formal analysis, but in fact more meaningful to the reader, can be achieved through the kinds of activities indicated above. It is also noticeable how much more power they give to the reader than the pedagogy derived from Prince's ideas.

Other reader-response theorists place more emphasis on the process of reading. Both Riffaterre (1966) and Fish (1970) note the significance of predictability and unpredictability, the reader's expectations and their frustration, in the reading process (Tompkins, 1980: xiii, xvi–xvii). For Fish, the meaning associated with reading *is* the experience of decision-making, revision, anticipation, surprise and recovery that readers experience. It is now well known that teachers can draw attention to and develop these experiences using DARTs, and that they can be sustained using reading logs, particularly where pupils' entries are supported by structured questions. Fish's arguments might even suggest that there is little value in translating the insights recorded in work of this kind into a formal essay: the log itself would be a more effective representation of the kinds of understanding that are possible in reading.

Some reader-response theorists have focused on ways in which readers and readings are constructed from outside the text. For Culler (1975), reading is dependent on institutional codes that determine what kind of reading of a text is acceptable. For example, when we read literature he notes that there is a rule of significance and an expectation of metaphorical coherence and thematic unity, from which readings are often constructed (Tompkins, 1980: xvii). Fish (1976) extends this argument when he insists that even commenting on apparently objective features in a text like rhyme is merely an effect of the interpretative strategies that readers have been given by the 'interpretative communities' to which they belong. We all recognise this in the observation that 'there is a lot of illiteration (*sic*) in this poem'. For Michaels (1977), the reading self is itself a text constructed through the interactions of various social and cultural sign systems (Tompkins, 1980: xxiv). The classroom can provide many opportunities for the exploration of these ideas. For example, readings of texts produced by different groups within a class can be a resource for considering the influences on how we read; the criteria for the assessment of public examination work on texts can be compared with the outcomes of work where pupils are given freedom to produce a response of whatever kind is most meaningful to them. These types of meta-reading activities may help pupils to understand the ways in which the different activities and tasks that they are given construct the writer–text–reader relationship. However, they will also point to the ways in which reading and writing are context-determined, and so undermine the idea that reader response can be allowed to operate in the classroom without reference to the insights of theories that primarily locate authority for meaning in those contexts.

The following conclusions can be drawn from this discussion of reader-response theory.

1   Different teaching strategies and classroom activities convey different messages regarding the 'slippery' author–text–reader relationships, about which there is ongoing debate. It follows that teachers need to choose activities designed to promote response with a critical alertness to the implications of their choices for pupils' developing understanding of those relationships.

2   Different reader-response theories promote and justify, at least on their own terms, different kinds of response to texts that pupils can be taught to produce. Rosenblatt's 'balance of power between writer and reader' may be difficult to achieve in a response to a text, and other reader-response theorists question its validity. It follows that a curriculum that is to continue to explore these relationships in ways that may benefit teaching and learning needs both a more open-minded attitude to what is an 'appropriate' response to a text, and more flexible approaches to assessment than those

that are current in the National Curriculum, SATs and other public examinations.

3   The multiplicity of reader-response theories is an effect of the differences between individual writers and readers and in the relationships between them. It follows that any complete theory of reading must pay more attention to the contexts of writing and reading than much reader-response theory does.

A revision of Meek's observation, with which this section began, would be that: we have to learn how to teach pupils about the different ways in which the power of the writer and the power of the reader can be balanced (or unbalanced) as part of teaching literacy in school.

Theories locating authority for meaning in the social, historical and cultural contexts in which texts are produced and received

> The meanings that are generated by the text will depend upon the relationships between the linguistic, narratological, cultural, experiential, ideological and cultural elements of the text and those of the reader.
>
> (Sarland, 1991: 129 [*sic*])

Sarland's *Young People Reading: Culture and Response* (1991) is an important examination of the interface between culture and response in young people's reading. A central finding of his research, which is voiced slightly differently above, is to confirm the findings of Crago and Crago (1983) that readers and texts both have 'ideological and cultural repertoires.' (Sarland, 1991: 131) These repertoires have important implications: a text's repertoire will affect the ability of readers to 'read *with*' or 'read *across* or in spite of' that text. For example, where 'the negotiation of cultural order and disruption ... constitutes a major theme', a book's repertoire is comparable to 'a similar negotiation that adolescents need to make as they grow up' (Sarland, 1991: 78), and this will often both enable them to access it and allow them to experience that access as valuable.

Sarland's conclusions, apart from providing a complex definition of 'response' which is enriched by this cultural perspective (Sarland, 1991: 129), largely focus on drawing out the implications of his findings for the choice of texts in schools, which should, he argues, be decentralised, allowing teachers to use popular literature and texts dealing with controversial issues; and also pedagogy, allowing them to move away from whole-class teaching methods that may not interact with the repertoires of individual pupils (131–3). However, building on these conclusions, it could be noted that one way of defining what the critical theories that locate authority for meaning primarily in context have in common is an insight into the fact that what Marxist criticism calls 'the ideological superstructure', is 'riven with contradiction and conflict, and so thus are the subjects constructed within it,' (Sarland, 1991: 136), a point that Sarland attributes to Belsey (1980). Sarland's case studies would suggest the possibility that adolescent readers could engage with the evidence of contradiction, conflict and disruption to be found in all texts, or in their relationships with the 'superstructure', at least with some appropriate teaching, which sets out to *extend* their cultural and ideological repertoires. This type of teaching could take the form of exposure to the theories that are most concerned with demonstrating the ways in which apparent meanings of texts are disrupted, or can be, by readings that take into account various forms of linguistic, social and economic exclusivity. This is at least part of the agenda that Marxist criticism, post-colonialism, feminism, Queer Theory and minority discourse(s) have in common. However, such theories may appear to create problems for the classroom teacher, precisely because they are often concerned with introducing texts for study, and with developing reading practices that privilege previously or currently marginalised groups of people or ways of thinking. Due to this radical preoccupation with changing thinking, the curriculum or society itself, their ideological character can be far more apparent than the hidden ideology of theories that are primarily concerned with the internal workings of a text. Commentators on these theories are often explicit about these ideological purposes: for example, Eagleton explains that he values Marxist criticism so highly because: 'unless we can relate past literature, however indirectly, to the struggle of men and women against exploitation, we shall not fully understand our own present and so will be less able to change it effectively' (1976: 76). Ashcroft *et al.* (1998: 1) point out that 'post-colonial analysis increasingly makes clear the nature and impact of inherited power relations, and their continuing effects on modern global culture and politics'. Similarly, Moi describes how Kristeva's negative definition of 'woman' is strategically constructed 'to undermine the phallocentric order that defines woman as marginal in the first place' (Moi, 1985: 163).

The introduction of such theoretical perspectives into classroom practice can therefore be felt to be interventionist, or even a kind of potentially illegal indoctrination, compared with which the practices of reader-response criticism and a pedagogy derived from them *seem* unproblematically neutral. The issue of legality and teachers' anxiety about it is raised specifically by Harris (1990), in a book which could be described as offering a classroom pedagogy for Queer Theory. Harris is as explicit about the radical aims of his book, as the 'academic' critics quoted in the last paragraph. He wants to provide: 'some concrete ideas for the teacher of English anxious to do 'something' in an attempt to combat homophobia' (Harris, 1990: 57). The language of conflict is used quite deliberately. Harris's scheme of work on Ireland's *Who Lies Inside* (1984) includes one lesson that begins by confronting students with the Nazi persecution of homosexuals as a deliberate means of controlling their response to a passage in the novel – a passage that is explicit about the physicality of homosexual attraction – in the second half of the lesson.

There are lots of issues here. Is there a difference between the expression of the kinds of challenge that critical theory makes to society in academic writing, often produced, paradoxically, from the security of academic tenure, in a discourse with other academics, and the expression of these same challenges in a school classroom in a discourse with young people, and indirectly with their parents, some of whom will receive a garbled account of 'what happened in English today'? Is the partially hidden controlling of response by pedagogical means as fascist as the persecution the lesson is intended to expose? Harris's answer to these questions is at least partly that a policy of anti-homophobic teaching needs to be established in a school, or at the very least, in a department, before such teaching takes place. This would legitimise both the content and pedagogy, because all content is political and all pedagogy is manipulative. Explicit policy would allow teachers, pupils and parents to develop a shared understanding that one of the aims of the English curriculum is to reassess the meanings in texts and culture, and to challenge society by doing so.

In *Cultural Politics – Queer Reading* Sinfield (1994) confirms that readings from what have been the margins can contribute to the reassessment of a whole culture. Writing specifically about Queer Theory, he notes that 'literary critics who want to concern themselves with culture will certainly discover crucial faultlines around homosexuality' (1994: 73). It is precisely because disjunction, contradiction, conflict and disruption of meaning are exposed when criticism engages with economics, power, gender, race, class and marginalisation, that the theories that locate the primary authority for meaning in context are at the cutting edge of practice. Moreover, in Sarland's terms, such theories demonstrate the cultural and ideological repertoires that reflect those that he found in adolescent readers.

Indeed, if there is a shared concern among critics who locate primary authority for meaning in context, regarding the effect of institutionalising the theoretical positions which they promote, it is that such an action can result in education and society paying mere lip-service to marginal groups and radical ideas, and that the established critical method will take only what it wants from a more radical mode of thinking, while at the same time formalising its absorption into the thinking practices of more established disciplines, so neutralising it. Eagleton expresses his concern like this: 'No doubt we shall soon see Marxist criticism comfortably wedged between Freudian and mythological approaches to literature, as yet one more stimulating academic 'approach' ... it is worth reminding ourselves [that] ... Marxism is a scientific theory of human societies and of the practice of transforming them' (Eagleton, 1976: vii).

The following conclusions can be drawn from this discussion of theories that locate primary authority for meaning in contexts.

1 Teachers engaging with such theories cannot disguise the fact that English teaching is a political activity. Since they will almost certainly be making their pupils aware of sets of attitudes that are new to them, and that may challenge their values, the values of their parents, their school and society

as a whole, departmental and school policies must support the adoption of the reading strategies promoted in the classroom.

2   The grounds for doing so may include: a model of citizenship that recognises the importance of challenging establishment power and values, and the recognition that the cultural and ideological repertoires of adolescents are likely to respond to models of reading that challenge the authority of texts, authors, schools, teachers and curriculum agencies to determine meaning.

3   Teachers should have control of the content of the reading curriculum, both so that they can choose texts that will engage the cultural and ideological repertoires of individual pupils and classes, and also so that they can teach them how extending those repertoires will allow them to engage with a widening range of texts, using strategies that challenge their authority.

4   A revision of the observation by Sarland with which this section began would be: 'teachers can develop the range and complexity of meanings which are generated by texts and readers in classrooms, by exposing and exploring the ideological and cultural elements of text and extending those of the reader.'

Theories locating primary authority for meaning in the text

seeing ourselves as the makers of our means of making meaning.

(Kress, 1995a: 94)

Kress (1995a), like Sarland, argues that a readerly repertoire is fundamental to developing literacy. However, whereas Sarland defines this key repertoire as 'cultural and ideological', Kress sees it as 'semiotic' (1995a: 87): for him, '"Development" has to be seen in intimate connection with the possibilities of representation' (Kress, 1995a: 88). Kress's means of balancing 'the power of the writer and the power of the reader' is partly by focusing on text and paying close attention to form: 'Meaning is produced in a constant and complex interplay between the meanings of the form read at this instant, and the meanings of the forms in the surrounding co-text, which includes, crucially, the meanings held by the reader who is herself a repository of meaning' (Kress, 1995a: 82). Kress offers a theory of response as at least culturally informed, if not culturally determined, in which critical alertness to the different ways in which forms represent or construct meanings is crucial to literacy.

Critical theories that locate the primary authority for meaning in the text provide many different kinds of framework that may help readers develop an awareness of textual structures and provide sets of terminology for describing and comparing them. In other words, exploring such critical theories may enable readers to investigate the representation of meaning through form and to articulate their findings about this. It may also be argued that this kind of understanding of the possibilities of representation also contributes to the development of an ability to generate new meanings by manipulating the forms that have been analysed.

The major questions that confront English teachers concern the choice of theory(ies) for describing forms to be used with particular groups of pupils. For example, should the textual theory(ies) be chosen using short-term criteria, such as suitability for discussing a particular text, or using long-term criteria, such as pupils' acquisition of a coherent, rather than haphazard, 'semiotic repertoire'? Should the parts of the terminology used in a particular critical framework be made explicit, and, if so, when and how should this be done? To return to an issue raised much earlier in this chapter, what will the use of a particular critical framework convey to pupils about the relative power of writers and readers?

Curriculum documents such as *English in the National Curriculum* (DfEE, 1995a) and *The National Literacy Strategy* (DfEE, 1998), particularly in its 'Technical Vocabulary List', often promote the use of sets of terminology that have strong links with theoretical approaches to reading, but these links have not been made explicit. For example, while much of the terminology promoted in the *National Literacy Strategy* (DfEE, 1998) is intended to provide pupils with a vocabulary for discussing language, the usefulness of this vocabulary could be defended in terms of its contribution to the articulation of analyses of texts adopting the methodology of stylistics (such as Widdowson, 1992). Other influences with a strong presence in recent curriculum documents include New Criticism (in terms like 'irony', 'imagery', 'metaphor' and 'symbol'), and genre theory (in terms like 'biography', 'limerick', 'novel' and 'parody'). What is not made explicit in the curriculum documents, is that the vocabulary that they promote is strongly biased towards the development of frameworks for reading, which, while text-centred, cast the writer as a deliberate manipulator of the effects produced in a text, and as an agent who has conscious control of a particular kind of 'semiotic repertoire', which perhaps has its origins in Classical rhetoric.

This is not to deny that some of the terminology promoted in these documents can be and has already been appropriated by critical theories that place different emphases on the location of power in the writer–text–reader relationship. Indeed, such activity merely illustrates the multi-accentuality of language proposed by Bakhtin (1929). For example, Moon (1992: 9) shows how, by prompting pupils with appropriate questions, teachers can promote a view of 'character' as something other than a coherent creation of an author, with consistent motivation. Pupils can be prompted to think about the ways in which intertextual references affect their reading of a character, or to search for gaps and inconsistencies in its presentation.

Nevertheless, it is clear that terminology derived from structuralism, post-structuralism, deconstruction and narratology, has achieved less status in official curriculum documents, despite the fact that there is good evidence of their effectiveness in pedagogy (e.g. Peim, 1993). Some of the key terminological frameworks from text-centred aspects of theory that are available to teachers, and that could be incorporated in nationally validated 'technical vocabulary lists' include:

- binary oppositions (especially those concerned with race (black/white) gender (masculine/feminine) and class (rich/poor));
- differance (*sic*) (meaning both permanently relative and deferred) (Derrida, 1967a);
- narrative codes (**hermeneutic**, i.e. promoting riddles and suspense; **semic**: presentation of, for example, character; **symbolic**: implied or stated classifications, oppositions; **proairetic**: promoting prediction and fulfilled expectation; **cultural**: representation of customs, assumptions; or **communication**: signs for people addressing each other) (Barthes, 1970);
- structural bundles of character/action relations (Levi-Strauss, 1963);
- different discourses operating within a single text (Foucault, 1975);
- the focalisation of narrative (time perspectives on events; the distance and speed of narration; the knowledge of the narrator(s)) (Genette, 1972);
- rhetorical and stylistic overcoding (the use of convention and cliché as a signal to the reader);
- plot and character types (Propp, 1928);
- textual gaps and silences (Iser, 1978).

Key distinctions worth addressing include those between:

- denotation and connotation;
- signifier and signified (de Saussure, 1974);
- monological and polyphonic texts (Bakhtin, 1929);
- open and closed, readerly and writerly texts (Barthes, 1970);
- 'fabula' (story; events in sequence) and 'sjuzet' (plot; finished arrangement) (Todorov, 1977).

Examples of practice that has made use of these terminological frameworks are now available, although there is only space here for one example to illustrate this point.

Exton (1984) describes how his understanding of Barthes' narrative codes informed his teaching of a short story in a manner that extended the semiotic repertoire of his pupils: 'the class were beginning to think about how a narrative worked rather than what it meant and how they felt about it' (1984: 72). The emphasis was on the structure of the text rather than the author's message or the pupils' response. However, the creative activities included in the work contributed to the empowerment of pupils, who were learning how to deploy 'the possibilities of representation', by, for example, writing their own endings for the story. Furthermore, questions derived from Todorov's account of the role of equilibrium and disruption in narrative, pointed pupils beyond structure to the social and cultural issues that were accessed via the discovery that structuralist analysis achieved – that the mother in the story had been marginalised (1984: 73)

The following conclusions can be drawn from this discussion of theories that locate primary authority for meaning in texts.

Exton's work suggests that investigations of texts which use frameworks derived from critical theories that acknowledge the significance of response and social and cultural contexts – while still focusing on the text as primary location for the authority of meaning – may provide one means of developing a pedagogy that promotes the status of text, reader and context as a corrective to the (still) writer-centred account of reading implied by the choice of terminological frameworks adopted in recent curriculum documents. It is nevertheless the case that future revisions of the curriculum must extend the range of the terminology and concepts that are used to support the teaching of reading, in order to include those listed above. This is a necessary step towards the development of the 'semiotic repertoire', which will enable pupils to see themselves as *makers of their means of making meaning.*

Conclusions

Theories that locate the primary authority for meaning in systems

> Criticism as appreciation is inescapably a product of the superstructure, is inescapably restricted to that sphere, and is one means among many by which the dominant ideology is reproduced from generation to generation.
>
> (Griffiths 1987: 57, on Althusser)

Due to the fact that post-structuralism is so concerned with exposing the power relationships in the systems in which meanings are made, it is obviously appropriate to finish this chapter by considering what type of insights into English teaching are offered by those theories that primarily locate authority for meaning in systems.

Griffiths (1992) has eloquently used conflicting ideas from Foucault and Bakhtin to discuss the effects that could result from providing pupils with an extending semiotic, cultural and ideological repertoire. His account of Foucault's interpretation of Bentham's 'Panopticon' has become more relevant to the analysis of British education systems since 1992, due to the increasing centralisation of the curriculum, and more overt and direct incursions of government policy into pedagogy. Griffiths argues that the principle of the panopticon is 'adaptable to all forms of mass social control in which the organisation of space and the distribution of activities through time lay within the control of a central monitoring and controlling power' (Griffiths, 1992: 14). Could there be a better metaphor for the literacy hour?

Griffiths notes that 'since orthodox behaviour can earn approval, and deviant activity can at any time call down punishment ["the prisoners"] internalise and put into practice the norms of the institution.' Some of the pressures that affect how teachers will convey what are likely to be perceived as the 'norms of the institution' that have been discussed in this chapter include: the problems involved in teaching overtly ideological theories without institutional support; the tendency of national curriculum documentation and assessment systems to promote textual analysis using terminology and frameworks derived from writer-centred theories; and the relative security with which apparently neutral, depoliticised versions of reader-response theory can be adopted. Even if teachers can make some use of some of the strategies of context and reader-centred frameworks for reading texts, it is at the systems level that the curriculum needs to be redefined before the most significant insights of contextual theories can contribute fully to English teaching.

However, Griffiths notes that the operation of a central controlling power is, for Foucault, constitutive of resistance. Bakhtin's notions of the dialogic and carnivalistic qualities of discourse, which always allow for an answer, or for existing power systems to be overturned, even with humour, are also significant for him (Griffiths, 1992: 103). In both cases, of course, these binary reversals are potentially features of the texts themselves, or of the reading of texts that can be accessed via structuralist methodology and concepts. In addition, as Sarland's work on the reading purposes of adolescents suggests, school pupils are particularly likely either to respond to the presence of these binary reversals, or to seek to construct them. Griffiths, like Kress, finally presents a vision of the literacy curriculum that stresses the need for an extending repertoire for pupils. However, Griffiths sees this specifically as a repertoire of genre manipulation: 'there can be for the pupils a significant and irreversible step from the state of having an unconscious knowledge of and command over an – inevitably finite – repertoire to the position of knowing something about the ways in which a (theoretically infinite) array of genres can be developed and used' (Griffiths, 1992: 103).

The concept of developing repertoires has linked all of the sections of this chapter. The teacher's repertoire of strategies must be employed with an awareness that any strategy offers an implicit view of the writer–text–pupil relationship. The function of the selection of a text or a pedagogical strategy, and the selection of a reading practice derived from a particular critical theory, should be to stimulate the extension of the semiotic, generic, cultural and ideological repertoires of pupils.

Questions for discussion

The questions that follow are an invitation to explore the issues considered in this chapter further through discussion.

1   To what extent, in practice, is 'authority for meaning' constructed by pupils as located in teachers, and by teachers as located in nationally imposed requirements of readers?
2   At what stage in pupils' reading development, and how, should 'context-centred' critical theory(ies) begin to influence pedagogy?
3   If teachers need to develop their own 'semiotic, generic, cultural and ideological repertoires', then how can this be achieved?

Further reading

For newcomers to literary theory, Culler (1997) is a readable, up-to-date introduction. Baldick (1990) and Moon (1992) are excellent reference works that define many terms in ways that will help teachers to make them comprehensible in the classroom.

14 What has sexuality got to do with English teaching?

Viv Ellis

Introduction

This chapter will investigate the responses of schooling to questions of sexuality and sexual identity. In particular, it will explore how sexuality has figured in the discourses of the subject of English, and it will try to identify what English teachers can take from recent theories of literary study and pedagogy, in order to develop their classroom practice, with the aim of empowering all pupils, whatever their sexual identity. Ironically, in view of the title of the book in which this chapter appears, it will contend that the presentation of sexuality in a reduced form as homosexuality, and as an 'issue', is counter-productive.

The three main questions that this chapter will address are:

1 How should sexuality be represented in schools?
2 How has sexuality been represented in the English curriculum?
3 How can English make use of recent theories and pedagogies concerned with sexuality, identity and critical literacy?

Given that the chapter's title would question any possible relationship between these two apparently separate areas of experience – and, as well as anticipating debate – it is probably best to set out here the context in which the key terms are used, and to offer my interpretation of the meanings of two in particular. Throughout the chapter, sexuality is taken to mean that area of experience in which sexual feelings, ideologies, desires and needs are integrated with one another and reconciled with modes of sexual expression and behaviour (Ellis and Forrest, 1999). Sexual identity, however, refers more specifically to the naming of certain formations of attitudes and self-representations. 'The heterosexual' and 'the homosexual' are sometimes regarded as the two poles of sexual identification, substituted by the names 'straight' or 'gay', sometimes with the possibility of bisexuality as a median point on a scale. Rather than being firm and fixed, however, I will assume that these identities are fluid, and that in fact there are many sexual identities (butch/femme, scene/non-scene, etc.) falling under these generic headings, and that they have changed, and continue to change, over time. Individuals may choose different sexual identities at different points in their lives. That is to say, sexual identities are cultural effects rather than categories of 'natural' or intrinsic behaviour. Throughout the chapter, however, I will use homophobia to refer to the violent bigotry produced by the hatred of difference in terms of assumed or declared sexual identity.

How should sexuality be represented in schools?

In 1998, the suicide of Darren Steele, a fifteen-year-old school pupil from Staffordshire, and the murder of the university student, Matthew Shepard, in Laramie, Wyoming, dramatically brought the virulence of the hatred produced by homophobia to the general public's attention. There was a telling difference between these events, however. Matthew Shepard identified himself as a gay man and had been entrapped by two 'straight' men, who had posed as potential partners. They took him out into the countryside, tied him to a fence and beat him to death. In their defence, they claimed to have felt their masculinity and heterosexuality to be threatened by their victim.

Darren Steele enjoyed singing in the choir, cooking and drama. He was small for his age. As far as is known, he hadn't made a declarative statement about his sexual identity. He was ruthlessly abused – physically and verbally – by some of his fellow pupils, until he could take no more. Perceived or assumed sexual identity is enough, it seems, to put some children at risk of homophobic bullying by other children who also believe their own sexual and gender identities to be under threat.

Recent surveys by Stonewall, a group that lobbies for lesbian and gay equality, and the Terrence Higgins Trust, a health education charity, have highlighted this problem in British schools. One survey of those teenagers under 18 who identified themselves as lesbian or gay found that 48% of respondents had suffered a violent attack and that 40% of these attacks took place in school (Stonewall, 1994: 2). The same report showed that 61% of respondents had suffered harassment, and over 10% had their property vandalised. A more recent report, based on a national survey of headteachers, found that 82% were aware that homophobic bullying did take place in their schools, and that this may involve physical violence (Douglas *et al*, 1998: 3).

In response to the death of Matthew Shepard, the US government was said to be considering widening 'anti-hate' legislation to include homophobic violence. In the UK, teachers, activists and politicians have responded to the death of Darren Steele – and the research into homophobic violence in schools – by calling for more effective anti-bullying policies and a programme of education for school-age pupils about homosexuality in the context of 'citizenship', in order to 'prevent' further violent attacks. The final report of the Qualifications and Curriculum Authority's Advisory Group on Citizenship (the Crick Report), published late in 1998, however, gives scant attention to questions of diversity in terms of sexuality. There are no explicit references in its recommendations, other than making 'equality and diversity' key concepts and the 'practice of tolerance' a key disposition. The most obvious implicit reference comes in the evidence submitted to the Advisory Group by the British Youth Council, who said:

The curriculum should consider the factors that lead to exclusion from society, such as bullying, colour and other forms of 'difference'. It should make students aware of the difficulties such exclusion can have on the individual and society and of the reasons why some people 'opt out' of the moral social set-up.

(Crick Report, QCA, 1998b: 19)

This is a good example of the dominant rhetoric around difference and diversity in educational contexts. Pupils are to be made aware of 'difference', and that this can lead to exclusion from society. Exclusion is not very nice and can make your life difficult. The implicit message is to be silent about difference. If, however, you voice difference, you can be seen to be making a conscious choice about 'opt[ing] out' of morality.

This has certainly been the treatment that sexual identity has received in countless classrooms. Sexuality itself has long been regarded as having no place in the classroom. If it must (because of concerns about bullying or health), it is reduced to homosexuality and is presented as an 'issue'. As soon as homosexuality/sexuality is presented as an issue, the aim of education seems to become the 'practice of tolerance'. But this, however noble an aim it may appear, does little other than reinforce the division between 'us/you' and 'them/me', and between those who practice tolerance and those who are tolerated. It is unfortunate that the Crick Report chose the phrase 'practice of tolerance', as this 'disposition' has been singled out by many who have written about education and equality as something that reinforces the tolerator/tolerated, oppressor/oppressed dyads (in terms of sexuality, see Britzman, 1995; Garber, 1995; Mac an Ghaill, 1996). The effect of this division, even in well-meaning educational endeavours, can be seen in this extract from a poem by a young gay man:

You can't be with me;
be seen with me and people will wonder.
I remain alone.
Friends?
I can't show friendship
for they suspect me.
Homosexual ... Gay ... Queer ...
That's me. Why me?

But I'm still a man with senses and feelings;
so please don't turn away, or laugh,
or show disgust and say I'm 'dirty'.
I'm still a man.
Homosexuality ... And me ...

Accept me – please.

(West Rhyl Young People's Project 1998: 39)

This poem is the product of what Ray Misson has called the ' "Gays are human, too" syndrome' (Misson, 1995: 30). The writer, through a process of education (this writing was undertaken as part of a lesbian and gay youth outreach project), has assumed the position of the subordinate, the excluded, seeking admission into the 'moral social set-up' from those who can give authorisation. The poem is addressed to a reader who can, if they wish, 'practice tolerance' (*sic*); it proposes that 'the power to accept or reject, the power to confer or deny humanity lies with the person [reading] it' (*ibid.*). Not only is this condescending, it is dangerous. It reproduces the conditions that have led to the formation of the identity given voice by the poem, conditions that make the exclusion and 'difference' of the poet possible.

It is often suggested that the formation of these kinds of 'tolerated' sexual and gender identities is partly a function of schooling (see, for example, Mac an Ghaill, 1994 and Epstein and Johnson, 1998). Marjorie Garber, in her provocative study of sexual identity and sexuality, *Vice Versa*, refers to one of the major functions of schooling as the 'normalisation of sexuality', that 'all schools are "normal schools" ' by which she means that all schools teach teaching (the ways in which to receive and respond to new knowledge) and normality (Garber, 1995: 326). 'Normality' is defined by 'the idea that it is "normal" to reach a settled sexual identity, and that that "identity" is either heterosexual or homosexual' (*ibid.*: 343). This is pervasive throughout the contexts and discourses of schooling – in pupil groupings, pastoral care, the model of the teacher, etc. – as well as in the texts and discourses of curriculum subjects. And even when sexuality, explicitly, is introduced on the curriculum, represented in a reduced and simple form as homosexuality, its purpose is to reinforce and confirm the already established binary heterosexuality/homosexuality, those who 'practice tolerance' and those who are tolerated. Deborah Britzman, in her seminal article 'Is There a Queer Pedagogy?' describes the liberal educational project represented, I believe, by the likes of the Crick Report, as one of an attempted 'identification with another'. But how, she asks, is this meant to occur 'if one is only required to tolerate and thereby confirm one's self as generous' (Britzman, 1995: 159).

I am suggesting that it is not homosexuality that needs to be presented as an 'issue' in schools, but rather that it is sexuality itself – complex, diverse, fluid and dynamic – and the representation of sexualities and sexual identities, which needs to be critiqued, beginning with the assumptions and conventions of normalised heterosexuality. I argue that the English classroom is an important site for this work.

How has sexuality been represented in the English curriculum?

One of the problems was that with the word 'gay' came a drive for positive images, but all the artists I knew and respected were involved with negative images

because that was the intelligent thing to do in a culture which promoted all that
false positivity through advertising and so on.

(Derek Jarman, 1992; quoted in Woods, 1994: 91)

The relatively recent interest in lesbian and gay studies in higher education
can be seen to have grown out of the political activism around civil rights and
sexual freedom during the 1960s. Interestingly, however, lesbian and gay studies
has most often found fertile ground for its development (and for its validation
by academia) in university English and Cultural Studies departments, where it
was deemed possible for the reading practices associated with particular
ideological positions to be allowed, and for non-canonical voices to be heard. (I
am not, however, suggesting that the incorporation of lesbian and gay studies or
even cultural studies into university English has been easy. Many departments
claim to have been 'torn apart' in the process. Many teachers in schools have
had similar experiences.)

Similarly, when questions of sexuality or sexual identity are addressed in
schools, this is often in English lessons. When Trenchard and Warren surveyed
young lesbian and gay teenagers in 1984, they found that 174 out of the survey
group of 416 recollected any 'mention' of homosexuality in school and, of this
group, just over a quarter recollected that 'mention' taking place in an English
lesson (Trenchard and Warren, 1984: 56). In his 1990 book, *Lesbian and Gay
Issues in the English Classroom*, Simon Harris speculates that 'English is, in some
ways, more amenable to the issue's inclusion than other areas of the curriculum'
(Harris, 1990: 29), and draws on research into classroom practice to support
this view. According to Harris, it is chiefly the opportunities for per-
sonal/autobiographical writing and discussion that have allowed for the 'issue's
inclusion' in so far as it has been included, bearing in mind that 242 people in
Trenchard and Warren's survey group (58.7%) recollected no 'mention' at all.

Harris's book was an important contribution to the debate around sexuality and education at the time it was written. However, it bears the deep scars
of Section 28 of the Local Government Act 1988: the notoriously clumsy
piece of legislation that attempted to 'prohibit the promotion of homosexuality' in maintained schools. Harris recommends the strategy of advancing
homosexuality as an 'issue' that needs to be tackled in schools and, after
discussing the place of homosexuality in the talk and writing of pupils in
English classrooms, offers a reading list of materials (fiction, poetry and
drama) that can be 'introduced'. Each of the entries in the list is identified as
having a gay male or lesbian theme, and an age range is suggested for each
text. Much of what is included could be regarded as what we may call
'becoming homosexual problem narratives', that is to say they are 'concerned
with self-realisation and with the outsider defining him/herself with/against
the group.' (Misson, 1995: 30).

An even broader category that can be used to describe these books is
'positive image texts'. Indeed, Harris took many of the materials in his reading
list from the Inner London Education Authority's (ILEA's) *Positive Images: a
Resources Guide for Teaching About Homosexuality*. This desire to provide

'positive images' for young readers can be seen as a continuation of the struggle for equality initiated by the rights movements in the 1960s. An early and infamous example of this kind of text is the picture book *Jenny Lives With Eric and Martin* by Susanne Bosche. To say that this book tells a story would be putting it too strongly, so it is probably more accurate to say it describes the day-to-day life of a little girl, Jenny, with her father and his male partner, the frequent visits from her kind and understanding mother who lives down the road, and the little gifts of freshly dug potatoes the boys give her for being so understanding. This book was never suggested as being suitable for use in schools by the ILEA (although not because it is such a dull story); rather it was kept in Resource Centres as an example of 'positive images' of gay men parenting, for teachers' edification. Nevertheless, the controversy surrounding the appearance of the book in ILEA Resource Centres is often identified as a factor that contributed to the enacting of Section 28.

Another text that suffered in the panic around Section 28 – although this time less deservedly – was the BBC 'Scene' drama *The Two of Us*. This told the story of the relationship between two teenage boys in a secondary school. One boy identified himself as gay, and the other was uncertain about having a single sexual identity and had a girlfriend too. Initially, the BBC banned the two-part drama and it was removed from the schedules. Then there were stories of re-editing to change the ending – in which the two boys – 'lived happily ever after', to one in which they lived on, but no-one knows how or with whom. Eventually, the programmes were broadcast in the revised version in the early hours of the morning, together with a heavy-handed message to teachers to ensure that they previewed the programmes before classroom use and that they sought their headteacher's permission.

All this was taking place at the same time as new curriculum and assessment initiatives were being introduced by English teachers. National Curriculum frameworks, lists of prescribed authors, national tests at ages seven, 11 and 14 and, later, the abolition of 100% course-work GCSEs, have all made it potentially more difficult (although not impossible) for individual teachers to read diverse and challenging texts with pupils in diverse and challenging ways. The added complication and symbolic power of Section 28 did not make it any easier for teachers to read particular texts or to teach reading in open and critical ways that allow for diversity and affirm difference in interpretation.

That said, English has always had a strong element of moral, spiritual and cultural training embedded in its discourses – however, and whenever, it has been conceived as a subject. This is not new or entirely driven by reactionary political initiatives. From its origins in the nineteenth century as a means of social cohesion: as a replacement for a religion that was no longer able to do the job (giving a sense of both national identity and of 'one's place'), English has traditionally sought to educate people in the right ways of speaking, listening, reading and writing; in identifying the right books; and training readers in the right response and the right feelings. As Michael Hurley has said:

> English studies is a moral technology, a series of social techniques, skills
> and trainings which produce and value a particular mode of subjectivity.
>
> (Hurley, 1990: 156)

The politically motivated changes to the English curriculum and assessment
mechanisms in schools in the early 1990s, combined with the symbolic effect of
Section 28 (and, of course, the unequal ages of consent for male homosexual
and heterosexual activity), have produced circumstances in which the silence
around sexuality in the English classroom has, at times, been deafening. This is
not to say, of course, that sexuality is absent from the classroom – in the texts
and discourses of the curriculum and in the bodies and desires of pupils and
teachers – merely that it has been silenced. To this extent at least, English
studies continues to effect a sort of moral training. The introduction of texts
with 'positive images' does not in itself do anything to change this if these texts
are read in ways that normalise sexuality as heterosexuality. It is not just that,
imaginatively, these texts create what Derek Jarman referred to as a 'false
positivity', and can be just plain bad, unstimulating and unattractive texts. Very
often the 'positive image' represented is a positive image of endurance,
tolerance of suffering, and coming to terms with being a tolerated 'other', and, if
read in an uncritical, closed and accepting way, simply acts to powerfully
reinforce the normalisation of heterosexuality. Drawing on the work of
Knoblauch and Brannon, and understanding the importance of 'representation,
the practices by which people name and rename the world' (Knoblauch and
Brannon, 1993: 3), Wendy Morgan suggests that effective work in the English
classroom around sexuality and sexual identity has 'two complementary aspects':

> One is analysis: scrutinising the ways language and image are used to give
> us a position for reading and desiring, for taking up a position as sexual
> beings. The other is imagination: understanding something of how the
> ideologies of our society are lived out in individuals in a specific time and
> place.
>
> (Morgan, 1997: 48)

In addition, as Misson points out, positive image texts are only really useful in
this kind of critical literacy pedagogy when they are used as material for
'examining how the inequality is reproduced in the society' (Misson, 1995: 30).
Even then, I would argue, teachers risk presenting sexuality simply as
homosexuality and as an 'issue'. This is the problem with texts conceived purely
to present (false, according to Jarman) positive images. Or, as Wilde put it, 'No
artist has ethical sympathies. An ethical sympathy in an artist is an unpardon-
able mannerism of style' (Wilde, 1999: xix).

So far, I have argued that this desire to create positive images arose out of the
lesbian and gay rights movement and the institutionalisation of a lesbian and
gay 'rights' position on representation. Next, I will briefly attempt to identify
what English teachers can take from what has become known as Queer Theory,

and critical literacy pedagogies, to enhance their classroom practice and to strive for the aim of social justice in terms of sexuality.

How can English make use of Queer Theory and critical literacy pedagogies?

Poppy Z. Brite's novel *Lost Souls* has occasionally figured in the comparative, extended essay course-work required by some A-level English Literature syllabuses. First published in 1992, it is an example of the new American Gothic horror genre, and provokes interesting points of comparison with nineteenth-century versions of the genre, especially discussion of the importance of sexuality in the discourses of vampire fiction. Students have written thoughtfully about *Lost Souls* in relation to, for example, Bram Stoker's *Dracula* and the novels of Anne Rice. At their best, students have taken the opportunity to analyse how language is used to form sexual identities and how sexuality figures in the representation of the vampire.

My purpose here, however, is to exemplify the effect of English as a 'moral technology', and of the process by which certain readings are allowed or denied. My concern is with the possibilities of reading rather than recommending *Lost Souls* as a text to 'use'. In this extract from the novel, the main character, 'Nothing', a fifteen-year-old goth from Maryland (known to his family as Jason), is enduring a lesson by his English teacher, Mrs Peebles:

In Nothing's English class the next day, Mrs Margaret Peebles plunged her hypodermic of higher learning into *Lord of the Flies* and sucked every drop of its primal magic, every trace of its adolescent wonder. Nothing knew half the class hadn't even read the book. If they were judging it by what the teacher said, he could hardly blame them. But he'd read it three years ago, one summer afternoon in bed with a fever, and when he had put the book down, his hands had been shaking. Those wild, salty-skinned little boys had tumbled through his head, and he had cried for them, so young, grown old so fast ...

'Jason.'

He sighed, Peebles was staring at him. The rest of the class paid no attention; they were elsewhere too, in their own worlds, driving away on their own roads.

'What? he said.

'We were discussing William Golding's *Lord of the Flies*. You have read the book?'

'I have.'

'Then perhaps you can tell me about the rivalry between Jack and Ralph. What allows it to grow so bitter?'

'Their attraction for each other,' Nothing said. 'Their love for each other. They had this fierce love, they wanted to be each other. And only when you love someone that much can you hate them too −'

A ripple of laughter went through the class. A couple of boys rolled their eyes at one another – what a fag!

Peebles pressed her thin lips together. 'If you had been paying attention, instead of doodling and staring out the window –'

Suddenly he was too tired to care what happened to him. This was empty, all empty useless crap. 'Oh fuck you,' he said, and felt the class suck in its breath and silently cheer him on.

(Brite, 1994: 29–31; © 1994 Penguin Books Ltd,
reproduced by permission)

There is only one possible reading of *Lord of the Flies* for Mrs Peebles and that is inside her head. There is only one reading of the rivalry between Jack and Ralph, and Mrs Peebles knows what it is, and it certainly isn't their 'fierce love.' It is perhaps the same reading that Mrs Peebles received from the lessons of her own English teacher, and that she feels impelled to reproduce. Or it could be that she feels duty-bound to reinforce what she believes to be the reading authorised by the system that will assess Nothing and his fellow high-school students and sanction their progress to the next stage of schooling? Perhaps Mrs Peebles' 'professional' readings are different to her personal ones, who knows? It is easy to be hard on Mrs Peebles, and how many English teachers can honestly say they have never had a Peebles moment?

What Nothing offers, however, is committed and personal, a powerful imaginative response based on a curious, independent reading which challenges Mrs Peebles' normalised reading. *Lord of the Flies* changed Nothing (if you'll pardon the pun) physically – he shook, he cried. There is no evidence of it having the same effect on Mrs Peebles or the rest of the class to whom she has 'introduced' this text, perhaps because she thought it would 'appeal to boys'. Indeed, the rest of the class, brought back into the classroom from their imaginative lives by Mrs Peebles' monitoring, know that Nothing's is not a permitted reading. They laugh in a way that says that schooling has had its intended effect on them. Nothing has chosen to voice a different reading, and is excluded from their shared 'moral social set-up'. Rather than feeling victimised by this exclusion, however, Nothing affirms his different reading and it is through this affirmation (in the expletive directed at the teacher) that he feels the rest of the class examine the authorised version as they 'suck in [their] breath'.

Nothing offered what could be described as a 'queer' reading in a number of senses. First of all, the word 'queer' has been used as a pejorative to describe lesbians and gay men. It retains some of the hostile connotations that have accrued to the word; Nothing's reading could be deemed to provide an unacceptably gay interpretation of the narrative. Second, 'queer' also signifies odd, misshapen, uncommon, out-of-place. Nothing appears to have an uncommonly odd view of *Lord of the Flies*. Third, it is queer in the sense of 'queer' as a verb: with 'queering' implying disruption and disturbance of settled understandings – queering the pitch, queering *Lord of the Flies*. Nothing has attempted to queer Mrs Peebles' reading of the novel.

It is these senses of 'queer' that inform the relatively recent interest in Queer Theory, a theory which, according to Deborah Britzman, insists on three methods of enquiry: 'the study of limits, the study of ignorance, and the study of reading practices' (Britzman, 1995: 155). It is Britzman's account of the study of reading practices that I believe will be especially useful here.

Drawing on the work of psychologists Shoshana Felman and Jacques Lacan, Deborah Britzman distinguishes between three 'analytic practices': practices of reading for alterity; practices of engaging in dialogue with the self as the self reads; and practices of theorising how one reads (Britzman, 1995: 163). 'Reading for alterity' involves acknowledging differences between readers, between readers and texts and between the reader's 'self' and 'another'. It begins, says Britzman, with 'an acknowledgement of difference as the grounds for identity' (*ibid.*) and for the possibility of the reader's multiple identities. In other words, reading shouldn't simply serve as a 'confirmation of identity' through the construction of resemblances:

> The question a reader might ask is: Who am I becoming through the inter-pretative claims I make upon another and upon myself?
>
> (*ibid.*)

This question leads into the second practice of 'engaging in a dialogue with the self as the self reads'. The key term here is *dialogue* – not just with other readers but with oneself as a reader. This is an aspect of many theoretical approaches to reading, where the knowledge that one brings to a text, and the intertextual dialogue with the self as reader, are seen as processes by which meanings are produced. The emphasis in this account, however, is on the privileging of the dialogue with the self over the 'intentions of the author or the reader' [my emphasis], so that the focus is on 'thinking through the structures of textuality as opposed to the attributes of the biography' (*ibid.*).

The third practice Britzman identifies is the 'theorizing [of] reading as always about risking the self' (*ibid.*: 164). Again, encouraging readers to develop their own 'theories of reading' is an important aspect of many approaches to literacy pedagogy, and it is generally assumed that progress in literacy education will involve an increasingly explicit theorisation of reading practices. Again, the difference here is that Britzman wants readers to 'confront one's own theory of reading' (*ibid.*), to unsettle the process by which meanings are produced, and to question the determinacy of their reading practices. This is consistent with the aim of all three analytic practices, which is:

> to point to the fact that there are no innocent, normal, or unmediated readings and that the representations drawn upon to maintain a narrative or a self as normal, as deviant, as unthinkable, are social effects of how discourses of normalization are lived and refused.
>
> (*ibid.*)

The highest aim of any queer cultural text or event should be to save lives.
(Woods, 1994: 92)

Queer Theory is sometimes seen by its detractors as a flippant, post-modern game. Those who are committed to a lesbian and gay 'rights' perspective often feel that 'queer' is used to challenge the political aims of the lesbian and gay 'community' and that 'queer' does nothing to fight for equality in terms of sexuality or to challenge homophobia. 'Queer', they say, implies confusion and inaction, it diffuses the strength of the 'rights' movement. However, there is a growing body of queer theorists and, more recently, queer pedagogues, who disagree with this viewpoint.

In this chapter, I have suggested that initiatives to combat homophobia in schools often reinforce unhelpful notions of 'us' and 'them', giving the normalised group the power to authorise and 'tolerate' the other. The introduction of positive image texts in the English classroom can often have this effect. The representation of sexuality (always, it seems, as homosexuality) as an 'issue' in English classrooms can be counter-productive, and rather than challenging pupils to scrutinise their assumptions about (hetero)sexuality, can lead to an entrenchment of the normalised position. My purpose has been to suggest that rather than seeking out texts that we hope will do the work of 'challenging' and 'confronting' homophobia for us, texts that appear to offer positive images of the 'others', we aim to empower, English teachers should focus on how we read and write sexuality. This involves us in re-examining our own reading practices and teaching our pupils to do the same. Many English teachers have taken this on in terms of gender, 'race' and social class, and have adopted many of the principles of critical literacy pedagogies to support their work, learning how discrimination and prejudice are read and written in the discourses of the world. Queer Theory, with its emphasis on the study of reading practices, allows us to begin the same work in terms of sexuality.

Questions for discussion, including suggestions for further reading

1   For further discussion of key terms such as sexuality and sexual identity, see Ellis and Forrest (1999) ' "One of Them or One of Us": sexuality, identity and equality', in M. Cole (ed.) (1999) *Equality, Human Rights and Education*.

2   *Batman Can't Fly*, by David Hines (1997), is published by Faber and Faber in their children's list. Apparently, even the author was surprised that sections dealing with the representation of sexuality made it into the published version. The central character becomes aware of his mother's prostitution, has a dominant, sexually demanding girlfriend and suffers a sexual assault by a swimming pool attendant. It is a powerful and provocative novel, with a compelling plot that cannot be summarised adequately in the few lines available to me here.

Does this novel have a place in the English classroom? And how should it be read?

3 In her book *Critical Literacy in the Classroom*, Wendy Morgan imagines a pedagogy 'that embraces desire and does not distance it' (Morgan, 1997: 45). How far does the curriculum unit outlined in chapter 2 of the book go towards achieving her aims?

4 *Same Difference*, edited by Simon Puttock (1998), is described by its publishers as a collection of short stories 'with lesbian or gay characters' by authors such as Anne Fine, Vivian French and Jan Mark. *Oliver Button Is a Sissy*, a picture book by Tomie dePaola (1979), is about a boy who does not conform to the conventions of 'masculine' behaviour displayed by other boys in his school, and is excluded by them. These difficulties are overcome when Oliver wins a dancing competition.

Is it fair to describe these texts as offering a 'false positivity'?

5 For some teachers, the question of 'coming out' in school to their pupils, and defining their sexual identity in a declarative statement, is a key decision. In a recent pairing of articles in *GLQ: a Journal of Lesbian and Gay Studies*, Jonathan G. Silin ('Teaching As A Gay Man') (1999) and Didi Khayatt (1999) ('Sex and Pedagogy') rehearse the opposing arguments.

15 Gender difference in achievement in English

A sign of the times?

Caroline Daly

Introduction

Gender has become a main focus of the current government campaign to raise literacy 'standards' within a prevalent political and economic discourse of 'school improvement'. This chapter offers a critical perspective on how gender differences are appropriated and contextualised by political and economic concerns, and amplified as such by the media. It examines critically the performance differential between girls and boys and the implications for their English teachers at all levels of compulsory schooling.

Teachers of English at primary and secondary level are charged with delivering national literacy targets, which rely on eradicating gender differences in performance in their classrooms:

> David Blunkett, the Education Secretary, has promised that 80 per cent of 11-year-olds will reach level 4 (in Standard Attainment Tasks for Reading and Writing) by 2002. This will be difficult unless boys make substantially more progress.
>
> (Pyke, 1998)

If a teacher were to consider the main obstacle to meeting the political imperative to 'raise standards' in the classroom, might that obstacle most accurately be described as 'boys'? Boys' underachievement in relation to girls has been a dominant strand within initiatives to improve literacy levels in the 1990s, and has led to the experience of girls being viewed unproblematically within a government initiative that prioritises the economic viability of the current generation of school-leavers. Within this discourse, girls are apparently working well, and quite happily performing in expected ways. In the 1998 Key Stage 2 SATs, girls achieved the national target, with 80% of them reading at Level 4. What are those female ways of working that appear to make it easier for girls to perform well? What relationship exists between girls' success in English, and their continued occupation of the poorest-paid, most insecure jobs in the world beyond school? Can we talk about amorphous groups of 'girls' and 'boys', setting aside other cultural influences, particularly social class and race, as though gender is the only factor determining their disposition to work at school?

These questions help to form the basis of three areas of enquiry to be explored in this chapter:

1   What is the nature of the differences in achievement that exist between boys and girls in English?
2   What is the relationship between gender, literacy and schooling?
3   What are the implications for pedagogy?

Contrasting discourses exist that offer varying and sometimes conflicting interpretations of the differences between girls and boys. Prominent political 'solutions' speak from within a historically capitalist discourse, with a male-oriented agenda for education and employment. Those who speak from outside this discourse do not attract equivalent political and media attention. However, work like Carrie Paechter's refocuses, in a critical way, the discussion surrounding boys' and girls' achievement:

> Given the recent concern about working class and black male disaffection and rejection of schooling, coupled with a decline in traditional areas of working class male employment, it is important to be aware of the evidence that the interests of girls remain subordinated in the school setting.
>
> (Paechter, 1998: 20)

Within English, the 'subordination of girls' might seem a surprising concept – yet the recent research of Elaine Millard makes it clear that interpretations of gender performance have to be seen in the light of their historical context, in which power relations are embedded:

> The difference in boys' and girls' performance in current language examinations may well be a sign that boys are already staking a claim to the more powerful means of communication by participating more actively in the biggest revolution of literacy practices since the introduction of print. It may therefore follow that, as men, they will continue to control entry to the most influential ways of making meaning through the interrelated media of film, computer and CD-ROM.
>
> (Millard, 1997: 181)

This seems a long way from prevalent apocalyptic visions of a de-skilled, semi-literate male workforce, unfit to carry Britain into the next millennium. Contemporary analyses of this issue must scrutinise the huge political concern about boys' underachievement. Who are the boys about which all this fuss is being made? Is the alarmist discourse to do with associating working-class male 'failure' at school with a moral panic in society about family breakdown and shifting values in a multicultural, multimedia world? Where do girls fit into these changes? Why is so little reported on the overall improvement in boys' examination results, and, when it is reported, why is it in terms of their poor performance in relation to girls?

The three areas for analysis in this chapter take up such questions within a broad discussion of how differences are 'problematised' in culturally specific ways, which are related to current political priorities for the curriculum.

Differences in the achievements of girls and boys

In order to make sense of the differing perspectives on the performance of boys and girls and their orientation towards English, it is important first to look at all the 'concerns' about gender and literacy within the particular political and social context of the late twentieth century. The current underperformance of boys forms part of a historical continuum, in which boys have consistently failed to achieve an elusive 'norm'. Michele Cohen's (1998) historical analysis exposes how the current scare about boys' recent decline is rooted in an inaccurate and mythologised version of the past:

> Stories about a 'Golden Age' of boys' achievement are particularly inter-esting for an historical perspective on boys' underachievement ... from the late seventeenth century to the present – boys have always 'underachieved' ... underachievement has never been treated as a problem of boys ... attributing boys' failure to a *method* has made it possible to explain away their poor results without implicating boys themselves.
>
> (Cohen, 1998: 20–3)

The contemporary focus on gendered differences in English has, however, been met with an unprecedented mobilisation of government policy and resources. Since the publication of the report, *Boys and English* in 1993, the decade has focused on boys as 'underachievers', whose failure to perform in English is a national issue, reflecting a wider concern about boys generally, and their fitness to carry Britain forward into the competitive global economy of the next century. The Report's findings were stark, and established a deficit model to describe male learners:

> Boys do not do as well as girls in English in schools. There are contrasts in performance and in attitudes towards the subject. The majority of pupils who experience difficulties in learning to write are boys. Boys' results in public examinations at 16 are not as good as girls', and many more girls than boys continue to study English beyond 16.
>
> (Ofsted, 1993b: 2)

The media have articulated an alarmist interpretation of these and related findings, through rhetorical headlines such as: 'Failing boys "public burden number one"' (Dean, 1998), and in the most summary of dismissals: 'Boys will be boys – and failures' (White, 1998). These comments are part of a discourse that relates the 'failure' of boys to fears about Britain's economic and social well-being. It is implied that the prosperity of the nation is the main responsibility for each generation of male school-leavers: 'Britain is losing out in the global market-place' was flashed as the chief concern of the Dearing Report (1996), which studied the poor literacy and numeracy levels of school-leavers – particularly working-class boys (Pyke, 1996a).

Statistical evidence about differential examination and end of Key Stage test performance, reveals a consistent shortfall in the attainment of boys in relation to girls. DfEE figures indicate that the shortfall exists across the Key Stages. In 1997, the KS 2 reading tests displayed a 7% difference between girls and boys aged eleven, with an 18% difference in writing. In the same year, there was a 17% discrepancy between girls and boys gaining grades A–C in English GCSE. What is also significant, is that statistics reflect *less* overall discrepancy in the performance of girls and boys at GCSE since 1994, than in the previous period of course-work assessment. Since the introduction of terminal examinations at GCSE level, the discrepancy between the numbers of girls and boys achieving grades A–C in English has varied annually between 13 and 18%. Despite national initiatives, boys' achievement is not a matter of simple incremental improvement.

Inspection evidence has produced statements about shortfalls in the performance of boys in English, with the notable exceptions of drama, media and argumentative essay-writing. It is important to consider the parameters in which inspection evidence operates: it can only report on pupils' performance within specified norm-referenced criteria. It cannot tell anything about boys' and girls' dispositions towards literacy, based on their experiences and behaviour in the world outside school. Neither statistical nor inspection evidence operates within a theoretical framework for understanding the differences that it reports. Such evidence frequently results in a binary conceptualisation of the achievements of male and female pupils, by comparing negatively the results of boys against girls. Within a binary opposition model, girls are the champions of the battle for higher standards, which boys constantly undermine.

An alternative to such binary interpretations of gender performance lies in understanding the *difference* in the literacy behaviours of boys and girls. This analysis acknowledges that all literacy behaviours are in fact cultural and social practices, and relates 'school' performance to the diversity of girls' and boys' literacy experiences in their broader social and cultural contexts (Millard, 1997). Pupils' orientations towards reading and writing are inextricably bound up with their experience of power relations in the gendered and classed world outside of school. Literacy forms part of their total sexual identity, and quantitative judgements of performance may tell us more about the political contests over what is to be assessed, than the differences in gender orientation towards English. This hypothesis is further developed in the next section.

Being 'good' at English – a gender issue?

The attribution of gender differences in performance in English to inherent ability is highly problematic, and the evidence is tenuous. Goodwyn's (1995) research into teachers' and pupils' perceptions of gender and ability dismisses the idea that girls have a greater natural aptitude for English as 'a minority view' among his respondents. Rather:

> the majority view is that there is no essential difference in ability. The difference is in attitude. Girls were seen as more mature than boys, especially in Years 7 to 9. This maturity is revealed not only in the quality of their writing and talking but also in their conscientiousness and thoroughness. Girls are seen as far more at ease with their achievements in English, they are open to their emotional reactions to reading and the fact that they read far more widely than boys gives them an 'extra dimension of experience'.
>
> (Goodwyn, 1995: 19–20)

Girls 'don't mind being good', whereas boys are 'more subject to peer pressure', and 'want to be funny all the time'. Overall, the research 'suggests a clear conviction amongst English teachers that the most able in the subject includes equal proportions of boys and girls and that differences are not to do with ability but with a marked difference in attitude. Boys' underachievement remains the key issue' (*ibid.*).

Where streaming exists, the concentration of boys in the lowest sets formalises their position at the bottom of a hierarchical conception of 'ability' – indicating that, generally, boys are 'worse' at English than the girls who dominate the top streams. 'Where classes were organised according to ability, there were more girls in the upper ability groups and more boys in the lowest in almost all the schools' (Ofsted, 1993b: 11). Streaming is a key means of identifying and reinforcing the idea that difference is a matter of 'ability' in schools, and there are attendant consequences for pupil attitudes, in terms of teacher and pupil expectations, peer pressure and motivation.

Contrasting with 'ability', the term 'attitude' is crucial, as it can disguise a whole spectrum of social and cultural factors that help to constitute gendered performance in the English classroom. Certainly, at government level, gender differences have been presented in terms of 'attitudes': raising boys' achievement is a matter of changing both students' and teachers' attitudes. According to *Boys and English*, 'sensitive' teachers do not have many problems in motivating working-class boys to learn English, because they are able to forge particularly effective relationships with them. This implies that each classroom has its own individual and identifiable features, determined by the relationships among the teacher, the content and the pupils.

A response to this perception that the 'problem' is one of 'attitudes', has been that if only teachers became more sensitive to boys' needs, and restructured their teaching accordingly, then there would be fewer problems. A flurry of INSET provision followed the Ofsted report, in a move to place responsibility for the solution squarely at the feet of teachers – by improving their practice. This strategy is apparent in government documents offering analysis and advice to English teachers, such as *Can Do Better* (QCA, 1998a) – (the title of which refers to the teachers as well as the boys). This document qualifies the deficit analysis of the earlier report, in its premise that boys' attitudes to literacy are attributable to the climate within a particular classroom. Such an assertion provides the basis for a powerful argument that better pedagogical 'strategies' are needed to improve boys' work. It assumes that 'underachievement' lies in the hands of English teachers, whose deficient pupils habitually transgress a universally agreed cultural norm. Of course, teachers have a huge effect on the motivation of students to learn – but this theory on its own does not begin to grapple with the context in which boys experience English, and which enshrines certain gendered prescriptions for what gets taught. A more complex conceptualisation of school literacy must include the fact that it is a powerful component of social agency, and carries with it a range of differing applications according to gender, race and class. The relationship of gender to literacy and schooling is critical – pupils are learning English along with learning about the different realisations of power available to men and women in an unequal and differentiated society. Such differences affect how girls and boys react to a prescribed English curriculum and its associated assessment methodology, and are explored in the next section.

The relationship between gender, literacy and schooling

English classrooms are complex microcosms of broader social relations. This section focuses on the interactions between curriculum, assessment and pupils, who are, of course, developing literacy as part of their social, economic and sexual identity. The nature of these interactions helps determine relative achievement between girls and boys.

Literacy is a social practice, and the learning of it in school relates to the formation of sexualised identities within the worlds of family and work beyond (Solsken, 1993; Turvey, 1996; Daly, 1999). What happens to students in the classroom is inextricably bound up with their experiences outside, and sexual identity is a critical factor in those experiences during the schooling years. Thus there is the need to complicate simplistic 'solutions' to inappropriate 'attitudes', by considering English teaching as part of the broader relations that exist between gender, literacy and schooling.

English as a gendered subject

A central theme of the gender debate has been the 'feminisation' of English teaching. From a feminist perspective, English as an academic subject has striven through an early history of marginalisation to win academic status in the universities, which is mirrored in the struggles of women teachers to win equal professional status with men in schools:

> The 'femaleness' of English lies partly in its uncertain status, its association with women, its potential as a 'civilising influence' rather than a rigorous course of study … Its character may also be read from ancient traditions of iconography and fairytale, which picture the acquisition and practices of early literacy as a wholly female terrain: domestic, parochial, consolatory and unthreatening.
>
> (Miller, 1996: 193)

The relative performance of boys and girls has been attributed to the 'feminisation' of English as a subject, which is populated by women teachers, offering a curriculum which validates emotional and subjective response, where girls feel at home. The problematisation of this 'feminisation' of English occurs within a patriarchal capitalist discourse, and appears in terms of a binary opposition, which sets 'girls' English' against 'boys' English'. This discourse argues that the incorporation of imaginative and empathetic responses offers an aspect to the English curriculum that amounts to female contamination. Girls, according to the discourse, are seen to be succeeding within a context of male disadvantage – and are making inroads on the traditional power relations embedded within education. The alienation of boys, it is argued, is compounded by a curriculum that contains a high percentage of literary material:

> many heads of department were dismayed by the change of direction in set-book selection for GCSE that has followed recent adjustments to the National Curriculum for English. They noticed that an increased emphasis on pre-twentieth century literature had been particularly prejudicial for boys of below average attainment and motivation.
>
> (Frater, 1997: 32)

This perspective views literature as gendered territory, the prevalence of which in models for assessment can be contested within a broader debate about the nature of the subject and its role within a competitive economy. An aspect of broader ideological tensions concerning the subject of English and its relationship to gender, is how it functions as a form of preparation for the world of work, in the millennium economy. It is argued that, for boys, much English subject-matter is far removed from their 'real world' concerns, which are enshrined in a utilitarian acceptance of acquiring adequate literacy skills; 'English is important for job prospects' (Ofsted, 1993b: 9).

A further dimension of the 'binary opposition' interpretation of the gender differences in achievement in English is connected with assessment requirements. A main contention from this position has been that examination content and allied assessment methods in English are gender-biased: this is a reaction against methods that have allowed girls (and greater numbers of boys) to succeed, where previously male success was assumed. The rhetorical headline 'Is English GCSE a girls' own paper?' (Pyke, 1996b) articulated a reactionary response to continued female success in English, even after the abandonment of 100% course-work examinations, which had seen girls make significant progress over boys, in the preceding few years. The findings of Punter and Burchell (1996) regarding the GCSE English Language exam were relayed within a discourse that attributed any unfairness to an *advantage* possessed by the girls, as illustrated by reporting in the *Times Educational Supplement* article:

> Examiners thought girls had an advantage in: extended pieces; answers to open-ended questions; showing audience awareness; writing reflectively; writing empathetically; writing imaginatively; discussing character motivation; conversation/drama; writing about poems, about literary prose and about drama; preparing for assignments; discussing assignments with teachers; and listening.
>
> (*ibid.*)

Boys scored better only in writing argumentatively; writing factually; and interpreting visual material.

Girls' success is interpreted as *unfair*, and is attributed to the assessment methodology rather than their greater command of a broader range of English skills than boys. Such an interpretation illustrates Cohen's historical point about 'attributing boys' failure to a *method*' and deflecting attention away from the boys themselves.

A post-war precedent for institutional intervention to distort the assessment of girls' and boys' abilities is the manipulation of grammar school places. Entry requirements for boys were lowered when fewer passed the eleven-plus than girls.

> In the British context, the 11-plus examinations, by which children used to be selected for secondary schooling, were deliberately skewed so that girls had to achieve better results than boys in order to gain entry to selective grammar schools. To do otherwise would have meant that grammar schools would have been overwhelmingly populated by girls.
>
> (Epstein *et al.*, 1998: 5)

This overt attempt to preserve male dominance within educational success, set out to disadvantage girls of comparable and higher ability. Similar institutional control over female success is invoked by the conclusion of Punter and Burchell: that assessment methods should be reviewed, so that criteria for assessing students should incorporate more of what boys are good at – in order to promote their success in a key area. This opens up a highly contentious area, about the contested nature of English as a subject, and whether it should be amended within a capitalist discourse whose concern is to protect the competitive advantage of boys. Who determines what counts as valid knowledge in a patriarchal society? The evolution of English as a 'gendered' subject is fraught with paradoxes. These reflect 'ways in which the history of English as a subject ... embodies the tensions and contradictions inherent in a national education system designed to promote ideals of maleness, but dependant [sic] on women for its delivery' (Miller, 1996: 190). The paradox lies partly in the ways in which English, historically, has been charged with delivering a basic, functional literacy to the mass working populace of a developed economy, while at the same time exercising a nurturing or 'a civilising influence', uneasily entrusted to the hands of women: 'teaching children in school was often perceived as continuous in certain respects with women's traditional relations with children in families' (*ibid*.: 191). A further contemporary paradox, is whether an allegedly 'feminised' curriculum, which values the imaginative and personally responsive areas of experience, is in fact the best preparation for girls to compete in the world of work. What is scarcely mentioned is the position of girls emerging from a 'feminised' curriculum, and whether what they appear to be succeeding in, is in fact valued in an entrepreneurial, competitive, technological and media-oriented society.

English teachers have been urged to resist the political manipulation of English to achieve gender parity between girls and boys. For example, Peter Thomas, Principal Examiner for NEAB GCSE, rejects the idea of amending English syllabuses to accommodate boys' needs and skills, condemning it as a process of 'dumbing down'. He prefers to maintain 'sensitivity towards ideas, language and imagined readers', which means that 'boys will do less well because they are boys, and less subtle and skilful than girls of an equivalent age' (Thomas, 1997: 23). This proposition implies a hierarchy of skills that are desirable in the subject of English – and if they favour girls, then it reflects a regrettable lack in boys, rather than an argument to alter the subject. The polarisation of 'boys' English' and 'girls' English' needs to be reconceptualised in terms of the opportunities that exist in the world beyond school for those who can utilise a whole range of language skills. In effect, methods have moved away from course-work-dominated assessment, which enhanced girls' achievement relative to boys, to terminal exams in which boys, supposedly, excel. The fact that the differential has subsequently fallen since 1993, reflects an improvement in boys' achievement, along with the fact that girls have been getting better at passing exams. It seems that the worries are not about boys failing to improve – for they are – but about them failing to catch up with the girls. The political imperative to do so, seems to supersede the desirability of the skills that course-work promotes in both boys and girls, and which have been praised by, for example, the CBI.

The problem with boys – sexualised identities in English

Underpinning the tensions in the relationships among gender, literacy and schooling, is the issue of pupils' sexualised identities at school. It is possible to identify two main perspectives on the causes of boys' underachievement within arguments centred on 'male' concepts of identity. One is to interpret boys as asserting their masculinity in the rejection of what it means to be 'good at English'. This is connected with concerns about a 'laddish culture', in which young males exhibit an anti-work ethos, or seek 'hard' or factual knowledge that will link directly to their status as dominant heterosexual males in a capitalist, patriarchal society, partly to affirm their employability in male areas. For those who want to 'get on', there is an instrumental understanding of what they are prepared to give in exchange for what they will gain. Literacy for 'getting a job' was enshrined by the male pupil respondents in *Boys and English* as the one area that English was good for. The compulsory study of, for example, Shakespeare at Key Stage 3, does not sit easily with an instrumental view of becoming literacy-skilled for the workplace. The 'laddish' culture has been met with a counter-offensive to 'raise standards', which includes government policies of 'target-setting' and 'zero tolerance' – all dominant male responses, according to a feminist interpretation of current educational policy-making. It is possible to identify the drive for standards as operating within a male arena, contextualised by patriarchal concerns, in what Reed calls the 'masculinisation' of educational policies and practices' (Reed, 1998: 60). It does not offer a very productive way forward – which is perhaps being realised in the reported 'plateauing out' of reading and writing results for 11-year-olds in the 1998 SATs, at a level that leaves boys consistently achieving less than girls. For example: 'A Government spokesman – confirmed that boys continued to cause concern' (Pyke, 1998).

An alternative way of looking at the effects of the heterosexual, dominant, male imperative is needed. Despite the Literacy Hour, SATs, league tables, national literacy targets and a rigorous inspection machine, boys' prospects at school are still problematic, according to studies of adolescent males in the 1990s. Mac an Ghaill's (1994) exploration of 'the processes involved in the interplay between schooling, masculinities and sexualities' stresses the complexity of the context of boys' apparent failure to achieve. For those who are striving, under the gaze of so many critical eyes, to motivate boys in literacy learning, it spells out the fact that boys' and girls' learning is inextricably bound up with their experience of class, race and sexuality, both in society at large and within schools in particular. For both working-class and middle-class boys, this is what characterises their discriminating approach to what is worth learning, despite how differently they regard school and each other. There is a common sense of 'bartering' – of seeing what can be got from the system, what the dividend might be in the real world of work. None of the boys in this study seem to find much at school that is inherently interesting or enriching in its own right. For the middle-class boys who want to 'get on', there is a tacit investment in certain aspects of the curriculum. For the working-class boys, a comparison with Willis's disaffected 'lads', from the 1970s study, *Learning To Labour*, shows how millennium panic is revisiting the same unresolved issues. Disaffected boys still offer a conventional endorsement of the conflicts between working-class male identity and school work: 'The work you do here is girls' work. It's not real work. It's just for kids. They [the teachers] try to make you write down things about how you feel – we live in the real world' (Mac an Ghaill, 1994: 59). But there is more to this than boys reacting against the so-called 'feminisation' of English teaching. This issue is about how what is taught fits in with what is on offer in the world outside with how boys and girls come to see themselves becoming men and women, in a world that offers little scope for them to transgress reductive sexual identities. Mac an Ghaill's research offers a different angle on the emotional, sexual and social individuals who are the objects of all the promotional literature about improving literacy, and calls for a fundamental rethink of the curriculum model on offer. This perspective points to the futility of a ' "race"- and gender-blind curricular approach' for boys, and there are important implications as to how the learning of literacy stands as a dubious goal for them during the secondary years.

Implications for pedagogy – how can English teachers enhance the learning of both boys and girls?

Both boys and girls stand to gain from the whole spectrum of reflective and active language learning, if they are to play the fullest parts in social and economic life. English teachers need to avoid a polarised literacy focus for girls and boys, and rather plan for the curriculum to be made accessible and enriching to all. The reductive concept of 'literacy' that accompanies the current political drive for boys' higher achievement needs critical treatment. However, it seems that some commentators believe that, for effective English teaching to appeal to working-class boys, it must happen covertly and be re-christened 'basic skills', or happen in a 'literacy hour'. In a government-sponsored response to current gender differences, the Basic Skills Agency has offered sound and practical advice based on classroom success with boys – but it is hard to see what there is about its findings that is exclusive to male learners; or to 'basic skills' as opposed to English:

> English departments took unusual care with planning and with the presentation of lessons ... they placed strong emphasis on the self-organisation of their pupils and on supporting them by adopting structured approaches to thinking, and to writing in particular.

> Special approaches included short, structured tasks with clear targets and deadlines ... storyboards and similar analytical techniques adopted from media studies ... the frequent use of DARTs ... offering systematic prompts to assist with re-drafting ...
>
> (Frater, 1997: 29–30)

Frater's recommendations look at gender achievement as embedded in the everyday practices of effective English teaching, within whole-school approaches to enhancing the achievement of pupils, rather than in special 'projects'. It is to be hoped that initiatives to improve boys' learning will enhance effective teaching for all – although we must dispute the contention that girls' needs are an insignificant additional outcome to the provision of a more motivating curriculum for boys.

Holistic pedagogical approaches offer a more productive way forward than the treatment of gender as a 'topic' in English, which can be fraught with conflicts within the sexualised domain of the classroom. When pupils' identities are so bound up with their gender, teachers need to be aware of the dangers of attempting systematic dismantling, and resist 'teaching approaches to gender work in schools that are based on a rigid polarization between victims and perpetrators' (Jackson, 1998: 83). A critique of gender roles can conflict in an unproductive way with the home cultures inhabited by pupils – in a world where stability can sometimes be precarious enough. Rather than looking at it as a 'topic' for study, this section will look at pedagogy differently – through considering gender in the everyday practice of English lessons, in pupils' dealings with language. Through language, pupils can see ways of positively identifying themselves, and more fully understand the nature of their gender identity – to see explicitly how it is manifested in the social interactions of speaking and listening, reading and writing. English is a subject where the content is itself the stuff of meaning, both reflecting what exists and helping its interpretation. Therefore, the final section of this chapter examines ways of intervening in the practice of literacy itself – in helping girls and boys to see the ways in which they are communicating, and to see learning within English as part of a progression to an ever-widening and refocused development of those skills.

Speaking and listening

Luke (1994) notes that in classrooms, boys out-talk girls by a ratio of 3:1, and girls' contributions are praised less than those of boys. Language is a form of social practice (Swann, 1992), and the ways in which it is regulated and used in school both reflect and prepare students for gender inequalities in language use in wider society (Paechter, 1998: 24).

This analysis of research into classroom talk in secondary schools indicates that boys dominate in turn-taking, time for talk, and attracting the teacher's invitations to speak: 'It would appear ... that girls are marginalised in two forms of classroom talk that are important learning contexts: learning through collaborative discussion in mixed groups and class discussion with the teacher' (*ibid.*: 25).

Accounts of the silencing of girls in mixed classrooms will be nothing new to any teacher who has taught in one: they have a particular resonance for English teachers who are charged with developing Speaking and Listening within a context of sexualised power relations. This complicates the rhetorical claims made by the BBC programme, Panorama, *The Future is Female* (BBC 1,

May 1995) that girls' superior oral communication skills make them more economically viable in the new generation of communications employment. The dimension of social class needs bringing to bear on the simplified term 'female'. Which females are making inroads on economic and political power-bases? Certainly not working-class girls, whose oral communication skills are chiefly denigrated in a culture that dismisses their talk as 'idle gossip', 'girl-talk' and 'chin-wagging'. The following points are rooted in the premise that all spoken English work occurs in classrooms that are a microcosm of a gendered society:

- Teacher-directed whole-class talk allows boys more opportunities to dominate: classroom discussion 'can ... be seen as competitive; in the rapid to and fro of student-teacher interaction it is usually the first to offer to respond (by raising one's hand or catching the teacher's eye) who gets to speak' – and the most successful at this are boys (Paechter, 1998: 25). Teachers need to ensure that this is not the main opportunity for talk, and that group and paired talk attract high-profile status as 'learning activities' – so that those who do not so confidently interact with the teacher in front of the whole class receive praise and feedback for their contributions.
- Where whole-class talk occurs, turn-taking can be an explicit learning aim, and boys' and girls' contributions can be monitored within this framework.
- Group discussion work requires careful choices about the composition of groups. In mixed groups, boys can dominate in turn-taking, while not developing collaborative learning as efficiently as girls (examination boards' trial-marking material for GCSE English oral grading 1988–94 reflected this repeatedly in its samples). Teachers need to make judicious decisions about when mixed groups are productive, and when they repro-duce patterns of dominance along gender lines – in terms of who talks, and how talk and scribing is conducted.
- In group talk, both boys and girls benefit from different speaking roles being made explicit to them, and also the criteria by which they are judged to be progressing, as well as criteria related to competent spoken perform-ance, e.g. encouraging others to speak; illustrating that they have listened to a particular point made by another speaker; supporting someone else's idea; offering an example to illustrate a point already made; initiating a new line of discussion.
- Opportunities should exist for students to examine the features of their own speaking and listening, and to reflect critically on them in terms of their gender. For example, work on a project such as the English and Media Centre's 'Language Autobiography' can be extended to give the opportu-nity for pupils to reflect on their spoken language related to gender, to augment broader work on individual language histories. Clearly, gender is a main factor in the oral skills at students' disposal, and can form an impor-tant additional aspect of such work, along with family history, region and

dialect. Students can be asked to consider how their own talk is conditioned by the expectations of others, self-regulation among gender peergroups, family and gendered talk, school talk, and how they relate to gendered social criteria regulating boys' and girls' talk, e.g. responding to terms like 'gossip'. Extensive examples of work like this can be found in published materials like *Language and Gender Packs 1 and 2* (Goddard, 1989).

For both boys and girls, reflection on gendered talk is a critical aspect of approaches to speaking and listening and language study: beyond the National Curriculum, such reflection can teach them how gender influences access to powerful and excluding spoken discourses.

Reading

In the National Year of Reading, boys were targeted through the positive images that leapt out from government publicity literature: they were depicted as eagerly reading, enjoying shared time with books, surrounded by committed adults, in a tacit acknowledgement that it was widespread concern about boys' reading that drove the initiative:

> recent studies of reading attitudes in English primary schools have concluded that the major difference in reading attitudes for Year 2, Year 4, and Year 6 children is ... located in the content of what was read rather than in a lack of interest in reading itself ... It has also been repeatedly recorded that gender differences in reading interests widen as pupils progress through school ...
>
> (Millard, 1997: 13)

Millard locates the origins of this disparity within the culture of early reading development in the primary school, which privileges narrative genre – which then continues to predominate in the secondary curriculum. This has been deemed a contributing factor to boys' alienation from reading: 'In all year groups girls read more fiction than boys' and 'Boys made less use of school libraries than girls' (Ofsted, 1993b: 2). In a masculinised society, emotion and imagination in fictionalised texts have little currency compared with fact. Factual texts offer more security about the viability of what will be learnt – the risk of 'wasted effort' is less, the reward more immediately tangible (Daly, 1999). In resisting a binary opposition of 'girls' reading' and 'boys' reading', we can ensure that girls benefit from the reading materials and strategies that boys prefer, and carry these benefits into a competitive world that demands multiliterate capabilities. There is surely much to be gained by boys, in developing a language to consider feelings, relationships and 'real people', all aspects of literature study that were considered irredeemably lost on them by advisory documents like *Can Do Better*.

The critical issue concerning teachers' power, is how reading is conceptualised in the classroom. Gender differences in attitudes towards reading are complex, and the following points can be made:

- Boys and girls can perceive the act of reading itself as a gendered form of behaviour. Much of the reading undertaken in classrooms is performed as a quiet, still, passive, compliant and constrained physical process. This conforms to stereotypical 'feminine' behaviour, at a time when adolescents are increasingly conscious of sexual identities (Daly, 1998: 109). Teachers need to reconceptualise reading as a behaviour in the classroom, to make opportunities for the active interrogation of texts, through dramatisation, media adaptation, Directed Activities Related to Texts, and group oral reading projects – for girls and boys to see themselves as variously skilled and behaving actively when they read, as well as reflecting introspectively.
- Female pupils find compensatory power in the lives of heroines in teenage romance novels, at a time when they are becoming more aware of gender differences in the economic power-roles in society (Rogers Cherland and Edelsky, 1993). Boys and girls need opportunities to develop critical reading about heroes and heroines who both transgress stereotypical embodiments of power, and conform to them.
- Male pupils are often alienated from the main texts that count as reading material, i.e. 'literature', in many classrooms. Their expressed reading preferences are infrequently met beyond occasional private reading opportunities. Science fiction, factual information books, hobby books, horror writing, graphic novels and comics are rarely given a high-profile whole-class focus. Teachers need to audit their reading environment, and ensure that such texts feature in book boxes and group sets for shared reading, as well as sometimes attracting whole-class attention.
- Close liaison with the school librarian is clearly vital, in order to construct a diverse reading environment for both girls and boys.
- A main emphasis on character study, personal response and empathy as approaches to literature is preferred by girls, while this is alienating to many boys. There is a need to teach girls – who find an empathetic response easier – that an over-reliance on this genre inhibits the practice of other analytical skills that have currency outside of English. Boys in general have expressed a greater interest in events and plot development, and analytical ways of writing about literature.
- Girls need to be introduced to a broad range of information texts, and taught to read them critically. Both boys and girls need to question the assumptions underlying 'hard knowledge' (Meek, 1997).

Writing

Anne Fine's novel for younger readers, *Bill's New Frock*, tells the story of the Kafkaesque Bill, who wakes up one morning to find he is transformed into a girl. At school that day his writing behaviour changes with his gender:

He wrote more than he usually did. He wrote it more neatly than usual too. If you looked back through the last few pages of his work, you'd see he'd done a really good job, for him.

(Fine, 1989: 16)

Gendered preferences and experiences in reading are frequently duplicated in choices of genre for writing: 'Girls, with their greater familiarity with a continuous prose style – that is not only the staple of their book reading, but which also permeates the style of the magazines they prefer ... – write narratives that fulfil teachers' implicit criteria of competence more readily' (Millard, 1997: 124–5). Instrumental writing offers more appeal to boys, once again figuring in the calculated decisions that many boys make related to employability: 'Writing will certainly help you when you apply for jobs' (Ofsted, 1993b), but this is not a prevalent genre in the English classroom.

Intervention in the writing process is critical, to make explicit to girls and boys the distinctions, strengths and weaknesses of gender-bound forays into writing. If a main purpose of writing is to assist the development of thinking as well as the manipulation of powerful written genres, effective teaching requires a judicious balance between modelling genre, and intervening to support pupils' own written language. When pupils are working with the writing process – through active drafting – there is much to be learnt from self-review, especially for pupils whose performance in continuous writing is limited. The development of ideas is afforded by those opportunities in writing to reflect, refine and rethink how they are articulated; there are implications affecting the learning of those (mostly boys), for whom continuous writing is problematic.

Thomas (1997) discusses the concept of 'solo potency' to describe the limitations of boys as narrative writers. In a persuasive metaphor, boys are likened to manic male drivers, who accelerate egotistically throughout their writing. The male hero wins over all, driving his story onwards, regardless of context or purpose:

Boys' stories often have pace and event at the expense of anything else ... It's the ability to respond to a passenger, and to the landscape, as well as to have a purpose for the journey which makes for good travelling. Screaming on two wheels from one action high spot to another is tiring, unproductive, and satisfying only to the driver.

(Thomas, 1997: 25)

There is much to consider about why boys find this packed factual narrative so satisfying, and relevant to their needs – but it reveals a lack of awareness of possible audiences, and an undeveloped understanding of the possibilities of genre. Thomas's point about intervening in composition is critical to the development of all writing – both girls' and boys': 'Good narrative composes events in a social or moral context. Boys' writing can be improved by connecting events with references to settings, other characters or authenticating detail.' (*ibid.*: 25).

Teacher intervention is the emphasis of his argument, and that teachers need to help pupils learn about criteria for redrafting text to make their interventions productive. These can become pupil interventions, where pupils learn in a conscious way about how they are writing – including understanding the influence of gender on the effectiveness of the results. The National Curriculum identifies drafting as a requirement of writing development, and paired drafting was already common practice in many schools since its promotion by the National Writing Project, but not usually with an emphasis on gender – the question of gendered authorship is generally not addressed within the writing process.

The following points support further planning for more effective writing within a range of genres for all pupils:

- 'Audience' needs to be clearly defined for particular pieces of writing, and articulation of that audience is critical; interventions need to make explicit how important it is to consider the audience for the writing, who may have different interests from the pupils.
- Criteria for effective writing need to be made explicit, but this does not mean issuing pupils with a prescriptive set of formulaic rules. Pupils can help formulate their own criteria by guided work that discusses the features of an effective sample text.
- Allow opportunities for neat *and* rough work. Discrimination about which type of work is appropriate for different occasions should be encouraged, and rough work should not be relegated to general notebooks or the backs of exercise books – it needs to be given full status as real and vital 'work'. For example, drafting books can be used, where pupils know they are expected to evaluate their writing against criteria before redrafting. Both boys and girls can benefit from critically re-appraising the false equation of neatness with quality.
- Build in a variety of ways for pupils to organise and develop ideas prior to writing, for example by using drama, story-boards and spidergrams.
- Build in opportunities for Information and Communications Technology to help composition and drafting, not just 'typing up' existing text.
- Encourage cross-gender authorship through collaborative writing games, for example by asking individuals or pairs to add a new line or paragraph to a piece of writing in a specified genre, which then passes on to the next authors to continue.
- Paired drafting can be extended to asking pupils to consider gendered features in their writing. For example, with creative writing, drafting criteria can refer to: the expectations of the intended audience; choices about verbs – active and passive; selection of nouns; narrative pace; features of characterisation.

Conclusions

The current prioritisation of boys' performance within a particular assessment model of English is at the expense of considering the implications of the demands for a broader conceptualisation of what it is to be 'good' at English in today's society. Millard (1997) reminds us of the need to widen the focus on gender issues and achievement:

> If we also consider the range of boys' literacy interests outside of school, and their greater interest in the new technologies it becomes clearer that girls also have a stake in our re-examination of literacy practices in the whole of schooling – Girls currently appear to be doing better than boys in terms of school work, but we need to question further whether their expressed literacy preferences are the best preparation for developments that are redirecting attention away from the page to the screen, from the pen to the mouse, and from a well-structured essay to a well-organised Web site.
>
> (Millard, 1997: 181)

Boys know what they need from English in instrumental terms, but boys and girls have complicated perceptions of what it means to be successful beyond school, and they continue to discriminate about what is useful. While teachers' energies are directed towards the achievement of boys, the factors that influence differentiated success in school and beyond go unchallenged – including questions about who determines what counts as English, and the ideological functions of English as an instrument of cultural continuity. There exist no plans to review what constitutes 'English' in this fundamental way, or how it is to be assessed. At the same time, the huge impact of Information and Communications Technology is seen as peripheral to assessing ability in English – but we must envisage the day when composing and publishing a web page may carry equal marks to the Shakespeare paper in the SATs for fourteen-year-olds – or indeed replace it. Relations among ICT, language and literature all remain unresolved, and form a vital aspect of differing gender performance in a subject in which there is so much cultural and economic investment. What is vital is to retain a critical perspective on current gender concerns, and understand them within a history of male privilege in educational discourse, which is always politically and economically determined.

Questions for discussion

1   The current alarmist discourse about gender and male underachievement draws on a reductive conceptualisation of 'literacy' and how to assess it. Consider the way in which English is conceptualised for assessment purposes in either the primary or secondary phase. Do decisions about what is assessed and how pupils are measured leave out other areas of ability that might be acknowledged as English? How does this absence affect the relative gender performance of pupils?

2   With the principles discussed in this chapter in mind, and with reference to the National Curriculum areas of speaking and listening, reading and writing, how might schemes of work be revised to ensure that pupils can access a curriculum that is empowering for both boys and girls?

3   How does the status of ICT in English departments affect conceptions of 'ability' in relation to boys and girls?

Further reading

Epstein, D., Elwood, J., Hey, V. and Maw, J. (1998) *Failing Boys? Issues in Gender and Achievement*, Buckingham: Open University Press.
This book offers a critique of contemporary discourses surrounding boys' underachievement, and explodes several myths: it looks at relative achievement in school within a broader understanding of gendered power relations.

Frater, G. (1997) *Improving Boys' Literacy*, London: Basic Skills Agency.
This booklet, provided free by the Basic Skills Agency, contains practical advice on teaching strategies to improve the motivation of boys in English. Importantly, it locates these strategies within whole-school approaches to more effective teaching for *all* pupils.

Millard, E. (1997) *Differently Literate*, London: Falmer Press.
Millard's study of gender differences in the learning of English has made a significant impact on the current debate, and broadens the focus to view literacy behaviour as being influenced by factors beyond the classroom. It provides research evidence based both in and out of school, to present a comprehensive picture of the diversity of literacy practices of both boys and girls.

Miller, J. (1996) *School for Women*, London: Virago.
In this analysis of the history of the relationship between females and education, Jane Miller manages to be both scholarly and vividly personal. Autobiographical, historical and critical – it makes a compelling read.

Paechter, C. (1998) *Educating the Other*, London: Falmer Press.
This book is a timely reminder of how the current discourse around boys' needs is reaffirming the position of male as Subject, to which female is the 'other'. What is vital about the book is the way it flies in the face of current 'macro' concerns, and positions them firmly within a continuum of the privileging of the male Subject in educational discourse. It asserts that individuals are required to collude in the privileging of male power as the prime agenda in education.

16 Literacy and social class

Jon Davison

> Dominant social and cultural groups have been able to establish their language, and their knowledge priorities, learning styles, pedagogical preferences, etc., as the 'official examinable culture' of school. Their notions of important and useful knowledge, their ways of presenting truth, their ways of arguing and establishing correctness, and their logics, grammars and language as institutional norms by which academic and scholastic success is defined and assessed.
>
> (Lankshear, 1997: 30)

The last decade of the twentieth century began with a Conservative Prime Minister announcing that society did not exist, and drew to a close with a New Labour Prime Minister announcing that we are now all members of the middle class. It has become unfashionable in recent years to discuss social class and education. There appears to be an underlying assumption that it is now passé to do so: the debate has moved on; social class is an irrelevance. However, it could be argued that the issue has never been properly tackled. In the early 1980s the Inner London Education Authority launched its 'Sex, Race and Class' initiative. While the ILEA did much work relating to the first two, for all its egalitarian zeal, it shied away from grasping the nettle of class.

However, government figures produced in 1991 showed that only 5% of children from skilled manual home backgrounds attended university (Social Trends, 1992), and, despite a claimed 30% increase in access to university, in 1998 only approximately 5% of those at university came from the poorest post-coded areas (Halsey, 1998). Despite the inception of the National Curriculum, which was designed to ensure an equal curricular entitlement for all pupils, children from working-class backgrounds are underachieving. OECD statistics (OECD, 1997) declared eight million adults in the United Kingdom to be 'functionally illiterate'. This chapter explores some of the reasons for this underachievement and the role that the teaching of English has played in promoting success or creating failure in pupils. While this chapter fully acknowledges that there are equal-opportunities issues concerning under-achievement relating to gender and race, a work of this length could not also attempt to address these issues without the risk of trivialisation.

A second aim of this chapter is to consider the importance of discursive practice in the social construction of knowledge, and the need to make educational discourses *visible* to pupils. Finally, the chapter argues the need for pupils to develop an empowering literacy.

Social class and educational policy-makers

The quotation that opens this chapter is taken from Colin Lankshear's exploration of sociolinguistics, *Changing Literacies*. He then goes on to say that the determination of 'the official examinable culture of the school' by dominant social and cultural groups is not necessarily a conscious process and far less a conspiracy:

> It is simply what tends to happen, with the result that Discourse and dis-courses of dominant groups become those which dominate education, and become established as major legitimate routes to securing social goods (like wealth and status). As a result, educational success is patterned along distinct lines of prior discursive experience associated with membership of particular social groups.
>
> (Lankshear *et al.*, 1997: 30)

While one might agree with Lankshear's observations regarding a conspir-acy, there is, nevertheless, a question of power relations to be answered when discussing dominant discourses. Gee defines Discourse as:

> a socially accepted association among ways of using language, of thinking, and of acting that can be used to identify oneself as a member of a socially meaningful group or 'social network'.
>
> (Gee, 1991: 21)

On examining official government documents it is difficult not to be struck by attitudes to the working class displayed by educational policy-makers throughout the twentieth century. Elsewhere, Baldick (1983), Davison and Dowson (1998), Eagleton (1983) and Palmer (1965) consider in detail how beliefs about working-class pupils shaped policy and practice in the English classroom during the twentieth century, but here it is useful, briefly, to remind ourselves of what these attitudes were.

> Many persons, most prominently social and economic leaders and social reformers, grasped the uses of schooling and the vehicle of literacy for the promotion of values, attitudes and habits considered essential to the main-tenance of social order and the persistence of integration and cohesion.
>
> (Graff, 1987: 7)

For Gossman (1981: 82) state education and the importance of English were 'advocated in a hard-headed way as a means of social control'. Poet and HMI, Matthew Arnold (1869: 105), saw the 'raw and half developed' working class living 'amidst poverty and squalor' as a threat to social stability, which would be averted by a high cultural, 'pure-English-as-civilising-agent' approach to education.

Concerns about the level of literacy among working-class children were addressed by the Board of Education (1910) *Circular 753*, which was instrumental in establishing the nature of English as it came to be taught in school, 'instruction in English in the secondary school aims at training the mind to appreciate English Literature and at cultivating the power of using the English Language in speech and writing' (para 2). With the founding of the Board of Education, and the establishment of what was – in reality – a national curriculum, during the first twenty years of the twentieth century, the successive circulars and reports promulgated beliefs in the power of English to civilise the masses. 'Pure English is not merely an accomplishment, but an index to and a formative influence over character' (Board of Education, 1910: para 2).

The importance of spoken English

The first major report into *The Teaching of English in England* was published in 1921, and it too was suspicious of the growing working class. The Newbolt Report (Board of Education, 1921), as it tends to be known after its chair, Sir Henry Newbolt, poet and Oxford Professor of Poetry, was sympathetic to elementary school teachers who had 'to fight against evil habits of speech contracted in home and street'. One senses the vehemence here in the choice of adjective to describe pupils' spoken English, which is referred to as 'disfigured' (para 67). The Report's hostility to working-class children is confirmed, when it describes the teacher's battle, which is 'not with ignorance but with a perverted power' (para 59). Children who do not use standard English are more than just untutored, they are 'evil' and 'perverted'.

There is not space, here, to discuss them in detail, but similar attitudes are be found in subsequent reports produced throughout the twentieth century. In the early years of the century, *Circular 753* lamented that pupils 'fall helplessly back on slang, the base coin of the language' (Board of Education, 1910: para 2), while a decade after the Newbolt Report, in the *Report on Secondary Education* (the Spens Report: Board of Education, 1938), pupils' spoken English is described as 'slovenly, ungrammatical, and often incomprehensible to a stranger' (p. 220). Half a century later, *English from 5 to 16* believed that pupils should 'Speak clearly, audibly and pleasantly, in an accent intelligible to the listener(s)' (DES, 1984: 10).

Three years after the inception of the National Curriculum, the draft proposals for a rewritten National Curriculum *English for Ages 5 to 16 (1993)* (DfE, 1993) stated that, from Key Stage 1, pupils 'should speak clearly using Standard English' and 'should be taught to speak accurately, precisely, and with clear diction'. Examples of accuracy and precision cited in the proposals include: 'We were (not was) late back from the trip'; 'We won (not winned) at cricket'; 'Pass me those (not them) books'; 'Clive and I (not me) are going to Wembley'; 'We haven't seen anybody (not nobody)' (pp. 9–23). In Chapter 7, Chris Davies examines the debate concerning 'correct' and 'appropriate' use of language.

The threat of the unions

For the members of the Newbolt Committee, not only were working-class children perceived as potentially dangerous, so too were members of 'organised labour movements', because they 'were antagonistic to, and contemptuous of literature … a subject to be despised by really virile men'. The writers of the Report learned that, 'a large number of thinking working men' believed literature to be as useful and relevant to their lives as, 'antimacassars, fish-knives and other unintelligible and futile trivialities of middle-class culture' and that it was taught in schools only 'to side-track the working movement' (para 233). Writing elsewhere, Newbolt Committee member George Sampson (1921) further stereotypes 'the extravagant British workman' and his 'moral, intellectual and emotional level', whose habits lead him to 'the newest and nudest revues' and who ends by 'being divorced'. Sampson believed that working-class children would only be saved by the correct teaching of English, because it would serve to educate them intellectually, morally and spiritually and 'very especially it will cover all that we at present leave naked and barbarous' (Sampson, 1921: 104–5). The teaching of correct English would do nothing to address the glaring social inequalities in society other than 'cover' them – an attitude that re-emerged in the *Report on Secondary Education*, the Spens Report: 'it should be possible for the spread of a common habit of English teaching to soften the distinctions which separate men and classes in later life' (Board of Education, 1938: 222).

(Un)Popular culture

The majority of official education policy documents in the twentieth century were antipathetic to popular culture. Not only was *Circular 753* (Board of Education, 1910) clear about the qualities instilled by an exposure to 'pure' English, it was also dismissive of popular, or working-class, culture: 'Boys and girls will read of their own accord many books – chiefly fiction. These … are only of transitory interest, and involve little or no mental effort' (*ibid.*: para 17).

Policy-makers espoused a moral, and almost evangelical approach to the teaching of 'Great Literature'. It was believed that nothing was more valuable, or indeed more civilising, than pupils connecting with the great minds of the past. Pupils were to be brought into the presence of the great works of Milton, Wordsworth, Coleridge, Swift and the like, in order to 'appreciate' the 'divine nature' of such texts (Davison and Dowson, 1998: 22). It was maintained that pupils 'should be taught to understand, not to criticise or judge' such great works (Board of Education, 1910: para 36). Thus, a version of English teaching that had as its purpose an induction into high culture, by definition must be antipathetic to popular culture. (In Chapter 12, Janet Maybin examines the role that canonical texts have played in the teaching of English and its 'official examinable culture'.)

It is unsurprising, therefore, that elsewhere, the adverse effects of cinema were deplored: 'the mental effect upon the children was to make them more fond of noise, ostentatious display, self-advertisement and change. The pictures excited their minds and created a love of pleasure and disinclination for steady work and effort' (*Times Educational Supplement*, 1915). Such attitudes can be found in official education documentation throughout the century: 'The pervading influences of the hoarding, the cinema, and a large section of the public press, are (in this respect as in others) subtly corrupting the taste and habits of the rising generation' (Board of Education, 1938: 222–3). This antipathy to the indulgence of children in popular culture can be traced to the present day in educational documents: from cinema through radio, television and video, to computer games. Although the Bullock Report *A Language for Life* (Department of Education and Science, 1975) helped to pave the way for media education, it contains the same attitudes displayed by the dominant social groups half a century earlier:

> Between them, radio and television spread the catch-phrase, the advertising jingle, and the frenetic trivia of the disc-jockey ... it is clear that the content and form of much radio and television utterance makes the teacher's job a great deal more difficult.
>
> (*ibid*.: para 2.8)

Twenty years later, at the Conservative Party conference on 7 October 1992, the then Secretary of State for Education, John Patten, railed against '1960s theorists', 'the trendy left', and 'teachers' union bosses', who were destroying 'our great literary heritage'. In a speech that attacked not only the trade unions but also popular culture, he warned: 'They'd give us chips with Chaucer. Milton with mayonnaise. Mr Chairman, I want William Shakespeare in our classrooms, not Ronald McDonald' (Patten, 1992).

The problem of 'naturalisation'

Even from this cursory examination of the development of the subject, it would appear that Lankshear's assertion is correct. For most of the twentieth century, dominant views about the nature of the subject have held sway. Particular 'notions of important and useful knowledge', clearly defined 'ways of arguing and establishing correctness' have formed the basis of school curricula, examination syllabuses, and the National Curriculum for English, which, in their assessment methodology, have established the 'institutional norms by which academic and scholastic success is defined and assessed'.

John Patten's speech fully endorses the view of English as a great literary tradition. The 1995 National Curriculum maintained the importance of standard English as the means of teaching and learning. Such attitudes have at their heart what has become the 'traditional' view of English teaching. For almost a century, a dominant version of the subject has prevailed, which, with the exception of a brief period during the 1960s and 1970s, has been, for the most part, accepted rather than challenged. With the passing of time, the re-iteration of a dominant view leads to the belief that the status quo is the natural order of things by some universal right. In other words, a particular curricular content, attitudes, values and practices are accepted as the very 'nature' of English itself, rather than interrogated to determine the underpin-ning value systems:

> A particular set of discourse practices and conventions may achieve a high degree of *naturalisation* – they may come to be seen as simply 'there' in a common-sense way, rather than socially put there.
>
> (Fairclough, 1992: 9)

Schooling and underachievement

> within societies like our own there is a tendency for forms of literacy to prevail which effectively maintain patterned inequalities of power within the social structure.
>
> (Lankshear, 1987: 79–80)

In the latter half of the twentieth century, a variety of aspects of school life have been examined in order to identify the causes of pupil underachievement: e.g. access, institutional structures and the nature of school knowledge. It is well documented that, despite the intentions of Education Acts from 1944 to 1988, children from the working class have continued to underachieve at school. Floud et al.(1966) exposed massive under-representation of working-class boys at grammar schools. Douglas (1964) showed how working-class pupils with the same IQ scores as middle-class children were failing to gain grammar school places, because of the bias of teachers in primary schools, while the IQ tests themselves were shown to have a middle-class bias in their content. It is also now well known that the eleven-plus scores of girls were adjusted down because they were far outstripping boys' achievement (see The Report of the Task Group on Assessment and Testing (TGAT) (DES, 1987: 40–53) for a discussion of these issues in relation to the establishment of the National Curriculum).

Hargreaves (1967), Lacey (1970) and Ball (1981) have cited the institu-tional structures of schools, such as streaming and banding, as influential in determining the performance of working-class pupils: a disproportionate number of whom were found to be represented in the lower streams and bands. For others, such as Brown (1973), Bourdieu (1973) and Bowles and Gintis (1976), it is the stratification of school knowledge that reproduces inequalities in 'cultural capital'.

This is not to say that working-class pupils are simply passive recipients of a dominant culture, for studies by Gaskell (1985) and Willis (1977, 1981) for example, have shown how pupils resist school culture – although Abraham's (1993) study reveals that resistance comes more from 'anti-school' pupils, whatever their social background. Abraham goes on to argue that:

> the organising and processing of school knowledge provides a setting which is not sufficiently critical of social class and gender divisions to discourage their reproduction in further schooling and out into the occupational structure.
>
> (1993: 136)

For Ball *et al.* (1990), Gee (1991) and Lankshear (1987, 1997), the challenge for those who would wish to address such issues lies in the development of an alternative to the dominant model of English, and in inculcating a 'proper' literacy that will empower pupils.

Forms of English as a school subject

The Cox Report (DES, 1989: para 2.21–5) identified the five broad versions of English that its writers found in schools: 'Personal Growth'; 'Cross-curricular'; 'Adult Needs'; 'Cultural Heritage', and 'Cultural Analysis'. Ball *et al.* (1990: 76) propose four main versions of the subject that have emerged since 1900: 'English as Skills'; 'English as the Great Literary Tradition'; 'Progressive English'; and 'English as Critical Literacy'. For Ball *et al.*, it is the first two models that have dominated.

Ball *et al.* go further and usefully link these versions of the subject to questions of power and conceptions of literacy, which they locate on a two-by-two matrix (see Figure 16.1 on p. 250). The horizontal axis – 'Self–Not self' – concerns relationships between people, and portrays the distance between a focus on the personal, private needs of the individual and the formal, rule-governed situations to which the individual might be subject: the essence of an individual living in a society. Put simply, this means individual needs versus collective need. The vertical axis concerns sources of power and the relationship between polarised authorities: 'Authority–Authenticity'. In essence, the polarity of power lies in the fact that it can be 'top down' or 'bottom up' – dictatorial or democratic. A top-down model is characterised by direction and prescription, whereas, in a bottom-up model, power is developed through negotiation and participation. Figure 16.1 is adapted from Ball *et al.* (1990), and shows the versions of English as a subject mapped into the sectors.

The 'English as Skills' version of the subject has at its heart the development of functionally literate individuals. There is a strong link here with the perceived needs of industry and commerce for individuals who are able to function in the workplace and earn an income. State education acts on behalf of employers and manufacturers by providing a functionally literate workforce of active consumers. Much of the drive for the introduction of the National Literacy Strategy came from a belief that workers in the UK were less literate

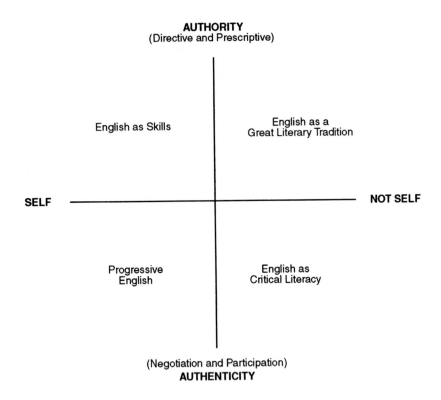

Figure 16.1   Versions of English

than their European counterparts – most notably those in Germany – and were, therefore, not only a symptom of, but also part of the cause of, the decline in British manufacturing industries.

Similarly, there were many complaints from employers that the level of literacy among school-leavers was in steady decline. This perception is, however, hardly surprising, when we consider the social changes that have occurred since, say 1960, and the growth in the literacy demands on individuals: for example, exponential growth in advertising has led to a need to decode sophisticated, complex advertisements in print alone. Increasingly, the demands made upon applicants for even the lowest-status jobs have increased during periods of high unemployment. As a consumer, the individual has had to develop complex skills, a change partly brought about by the transition of corner grocery shops into out-of-town supermarkets filled with a plethora of signs and aisle guides, with shelves containing an abundance of groceries in sophisticated packaging, bearing complex instructions. Similarly, the 'packaging' of political messages in the 'infomercial', the increasing delivery of political pamphlets to the home, and sophisticated, enigmatic advertising poster campaigns, have all placed increasing literacy demands on the individual.

Moreover, in the home, every major electrical appliance comes complete with its own forty-eight page guide in six languages. Lankshear (1987) observes that:

> Even if schools improved their current performance to the point where they matched the functional demands of the present day, changes occurring *outside* the school – in technology, economic production, commerce, communications, consumerism, cultural life, etc., – would tend towards creating a rate of illiteracy in the future by simply continuing to raise the minimum required level of print competence.
>
> (*ibid.*: 135)

The National Literacy Strategy and the Literacy Hour are prime manifestations of the English as Skills version of English: a top-down model of prescription and direction, and one which, in its emphasis on print-based literacy, is, in Lankshear's analysis, doomed to failure. John Patten's (1993) *Literacy in the Opportunity Society* is a useful example of the discourse, which promotes this version of English.

The version of 'English as Great Literary Tradition' is likewise constructed on direction and prescription. Ultimately, the high-cultural model is anti-democratic. A selected élite agree the canon of great works into which educated members of society are inducted. As we saw earlier, this is the literacy of morality. The great texts speak of the divine nature of humankind, the virtues, duty and citizenship. They cultivate the intellectual, emotional and moral aspects of life. It is in this version, too, that an emphasis on correctness, on grammar and standard English is located, because the 'standard form is identified with cultivation and national identity, and acts as a form of social closure and social exclusion' (Ball *et al.*, 1990: 79). A prime treatise on this version of English can be found in Marenbon's (1987) *English, Our English.*

Both versions of English are underpinned by models of what Lankshear (1987, 1997) calls 'improper literacy', because the learner is passive – the individual is neither empowered nor invited to engage in the construction of knowledge, nor to debate it. The individual simply learns to conform to a defined set of rules; to regurgitate a predetermined set of attitudes about a prescribed body of texts; to appreciate rather than to critique; and to acquire rather than to actively generate knowledge.

'Progressive English', or the 'Personal Growth' model as Cox referred to it, places an emphasis on the development of the individual and the link between language and learning: the English of self-expression, the personal voice, of creativity and discovery. Here, literature is a source for the development of the individual's imagination and aesthetic sensibilities. Personal responses to stimuli are valued and developed. During the 1960s and 1970s, the development of 100% course-work examinations, of Mode 3 CSEs, which were set and marked by teachers in schools, the development of materials by the Inner London Education Authority's English Centre, and the work of the London Association of the Teaching of English, all helped to develop a more democratic version of the subject. Contemporary culture, mass media, youth culture and popular cultural artefacts were regarded as objects of study – equally as valid as 'traditional' literary texts. John Dixon's (1967) *Growth Through English* was particularly influential in promoting this version of English.

'English as Critical Literacy' is a 'radical' version of the subject. Unquestionably, it acknowledges the political nature of the subject and of schooling. Schooling and Education (two different things) are problematised and debated. 'This version of English is assertive, class-conscious and political in content. Social issues are addressed head-on. The stance is oppositional, collective aspirations and criticisms become the basis for action ... The critical gaze is turned upon the school itself and the processes of schooling' (Ball *et al.*, 1990). Given its nature, it is scarcely surprising that this version of English is attacked with vehemence by right-wing commentators such as Marenbon, Patten and Phillips. It is a model, however, that more closely matches Lankshear's 'proper literacy': 'Literacy is essential for generating and transmitting information, and for organising, lobbying, articulating grievances and so on' (Lankshear, 1987: 144). Chris Searle's *Stepney Words* (1971) and *Heart of Sheffield* (1995) are testaments to the power of a radical version of English teaching.

Discourse and schooling

Gee (1991) makes a distinction between what he calls 'primary' and 'secondary' Discourses and between 'Discourses' and 'discourses'. He defines 'discourses' as the 'connected stretches of language that make sense, like conversations, stories, reports, arguments, essays', as such, they may be found within, appropriate to and different across, Discourses (Gee, 1990: 143). For Gee, Discourse is always greater than language, and incorporates beliefs, values, ways of thinking and behaving, and ways of using language.

An individual's primary Discourse is most often acquired through socialisation into the family: the acquisition of thoughts, values, attitudes and ways of using language that create a world view. Engagement here is most likely to be one-to-one, face-to-face. Discourses incorporate beliefs, values, ways of thinking, of behaving and of using language, and therefore different social groups are likely to have very different primary Discourses.

It is important to recognise that there may not be a congruence between an individual's primary Discourse and secondary Discourses encountered during the process of schooling. Secondary Discourses may be in complete contrast, or in direct opposition, to primary Discourses, and, as such, have relevance to the earlier discussion of working-class underachievement, because it is likely that such a clash of primary and secondary Discourses will 'effectively maintain patterned inequalities of power within the social structure' (Lankshear, 1987: 79–80). Furthermore, such a situation is likely to be exacerbated precisely because the ground rules of the secondary 'educated' Discourse remain invisible.

For Freire (1972, 1976), human beings develop through a process of reflection upon action: a conscious objectification of their own and others' actions through investigation, contemplation and comment. By engaging in such a process, they become historical and cultural agents, which is an active, rather than passive, role. This 'becoming', however, is not achieved in isolation, but through a process of 'dialogue' (Freire, 1985: 49–59):

> becoming is the ontological vocation of human beings: of *all* humans equally. To deny any human beings the right to name the world on equal terms is to dehumanise those people, to subvert their ontological vocation, to rule them out of the process of becoming. This is for them to be made by others, as objects, rather than for them as subjects to make themselves, and in making themselves to become, and thus to *be*, human. Consequently, human becoming must be a process in which all people have an equal right to their voice.
>
> (Peters and Lankshear, 1994)

One context of dialogue is in the meeting of primary and secondary Discourses. Secondary Discourses are encountered through engagement in different social institutions: schools; churches; societies; clubs; through being a football supporter; through participation in aspects of popular culture, etc. Such secondary Discourses also involve uses of language, ways of thinking, believing, valuing and behaving, which offer human beings new and different ways of seeing the world.

> Education, socialisation, training, apprenticeship and 'enculturation' are among the terms we use to refer to processes by which individuals are initiated into the Discourses of their identity formations ... knowledge of Discourses is not innate. Initiation into Discourses is a cultural activity, and the Discourses themselves are, simultaneously, means and outcomes of cultural process.
>
> (Lankshear *et al.*, 1997: 17)

Schools are discourse communities: in Mercer's (1995) terms, they are the site of 'educational discourse'. The language, values, ways of being and membership of various facets of the school, whether by staff or pupils, define and are defined by individuals' engagement with Discourses. In Gee's terms above, they are ways of using language, of thinking, and of acting' that identify the individual as 'a member of a socially meaningful group'. Furthermore, each curriculum subject will have its own particular Discourse (for example, Mathematics or Science) and the 'official discourse' (Mercer, 1995) of any classroom will result from the teachers' interaction in a 'dialogue of educational discourses', which will determine their position on teaching and learning (Arthur *et al.*, 1997). As Kress (1988: ii) observes, 'social structures and linguistic forms are intimately intermeshed'. Engagement with learning will result from an induction into 'educated discourse', success in which will determine future acquisition of social 'goods': for example, particular employment paths, higher education, power, status, wealth, and so on.

Awareness, or knowledge, of Discourses is not innate. While, in general terms, a school may make statements concerning ethos and values, the very values, beliefs and ways of thinking that underpin the Discourse of the version of English that pupils encounter in the classroom, for example, are rarely – if ever – made explicit. Coupled with the fact that much of what comprises classroom interaction arises from versions of English that are shown in the top two quadrants of Figure 16.1 – versions underpinned by prescription and direction – it is unsurprising that social inequalities are maintained, precisely because pupils are not 'becoming' in Freirean terms. In other words, they are not empowered through critique and debate; they are not active subjects engaging in 'dialogue' to generate knowledge, but are passive objects, who might engage in 'educated discourse' by taking notes, writing essays, reports, etc., without learning.

Literacy and empowerment

Research evidence from New Zealand, produced by Jones (1986, 1991), clearly exemplifies the problems raised in the previous paragraph. Jones studied two streamed classes of girls – 5M and 5S. Girls in both groups were committed to work hard in order to achieve academic success, which they perceived to be the route to better life chances. Class 5M comprised working-class girls of a low-to-middle academic ability, while 5S girls were overwhelmingly middle-class, higher-ability girls. Unsurprisingly, the two groups had very different views of the work, which corresponded with two very different views of how to operate language within learning, based upon two contrasting primary Discourses.

Within their primary Discourse, the 5M girls' model of education was hierarchical and 'top-down': the teacher was seen as the source of authority and knowledge. Such a view demanded an academic and examination-oriented literacy, characterised by gaining the knowledge that the teacher held about texts, through assiduous note-taking: 'they had no apparent idea that claims advanced as knowledge/information should be checked for accuracy and sense against recognised authoritative sources. Yet this is an essential aspect of enacting the appropriate "saying (writing)–believing–valuing–doing combinations" involved in academic-exam literacy specifically and academic Discourse generally' (Lankshear *et al.*, 1997: 28). Consequently, if teachers attempted discursive practice in the class through, for example, question and answer sessions, 5M did not value it as 'real work', and therefore tended to be disruptive. Therefore, teachers reinforced the girls' view of teacher-as-authority, teacher-as-source-of-knowledge by relying heavily upon dictation as a means of control. In complete contrast, however, within their primary Discourse, the 5S girls saw the teacher as just one of the sources of knowledge available to them, and insisted that sessions were structured by discussion and critique that challenged teachers' assertions. The 5S girls played an active role in the construction of knowledge through discussion and debate in the classroom. Ultimately, 5S students passed their School Certificate examinations precisely because the attitudes, values and beliefs enshrined in the Discourse of the official examinable culture of the school were closer to their experiences within their primary Discourse, whereas, almost without exception, 5M girls, whose view of education was the product of a contrasting primary Discourse, failed their examinations:

> The kinds of difference in language and literacy in Jones's study are closely associated with systematic patterns of academic success and failure ... Scholastic achievement draws heavily on discursive practices and associated language use which emphasise developing positions and viewpoints by demonstrating flair in arguing a point of view; manipulating and relating abstract ideas; and assuming detached standpoints when matters of objectivity or hypothesis arise.
>
> (Lankshear *et al.*, 1997: 29–30)

The modes of thinking, writing and speaking, and the appropriate registers, come much more easily to those students in the same social groupings as 5S. The difficulty for 5M students was that in adopting a 'scholastic pose', by doing or appearing to do what is believed to be educationally literate (or, indeed, doing what *they* believed to be scholastic activity, i.e. taking notes) without an understanding of the underlying principles and values, the activities, such as note-taking, become an end in themselves. By devolving all power and responsibility to the teacher as the fount of all knowledge, the class was not learning or understanding (Lankshear, 1987: 164). As knowledge of discourse is not innate, and nobody had ever made the ground rules visible, 5M students were much more likely to fail. They simply did not control the secondary language uses of the secondary Discourse. However, the 5S students were more able to master the dominant literacy of writing exams precisely because their primary Discourses and cultural capital privileged them in relation to students from the same social grouping as the 5M students, whose parents did not have access to secondary Discourses.

The guided construction of knowledge

Research in the United Kingdom, carried out by Mercer (1995), confirms Gee's assertions, and suggests a way in which to facilitate access to secondary Discourses. In *The Guided Construction of Knowledge*, Mercer examines language as a social mode of thinking. He argues that, while, in Vygotskian terms, language can be described as a psychological tool, it is also, essentially, a cultural tool. The two functions of language: the psychological – thinking – and the cultural – communication, are inextricably conjoined, and enable each of us to make sense of the world (in Freirean terms enabling us to 'become'): 'Language is therefore not just a means by which individuals can formulate ideas and communicate them, it is also a means for people to think and learn together' (Mercer, 1995: 4).

Mercer envisages the classroom as a 'discourse village', which he describes as 'a small language outpost from which roads lead to larger communities of educated discourse'. The teacher is a 'discourse guide', who uses 'educational discourse to organise, energise and maintain a local mini-community of educated discourse'. Mercer goes on to exemplify the key role of the teacher:

> teachers have to start from where the learners are, to use what they already know, and to help them go back and forth across the bridge from 'everyday discourse' into 'educated discourse'.
>
> (Mercer, 1995: 83–4)

While Mercer's terminology, perhaps, simplifies the linguistic complexities of the classroom – 'everyday discourse' is, in fact, likely to be a dialogue of a multiplicity of multicultural primary Discourses, and 'educated discourse' is a complex web of the secondary Discourses of teaching and learning – Mercer's extended metaphor is describing the process of induction, in Gee's terms, from primary to secondary Discourses. But what is of particular interest is that Mercer's research describes a methodology through which the secondary Discourse is made visible to learners by making visible not only the language structures, but, significantly, the values and beliefs inherent in the secondary Discourse.

Based on the examination of classroom talk in problem-solving situations, Mercer typifies three ways of talking and thinking: 'disputational talk', which is characterised by disagreement and individualised decision-making; 'cumulative talk', which is characterised by speakers' uncritical positive support of each other to construct a 'common knowledge' by accumulation; and 'exploratory talk', which is characterised by a critical, constructive engagement with each others' ideas. Exploratory talk is of particular significance because 'knowledge is made more publicly accountable and reasoning is more visible in the talk' (Mercer, 1995: 104).

Through his analysis, Mercer attempts to elaborate these models of talk into three 'distinctive social modes of thinking' by using three levels of analysis to describe and evaluate the types of talk: the 'linguistic level', the 'psychological level' and the 'cultural level'. This chapter cannot attempt to relate Mercer's analysis in full. Therefore, this part of the chapter will focus only on the 'cultural' level of analysis, because it involves a consideration of the nature 'of "educated" discourse and of the kinds of reasoning that are valued and encouraged in the cultural institutions of formal education' (Mercer, 1995: 106).

Mercer's analysis highlights the importance of exploratory talk:

> It typifies language which embodies certain principles – of accountability, of clarity, of constructive criticism and receptiveness to well-argued pro-

posals – which are highly valued in many societies. In many of our key social institutions – for example, the law, government, administration, research in the sciences and arts, and the negotiation of business – people have to use language to interrogate the quality of the claims, hypotheses and proposals made by each other, to express clearly their own understandings, to reach consensual agreement and make joint decisions ... it is language in which reasoning is made visible and in which knowledge is made accountable – not in any absolute terms, but in accord with the 'ground rules' of the relevant discourse community.

(*ibid.*)

Here Mercer identifies the beliefs and values that underpin the secondary Discourses of education and schooling. Having exemplified the ground rules of exploratory talk, the next part of the research involved making pupils aware of them in order to encourage exploratory talk, thereby enabling them to enter the secondary Discourse. These ground rules included: sharing relevant information; providing reasons for any assertions or opinions; asking for reasons where appropriate; reaching agreement; and accepting that the group, rather than any individual, was responsible for decisions and actions and ultimately for any ensuing success or failure (Mercer, 1995: 108).

The results of Mercer's research have shown that, not only did the quality of classroom talk improve, and not only was collective problem-solving more successful, but also pupils' scores in tests of non-verbal reasoning improved significantly – establishing a tangible link between thinking and learning (Mercer *et al.*, 1999). Furthermore, such learning also exemplifies Gee's claim that: 'The learning they are doing, provided it is tied to good teaching, is giving them not the literacies, but the meta-level cognitive and linguistic skills that they can use to critique various discourses throughout their lives' (Gee, 1992: 26).

Powerful literacies

Gee defines literacy as 'control of secondary uses of language (i.e. uses of language in secondary discourses)'. Thus, he argues, 'there are as many applications of the word "literacy" as there are secondary discourses'. He goes on to define 'powerful literacy' as:

control of a secondary use of language used in a secondary discourse that can serve as a meta-discourse to critique the primary discourse or other secondary discourses, including dominant discourses.

(Gee, 1992: 25–6)

Powerful literacy, then, is not a particular literacy, *per se*, but a particular use of a literacy. Pupils are empowered through learning the meta-level linguistic cognitive and linguistic skills, as opposed to acquiring the language of the secondary Discourse. The differences between the success of 5S and 5M ably demonstrate this difference. Lankshear sums up the importance of this meta-level knowledge as:

> knowledge *about* what is involved in participating in some Discourse(s). It is more than merely knowing *how* (i.e. being able) to engage successfully in a particular discursive practice. Rather, meta-level knowledge is knowing about the nature of that practice, its constitutive values and beliefs, its meaning and significance, how it relates to other practices, what it is about successful performance that makes it successful, and so on.
>
> (Lankshear *et al.*, 1997: 72)

Lankshear further argues that such knowledge empowers in at least three ways. First, it enhances the individual's level of performance within the Discourse and increases the chances of access to social 'goods'. It is easy to relate this mode of empowerment to success in the education system. Second, the ability to control secondary language uses provides the means by which a Discourse may be analysed to see how skills and knowledge may be used in new ways and directions within that Discourse. Finally, the meta-level knowledge of secondary Discourses makes it possible to critique and transform a secondary Discourse. Critical awareness of alternative Discourses allows the possibility of *choice* among them. To be enabled to critically choose among Discourses rather than simply to acquire or to reject Discourses without such learning and understanding, is to be empowered: it is the essence of powerful literacy.

Conclusions

The dominant Discourse of Government documents that established the education system in England and Wales was high-cultural and displayed an antipathy to working-class children and to popular culture. In the 1990s, the central metaphor of the National Curriculum was 'delivery'. Eisner (1984) reminds us that the metaphors that we use shape our understanding of the concepts we study. A curriculum to be 'delivered' by a teacher is disempowering of pupils and teachers alike. It is a view of knowledge that is hierarchical, top-down, and is characterised by prescription and direction. Consequently, it is unsurprising that the 'official examinable culture' of school – the language, knowledge priorities, learning styles, pedagogical preferences – is that of the dominant social and cultural groups. It is also well documented that children from the working class underachieve disproportionately.

The National Literacy Strategy is a product of the dominant Discourse. The methodology of the 'Literacy Hour' epitomises the official examinable culture of the school described above and, while it is likely to provide the desired higher SATs scores for the government, to what degree it will empower pupils remains to be seen. The work of Gee, Lankshear, Mercer and others offers teachers the possibility of empowering pupils through developing powerful literacies:

through participation, collaboration and negotiation; by making Discourses visible; by exposing the ground rules, the underpinning values and beliefs. As a result, pupils and teachers are more likely to recognise, critique and value aspects of their primary Discourses, and less likely to uncritically take on the language and attitudes of the secondary Discourses that they encounter:

> Learning should lead to the ability for all children ... to critique their primary and secondary discourses, including dominant secondary discourses. This requires exposing children to a variety of alternative primary discourses and secondary ones (not necessarily so that they acquire them, but so that they learn about them). It also requires a realising explicitly that this is what good teaching and learning is good at.
>
> (Gee, 1992: 27)

Questions for discussion

1   Is it appropriate to regard the teaching of English as political as well as cultural?
2   Are all types of culture equally valid? Should cultural studies cross class divisions?

Further reading

Lankshear, C. (1987) *Literacy, Schooling and Revolution*, London: Falmer Press.
    This book explores the politics of education in relation to the way in which reading and writing are shaped and transmitted within dominant discourses. The inherently political character of literacy is argued for, and assumptions about the nature and value of reading and writing are challenged.

Shannon, P. (ed.) (1992) *Becoming Political: Readings and Writings in the Politics of Literacy Education*, Portsmouth, New Hampshire: Heinemann.
    This book contains seminal readings on the politics of literacy education, by authors such as Gee, Brice Heath, Bloome and Giroux, and is an excellent starting point for anyone interested in the issues related to literacy and power.

Bibliography

Abbs, P. (1994) *The Educational Imperative*, Brighton: Falmer Press.

Abraham, J. (1993) *Divide and School: Gender and Class Dynamics in Comprehensive Education*, London: Falmer Press.

Achebe, C. (1965) 'English and the African writer', in A. Mazrui, *The Political Sociology of the English Language*, The Hague/Paris: Mouton (see Appendix B).

Adam, B. and Allan, S. (eds), *Theorising Culture: an Interdisciplinary Critique After Postmodernism*, London: University College London Press, pp. 149–64.

Ahmad, A. S. and Donnan, H. (1994) 'Islam in the age of postmodernity', in A. S. Ahmad and H. Donnan (eds) *Islam, Globalisation and Postmodernity*, London: Routledge, pp. 1–20.

Aitchison, J. (1997) *The Language Web: The Power and Problem of Words. The 1996 BBC Reith Lectures*, Cambridge University Press, Cambridge.

Apple, M. W. (1990) *Ideology and the Curriculum*, 2nd edn, New York: Routledge.

Applebee, A. N. (1978) *The Child's Conception of Story*, Chicago: University of Chicago Press.

Applebee, A. N. (1984) *Contexts for Learning to Write*, Norwood: N. J. Ablex.

Arnold, M. (1869) *Culture and Anarchy*, London: Penguin (1969 edn).

Arnot, M. *et al.* (1998) *Recent Research on Gender and Educational Performance*, London: HMSO.

Arthur, J., Davison, J. and Moss, J. (1997) *Subject Mentoring in the Secondary School*, London: Routledge.

Arts Council (1992) *Drama in Schools*, London: ACGB.

Arts in Schools Project Team (1990a) *The Arts 5–16: A Curriculum Framework*, London: Oliver and Boyd for the NCC.

Arts in Schools Project Team (1990b) *The Arts 5–16: Practice and Innovation*, London: Oliver and Boyd for the NCC.

Ashcroft, B., Griffiths, G. and Tiffin, H. (1998) *Key Concepts in Post-Colonial Studies*, London: Routledge.

Ashley, B. (1995) *Johnnie's Blitz*, London: Penguin.

Baker, D., Clay, J. and Fox, C. (eds) (1996) *Challenging Ways of Knowing: in English, Maths and Science*, London: Falmer Press.

Bakhtin, M. (1929) (trans. 1973) *Marxism and the Philosophy of Language*, London: Seminar Press.

Baldick, C. (1983) *The Social Mission of English Criticism*, Oxford: Oxford University Press.

Baldick, C. (1990) *The Concise Oxford Dictionary of Literary Terms*, Oxford: Oxford University Press.

Ball, S. (1981) *Beachside Comprehensive: A Case Study of Secondary Schooling*, London: Cambridge University Press.

Ball, C. (1994) *The Importance of Early Learning*, London: RSA.

Ball, S., Kenny, A. and Gardiner, D. (1990) 'Literacy, Politics and the Teaching of English', in I. Goodson and P. Medway (1990) *Bringing English to Order*, London: Falmer Press.

Banks, R. A. and Marson, P. (1998) *Drama and Theatre Arts*, London: Hodder and Stoughton.

Barnes, D. (1976) *From Communication to Curriculum*, Harmondsworth: Penguin.

Barnes, D. and Todd, F. (1977) *Communication and Learning in Small Groups*, London: Routledge and Kegan Paul.

Barnes, D., Britton, J. and Rosen, H. (1969) *Language, the Learner, and the School*, Harmondsworth: Penguin.

Barrs, M. and Pidgeon, S. (1998) *Boys and Reading*, London: Centre for Language in Primary Education.

Barthes, R. (1970) (trans. 1974) *S/Z*, New York: Hill and Wang.

Barthes, R. (1973) *Mythologies*, St Albans: Paladin Granada.

Basic Skills Agency (1999) http//www.basic-skills.co.uk (14 May 1999).

Bauer, L. (1994) *Watching English Change*, Longman: Harlow, Essex.

Baumann, G. (1996) *Contesting Culture*, Cambridge: Cambridge University Press.

Baxter, J. (1998) 'Teaching the Classics', in A. Goodwyn (ed.) *Literary and Media Texts in Secondary English: New Approaches*, London: Cassell.

Beard, R. (1999) 'Influences on the Literacy Hour', *Reading*, **33(1)**: 7.

Bearne, E. (1994) *Raising Reading Standards: Course Evaluation*, London: Southwark Council.

Bearne, E. (ed.) (1998a) *Literacy Across the Primary Curriculum*, London: Routledge.

Bearne, E. (ed.) (1998b) *Literacy Across the Secondary Curriculum*, London: Routledge.

Bearne, E. (ed.) (1998c) *Use of Language Across the Secondary Curriculum*, London: Routledge.

Bearne, E. and Elding, S. (1996) 'Speaking and listening, describing Progress', *The Primary English Magazine*, **2(2)**.

Belsey, C. (1980) *Critical Practice*, London: Methuen.

Bennett, J. (1991) *Learning to Read with Picture Books*, 4th edn, Stroud: Thimble Press.

Bennett, N. and Dunne, E. (1992) *Managing Classroom Groups*, London: Simon and Schuster.

Benton, M. (1992) *Secondary Worlds: Literature Teaching and the Visual Arts*, Buckingham: Open University Press.

Benton, M., Teasey, J., Bell, R. and Hurst, K. (1988) *Young Readers Responding to Poems*, London: Routledge.

Bereiter, C. and Scardamalia, M. (1987) *The Psychology of Written Composition*, New Jersey: Lawrence Erlbaum Associates.

Bernstein, B. (1971a) 'On the classification and framing of educational knowledge', in M. F. D. Young (ed.) *Knowledge and Control*, London: Collier-Macmillan, pp. 47–69.

Bernstein, B. (1971b) *Class, Codes and Control*, London: Routledge and Kegan Paul.

Biggs, A. P. and Edwards, V. (1994) 'I treat them all the same: teacher–pupil talk in multi-ethnic classrooms', in D. Graddol, J. Maybin and B. Stierer (eds) *Researching*

Language and Literacy in Social Contexts, Avon: Open University/Multilingual Matters.

Black, P. and Wiliam, D. (1998) *Inside the Black Box: Raising Reading Standards Through Classroom Assessment*, London: Kings College School of Education.

Bloom, H. (1995) *The Western Canon*, London: Macmillan.

Blunkett, D. (1999) *Times Educational Supplement*, 16 April 1999, London: Times Newspapers.

Board of Education (1910) *Circular 753*, London: HMSO.

Board of Education (1921) *The Teaching of English in England* [Newbolt Report], London: HMSO.

Board of Education (1938) *Report on Secondary Education* [Spens Report], London: HMSO.

Bolinger, D. (1980) *Language: The Loaded Weapon*, London and New York, Longman.

Bolton, G. (1992) *New Perspectives on Classroom Drama*, London: Simon and Schuster.

Bouchard, R. E. and Giles, H. (1982) *Attitudes Towards Language Variation*, Edward Arnold, London.

Bourdieu, P. (1973) 'Cultural Reproduction and Social Reproduction', in R. Brown (ed.) (1973) *Knowledge, Education and Cultural Change*, London: Tavistock.

Bourdieu, P. (1993) *The Field of Cultural Production*, Cambridge: Polity Press.

Bowles, S. and Gintis, H. (1976) *Schooling in Capitalist America: Education and the Contradictions of Economic Life*, London: Routledge and Kegan Paul.

Brathwaite, K. (1981) 'English in the Caribbean: notes on nation, language and poetry', in L. A. Fiedler and H. A. Baker Jr, *English Literature: Opening Up the Canon*, Baltimore: Johns Hopkins University Press.

Brice Heath, S. (1983) *Ways with Words: Language, Life and Work in Communities and Classrooms*, Cambridge: Cambridge University Press.

Brice Heath, S. (1986) 'Critical factors in literacy development', in S. de Castell, A. Luke and K. Egan (eds) *Literacy, Society and Schooling, a Reader*, Cambridge: Cambridge University Press.

Brindley, S. (ed.) (1994) *Teaching English*, London: Routledge/Open University.

Brite, P. Z. (1994) *Lost Souls*, Harmondsworth: Penguin.

Britton, J. (1970) *Language and Learning*, Harmondsworth: Penguin.

Britton, J. (1982) *Prospect and Retrospect: Selected Essays of James Britton*, Montclair: Boynton/Cook.

Britton, J. (1993) *Literature in Its Place*, Portsmouth, NY: Boynton and Cook/Heinemann.

Britton, J., Burgess, A., Martin, N., Macleod, A. and Rosen, H. (1975) *The Development of Writing Abilities, 11–18*, London: Macmillan.

Britzman, D. (1995) 'Is there a queer pedagogy? Or, stop reading straight', *Educational Theory*, **45(2)**: 151–65.

Brooke, R., Mirtz, R. and Evans, R. (1995) *Small Groups in Writing Workshops: Invitations to a Writer's Life*, New York: NCTE.

Brooks, G., Pugh, A. K. and Schagen, I. (1996) *Reading Performance at Nine*, Slough: NFER.

Brooks, L. (1999) 'Modern Britain: Young, Gifted and Extremely Cautious with the Cash', *Guardian*, Wednesday 20 January, 1999.

Brown, R. (ed.) (1973) *Knowledge, Education and Cultural Change*, London: Tavistock.

Brown, R. (1983) *A Dark Dark Tale*, London: Scholastic.

Bruner, J. (1960) *The Process of Education*, New York: Vintage.

Bruner, J. (1966) *Toward a Theory of Instruction*, Cambridge, MA: Harvard University Press.

Bruner, J. S. (1975) 'The ontogenesis of speech acts', *Journal of Child Language*, 2: 1–19.

Bruner, J. S. (1985) 'Vygotsky: a historical and conceptual perspective', in J.V. Wertsch (ed.) *Culture, Communication and Cognition: Vygotskian Perspectives*, Cambridge: Cambridge University Press.

Bruner, J. S. (1986) *Actual Minds, Possible Worlds*, Cambridge, MA: Harvard University Press.

Buckingham, D. (1999) 'Superhighway or road to nowhere? Children's relationships with digital technology', *English in Education*, **33(1)**: 3–12.

Burbules, N. (1998) 'Rhetorics of the Web: hyperreading and critical literacy', in I. Snyder (ed.) *From Page to Screen: Taking Literacy into the Electronic Era*, London: Routledge.

Butler, M. (1987) *Literature as a Heritage*, London: Cambridge University Press.

Campbell, A. (1999) 'An Integrated Curriculum for English, Media and Drama at KS 4', *English in Education*, **33(1)**: 13–23.

Cassidy, S. (1999) 'Blunkett orders books for boys', *Times Educational Supplement*, 23 April, 1–2.

Cazden, C. (1988) 'Social interaction as scaffold: the power and limits of a metaphor', in M. Lightfoot and N. Martin *The Word for Teaching is Learning*, London: Heinemann.

Cheshire, J. and Edwards, V. (1993) 'Sociolinguistics in the classroom', in J. Milroy and L. Milroy (1993) *Real English. The Grammar of English Dialects in the British Isles*, pp. 34–52.

Christie, F. and Misson, R. (1998) *Literacy and Schooling*, London: Routledge.

Christian-Smith, L. K. (ed.) *Texts of Desire: Essays on Fiction, Femininity and Schooling*, London: Falmer Press, pp. 28–44.

Clark, R. (1992) 'Principles and practice of CLA in the classroom', in N. Fairclough (ed.) *Critical Language Awareness*, London: Addison Wesley Longman.

Clark, R. and Ivanic, R. (1997) *The Politics of Writing*, London: Routledge.

Coates, J. (1986) *Women, Men and Language: A Sociolinguistic Account of Sex Differences in Language*, London: Heinemann.

Coates, J. (1993) *Women, Men and Language*, Harlow, Essex: Addison Wesley Longman.

Coggle, P. (1993) *Do you speak Estuary?* London: Bloomsbury.

Cohen, M. (1998) 'A habit of healthy idleness: boys' underachievement in historical perspective', in D. Epstein, J. Elwood, V. Hey and J. Maw (1998) *Failing Boys? Issues in Gender and Achievement*, Buckingham: Open University Press, pp. 19–34.

Cole, M. J. (1995) 'Critical thinking, talk and a community of enquiry in the primary school', *Language and Education*, **9(3)**: 161–177.

Cole, M. (ed.) (1999) *Equality, Human Rights and Education*, London: Falmer Press.

Cook, C. (1917) *The Play Way*, London: Heinemann.

Cooper, R. and Cooper, N. (1991) *Culture Shock! Thailand and How to Survive It*, London: Kuperard.

Cooper, S. and Mackey, S. (1995) *Theatre Studies: an Approach for Advanced Level*, AEB.

Cope, B. and Kalantzis, M. (eds) (1993) *The Powers of Literacy: A Genre Approach to Teaching Writing*, London: Falmer Press.

Corcoran, B. and Evans, E. (1987) *Readers, Texts, Teachers*, Milton Keynes: Open University Press.

Cox, B. (1991) *Cox on Cox*, London: Hodder and Stoughton.

Cox, B. (1995) *The Battle for the English Curriculum*, London: Hodder and Stoughton.

Crago, M. and Crago, H. (1983) *Prelude to Literacy*, Edwardsville, Illinois: Southern Illinois University Press.

Crinson, J and Leake, L. (ed.) (1993) *Move Back the Desks*, Sheffield: NATE.

Crystal, D. (1976) *Child Language, Learning and Linguistics*, London: Edward Arnold.

Crystal, D. (1994) *The Cambridge Encyclopedia of Language*, Cambridge: Cambridge University Press.

Culler, J. (1975) *Structuralist Poetics*, London: Routledge and Kegan Paul.

Culler, J. (1997) *Literary Theory*, Oxford: Oxford University Press.

Czerniewska, P. (1992) *Learning about Writing*, Oxford: Basil Blackwell.

Daiker, D. and Morenberg, M. (1990) *The Writing Teacher as Researcher*, Portsmouth, New York: Boynton and Cook/Heinemann.

Daly, C. (1998) 'Reading', in J. Davison and J. Dowson (eds) (1998) *Learning to Teach English in the Secondary School: A Companion to School Experience*, London: Routledge.

Daly, C. (1999) 'Reading boys', *Changing English: Domains of Literacy*, vol. 6, no. 1, University of London Institute of Education.

D'Arcy, P. (1989) *Making Sense, Shaping Meaning*, Portsmouth, New Hampshire: Boynton and Cook.

Davies, C. (1996) *What is English Teaching?* Buckingham: Open University Press.

Davies, H. (1997) unpublished assignment for the Essex Reading Project.

Davison, J. and Dowson, J. (eds) (1998) *Learning to Teach English in the Secondary School: A Companion to School Experience*, London: Routledge.

Day, R. (1982) 'Children's attitudes toward language', in E. Bouchard, E. Ryan and H. Giles (1982) *Attitudes Towards Language Variation*, London: Edward Arnold, pp. 116–31.

Dean, C. (1998) 'Failing boys "public burden number one" ', *Times Educational Supplement*, 27 November, 1.

Dearing, R. (1996) *Review of Qualifications for 16 to 19-Year-Olds*, London: SCAA.

dePaola, T. (1979) *Oliver Button is a Sissy*, San Diego: Voyager Books.

Department for Education (1993) *English for Ages 5 to 16 (1993)*, London: HMSO.

Department for Education (1994) *Code of Practice on the Identification and Assessment of Special Educational Needs*, London: DfE.

Department for Education (1995a) *English in the National Curriculum*, London: HMSO; Cardiff: Welsh Office Education Department.

Department for Education (1995b) *Key Stages 1 and 2 of the National Curriculum*, London: HMSO.

Department for Education and Employment (1997a) *Excellence in Schools: A White Paper*, London: DfEE.

Department for Education and Employment (1997b) 'Annex B: Initial Teacher Training National Curriculum for English Teaching', in *High Status, High Standards of the Teacher Training Agency*, London: DfEE.

Department for Education and Employment (1998) *The National Literacy Strategy: Framework for Teaching*, Sudbury: DfEE Publications.

Department for Education and Employment (1999) 'Education Action Zones', http://www/dfee/gov.uk/education/edaction (29 January 1999).

Department of Education and Science (1975) *A Language for Life. Report of the Committee of Inquiry Appointed by the Secretary of State for Education and Science* [The Bullock Report], London: HMSO.

Department of Education and Science (1984) *English from 5 to 16*, London: HMSO.

Department of Education and Science (1987) *The Report of the Task Group on Assessment and Testing (TGAT)*, London: HMSO.

Department of Education and Science (1988) *Report of the Committee of Enquiry into the Teaching of the English Language* [The Kingman Report], London: HMSO.

Department of Education and Science (1989) *English for Ages 5–16* [The Cox Report], London: HMSO.

Derewianka, B. (1990) *Exploring How Texts Work*, Melbourne, Australia: PETA.

Derrida, J. (1967a) (trans. 1974) *Of Grammatology*, Baltimore: Johns Hopkins University Press.

Derrida, J. (1967b) (trans. 1978) *Writing and Difference*, London: Routledge and Kegan Paul.

Dias, P. and Hayhoe, M. (1988) *Developing Response to Poetry*, Milton Keynes: Open University Press.

Dixon, J. (1967) *Growth Through English*, Oxford: Oxford University Press.

Dixon, J. (1975) *Growth Through English: Set in the Perspective of the Seventies*, Oxford: Oxford University Press.

Doddington, C. (1998) 'Significant speech', in E. Bearne *Use of Language Across the Primary Curriculum*, London: Routledge.

Doherty, B. (1995) *The Golden Bird*, London: Heinemann.

Dollimore, J. and Sinfield, A. (1985) *Political Shakespeare*, Manchester: Manchester University Press.

Dombey, H. (1998) 'Changing literacy in the early years of school', in B. Cox (ed.) (1998) *Literacy is Not Enough: Essays on the Importance of Reading*, Manchester: Manchester University Press.

Doughty, P., Pearce, J. and Thornton, G. (1971) *Language in Use*, London: Edward Arnold.

Douglas, J. (1964) *The Home and the School*, London: MacGibbon and Kee.

Douglas, N., Warwick, I., Kemp, S. and Whitty, G. (1998) *Playing it Safe ('Research in Brief')*, London: Institute of Education.

Doyle, B. (1989) *English and Englishness*, London: Routledge.

Durst, R. K. and Newell, G. E. (1989) 'The Uses of Function: James Britton's Category System and Research on Writing', *Review of Educational Research*, **59(4)**: 75–94.

Eade, J. (1997) 'Using a core text with bilingual children', *English in Education*, **31(3)**.

Eagleton, T. (1976) *Criticism and Ideology*, London: Verso.

Eagleton, T. (1983) *Literary Theory: an Introduction*, Oxford: Basil Blackwell.

Easthope, A. (1991) *Literary into Cultural Studies*, Routledge: London.

Edwards, J. (1982) 'Language attitudes and their implications among English speakers', in R. E. Bouchard and H. Giles, (1982) *Attitudes Towards Language Variation*, Edward Arnold, London, pp. 120–33.

Edwards, A. D. and Furlong, V. J. (1978) *The Language of Teaching*, London: Heinemann.

Edwards, A. and Mercer, N. (1987) *Common Knowledge: The Development of Understanding in the Classroom*, London: Methuen/Routledge.

Edwards, A. and Westgate, D. (1987) *Investigating Classroom Talk*, London: Falmer Press.

Eisner, E. (1984) *Cognition and Curriculum*, London: Longman.

Elbow, P. (1973) *Writing without Teachers*, New York: Oxford University Press.

Elbow, P. (1981) *Writing with Power*, New York: Oxford University Press.

Elbow, P. and Belanoff, P, (1995) *A Community of Writers: A Workshop Course in Writing*, 2nd edn, New York: McGraw-Hill.

Ellingham, M., McVeigh, S. and Grisbrook, D. (1998) *Morocco: The Rough Guide*, London: Penguin.

Ellis, V. and Forrest, S. (1999) ' "One of them or one of us": sexuality, identity and equality', in M. Cole (ed.) (1999) *Equality, Human Rights and Education*, London: Falmer Press.

Engel, D. M. and Whitehead M. R. (1996) 'Which English? Standard English and language variety: some educational perspectives', *English in Education*, **30(1)**: 36–49.

Epstein, D. and Johnson, R. (1998) *Schooling Sexualities*, Buckingham: Open University Press.

Epstein, D., Elwood, J., Hey, V. and Maw, J. (1998) *Failing Boys? Issues in Gender and Achievement*, Buckingham: Open University Press.

Evans, T. (1984) *Drama in the English Classroom*, Manchester: Croom Helm.

Exton, R. (1984) 'The language of literature', in J. Miller (ed.) (1984) *Eccentric Propositions: Essays on Literature and the Curriculum*, London: Routledge.

Fairclough, N. (1989) *Language and Power*, London: Addison Wesley Longman.

Fairclough, N. (1992) *Critical Language Awareness*, London: Longman.

Fairclough, N. (1995) *Critical Discourse Analysis: The Critical Study of Language*, London: Addison Wesley Longman.

Fiedler, L. A. and Baker, J. R. (eds) (1981) *English Literature: Opening Up the Canon*, Baltimore, Maryland and London: Johns Hopkins University Press.

Fine, A. (1989) *Bill's New Frock*, London: Mammoth.

Fine, A. (1998) *Loudmouth Louis*, London: Penguin.

Fish, S. (1970) 'Literature in the Reader: Affective Stylistics', in J. P. Tompkins (ed.) (1980) *Reader-Response Criticism*, Baltimore: Johns Hopkins University Press, pp. 70–100.

Fish, S. (1976) 'Interpreting the *Variorum*', in J. P. Tompkins (ed.) (1980) *Reader-Response Criticism*, Baltimore: Johns Hopkins University Press, pp. 164–84.

Fiske, J. (1987) *Television Culture*, London: Routledge.

Flanders, N. A. (1970) *Analyzing Teacher Behaviour*, Reading: Addison-Wesley.

Fleming, M. (1997) *The Art of Drama Teaching*, London: Fulton Press.

Floud, H. A. and Martin, F. (1966) *Social Class and Educational Opportunity*, Bath: Chivers.

Foucault, M. (1975) (trans. 1977) *Discipline and Punish: The Birth of the Prison*, Harmondsworth: Penguin.

Foucault, M. (1977) *The Archaeology of Knowledge*, London: Tavistock.

Foucault, M. (1981) 'The Order of Discourse', in R.Young (ed.) *Untying the Text*, London: Routledge and Kegan Paul, pp. 48–78.

Foucault, M. (1988) 'What is an Author', in D. Lodge (ed.), *Modern Criticism and Theory*, London: Longman.

Francis, P. (1999) 'Do it yourself soap', *The Secondary English Magazine*, **2(4)**: 18.

Frater, G. (1997) *Improving Boys' Literacy*, London: Basic Skills Agency.

Freeborn, D. (1992) *From Old English to Standard English*, Basingstoke: Macmillan.

Freedman, A. and Medway, P. (1994) *Genre and the New Rhetoric*, London: Taylor and Francis.

Freire, P. (1972) *Pedagogy of the Oppressed*, Harmondsworth: Penguin.

Freire, P. (1976) *Education: The Practice of Freedom*, London: Readers and Writers.

Freire, P. (1985) *The Politics of Education: Culture, Power and Liberation*, London: Macmillan.

Freire, P. and Macedo, D. (1987) *Literacy: Reading the Word and the World*, London: Routledge and Kegan Paul.

French, J. and French, P. (1984) 'Gender imbalances in the primary classroom: an international account', *Education Research*, **22**: 127–136.

Fulwiler, T. (ed.) (1987) *The Journal Book*, Portsmouth, New Hampshire: Boynton and Cook.

Garber, M. (1995) *Vice Versa: Bisexuality and the Eroticism of Everyday Life*, New York: Simon and Schuster.

Gardner, P. (1984) *The Lost Elementary Schools of England*, London: Croom Helm.

Gaskell, J. (1985) 'Course enrollment in high school: the perspective of working class females', *Sociology of Education*, **58(1)**: 48–59.

Gee, J. P. (1990) *Social Linguistics and Literacies: Ideology in Discourses*, London: Falmer Press.

Gee, J. P. (1991) 'What is literacy?', in C. Mitchell and K. Weiler (1991) *Rewriting Literacy: Culture and the Discourse of the Other*, New York: Bergin and Garvey.

Gee, J. P. (1992) *The Social Mind: Language, Ideology and Social Practice*, New York: Bergin and Harvey.

Genette, G. (1972) (trans. 1980) *Narrative Discourse*, Oxford: Basil Blackwell.

Gibson, W. (1950) 'Authors, Speakers, Readers and Mock Readers', in J. P. Tompkins (ed.) (1980) *Reader-Response Criticism*, Baltimore: Johns Hopkins University Press, pp. 1–6.

Gilham, B. (ed.) (1986) *The Language of School Subjects*, London: Heinemann.

Goddard, A. (1989) *The Language Awareness Project, Years 4 and 5: Language and Gender*, Lancaster: Framework.

Goelman, H., Oberg. A. and Smith, F. (eds) (1984) *Awakening to Literacy*, London: Heinemann.

Goodman, S. and Graddol, D. (1996) *Redesigning English: New Texts, New Identities*, London: Routledge.

Goodson, I. and Medway, P. (1990) *Bringing English to Order*, London: Falmer Press.

Goodwyn, A. (1995) *English and Ability*, London: David Fulton.

Goodwyn, A. (1997) *Developing English Teachers: The Role of Mentorship in a Reflective Profession*, Buckingham: Open University Press.

Goodwyn, A. (1998a) 'Adapting to the textual landscape: bringing print and visual texts together in the classroom', in A. Goodwyn (ed.) (1998b) *Literary and Media Texts in Secondary English: New Approaches*, London: Cassell.

Goodwyn, A. (ed.) (1998b) *Literary and Media Texts in Secondary English: New Approaches*, London: Cassell.

Gorak, J. (1991) *The Making of the Modern Canon: Genesis and Crisis of a Literary Idea*, London: Athlone Press.

Gossman, L. (1981) 'Literature and education', *New Literary History*, **13**.

Graddol, D. (1997) *The Future of English?* London: British Council.

Graddol, D., Leith, D. and Swann, J. (eds) (1996) *English: History, Diversity and Change*, London: Routledge.

Graff, H. J. (1987) *The Legacies of Literature: Continuities and Contradictions in Western Society and Culture*, Bloomington: Indiana University Press.

Grainger, T. (1998) 'Drama and reading: illuminating their interaction', *English in Education*, **32(1)**.

Graves, D. (1982) *Writing: Teachers and Children at Work*, London: Heinemann.

Griffiths, P. (1987) *Literary Theory and English Teaching*, Milton Keynes: Open University Press.

Griffiths, P. (1992) *English at the Core: Dialogue and Power in English Teaching*, Milton Keynes: Open University Press.

Gulbenkian Foundation (1982) *The Arts in Schools*, London: Gulbenkian.

Hall, C. and Coles, M. (1999) *Children's Reading Choices*, London: Routledge.

Hallberg, R. von (ed.) (1984) *Canons*, Chicago: University of Chicago Press.

Halliday, M. A. K. (1978) *Language as Social Semiotic*, London: Edward Arnold.

Halsey, A. H. (1998) 'Leagues Apart', in *The Times Higher Education Supplement*, 6 February 1998, p. 17, London: Times Newspapers.

Harding, D. W. (1960) 'Psychological Processes in the Reading of Fiction', in *British Journal of Aesthetics*, **2(2)**.

Hargreaves, D. (1967) *Social Relations in the Secondary School*, London: Routledge and Kegan Paul.

Harland, R. (1987) *Superstructuralism*, London: Routledge.

Harris, S. (1990) *Lesbian and Gay Issues in the English Classroom*, Buckingham: Open University Press.

Harvey, D. (1991) *The Condition of Postmodernity*, Oxford: Basil Blackwell.

Hatton, E. J. (1988) 'Teachers' work as bricolage: implications for teacher education', *British Journal of Sociology of Education*, **9(3)**: 337–57.

Hawke, J. (1991) 'Aspects of dialogue and learning in a junior school', unpublished MA thesis, Canterbury Christ Church University College.

Hawkes, T. (1992) *Meaning by Shakespeare*, London: Routledge.

Haworth, A. (1992) 'Towards a collaborative model of learning', *English in Education*, **26(3)**.

Hayhoe, M. and Parker, S. (eds) (1990) *Reading and Response*, Milton Keynes: Open University Press.

Heathcote, D. (1980) *Signs and Portents?* in L. Johnson and C. O'Neill (1984) *Dorothy Heathcote: Collected Writings on Education and Drama*, London: Hutchinson.

Heathcote, D. and Bolton G. (1995) *Drama for Learning: an Account of Dorothy Heathcote's Mantle of the Expert*, Portsmouth, NH: Heinemann.

Hines, D. (1997) *Batman Can't Fly*, London: Faber.

Hirsch Jr, E. D. (1987) *Cultural Literacy: What Every American Needs to Know*, Boston: Houghton Mifflin.

Holbrook, D. (1961) *English for Maturity*, Cambridge: Cambridge University Press.

Holderness, G. (ed.) (1988) *The Shakespeare Myth*, Manchester: Manchester University Press.

Holland, N. (1975) 'Unity, Identity, Text, Self', in J. P. Tompkins (ed.) (1980) *Reader-Response Criticism*, Baltimore: Johns Hopkins University Press, pp. 118–33.

Holliday, A. R. (1994a) *Appropriate Methodology and Social Context*, Cambridge: Cambridge University Press.

Holliday, A. R. (1994b) 'Student culture and English language education: an international context', *Language, Culture and Curriculum*, **7(2)**: 125–43.

Holliday, A. R. (1996) 'Otherisation in British education and media', in D. Hayes, (ed.) *Debating Education: Issues for the New Millennium?*, Canterbury: Department of Education, Canterbury Christ Church University College, pp. 139–42.

Holliday, A. R. (1998) 'Autonomy and discipline in content-based learning', Paper presented at the 14th Summer Institute of English – *Content-Based Instruction in Moroccan ELT*, Rabat, Morocco.

Holliday, A. R. (1999) 'Small cultures', *Applied Linguistics*, **20(2)**.

Holmes, J. (1992) *An Introduction to Sociolinguistics*, London: Longman.

Hornbrook, D. (1989) *Education and Dramatic Art*, Oxford: Basil Blackwell.

Hornbrook, D. (1991) *Education in Drama: Casting the Dramatic Curriculum*, Brighton: Falmer Press.

Housego, E. and Burns, C. (1994) 'Are you sitting too comfortably? A critical look at 'Circle Time' in primary classrooms', *English in Education*, **28(2)**.

Hughes, A. and Trudgill, P. (1979) *English Accents and Dialects*, Edward Arnold, London, 1st edn.

Hughes, A. and Trudgill, P. (1996) *English Accents and Dialects*, Edward Arnold, London, 3rd edn.

Hurley, M. (1990) 'Homosexualities: fiction, reading and moral training', in T. Threadgold and A. Cranny-Francis (eds) *Feminine/Masculine and Representation*, Sydney: Allen and Unwin.

Hurt, J. (1972) *Education in Evolution: Church, State, Society and Popular Education 1800– 1870*, London: Paladin.

Ireland, T. (1984) *Who Lies Inside*, Gay Men's Press.

Iser, W. (1978) *The Act of Reading*, London: Routledge and Kegan Paul.

Jackson, D. (1998) 'Breaking out of the binary trap', in D. Epstein *et al. Failing Boys? Issues in Gender and Achievement*, Buckingham: Open University Press, pp. 77–95.

Jakobson, R. (1960) 'Linguistics and Poetics', in T. Sebeok (ed.) *Style and Language*, Cambridge, USA: MIT Press.

Johnson, L. and O'Neill, C. (eds) (1984) *Dorothy Heathcote: Collected Writings on Education and Drama*, London: Hutchinson.

Jones, A. (1986) 'At school I've got a chance: ideology and social reproduction in a secondary school', cited in C. Lankshear, P. J. Gee, M. Knobel and C. Searle (1997) *Changing Literacies*, Buckingham: Open University Press.

Jones, A. (1991) *At School I've Got a Chance: Culture/Privilege: Pacific Islands and Pakeha Girls at School*, Palmerston North: Dunmore Press.

Jones, P. (1988) *Lipservice: The Story of Talk in Schools*, Milton Keynes: Open University Press.

Jordan, G. and Weedon, C. (1995) 'The celebration of difference and the cultural politics of racism', in B. Adam and S. Allan (eds), *Theorising Culture: an Interdisciplinary Critique After Postmodernism*, London: University College London Press, pp. 149–64.

Kabbani, R. (1988) *Devise and Rule: Europe's Myths of Orient*, London: Pandora Press (first published 1986, London: Macmillan).

Kachru, B. (1992) *The Other Tongue: English Across Cultures*, London: University of Illinois Press.

Kempe, A. (1997) *The GCSE Drama Coursebook*, Cheltenham: Stanley Thornes.

Khayatt, D. (1999) 'Sex and Pedagogy: Performing Sexualities in the Classroom', *GLQ: A Journal of Lesbian and Gay Studies*, **5(1)**: 107–13.

Knight, R. (1996) *Valuing English: Reflections on the National Curriculum*, London: David Fulton.

Knoblauch, C. and Brannon, L. (1993) *Critical Teaching and the Idea of Literacy*, Portsmouth, New Hampshire: Boynton/Cook.

Krashen, S. (1982) *Principles and Practices in Second Language Acquisition*, Oxford: Pergamon.

Kress, G. (1988) *Communication and Culture*, Kensington: University of New South Wales.

Kress, G. (1994) *Learning to Write*, London: Routledge.

Kress, G. (1995a) *Writing the Future: English and the Making of a Culture of Innovation*, NATE: Sheffield.

Kress, G. (1995b) *Making Signs and Making Subjects: The English Curriculum and Social Futures*, Inaugural Lecture, Institute of Education, University of London.

Kress, G. and van Leween, T. (1996) *Reading Images: The Grammar of Visual Design*, London: Routledge.

Kureishi, H. (1997) *Love in a Blue Time*, London: Faber and Faber.

Labov, W. (1973) 'The logic of nonstandard English', in J. Young (ed.) *Tinker, Tailor – the Myth of Cultural Deprivation*, Harmondsworth: Penguin (recently reprinted on Labov's homepage as 'Black Intelligence and Academic Ignorance').

Lacan, J. (1992) *The Ethics of Psychoanalysis*, London: Routledge.

Lacey, C. (1970) *Hightown Grammar*, Manchester: Manchester University Press.

Lambirth, A. (1998) 'Attitude Changers', *The Primary English Magazine*, **4(2)**: 29.

Langer, S. (1999) 'Advanced Certificate in Language and Literacy', unpublished portfolio, Canterbury: Christchurch University College.

Lankshear, C. (1987) *Literacy, Schooling and Revolution*, London: Falmer Press.

Lankshear, C., Gee, P. J., Knobel, M. and Searle, C. (1997) *Changing Literacies*, Buckingham: Open University Press.

Lansley, C. (1994) ' "Collaborative development": an alternative to phatic discourse and the art of co-operative development', *ELT Journal*, **48(1)**: 50–6.

Lawlor, S. (1988) *Correct Core*, London: Centre for Policy Studies.

Lawn, M. (1996) *Modern Times? Work, Professionalism and Citizenship in Teaching*, London: Falmer Press.

Leavis, F. R. (1948) *The Great Tradition*, London: Chatto and Windus.

Leech, G. and Svartvik, J. (1994) *A Communicative Grammar of English*, 2nd edn, London: Longman.

Leith, D. and Graddol, D. (1996) 'Modernity and English as a national language', in D. Graddol, D. Leith and J. Swann (eds) *English: History, Diversity and Change*, London: Routledge.

Levine, J. (ed) (1990) *Bilingual Learners and the Mainstream Curriculum*, Basingstoke: Falmer Press.

Levi-Strauss, C. (1963) *Structural Anthropology*, Harmondsworth: Penguin.

Lewis, M. and Wray, D. (1995) *Developing Children's Non-Fiction Writing: Working with Writing Frames*, Leamington Spa: Scholastic.

Luke, C. (1994) 'Women in the Academy: the politics of speech and silence', *British Journal of Sociology of Education*, **15(2)**: 211–30.

Lunn, E. (1982) *Marxism and Modernism*, Berkeley: University of California Press.

Lyotard, J.-F. (1986) *The Postmodern Condition*, Manchester: Manchester University Press.

Mac an Ghaill, M. (1994) *The Making of Men: Masculinities, Sexualities and Schooling*, Buckingham: Open University Press.

Mac an Ghaill, M. (1996) 'Deconstructing Heterosexualities within School Arenas', *Curriculum Studies*, **4(2)**: 191–209.

MacCabe, C. (1987) 'The state of the subject English', *Critical Quarterly*, **21(4)** (Winter).

Mackey, M. (1999) 'Popular Culture and Sophisticated Reading: *Men in Black*', in *English in Education*, **33(1)**: 47–57.

McLaren, P. and Lankshear, C. (eds) (1994) *Politics of Liberation: Paths from Freire*, London: Routledge.

McTear, J. (1981) 'Towards a model for the linguistic analysis of conversation', *Belfast Working Papers in Language and Linguistics*, no. 5, Belfast: Ulster Polytechnic, pp. 79–92.

Mail on Sunday, 31 January 1993.

Manguel, A. (1996) *A History of Reading*, London: HarperCollins.

Marciano, F. (1998) *Rules of The Wild*, London: Jonathan Cape.

Marenbon, J. (1987) *English Our English*, London: Centre for Policy Studies.

Marenbon, J. (1994) 'The new orthodoxy examined', in S. Brindley (ed.) *Teaching English*, London: Routledge/Open University.

Martin, N., Williams, P., Wilding, J., Hennings, S. and Medway, P. (1976) *Understanding Children Talking*, London: Penguin.

Martin, T. and Leather, B. (1994) *Readers and Texts in the Primary Years*, Buckingham: Open University Press.

Mathieson, M. (1975) *The Preachers of Culture*, London: George Allen and Unwin.

Maybin, J. (1996) 'An English canon?', in J. Maybin and N. Mercer (eds) *Using English: from Conversation to Canon*, London: Routledge.

Medwell, J., Wray, D., Poulson, L. and Fox, R. (1998) *Effective Teachers of Literacy: A Report of a Research Project Commissioned by the Teacher Training Agency*, Exeter: University of Exeter.

Meek, M. (1988) *How Texts Teach What Readers Learn*, Stroud: Thimble Press.

Meek, M. (1991) *On Being Literate*, London: Bodley Head.

Meek, M. (1994) 'How do they know it's worth it? The untaught reading lessons', in S. Brindley (ed.) *Teaching English*, London: Routledge/Open University.

Meek, M. (1996) *Information and Book Learning*, Stroud: Thimble Press.

Meek, M. (1997) 'Rhetorics about reading', in *Changing English: Domains of Literacy*, vol. 4, no. 2, University of London Institute of Education.

Mercer, N. (1995) *The Guided Construction of Knowledge*, Clevedon: Multilingual Matters.

Mercer, N., Wegerif, R. and Dawes, L. (1999) 'Children's talk and the development of reasoning in the classroom', *British Educational Research Journal*, **25(1)**: 95–111.

Michaels, W. B. (1977) 'The interpreter's self', in J. P. Tompkins (ed.) (1980) *Reader-Response Criticism*, Baltimore: Johns Hopkins University Press, pp. 185–200.

Millard, E. (1997) *Differently Literate*, London: Falmer Press.

Miller, J. (1996) *School for Women*, London: Virago.

Mills, C. (1994) 'Texts that teach', in D. Wray and J. Medwell (eds) *Teaching Primary English: The State of the Art*, London: Routledge.

Milroy, J. and Milroy, L. (1985) *Authority in Language*, London: Routledge and Kegan Paul.

Milroy, J. and Milroy, L. (1991) *Authority in Language: Investigating Language Prescription and Standardisation*, 2nd edition, London: Routledge.

Milroy, J. and Milroy, L. (1993) *Real English. The Grammar of English Dialects in the British Isles*, Harlow, Essex: Longman.

Misson, R. (1995) 'Dangerous lessons: sexuality issues in the English classroom', *English in Australia*, **112 (July)**: 25–32.

Mitchell, C. and Weiler, K. (1991) *Rewriting Literacy: Culture and the Discourse of the Other*, New York: Bergin and Garvey.

Moeran, B. (1996) 'The Orient strikes back: advertising and imagining in Japan', *Theory, Culture and Society*, **13(3)**: 77–112.

Moi, T. (1985) *Sexual–textual politics: feminist literary theory*, London: Methuen.

Moon, B. (1992) *Literary Terms: A Practical Glossary*, London: English and Media Centre.

Morgan, W. (1997) *Critical Literacy in the Classroom: The Art of the Possible*, London: Routledge.

Morgan, C. and Morris, G. (1999) *Good Teaching and Learning: Pupils and Teachers Speak*, Buckingham: Open University Press.

Morris, P. (1993) *Literature And Feminism*, Oxford: Basil Blackwell.

Moss, J. (1998) 'Which English?', in J. Davison and J. Dowson *Learning to Teach English in the Secondary School: A Companion to School Experience*, London: Routledge, pp. 1–17.

National Literacy Trust (1999) http//www.literacytrust.org.uk (14 May 1999).

NCC (1990) English: Non-Statutory Guidance for Schools, London: HMSO.

Neelands, J. (1990) Structuring Drama Work, Cambridge: Cambridge University Press.

Neelands, J. (1992) Learning through Imagined Experience, London: Hodder and Stoughton.

Neelands, J. (1998) Beginning Drama 11–14, London: Fulton Press.

Ngugi wa Thiong'o (1981) Education for a National Culture, Harare: Zimbabwe Publishing House.

Nkosi, L. (1965) Home And Exile, London: Longman.

NOP (1991) Teaching Talking and Learning in Key Stage Two, York: NCC.

Norman, K. (ed.) (1992) Thinking Voices, London: Hodder and Stoughton.

O'Brien, A. (1999) 'The future of English', Paper presented at The Best of British ELT: The ELT Kaleidoscope, Conference, British Council, Mexico City.

Organisation for Economic Cooperation and Development/Human Resources Development Canada (OECD) (1997) Literacy Skills for the Knowledge Society: Further Results from the International Adult Literacy Survey, Paris: OECD.

Ofsted (1993a) Handbook for the Inspection of Schools, London: Office for Standards in Education.

Ofsted (1993b) Boys and English, Ref. 2/93 NS 1993, London: Office for Standards in Education.

Ogilvy, C., Boath, E., Cheyne, W., Jahoda, G., and Schaffer, H. (1992) 'Staff–child interaction styles in multi-ethnic nursery schools', British Journal of Developmental Psychology, 19: 85–87.

O'Neill, C. (1995) Drama Worlds, Portsmouth, New Hampshire: Heinemann.

Ong, W. (1982) Orality and Literacy: The Technologizing of the Word, London: Methuen.

O'Toole, J. (1992) The Process of Drama, London: Routledge.

O'Toole, J. and Haseman, B. (1987) Dramawise, London: Heinemann.

Paechter, C. (1998) Educating the Other, London: Falmer Press.

Palmer, D. (1965) The Rise of English Studies, Oxford: Oxford University Press.

Parker, D. (1999) 'You've read the book, now make the film: moving image media, print literacy and narrative', in English in Education, 33(1): 24–35.

Patten, J. (1992) Speech to Conservative Party Annual Conference: 7 October 1992.

Patten, J. (1993) Literacy in the Opportunity Society, London: Conservative Party Information Office.

Peim, N. (1993) Critical Theory and the English Teacher, London: Routledge.

Pennac, D. (1994) Reads Like a Novel, London: Quartet Books.

Pennycook, A. (1994) The Cultural Politics of English as an International Language, London: Addison Wesley Longman.

Perera, K. (1994) 'Standard English: the debate', in S. Brindley Teaching English, London: Routledge, pp. 79–88.

Peters, M. and Lankshear, C. (1994) 'Education and hermeneutics: a Freirean perspective', in P. McLaren and C. Lankshear (1994) Politics of Liberation: Paths from Freire, London: Routledge.

Phillips, T. (1992) 'Why? The neglected question in planning for small group discussion', in Norman, K. (ed) Thinking Voices: The Work of the National Oracy Project, London: Hodder and Stoughton.

Piaget, J. (1971) Science as Education and the Psychology of the Child, London: Longmans.

Piaget, J. and Inhelder, B. (1969) The Psychology of the Child, New York: Basic Books.

Pilger, J. (1992) Distant Voices, London: Vintage.

Pilling, A. (1984) The Year of the Worm, Harmondsworth: Puffin.

Plowden Report (1967) *Children and their Primary Schools*, London: Central Advisory Council for Education.

Poulet, G. (1972) 'Criticism and the Experience of Interiority', in J. P. Tompkins (ed.) (1980) *Reader-Response Criticism*, Baltimore: Johns Hopkins University Press, pp. 41–9.

Poulson, L. (1998) *The English Curriculum in Schools*, London: Cassell.

Prasad, U. (1998) *My Son the Fanatic*, London: Faber and Faber.

Prince, G. (1973) 'Introduction to the Study of the Narratee', in in J. P. Tompkins (ed.) (1980), *Reader-Response Criticism*, Baltimore: Johns Hopkins University Press, pp. 7–25.

Propp, V. (1928) (trans. 1968) *Morphology of the Folk Tale*, Austin: Texas University Press.

Protherough, R. (1983) *Developing Response to Fiction*, Milton Keynes: Open University Press.

Protherough, R. and Atkinson, J. (1994) 'Shaping the image of an English teacher', in S. Brindley (ed.) *Teaching English*, London: Routledge/Open University.

Punter, A. and Burchell, H. (1996) 'Gender issues in GCSE English assessment', *British Journal of Curriculum and Assessment*, **(6)2**: 20–4.

Puttock, S. (ed.) (1998) *Same Difference*, London: Mammoth.

Pye, J. (1988) *Invisible Children: Who Are the Real Losers at School?*, Oxford: Oxford University Press.

Pyke, N. (1996a) 'Sir Ron rides to country's rescue', *Times Educational Supplement*, 29 March, 6.

Pyke, N. (1996b) 'Is English GCSE a girls' own paper?', *Times Educational Supplement*, 24 May, 2.

Pyke, N. (1998) 'Results hide fall in boys' reading', *Times Educational Supplement*, 16 October, 1.

Qualifications and Curriculum Authority (1997) *Optional Assessment Units During Key Stage 2*, London: Qualifications and Curriculum Authority.

Qualifications and Curriculum Authority (1998a) *Can Do Better: Raising Boys' Achievement in English*, London: QCA.

Qualifications and Curriculum Authority (on behalf of the Advisory Group on Citizenship) (1998b) *Education for Citizenship and the Teaching of Democracy in Schools*, London: QCA [Crick Report].

Qualifications and Curriculum Authority (1998c) 'Standards at Key Stage 3: English Report on the 1998 National Curriculum Assessments for 14-Year-Olds', QCA Ref.: QCA/98/279, London: QCA.

Qualifications and Curriculum Authority (1998d) *Standards at Key Stage 1 English and Mathematics: Report on the 1998 National Curriculum Assessments for 7 Year Olds*, London: QCA.

Qualifications and Curriculum Authority (1998e) *Standards at Key Stage 2 English and Mathematics: Report on the 1998 National Curriculum Assessments for 11 Year Olds*, London: QCA.

Raban-Bisby, B. (ed.) (1995) *Developing Language and Literacy in the English National Curriculum*, London: Trentham Books.

Rao, R. (1938) *Kanthapura*, London: George Allen and Unwin.

Reed, L. R. (1998) 'Zero tolerance: gender performance and school failure', in D. Epstein, J. Elwood, V. Hey and J. Maw (1998) *Failing Boys? Issues in Gender and Achievement*, Buckingham: Open University Press.

Reid, J. A., Forrestal, P. and Cook, J. (1989) *Small Group Learning in the Classroom*, London: English and Media Centre.

Reid, M. (ed.) (1999) *English in Education*, **33**(1).

Resnick, D. and Resnick, L. (1977) 'The nature of literacy: an historical explanation', in *Harvard Educational Review*, **47**(3): 370–85.

Riffaterre, M. (1966) 'Describing poetic structures', in J. P. Tompkins (ed.) (1980) *Reader-Response Criticism*, Baltimore: Johns Hopkins University Press, pp. 26–40.

Roberts, P. (1995) 'Defining literacy: paradise, nightmare or red herring?' *British Journal of Educational Studies*, **XXXXIII**(4): 412–32.

Robinson, J. (1990) *Conversations on the Written Word: Essays on Language and Literacy*, Portsmouth, New Hampshire: Boynton and Cook/Heinemann.

Robinson, M. (1997) *Children Reading: Print and Television*, London: Falmer Press.

Rogers Cherland, M. and Edelsky, C. (1993) 'Girls and reading: the desire for agency and the horror of helplessness in fictional encounters', in L. K. Christian-Smith (ed.) *Texts of Desire: Essays on Fiction, Femininity and Schooling*, London: Falmer Press, pp. 28–44.

Rosen, C. and Rosen, H. (1973) *The Language of Primary School Children*, Harmondsworth: Penguin.

Rosen, H. (1993) 'How Many Genres in Narrative?' in *Changing English: Domains of Literacy*, vol. 1, no. 1, University of London Institute of Education.

Rosenblatt, L. (1970) *Literature as Exploration*, London: Heinemann.

Rosenblatt, L. (1978) *The Reader, the Text, the Poem*, Carbondale, Illinois: Southern Illinois University Press.

Russell, S. (1997) *Grammar, Structure and Style*, Oxford: Oxford University Press.

Said, E. (1978) *Orientalism*, London: Routledge and Kegan Paul.

Said, E. (1993a) *Culture and Imperialism*, London: Chatto and Windus.

Said, E. (1993b), 'The Idea of Empire', *Arena*: 12 February 1993, London: BBC [TV programme].

Sampson, G. (1921) *English for the English*, Cambridge: Cambridge University Press.

Sarangi, S. (1995) 'Culture', in J. Vershueren, J. Östman and J. Blomaert (eds) *Handbook of Pragmatics*, Amsterdam/Philadelphia: John Benjamin.

Sarland, C. (1991) *Young People Reading: Culture and Response*, Milton Keynes: Open University Press.

Saussure, F. de (1974) *Course in General Linguistics*, London: Fontana.

SCAA (1996a) *Monitoring the School Curriculum*, London: SCAA.

SCAA (1996b) *Speaking and Listening: Key Stages 1 to 3, Levels 1 to 8, Exemplification of Standards*, London: SCAA.

SCAA (1997a) *Use of Language: A Common Approach*, London: SCAA.

SCAA (1997b) *Planning Progression in English at Key Stages 1 and 2*, London: SCAA.

Scholes, R. (1989) *Protocols of Reading*, New Haven and London: Yale University Press.

Searle, C. (ed.) (1971) *Stepney Words*, London: Reality Press.

Searle, C. (1995) *Heart of Sheffield*, Sheffield: Earl Marshall School.

Sebeok, T. (ed.) *Style and Language*, Cambridge, USA: MIT Press.

Sedgwick, E. K. (1994) *Epistemology of the Closet*, Harmondsworth: Penguin.

Seldon, R. and Widdowson, P. (1993) *Contemporary Literary Theory*, Brighton: Harvester Wheatsheaf.

SHA (1998) *Drama Sets You Free!*, Leicester: SHA.

Shannon, P. (ed.) (1992) *Becoming Political: Readings and Writings in the Politics of Literacy Education*, Portsmouth, New Hampshire: Heinemann.

Sheeran, Y. and Barnes, D. (1991) *School Writing: Discovering the Ground Rules*, Milton Keynes: Open University Press.

Showalter, E. (1986) *New Feminist Criticism: Essays on Women, Literature and Theory*, London: Virago.

Sinfield, A. (1994) *Cultural Politics – Queer Reading*, London: Routledge.

Slade, P. (1954) *Child Drama*, London: Cassell.

Silin, J. K. (1999) 'Teaching as a Gay Man: Pedagogical Resistance or Public Spectacle? *GLQ: A Journal of Lesbian and Gay Studies*, **5**(1): 95–106.

Smith, F. (1984) *Joining the Literacy Club*, Reading: Centre for the Teaching of Reading, University of Reading.

Smith, F. (1990) 'Backs against the wall', *Times Educational Supplement*, 2 February 1990, London: Times Newspapers.

Smith, R. and Curtin, P. (1998) 'Children, computers and life online: education in a cyber-world', in I. Snyder (ed.) (1998) *From Page to Screen: Taking Literacy into the Electronic Era*, London: Routledge.

Snyder, I. (ed.) (1998) *From Page to Screen: Taking Literacy into the Electronic Era*, London: Routledge.

Social Trends (1992) *Social Trends – 21: 1991*, ed. T. Griffin, London: HMSO.

Solsken, J. (1993) *Literacy, Gender and Work in Families and in School*, New Jersey: Ablex.

Soueif, A. (1992) *In the Eye of the Sun*, London: Bloomsbury.

Spratt, N. and Sturdy, R. (1998) 'Reading and gender', in E. Bearne (ed.) (1998) *Use of Language Across the Secondary Curriculum*, London: Routledge.

Stonewall (1994) *Arrested Development*, London: Stonewall.

Storey, J. (1993) *Cultural Theory and Popular Culture*, London: Harvester Wheatsheaf.

Street, B. (1984) *Literacy in Theory and Practice*, Cambridge: Cambridge University Press.

Stubbs, M. (1976) *Language, Schools and Classrooms*, London: Methuen.

Stubbs, M. (1986) *Educational Linguistics*, Oxford: Basil Blackwell.

Styan, J. L. (1981) *Modern Drama in Theory and Practice*, vols 1–3, Cambridge: Cambridge University Press.

Styles, M., Bearne, E. and Watson, V. (1996) *Voices Off*, London: Cassell.

Swann, J. (1992) *Girls, Boys and Language*, Oxford: Basil Blackwell.

Tannen, D. (1994) *You Just Don't Understand*, London: Ballantine Books.

Taylor, M. (1999) 'Platform: Freedom to succeed', *Times Educational Supplement*, 26 February 1999, 13.

Thomas, P. (1997) 'Doom to the red-eyed Nyungghns from the Planet Glarg: boys as writers of narrative', *English in Education*, **31**(3).

Threadgold, T. and Cranny-Francis, A. (eds) *Feminine/Masculine and Representation*, Sydney: Allen and Unwin.

Times Educational Supplement (1915) *Report on Lancashire Headteachers' Report*, London: Times Newspapers.

Tizard, B. and Hughes, M. (1984) *Young Children Learning: Talking and Thinking at Home and School*, London: Fontana.

Todorov, T. (1977) *The Poetics of Prose*, New York: Cassell.

Tompkins, J. P. (ed.) (1980) *Reader-Response Criticism*, Baltimore: Johns Hopkins University Press.

Trenchard, L. and Warren, H. (1984) *Something to Tell You*, London: London Gay Teenage Group.

Trevarthen, C. and Hubley, P. (1975) 'Secondary intersubjectivity', in A. Lock (ed) *Action, Gesture and Symbol*, London: Academic Press.

Trilling, L. (1982) *Matthew Arnold*, Oxford: Oxford University Press.

Trudgill, D. (1975) *Accent, Dialect and the School*, London: Edward Arnold.

Turvey, A. (1996) 'Either reading or writing or praying: the story of a good girl', *Changing English: Domains of Literacy*, vol. 3, no. 2, University of London Institute of Education.

Viswanathan, G. (1990) *Masks of Conquest*, Faber and Faber: London.

Vulliaumy, E. (1993) Everyman: 11 April 1993, London: BBC [TV programme].

Vygotsky, L. S. (1962) *Thought and Language*, Cambridge, MA: MIT Press.

Vygotsky, L. S. (1978) *Mind in Society: The Development of Higher Psychological Processes*, Cambridge, MA: Harvard University Press.

Vygotsky, L. S. (1986) *Thought and Language*, rev. edn, Cambridge, MA: MIT Press.

Wallace, C. (1992) 'Critical literacy awareness in the EFL classroom', in N. Fairclough (ed.) *Critical Language Awareness*, London: Addison Wesley Longman.

Wallbank, M. (1979) 'Eighteenth century public schools and the education of the governing elite', *History of Education*, 8(1): 1–20.

Way, B. (1968) *Development through Drama*, London: Longman.

Weedon, C. (1987) *Feminist Practice and Poststructuralist Theory*, Oxford: Basil Blackwell.

Wegerif, R. and Scrimshaw, P. (1997) *Computers and Talk in the Primary Classroom*, Clevedon: Multilingual Matters.

Wells, G. (1985) *The Meaning Makers: Children Learning Language and Using Language to Learn*, London: Hodder and Stoughton.

Wells, G. and Chang-Wells, G. N. (1992) *Constructing Knowledge Together: Classrooms as Centers of Inquiry and Literacy*, Portsmouth, New Hampshire: Heinemann.

West, A. (1986) 'The Production of Readers', *The English Magazine*, 17 (Autumn): 4–9, London: ILEA English Centre.

Westbrook, J. (1990) 'The Shared Reader in the Secondary Classroom', unpublished MA dissertation, Institute of Education, University of London.

Westbrook, J. (Project Co-ordinator), Godfrey, R., Robertson, C. and Tod, J. (1998) *Factors Relating to Pupils Who Attain Below the Expectation in English at Key Stage 3*, Project funded by the Quaiifications and Curriculum Authority as part of their review of the school curriculum, London: Qualifications and Curriculum Authority.

West Rhyl Young People's Project (1998) 'Stories which give shape to life'.

White, L. (1998) 'Boys will be boys – and failures', *Sunday Times*, News Review, 11 January, 5.

Whitehead, F. *et al.* (1977) *Children and their Books: The Final Report of the Schools Council Project on Children's Reading Habits, 10–16*, Basingstoke: Evans/Methuen Educational.

Widdowson, H. G. (1992) *Practical Stylistics: an Approach to Poetry*, Oxford: Oxford University Press.

Wilde, O. (1999) *The Picture of Dorian Gray*, ed. E. White, Oxford: Oxford University Press.

Wilkinson, J. (1995) *Introducing Standard English*, London: Penguin.

Wilkinson, A. and Berrill, D. (1990) 'Truth to tell: criteria for judgement', in A. Wilkinson, A. Davies and D. Berrill *Spoken English Illuminated*, Milton Keynes: Open University Press.

Wilkinson, A., Davies, A. and Atkinson, D. (1965) 'Spoken English', *Education Review*, occasional publication, no. 2, University of Birmingham, School of Education.

Williams, R. (1973) *The Country and the City*, London: Chatto and Windus.

Willinsky, J. (1990) *The New Literacy: Redefining Reading and Writing in the Schools*, New York: Routledge.

Willis, P. (1977) *Learning to Labour: How Working Class Kids Get Working Class Jobs*, Farnborough: Saxon Press.

Willis, P. (1981) 'Cultural production is different from cultural reproduction ...' *Interchange*, **12(2–3)**: 48–67.

Wilson, T. (1998) 'Great debate', in E. Bearne *Use of Language Across the Primary Curriculum*, London: Routledge.

Wood, D. J. and Wood, H. A. (1989) 'Questioning student initiative', in J. Dillon (ed) *Questioning and Discussion*, Northwood, NJ: Ablex.

Woods, G. (1994) *This is No Book: A Gay Reader*, Nottingham: Five Leaves Publications.

Wragg, E. and Wragg, C. (1998) *Improving Literacy in the Primary School*, London: Routledge.

Wray, D. (1994) 'Reviewing the reading debate', in D. Wray and J. Medwell (eds) (1994) *Teaching Primary English: The State of the Art*, London: Routledge.

Wray, D. and Medwell, J. (eds) (1994) *Teaching Primary English: The State of the Art*, London: Routledge.

Zetzel, J. E. G. (1983) 'Recreating the canon: Augustan poetry and the Alexandrian past', in R. von Hallberg (ed.) *Canons*, Chicago: University of Chicago Press.

Index

Hurley, M. 217–18
Hurt, J. 92
hybridity 165–6

identity: sexual identities 212–13;
    sexualised identities 232–4; subject
    identity 164–5, 170–1, 177–9; teachers'
    professional identity 169–71, 177–9
ideological repertoire 203–4, 209–10
ideological superstructure 203–4
ideology, naturalisation of 136–8
In the Eye of the Sun (Soueif) 144–5
India 188
information and communications
    technology (ICT) 115, 241; literacy
    and 99–100; and NLS 101–2; and oracy
    67
Inner London Education Authority
    (ILEA): *Positive Images* 216–17; 'Sex,
    Race and Class' initiative 243
innocent ideology 136–8
inspection evidence 227
interpretative communities 202
intervention strategies 54; concerns over
    51–2
Ireland, T.: *Who Lies Inside* 204
Iser, W. 163, 208
Ivanic, R. 140

Jakobson, R. 95
Japanese 127, 132
Jarman, D. 215–16
Jenny Lives with Eric and Martin (Bosche)
    217
Johnson, L. 78
Johnson, S. 183
Jones, A. 254
Jordan, G. 141, 147
journals: leading logs and talk diaries 70;
    reading journals 16–18, 201–2; think
    books 29, 33–4
Joyce, J. 182

Kachru, B. 127
Kalantzis, M. 41
Kempe, A. 89
key skills 45–6
Key Stage 1 29–32
Key Stage 2 19, 32–3, 227
Khayatt, D. 223

King James Version of the Bible 183
Kingman Report 180
Knight, R. 194–5
Knoblauch, C. 218
knowledge: explicit knowledge about
    writing 28–33; guided construction of
    255–7; about talk 68–70
Krashen, S. 111–12
Kress, G. 21, 46, 115, 206, 253; drama as
    English 83; escaping linguistic
    parochialism 133–4, 146
Kureishi, H.: 'My Son the Fanatic' 142–4

Labov, W. 174
Lacan, J. 163, 171, 221
Lacey, C. 248
'laddish' culture 233
Lambirth, A. 53
language: change today 127–8; making
    language work for you 126–7; and
    music 100–1; post-structuralist theory
    171–3; student teachers' definitions of
    English 152–3; subject development
    178–9
language acquisition 111–12
'language across the curriculum' 42
language development 95–6
language guardians 124
language rules 111–12
language use 95–6, 113, 114, 116
Language in Use project 107
language variation *see* variation
Lankshear, C. 248, 249, 251, 253;
    discourses and empowerment 254, 255,
    258, 259; dominant groups 243, 244;
    improper and proper literacy 251, 252;
    language as social practice 139
Lansley, C. 138
Lawlor, S. 107, 112
Leake, L. 89
learning: drama as a method of 75, 76,
    77–9; home oracy 58–9; school oracy
    59
learning logs 70
Leather, B. 199, 200
Leavis, F.R. 168, 185
Leavisites 185–7
Leech, G. 118
Leith, D. 194
lesbian and gay rights movement 216–18

role-play 70
Romanticism 184–5
Romeo and Juliet 12, 99
Rosen, H. 41, 84
Rosenblatt, L. 199–200
rules, language 111–12
Russell, S. 118

Said, E. 140–1
Sampson, G. 166–7, 168, 246
Sarangi, S. 141–2
Sarland, C. 203–4
Saussure, F. de 163, 208
SCAA 59; *Framework for Planning and Progression in English* 66, 67
scaffolding 59
Scardamalia, M. 117
Scholes, R. 21
school culture: defining literacy and 3, 42–56
school oracy 59
school placements 159–60
schooling: discourse and 252–4; gender, literacy and 229–34; and underachievement 248–9
Scrutiny 186
SCYPT (Standing Conference of Young People's Theatre) 78
Searle, C. 252
Secondary Heads Association (SHA): *Drama Sets You Free!* 86–8, 89
secondary schools 94–5; defining literacy 50–5
secondary student teachers *see* student teachers
Section 28 216–17
Seldon, R. 171, 179
self: articulating self as writer 38–9; engaging in a dialogue with the self as the self reads 221; self and power matrix 249–52
semic code 176–7
semiotic repertoire 206–9, 209–10
semiotics 178–9
service subject, English as 153
sexual identities 212–13
sexualised identities 232–4
sexuality 6, 212–23; representation in the English curriculum 215–19; representation in schools 213–15; use of

Queer Theory and critical literacy pedagogies 219–22
Shakespeare, W. 164, 183; *see also Hamlet, Romeo and Juliet*
Shannon, P. 259
shared reading and writing 30–2, 34–5, 47–8
Sheep-Pig, The 98, 99
Shelley, P.B. 185
Shepard, M. 213
Showalter, E. 190
Silin, J.G. 223
Sinfield, A. 164, 205
Singapore 132
skills, English as 249–51
Slade, P. 77
Slavin: *Success for All* 47, 49
Smith, F. 42
Smith, R. 102
Snyder, I. 104
soap operas 165
social class *see* class
social context 203–6
social and personal learning 75; *see also* personal growth
society 45
sociolinguistics 107–8, 174
solidarity 124–5
solo potency 239
Solsken, J. 13
Soueif, A.: *In the Eye of the Sun* 144–5
Southey, R. 186
Soyinka, W. 187
Special Educational Needs (SEN) pupils 43, 45–6
specialist teachers 88
spectator role 26–7, 34–5
speech *see* talk/talking
Spens Report 245, 246
Spenser, E. 183
Spratt, N. 12
Standard Attainment Tasks (SATs) 19, 161, 224
standard English: canon and 182–3, 192; 'correct' vs 'appropriate' debate 4, 105–18; cultural politics 166–7, 168; dialect, accent and 126
standards 45, 233
Stanford University 191
status 125

36526

9 780415 206655